Time Out

London Calling

High art and low life in the capital since 1968

timeout.com

Published by Time Out Guides Ltd, a wholly owned subsidiary of Time Out Group Ltd.
Time Out and the Time Out logo are trademarks of Time Out Group Ltd.

© **Time Out Group Ltd 2008**

10 9 8 7 6 5 4 3 2 1

This edition first published in Great Britain in 2008 by Ebury Publishing
A Random House Group Company
20 Vauxhall Bridge Road, London SW1V 2SA

Random House Australia Pty Limited 20 Alfred Street, Milsons Point, Sydney, New South Wales 2061, Australia
Random House New Zealand Limited 18 Poland Road, Glenfield, Auckland 10, New Zealand
Random House South Africa Pty Limited Isle of Houghton, Corner Boundary Road & Carse O'Gowrie,
Houghton 2198, South Africa

Random House UK Limited Reg. No. 954009

Distributed in USA by Publishers Group West
1700 Fourth Street, Berkeley, California 94710

Distributed in Canada by Publishers Group Canada
250A Carlton Street, Toronto, Ontario M5A 2L1

For further distribution details, see www.timeout.com

ISBN: 978-1-84670-109-2

A CIP catalogue record for this book is available from the British Library

Printed and bound in Singapore by Tien Wah Press Ltd

The Random House Group Limited supports The Forest Stewardship Council (FSC), the leading international
forest certification organisation. All our titles that are printed on Greenpeace approved FSC certified paper
carry the FSC logo. Our paper procurement policy can be found at www.rbooks.co.uk/environment

Time Out carbon-offsets all its flights with Trees for Cities (www.treesforcities.org).

On 12 August 1968, the first issue of a new London listings magazine appeared. Originally to be called *Where It's At*, the title was changed just before it went to press. The publication told Londoners what was going on where, and how to make the most of their city.

Forty years later, a lot has changed: the street life, the nightlife, the people, the skyline. From naked theatre to snail porridge, street protests to terrorist attacks, the devastating closure of the docks to the rampant gentrification of working-class neighbourhoods, London has seen it all.

At the same time, much has stayed the same. One constant has been *Time Out*, chronicling London life during the past four decades. This book tells the story of this city and those changes, seen through the prism of that magazine.

Time Out Guides Limited
Universal House
251 Tottenham Court Road
London W1T 7AB
Tel + 44 (0)20 7813 3000
Fax + 44 (0)20 7813 6001
Email guides@timeout.com
www.timeout.com

Editorial

Editors Jessica Cargill Thompson, Jonathan Derbyshire
Proofreader Simon Cropper
Indexer Sally Davies

Managing Director Peter Fiennes
Financial Director Gareth Garner
Editorial Director Sarah Guy
Series Editor Cath Phillips
Editorial Manager Holly Pick
Assistant Management Accountant Ija Krasnikova

Design

Art Director Scott Moore
Art Editor Pinelope Kourmouzoglou
Senior Designer Henry Elphick
Graphic Designer Gemma Doyle, Kei Ishimaru
Digital Imaging Tessa Kar
Ad Designer Jodi Sher
Cover Designer John Oakey

Picture Desk

Picture Editor Jael Marschner
Deputy Picture Editor Katie Morris
Picture Researcher Gemma Walters
Time Out London Picture Editor Allyce Hibbert

Archives

Librarian Paul Fairclough
Picture Librarian Abigail Lelliott

Advertising

Commercial Director Mark Phillips
Sales Manager Alison Wallen
Advertising Assistant Kate Staddon

Marketing

Marketing Manager Yvonne Poon
Sales & Marketing Director North America Lisa Levinson
Senior Publishing Brand Manager Luthfa Begum
Marketing Designers Anthony Huggins, Nicola Wilson

Production

Group Production Director Mark Lamond
Production Manager Brendan McKeown
Production Controller Damian Bennett
Production Coordinator Julie Pallot

Time Out Group

Chairman Tony Elliott
Group General Manager/Director Nichola Coulthard
TO Communications Ltd MD David Pepper
Time Out International MD Cathy Runciman
Group IT Director Simon Chappell
Head of Marketing Catherine Demajo

The Editors would like to thank Jim Haynes, Charlie Godfrey-Faussett, Lynn Chambers, Tamarin Marriott Wilkinson, CND, the Roundhouse, Oval House Theatre, Esme, Max and Jay. Thanks, also, to staff and contributors to *Time Out* past and present for 40 years of entertaining, informative and provocative writing, and for their input and advice on this project. Special thanks to Tony Elliott, for taking a good idea and turning it into a global phenomenon. We would also like to pay tribute to the millions of Londoners and visitors to the capital who have made, and continue to make, London the rich and diverse city we know and love.

Articles reproduced from the *Time Out* archives are edited extracts from the original features. Every effort has been made to contact the copyright holders. The publishers will be glad to deal with any queries.

Photography & illustration credits

Contents

What
Londoners
take when
they
go out.

Time Out
London
EVERY WEEK

YOU have
one week
to live.

Time Out Out Wednesday
http://www.timeout.co.uk

NO OTHER MAGAZINE

TELLS YOU MORE ABOUT

WHAT'S HAPPENING IN

LONDON EVERY WEEK

AND THAT'S ONLY HALF THE STORY.

Where do you find
out what's happening
in London?

Time Out London's biggest-selling
weekly entertainment guide.

HEDONISM **INTRODUCTION**
SEX CITYSCAPE FASHION
SOCIETY SHOPPING COMEDY
DRAMA PROTEST & POLITICS
VISUAL ARTS PERFORMANCE
LITERATURE GANGS OPINION
COCKNEYS BARS ON SCREEN
DANCE MUSIC TELEVISION
BUILDINGS CLUBS NIGHTLIFE
SPORT & FITNESS MEMORIES
STYLE FOOD & DRINK GIGS
CONSUME RIOTS REFERENCE

Forging the future

In 1968, the air was thick with revolution. While it is the protests and the politics that enchant historians of recent social history, it was the consumer revolution, led by a generation of young entrepreneurs sympathetic to the prevailing counterculture, that propagated the London of today.

By Tony Elliott

INTRODUCTION

G rowing up in Gloucester Road, South Kensington, in a slightly sheltered background, I found London quite genteel. For a teenager in the mid '60s, there weren't a lot of interesting, accessible options for entertainment. There were clubs for grown-ups and high-profile casinos, but for someone who was 15, 16 or 17, there were very few venues.

Cafés were the focal point of our social life: we frequented one called the Witches' Cauldron in Belsize Park. Richmond had a lot of places, but it was a bit of a trek if you lived in the centre of town. Earl's Court was slightly rough, but always very lively, with interesting pubs. Fulham and Chelsea were more bohemian – the people there wore jeans and had longer hair. Restaurants were usually too expensive. There were a few accessible places such as Conran's Chelsea Kitchen on the King's Road and the Presto Bar in Notting Hill.

Most of the time I went to a club called Café des Artistes, in a basement at 266A Fulham Road (now the K Bar Chelsea), which had live music and a very cosmopolitan group of people. It was famous for being where the au-pairs went. The Marquee on Wardour Street was extremely important for the current rock acts, and there were certain pubs on the entertainment circuit (mainly in Soho and Hampstead). Otherwise, we relied on the art colleges, which put on great bands – I remember seeing the Animals performing in the underground car park at Central School of Art. Things were

The City of London, 2007. Since 1968, the skyline has been transformed by skyscrapers such as the Gherkin, Tower 42, the Barbican and the Commercial Union Building, as well as the Wembley Stadium arch, visible in the distance.

happening, and everyone was hungry for new experiences, but you had to know where to go.

When I left Keele University in 1968 to set up *Time Out*, there were two strands to London's cultural life. First, there was a continuation of semi-established cultural places that were showing interesting things. In cinema there was the Everyman (which is still around), the Paris Pullman, the Academy, and the Classic cinema chain (which showed good late-night movies at the weekend), which would be showing films from Italy and France alongside the British New Wave: Tony Richardson, Joe Losey, Lindsay Anderson and others. The Tate had shows by Andy Warhol, Giacometti and Naum Gabo: significant landmarks that anyone who was interested in quality culture would go to. In theatre there was Peter Hall, Peter Brook, the Royal Shakespeare Company at the Aldwych, and David Warner's *Hamlet*.

The counterculture

And then there was another tribe of people who were referred to as the 'alternative society', or the 'counterculture', or 'the underground'. People who were involved in a mix of projects that were largely being invented or discovered on the run. It included influences from America, and people packaging up gems such as Jean Genet plays. Jim Haynes was running the Arts Lab on Drury Lane, which was multi-arts-based: it had live theatre; it showed movies; there was a coffee bar; people did talks.

It was the ultra-hip version of the ICA. At the same time, the ICA itself reopened in the summer of 1968 in new premises on the Mall (the cover image of the first ever *Time Out* was based on its opening exhibition, Cybernetic Serendipity). At that time, it was run by Michael Kustow (later a founding commissioning editor of Channel 4 when it launched in 1982) who, like a lot of the people involved with the counterculture, was not an underground radical but a well-educated intellectual, interested in things that were experimental and avant-garde.

The Roundhouse, now seen as a mainstay of that counterculture, did not, in fact, initiate many of its own events, but was a venue for hire. It was clubs such as UFO, originally housed in a basement on Tottenham Court Road, that set the tone, renaming itself Middle Earth when it took up residence in the Chalk Farm engine shed. It was also where theatre producer Michael White put on Kenneth Tynan's *Oh! Calcutta!*, before going on to stage *The Rocky Horror Show* in the Classic on the King's Road, a typical example of the more experimental end of theatre meeting the new-wave avant-garde and creating a phenomenon.

The notion that the hippy culture was the prevailing mood is not the exact truth. It was a phase and was clearly represented in the clothes people wore, the music they listened to, the free

'Things were happening, and everyone was hungry for new experiences, but you had to know where to go.'

concerts, and the smoking of dope in public. Within that milieu there were unquestionably a number of very committed idealists, who were seeking some kind of alternative way of living life by experimenting with things like living in communes, but they were not the majority. There were bookshops and magazines, such as Gandalf's Garden at World's End in Chelsea, catering to the pure hippy spirit – worthy, but basically irritating. Ultimately, it was a bit of a dead end.

The consumer revolution

If 1968 was a time of revolution, it was a consumer one. There was a cultural economy demanding new things, be it poetry, music, theatre, art or fashion. And there was quite a lot of money around to sustain this boom in new businesses.

Some of the best events and venues were being run by young, but slightly traditional entrepreneurs, who were in it to make money. The heroes of the counterculture were mostly businessmen, and often from the establishment.

Piccadilly Circus in 1968; Coca-Cola is the only advertiser still on site.

Carnaby Street in 1968, at the time the hippest street in the world.

Island Records was very stylish and the home for a lot of important acts, but it was set up by Chris Blackwell of Cross & Blackwell – at one stage, his family owned a huge chunk of Jamaica. Nigel Samuel, the financial supporter of hip countercultural entities such as Indica Books and *International Times*, was from the banking family. Benny Gray, who started Kensington Market, was arguably just a property guy who was shrewd enough to rent stalls to creative people selling stuff you wouldn't find anywhere else.

Events such the Doors and Jefferson Airplane playing the Roundhouse in 1968 have become the stuff of countercultural legend, but, ultimately, it was a ticketed event by the bands of the moment, supported by a big record label. Even Biba, often seen as the embodiment of '60s bohemia, was basically a commercial fashion business, just one with very unique content. People lapped it up because there was such a wealth of talent that it all felt fantastically new.

Anti-establishment

Politics were there, but they weren't the be-all and end-all. There were people who were undoubtedly very hardline, whose reference points were Trotsky or Marx or International Socialism. But between them they lacked the coherent, sustainable political view of the world to effect any permanent change.

The prevailing mood was not so much political as simply anti-establishment. The Vietnam War drew widespread opposition and led to headline-making riots in Grosvenor Square, but there were also a lot of emerging domestic issues that today we take for granted: issues to do with abortion – which was still only semi-illegal (we all supported the general principle that abortion on demand was something that was desirable and should be allowed) – draconian drug laws, and the appalling behaviour of the police against black people.

There was a strong feeling of generational conflict. The slightly challenging and chaotic nature of the youth culture and the underground

London Calling **Time Out** 13

drove the police into behaving in extraordinarily clumsy ways, which fuelled anti-police cynicism. As young people, we felt very much that we were on our own. You didn't trust the authorities or the older generation to take you seriously. The more of London we could colonise, map out and put under our control, the more we could protect our own interests. It made us go out and take risks.

Everybody of a certain age and education got the scent of worthwhile and positive long-term change. That's what we were all building in lots of different ways. There were publications such as *International Times* trying to forge a way: genuine alternative newspapers for an alternative way of looking at the world. To some degree, *Time Out* was part of that milieu.

When *Time Out* started, it was a way of telling people about everything that was going on in London's culture, not just arts events but also information on shops and organisations. Very quickly we realised that by listing something, it was a three-way win: you were helping that entity do something, the people who were buying the magazine were pleased to hear about it, and it was bolstering the position of the magazine. It wasn't all about what was alternative or independent; people just wanted what was new, good and worthwhile.

If certain social changes were instigated in 1968, a second force came nearly ten years later with punk. It lit a long fuse and established a lot of talent. The people who have held power in London over the past decade have largely come from those two periods – the late '60s and the late '70s –

Gandalf's Garden: World's End shop, New Age commune and headquarters of an eponymous magazine – led by Muz Murray (centre). Eventually, members decided Chelsea was 'too constricting' and decamped to Norfolk.

and their sensibilities, shaped in those periods, are what has formed 21st-century London.

London, 2008

Today, the world is far more sophisticated than it ever was. Everything that exists you can find out about through the internet or TV. The sheer spectrum of what people do has widened massively. In fashion or design or music, what existed in the '60s was only a quarter of the range of what exists now. What is quite remarkable is that London, on the whole, has remained at the leading edge of most fields of creativity, while cities such as Paris and even Barcelona now seem one-dimensional by comparison.

The most surprising, and one of the greatest pleasures, is that we've become, in very loose terms, a Continental city. Instead of dirty, smoke-filled pubs, we have bars and coffee houses. You can go to any part of London and get a decent cup of coffee, or get a drink at any time of day. There are shops everywhere, open late or on a Sunday.

Twenty-first century London is a very different creature from the London of the 1960s and '70s, but its current form was shaped by the energy and vision of those times. And 40 years on, *Time Out* strives each week to maintain its original commitment to being London's independent window on what's the best in the city at any moment.

Tony Elliott set up *Time Out* in 1968. He remains the company's chairman.

TIMELINE

1968
The price of a tube ticket between central London stations is four pence (about 21p in today's money). In 2008, without an Oyster card, a single fare in Zones 1 and 2 costs £4.

Sir John Rennie's 1823 London Bridge is dismantled and shipped to Arizona. The present bridge, by architects Matt, Hay & Anderson, opened in 1972.

1973
A one-day national strike is called by the Trades Union Congress, with more than 1.5 million workers downing tools in protest at pay and prices.

1975
Ross McWhirter, editor of the *Guinness Book of Records*, is shot at his home in north London by IRA terrorists. His killers, responsible for dozens of attacks throughout London,

are later cornered in a six-day siege in Balcombe Street.

1978
Saatchi & Saatchi designs the now-famous 'Labour isn't working' poster. It contributes to the Conservatives' success in the elections that follow, and has since been voted the poster advertisement of the century.

The Central London Mosque in Regent's Park opens.

1979
The Conservative Party gains power and Margaret Thatcher becomes the first female prime minister. Unemployment soars.

1981
Prince Charles and Lady Diana Spencer are married in St Paul's Cathedral. Some 600,000 well-wishers line the streets and an estimated 750 million worldwide watch on TV.

1982
Britain sends a naval taskforce to reclaim the Falkland Islands from Argentina.

1985
The first organised Chinese New Year celebrations take place in Chinatown.

1986
The left-wing Greater London Council (GLC), led by Ken Livingstone since 1981, is abolished by the Conservative government.

1990
Prime Minister Margaret Thatcher stands down and is replaced by John Major.

1994
Nelson Mandela becomes the first black president of South Africa after some 300 years of white rule.

The National Lottery is founded. Profits put towards good causes so far total some £20bn.

1997
Tony Blair becomes prime minister as Labour win their first general election for 24 years.

On 31 August, Diana, Princess of Wales is killed in a late-night car crash in a Paris underpass. Mourners queue down the Mall to leave flowers and sign a book of condolence.

1998
The British Library moves from the British Museum to new premises at St Pancras. The famous round Reading Room, where Marx wrote *Das Kapital*, becomes an exhibition space.

2003
Ken Livingstone introduces the congestion charge. Initially unpopular, it has since been credited with reducing by 70,000 the number of vehicles entering central London each day.

2005
The traditional Routemaster buses are withdrawn. They are replaced with unpopular bendy buses.

In May, Tony Blair secures an historic third term in office for the Labour government. The severe reduction in the government's majority is largely attributed to the prime minister's policy on Iraq.

On 7 July, Islamic extremists detonate three bombs on the tube, and another on a bus in Tavistock Square, during the morning rush hour. Fifty-six people are killed, including the four terrorists, and some 700 are injured.

2008
Conservative candidate Boris Johnson replaces Ken Livingstone as Mayor of London.

TIME OUT
London
Aug 12-Sept 2

1s

Time Out, issue number 1
The first ever issue of *Time Out* was published on 12 August 1968, with a cover price of one shilling. Printed as a double-sided A2 sheet, it was folded down into an A5 magazine, which readers then had to open out again to read. The cover image was taken from the ICA's recently opened exhibition, Cybernetic Serendipity. The magazine came as a fold-out for one more issue before adopting a more conventional format from 23 September. Frequency was increased from every three weeks to fortnightly in August 1969, but it wasn't until 1971 that the magazine grew to A4 and went weekly. Overleaf is a reduced-size facsimile of the first issue.

Tony Elliott, 1973

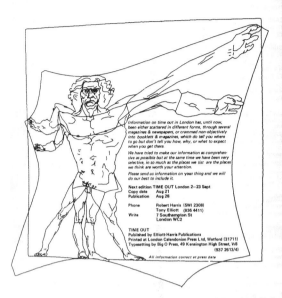

Information on time out in London has, until now, been either scattered in different forms, through several magazines & newspapers, or crammed non-objectively into booklets & magazines, which do tell you where to go but don't tell you how, why, or what to expect when you get there.

We have tried to make our information as comprehensive as possible but at the same time we have been very selective, in so much as the places we list are the places we think are worth your attention.

Please send us information on your thing and we will do our best to include it.

Next edition TIME OUT London 2–23 Sept
Copy date   Aug 21
Publication   Aug 28

Phone   Robert Harris   (SWI 2308)
         Tony Elliott   (836 4411)
Write   7 Southampton St
         London WC2

TIME OUT
Published by Elliott-Harris Publications
Printed at London Calendonian Press Ltd, Watford (31711)
Typesetting by Big O Press, 49 Kensington High Street, W8
                                          (937 2613/4)

All information correct at press date

TIME OUT
London
Aug 12–Sept 2

1s

Buildings

ROYAL COLLEGE OF PHYSICIANS, St Andrews Place, NW1
Place NW1. Gt Portland St tube. massive white facade, slit windows, 2 slender square column. Strange asymetric lecture theatre in dark grey brick; most powerful piece of modern architecture in London. Explore inside on Tuesdays; phone WEL 1174 for appointments.

ST. PANCRAS STATION
Sympathise with the mass of ridiculous little towers on its roof, then go inside and look at the huge delicate iron work roof over the trains, and the iron work of the old gasworks it frames.

THE MONUMENT
Monument tube station. London from above is pale, grey and gentle. Pay 6d and climb 311 steps.

Immediate Event

FOR ANNE

With Annie gone,
Whose eyes to compare
With the morning sun?

Not that I did compare
But I do compare
Now that she's gone.

Leonard Cohen

Classical Music

OPEN AIR CONCERTS IN HOLLAND PARK, W8
Seats bookable at Cavell House, 2a Charing Cross Road.
Deckchairs 6/-, other chairs 4/-
Booking closes at noon on Saturdays.
Buses: 9,12, 27, 28, 31, 49, 73, 88, 207a
Tube: Holland PARK, High St Kensington

11 Aug **London Philharmonic** with Brian Briestman
Overture 'Barber of Seville' **Rossini**
Slavonic Rhapsody No 3 **Dvorak**
Theme and Variations, Suite No 3 **Tchaikovsky**
Symphony 2 in D **Brahms**

18 Aug **Royal Philharmonic Orchestra** with Stanley Pope
Overture Magic Flute **Mozart**
Symphonic dances Op 64 **Grieg**
Capriccio Halien **Tchaikovsky**
Symphony No 5 in E flat **Sibelius**

Bookshops

INDICA, 102 Southampton Row WC1 (HOL 5824)
Little mags, posters, LP's and nice books. Atmosphere friendly and informal

BETTER BOOKS, 94 Charing Cross Road WC1 (836 6944)
Formal purchasing upstairs informal browsing in the basements. Many small mags and superb sections on cinema and poetry also posters. (Open daily 10am–6.20pm)

LONDON ART BOOKSHOP, 72 Charlotte Street W1 (636 8565)
Probably the most comprehensive selection on Art and Architecture in the world. Atmosphere appalling. (Open 9am–6pm not Saturdays)

FREE BOOKSHOP, Colherne Mews, Wharfedale Street SW10 (PAD 2409)
for Free books! (Open 6pm–9pm 10am–6pm Sat & Sun)

Ballet

ROYAL FESTIVAL HALL, South Bank (928 3191)
London's Festival Ballet in 'The Sleeping Beauty' by Tchaikovsky. Seats 28/- to 7/6d
Mon–Fri 7.30pm Sat 4 and 8pm. Until 31 Aug.

Electronic Music

COMPUTER MUSIC
29 Aug 'Music composed with and played by Computer'.
Concert of taped computer music from the Experimental Music Studio at the University of Illinois, with works by Lejaren A. Hiller, Herbert Brun, Gary Grossman, James Cuomo etc.
ICA, Nash House, The Mall W1 (WHI 6393) 8pm Members 5/-, others 7/6d

ELECTRONIC MUSIC STUDIO SURVEY
The Arts Council is undertaking research into the present state of electronic music facilities in Great Britain. Certain studios are known of, but if readers know of studios either privately or collectively owned, could they please contact Keith Winter, Music Assistant, 105 Piccadilly W1.

This publication would like to list performances and performers of **Electronic music** in future editions. Would anyone with any information please contact us.

Records

MUSICLAND, 44 Berwick St., W1 (734 5626)
One of the best record shops of London. Incredible number of really good imported LP's. Coming, new albums from Hendrix, Grateful Dead, Tim Buckley and Apple Tree Theatre.

ONE STOP RECORDS, 40 South Moulton Street W1 (629 4200)
Any American record to order. Had 'Satanic Majesties' LP sleeve a week before Mick Jagger had seen it. Very good selection of imports.

COLLETTS, 70 New Oxford St., W1 (636 3224)
Really good selection of modern and obscure folk records and information.

DOBELLS JAZZ RECORD SHOP, 77 Charing Cross Road WC2 (437 3075)
Widest selection of Jazz in London. Also comprehensive choice of folk LP's.

Jazz

RONNIE SCOTT'S, 47 Frith St., W1 (437 4
12/6 before 9.30pm, £1 thereafter
Sat–Sun 25/- to 30/-
To 17 Aug **Blossom Dearie** with Alan Haven
17 Aug–7 Sept **Joy Marshall** with Ronnie S
Band (8 piece)

August

12	Chris McGregor 100 Club
13	Ken Colyer 100 Club
14	Ronnie Ross Quintet Phoenix
15	Dis Disley 100 Club
16	Dick Morrissey Old Gatehouse
18	Alan Elsdon's Band 100 Club
19	Alan Haven Trio Bull's Head
21	Michael Garrick Phoenix
23	Johnnie Scott Old Gatehouse
24	Alex Welsh 100 Club
26	Mike Westbrook 100 Club
27	Ken Colyer 100 Club
28	Ken Colyer 100 Club
31	Alex Welsh 100 Club

Maynard Ferguson

1 Sept Maynard Ferguson 100 Club

100 CLUB, 100 Oxford Street, W1 (MUS 0933) Membership 2/6d for three m Entrance approx 7/6d

THE PHOENIX, Cavendish Sq., W1 (MAY 1700) Wednesdays 6/-, Students 4/-

OLDE GATEHOUSE, North Road N6 (340 2154) 4/- to 7/6d

BULL'S HEAD, Barnes Bridge, SW13 (PRO 5241) Alan Haven 10/-
Tues, Wed, Thurs Tony Lee/Phil Seeman
Fri, Sat, Sun, Bill Lesarge + guests

TALLY HO, Fortess Road, Kentish Town, (485 1210)
Mondays Dixieland
Tues, Wed, Modern
Thurs New Orleans
Fri, Sat, Jazz Trio

LITTLE THEATRE CLUB, Garrick Yard (COV 0660) Jazz Club
Thurs–Sat 10.30–1am
Membership students free, others 10/-
Entrance: Members 4/-, others 6/-

Marches/Meet the fuzz

August Demonstrations
Nothing much on this month

'THE GREEN BERET', John Wayne's film about the early American involvement in Vietnam opens at the Warner from Aug 8. This is the first Vietnam glorification film, let it be the last!

BANK HOLIDAY WEEKEND, 30 Aug–2 Sept
The 4 Cathedrals March from Canterbury Cathedral to St Pauls, organised by Kent Youth for Peace in Vietnam organisation. Details from 606 1705, The British Council for Peace in Vietnam.

22 Sept **BOAT TRIP TO FRANCE** organised by the British Council for Peace in Vietnam (606 1905). Folkestone to Boulogne in boat carrying 1000 people. Meeting there with representatives of the North Vietnamese delegation in Paris.

Help

CITIZENS ADVICE BUREAU, 26 Bedford Sq., WC1 (636 4066)
Also FULham 1322, HAMpstead 0048, PARk 8170, CUNningham 4815 and EUSton
Advice on almost any problem   2739

RELEASE 603 8654 (Emergencies) 229 7753 (Offices)
52 Princedale Road, W11 (10–5pm
Call this number if you are busted for drugs

THE CENTRAL INFORMATION BUREAU, 7/9 Baker St., W1 (935 8490)
Help for girls: long term and emergency accomodation

THE SAMARITANS (626 9000)
Round the clock service to tempt would-be suicides away from heaven

BIT INFORMATION SERVICE (229 0053) 24 hours
Call any time and ask for what you want, you might get it

SIMON COMMUNITY, 129 Malden Road NW5 (485 6639)
Hospitality to the homeless and restless

Last Trains

OXFORD CIRCUS Central Line
Westbound 12.31am
Eastbound 12.14am
Bakerloo Northbound 12.36am
Southbound 12.29 am
LEICESTER SQUARE
Northern Line Northbound 12.39am,
Southbound 12.31am
Piccadilly Westbound 12.18am
Eastbound 12.23am

Night Buses

PICCADILLY CIRCUS
Piccadilly Line Westbound
12.21am, Eastbound 12.21am
Bakerloo North 12.33am, South 12.34am
N90 Camden Town, Trafalgar Sq.,
Victoria, Pimlico
N91 Willesden, Paddington, Marble Arch
Oxford Circus., Trafalgar Sq., Strand.
N93 Trafalgar Sq., Kings X, Hampstead
Heath.

Folk

INCREDIBLE STRING BAND
25 Aug Magical Mystery Tour
Oct Round the Country—more details next
WHERE IT'S AT

PENTANGLE
26–31 Aug nightly 10.45
Edinburgh Festival, New University Theatre,
George Sq.,

ROY HARPER
24 Aug Les Cousins

LES COUSINS, 49 Greek Street, W1 (GER 5413)
2/6 membership; entrance 5/- and 7/6
Wed, Fri, Sat, 7.30 (Sat all night 12–7)
Coming Aug Stefan Grossman, Tom and Smiley and
others.

THE SINGERS FOLK CLUB, The Union Tavern
52, Lloyd Baker St., WC1 (TER 0421)
Sundays 7.45 Programmes usually settled last
minute, phone 7pm Sats. Often Peggy Seeger and
Ewan McColl

BUNJIES FOLK CELLAR, 27 Lichfield St., WC2
(240 1796) 7.30 every evening
Members 2/- others 4/-

THE TROUBADOR, 265 Old Brompton Road SW5
(FRE 7872) closed until Sept 2

THE ENTERPRISE, 2 Haverstock Hill NW3
(794 2233) Membership 2/-, entrance 4/-, 5/-.
Residents Terry Gould, Marion McKenzie and Don
Benito. Sundays.

Late Shopping

CHEMISTS

JOHN BELL AND CROYDON, 50 Wigmore Street, W1
open to 9.50pm   (935 5555)

BAYSWATER PHARMACY, 108 Westbourne Grove W2
Mon–Sat to 11pm; Sun to 8.30pm   (PAR 4083)

FOOD AND BITS

VINCE'S FOOD STORES, 72 Gloucester Road SW7
9am to midnight every day   (opp tube)

FUTURE STORES LTD., 286 Brompton Road SW3
8am to midnight every day

CENTRA MINI MARKET, 60 Belsize Lane, NW3
10am to 11–11.30pm

Fairs

HAMPSTEAD FAIR,
Hampstead Heath
30 Aug to Sept 2

Swimming

THE SERPENTINE, HYDE PARK
Free 6–10am, then 1/6d Outdoors
THE OASIS, Endell St., W1 (836 9555)
Open 9.30am 1/6d Indoors and out-
doors. Sunroof.
CHELSEA MANOR BATHS, Kings Road.
(FLA 6985) Indoors.
Small pool 9am–6.20
Large 9am–8pm.
1/6d weekdays, 2/- Sat-Sun

SWISS COTTAGE, Central Library
(586 0061)
Mon—Fri 8am–9.30pm 1/6d
Sat 8am–6.30 2/-
Sun 8am–5.30 2/-

SEYMOUR HALL, Seymour Place, W2
(723 8018) 1/6d
9am—7.30 Indoors

THE SEASIDE, BRIGHTON.
Trains from Victoria (928 5100)
Cheap day 15/9d, single 14/-, return 28/-
Fast trains (55 mins) every hour
Slow (70 mins) 28 past the hour

Groups/Gigs/Events

BRIAN AUGER JULIE DRISCOLL & THE TRINITY
Live each Sunday on David Frost programme.

AYNSLEY DUNBAR RETALIATION
20 Aug   Klooks Kleek, 100 West End Lane NW6

JEFF BECK
In America during Aug/Sept

BLONDE ON BLONDE
24 Aug   Black Sheep, Whitehall SW1
25   Middle Earth Magical Mystery Tour.

ARTHUR BROWN
17 Aug   Roundhouse, Chalk Farm NW1.

31   Fishbourne IOW. (See large notice)

CHICKEN SHACK
16 Aug   Manor House (Bluesville '68), 316 Green Lanes, WHO
                        N4 (800 4678)

JOE COCKER & THE GREASEBAND
14 Aug   Marquee, 90 Wardour Street, W1 (GER 2375)
18   Blaise's, 121 Queen's Gate SW7 (589 6228)
21   Marquee
28   Marquee

SPENCER DAVIS GROUP
16 Aug   Pavillion, Hemel Hempstead

DR K'S BLUESBAND
16 Aug   Blaise's
24   Magical Mystery Tour
30   Black Sheep
31   Fishbourne IOW

FREE
21 Aug   Blaise's
24   Magical Mystery Tour

GLASS MENAGERIE
20 Aug   Marquee
26   Marquee

PETER GREEN'S FLEETWOOD MAC
30 Aug   Manor House (Bluesville '68)

ELMER GANTRY'S VELVET OPERA
21 Aug   Hampstead Country Club

JETHRO TULL
23 Aug   Marquee
27   Blaise's
28   Hampstead Country Club, 210a
                        Haverstock Hill,
JIMI HENDRIX   NW3
In America during Aug/Sept

MARMALADE
23 Aug   Tottenham Royal
27   Marquee

JOHN MAYALL AND THE BLUESBREAKERS
13 Aug   Marquee
23   Middle Earth, Roundhouse.
23   Manor House, (Bluesville '68)

THE NICE	14 Aug	Hampstead Country Club
	22	Marquee
	5 Sept	Marquee
PINK FLOYD		In USA and Belgium during Aug/Sept
PRETTY THINGS	24 Aug	Magical Mystery Tour
TEN YEARS AFTER	16 Aug	Marquee
	30	Marquee
TRAFFIC	24 Aug	Magical Mystery Tour
	29	Victoria Ballroom, Dartford
TYRANNOSAURUS REX	31 Aug	Fishbourne IOW
SELOFANE	18 Aug	Bag O'Nails, 9 King Street W1
	19/20	Bag O'Nails
WHO		In USA during August. Will be back in Britain mid-Sept. for big concert with Arthur Brown in October. Watch Time Out.

Shops

BODIMA, William St., SW1 (BEL 3905)
Beautiful patterned and raw silks 44" wide,
49/11 and 59/6
Cottons 5/-, 10/-
Best printed sheets and towels in London. Lime
on turquoise etc. 2 sheets 72" x 108" 110/-
Towels 3/6–43/6
Double bedspreads, blues, purples etc 65/-
Closes 1pm Sat.
CRAFT GALLERY, Kensington Church St.,
Nr Notting Hill Gate.
Silver and other jewellery by good designers—
Gillian Packard and Brean O'Casey
Terrific pottery, some very cheap
Handprinted silk scarves about 30/-
Some folksy stuff, but mostly good.
WAY-IN, Harrods
Quantity rather than character. Convenient,
everything on show, one place, open to 7pm.
Clothes usually well made, unusually expensive.
Beautiful bras and things (Rosy/Emanuelle Khan)
cosmetics, wrapping paper, cards books
(specially chosen for idiots) records (good
selection—surprising after choice of piped music)
shoes and bags are exclusive, well made, dull.
Big posters made of you for 39/6. Prints 10/6
LAURENCE CORNER, Hampstead Road.
Nr Warren St tube
Use imagination and dylon long wool vests 12/6
Flaired high waisted trousers, white or navy 13/6
Jackets 11/6d–29/6d
Blue worsted waistcoats 6/6d belts,hats, bags, m

Food

STOCKPOT, 14 Hogarth Place, SW5 (373 2407)
Kidneys in red wine 4/6d
2 can eat weel for 12/-
BISTRO VINO, 5 Clareville St., SW7 (373 3903)
Superb value.
Onion soup 2/-
Chicken Chasseur 7/6d
Creme Caramel 2/6d
Entertainment provided by other customers.
JIMMY'S, Frith St., W1.
Goodish, cheapish, plainish. 'Special' each day.
Beef stew 5/6d
HARRODS!, Knightsbridge.
Way-In does jumbo salads–chicken, beef etc
for 6/-
Plain salads 3/6d
Coffee, cream, croissant 1/-
French bread and jam 6d
Open to 7pm

Rabbit Food

CAPRINI'S, SNACK BAR ,Notting Hill Gate.
Huge salads 3/6d
CRANK'S, 22 Carnaby St., W1.
Still good. Salads about 5/-
THE FLYING DRAGON, 436, Kings Road, SW3
11.30am–2am. Macrobiotic.

Middle Earth
The New Roundhouse, Chalk Farm, NW1
(636 6311)

17 Aug   ARTHUR BROWN
23 Aug   JOHN MAYALL
24/25   MAGICAL MYSTERY TOUR
         (to unknown destination)
with: TRAFFIC
         BONZO DOG DOODAH BAND
         FAMILY
         DR K'S BLUES BAND
         FREE
         HURDY GURDY
         DEVIANTS
         INCREDIBLE STRING BAND
         FAIRPORT CONVENTION
         BLONDE ON BLONDE
         BLOSSOM TOES
         PRINCIPLE EDWARDS MAGIC THEATRE

food stalls, fairground, sweet shop and side shows. Events and happenings. 50 buses from Middle Earth with groovy conductors to take you fare. £3. Camping space provided. Buses leave at 10.30. Phone for further information.

EVENT
31 Aug

Fishbourne, Isle of Wight open air concert with Jefferson Airplane, Arthur Brown, Tyrannosaurus Rex and others

Trains:
At 10 and 20 past each hour from Victoria to Portsmouth and then to Rhyde IOW. Trains back 10 minutes to the hour, each hour on Sept 1. Phone WAT 5100 for further information.

New Cinema Club

THE NEW CINEMA CLUB, 122 Wardour St., W1 (734 5888)
Membership 21/- Tickets from above

The Switchboard Operator

14 **Evening Underground** 6.30 ICA, Nash House, W1 8/6d
Evening includes 'Scorpio Rising' and 'Relativity'
14 **The Switchboard Operator** 9.0 ICA 8/6d
Dusan Makavejev's film without cuts
16 **The Complete Picture** Midnight NFT 21/-
Showing of 'The Chelsea Girls' and 'Rush to Judgment'
21 **Something Different** 6.30 ICA 8/6d
Vera Chytilova's study of two yearning women
21 **The Brig** 9.0 ICA 8/6d
Mekas brothers documentary of US military prison. Frightening and noisy
28 **The Switchboard Operator** 6.30 ICA 8/6d
28 **Evening Underground** 9.0 ICA 8/6d

Classics

MARX BROTHERS SEASON
Baker Street, W1 (935 8836)

11–14 Animal Crackers
Sun 2.30, 4.35, 6.40, 8.50
Daily 12.50, 2.25, 4.35, 6.40, 8.50

15–17 Monkey Business
12.50, 2.20, 4.45, 6.35, 8.50

SUNDAY 11th 7 days
CHELSEA, Kings Road, SW3 (352 4388)
The Brothers Karamazov
2.0, 4.50, 7.50

HAMPSTEAD, Pond Street, NW3 (794 4000)
No Way To Treat A Lady (X)
Sunday 4.25, 8.40, Daily 4.45, 9.0
Yesterday, Today and Tomorrow
Sunday 6.20 Daily 2.20, 6.35

NOTTING HILL GATE, W11 (PAR 5750)
The Barrets of Wimpole St
Sunday 4.25, 6.30, 8.40
Daily 1.0, 3.25, 5.55, 8.20

PRAED STREET, W2 (723 5716)
Echo of the Jackboot
Sunday 4.55, 8.55, Daily 1.10, 5.05, 8.55
The Party's Over
Sunday 3.15, 7.10 Daily 3.20, 7.15

SUNDAY 18th 7 days
BAKER ST., W1 (935 8836)
Darling (X)
Sunday 1.45, 3.50, 6.15, 8.40
Daily 12.40, 3.10, 5.45 8.25

KINGS ROAD, SW3 (352 4388)
The Barretts of Wimpole St.
2.20, 4.20, 6.25, 8.40

HAMPSTEAD, Pond St., NW3 (794 4000)
The Taming of the Shrew
Sunday 4.0, 7.30 Daily 2.15, 7.30

NOTTING HILL GATE, Upper Tooting Rd.,
(627 5566)   SW17
Dracula–Prince of Darkness (X)
Sunday 5.45, 9.0 Daily 2.35, 5.50, 9.05
Frankenstein Conquers the World (X)
Sunday 4.10, 7.25 Daily 1.0, 4.15, 7.30

SUNDAY 25th 7 days
BAKER ST., W1 (935 8836)
The Moving Target
Sunday 2.0, 4.0, 6.20, 8.40
Daily 1.0, 3.25, 5.55, 8.30
CHELSEA, Kings Road, SW3 (352 4388)
Madame Bovary
2.15, 4.10, 6.20, 8.35
HAMPSTEAD, Pond St., NW3 (794 4000)
Exodus
Sunday 3.30, 7.05, Daily 3.05, 6.40
NOTTING HILL GATE, W11 (PAR 5750)
The Firefly
Sunday 3.30, 5.40, 8.20,
Daily 12.50, 3.15, 5.45, 8.20

Cinemas

PARIS PULLMAN, Drayton Gdns, SW10
(FRE 5898)
'Order of the Daisy'
Cinema Club
13 August 7.30 film about the sculpture of
Picasso by Sir Ronald Penrose

21 August 'Father' (Szabo) 11am

EVERYMAN, Hampstead (HAM 1525)
12–18 August The Millionairess
19–25 August The Importance of Being Earnest
26–1 September The Third Man.

N. LONDON FILM THEATRE
104 Crouch Hill, N8
(340 5885)
Membership 3 months 10/-d
17 August Intimate Lighting (Ivan Passer)

ICA, Nash House, The Mall, W1
Throughtou August Thurs–Fri 6 & 8pm
Sat–Sun 3.30, 6 & 8pm
Members only 7/6d and 10/-d
Godard's Weekend

TV Films

BBC 2 'World Cinema' Tuesday evenings
13 August 'Shop on the High St' (1964)
20 August 'The Trial' (1962 Orson Welles)

Ronald Reagan

DYNAMIC RONALD REAGAN 'B' MOVIES!

PRAED ST Classic, W2
18 August 7 days
Ronald Reagan, Barbara Stanwyck
Cattle Queen of Montana (U)

STOCKWELL Classic, Clapham Rd., SW9
19 August 3 days only
Ronald Reagan, Patricia Neal
The Hasty Heart (U)

BLUEish Films

DILLY CINE CLUB, Gt Windmill St, W1
(437 6266)
To 17 August 'Venus in Furs'
Membership and entrance both 12/6d

COMPTON CINE CLUB, Old Compton St, W1
(437 4555)
Ring for programme
Membership and entrance 10/-d

Premieres

15 Aug 'Helga', Prince of Wales: Sex Education film

10 Sept 'Gone With The Wind' Bach at the Empire.

National Film Theatre

NATIONAL FILM THEATRE, South Bank, Waterloo
Box Office 928 3232/33
Associate membership 10/6d
Full membership £1 12 6

Autumn programme

12 **Nazarin** (Luis Bunuel 1958) 6.15 and 8.30
13 **The War Lord** (F Schaffner 1965) 6.15 and 8.45 Charlton Heston as Norman warrior in conflict
between paganism and Christianity. Spectacular medaeval battle.
14 **Nazarin** 6.15 and 8.40
15 **Summer Interlude** (I Bergman 1951) 6.15 and 8.30 'the special sweet sadness remains unforgettable'
16 **To Be And Not To Be** (E Lubnitsch 1942) 4, 6.20 and 8.45. Brilliant comedy with Jews and fascists.
17 **Le Beau Serge** (Chabrol) and **Les Mistons** (Truffaut) 4, 6.20 and 8.45. 2 historic films, part of
'Free Cinema'; mark official birth new era
18 **To Be And Not To Be** 4, 6.15 and 8.30
19 **Shorts 1** 6.15 includes 'Vive Beau' photographed by Raoul Coutard
20 **Shorts 2** 6.15 includes 'Experience' a stunning visual-record and analysis of Jimi Hendrix. **Shorts 1** 8.30
21 **Shorts 3** 6.15 includes Don Levy's 'Opus'
Shorts 4 8.30 includes the surreal 'les Corbeaux'
22 **Shorts 5** 6.15
Shorts 3 8.30
23 **Shorts 4** 6.15
Shorts 5 8.30
Shorts 6 11.30 All night show
24 **Shorts 7** 4.0
Shorts 8 6.15 includes 'Warhol's Exploding Plastic Invitable'
The Ernie Game (Don Owen 1967) 8.30
25 **Shorts 9** 4.0 includes 'Edith Piaf'
Shorts 10 6.15 includes Don Levy's 'Five Short Films'
The Illiac Passion (G Markopolous 1967) 8.30
26 **Boule de Suif** 1934 version of Maupassant's story (Russian) 6.15 and 8.30
27 **Major Dundee** (S Peckingpah 1964) good epic western 6 & 8.45
28 **Boule de Suif** 6.15
Palm Beach Story (Preston Sturges 1942) 8.30
29 **Palm Beach Story** 6.15 & 8.30
30 **Johnny O'Clock** (Rossen 1946) and **The Hanged Man** (Don Siegal 1964) 7.0
31 **Les Parents Terribles** (J Cocteau 1949) 4,6.15 and 8.30
1 **Olympiad Part 2, Tokyo Olympiad** 2.0
The Deadly Companions (S Peckinpah 1961) western 6.30 and 8.45

Shorts 5

Late Night Cinema

LATE NIGHT FILMS AT THE CLASSICS

CHELSEA Mon–Fri 11.15
12–17 Aug Hot Enough For June
19–25 Aug Harakiri
26–30 Aug The War Is Over

NOTTING HILL GATE Mon –Fri 11'15
12–17 Caged
19–25 4 Kinds of Love
26–30 Viridiana

SATURDAY AUGUST 17
Days of Wine and Roses–Cameo Victoria 11.15
And So To Bed–Hampstead 11pm
This Sporting Life–Hendon 11.15
4 for Texas–Tooting 11.15
Monkey Business–Baker St. 11.15
The Lady With the Little Dog–Paris Pullman 11

SATURDAY AUGUST 24
Darling–Baker St. 11.15
The Girl Rosemarie–Cameo victoria 11.15
Days of Wine and Roses–Hampstead 11
Dr Crippen–Tooting 11.15
Shakespeare Wallah–Paris Pullman

SATURDAY AUGUST 31
The moving Target–Baker St. 11.15
Paris Vu Par–Cameo Victoria 11.15
Viridiana–Chingford 11pm
Cry The Beloved Country–Hampstead 11
Vivre Sa Vie–Hendon 11.15
The Peach Thief–Paris Pullman 11

ARTS LABORATORY, 182 Drury Lane WC2 (242 3407)
THEATRE

Nightly/indefinitely 'Shouts and Murmurs' Osborne and Tynan
Saturdays 9pm Lecture to An Academy Kafka
13 Aug (2 Weeks) 'Hakuim and Events in Uncle Harry's Head' with Bazkershaw, Mike Dean,
Will Sporr
13 Aug (2 Weeks) 'Drama in a Wide Media Environment' (Malcolm Legrice)

DANCE
24–30 Aug Edith Stephen Dance Company

MUSIC
Sundays 6pm New Music Concepts
Fridays Midnight Music selected by John Peel

POETRY
Wednesdays Readings and discussion. Guerilla poets
24 Aug Experimental Phonetic and Concrete Lily Greenham

EXCHANGES
Tuesdays 9.45pm Series of Dialogues
27 Aug Newspaper/magazine editors discuss their policies
22 Aug Macrobiotic Congress

CINEMA
Tuesdays open screening
14–17 'Loi de Vietnam' Godard, Chabrol, Renais, Marker, Klein etc 8
17 Late show 'Hallelujah The Hills' (Mekas Brothers)   and 10pm
'Hunchback of Notre Dame'
18 Paris Cine Tracks
21–22 Open to visiting film makers
23 Films from RCA
24 Late show 'An Actor's Revenge' (Kon Ichikawa)
'Rocketship X–M' 'Further out than 2001'
28–31 Warhol's 'The Chelsea Girls' 2 Screens 3¾hrs 7pm (ends 12)
31 Late Show Lang's 'Cloak and Dagger' Gary Cooper and Lilli Palmer

Poetry-Readings

17 Aug **Guerilla Poets** take part in children's entertainment at the motorway playsite, Ladbroke
Grove, W10

STREET READINGS Organised by Guerilla poets
25 Aug Petticoat Lane meet noon outside Whitechapel Art Gallery
29 Aug Soho Meet 8pm in 'Yorminster' pub, Dean St., W1

POETRY WORKSHOPS AND READINGS

Arts Lab., 182 Drury Lane, WC2 (242 3407)
Readings and discussion. Free every Wednesday.

Ladbroke Hotel, Talbot Grove, W11
Jazz, Poetry and Music every Wed 8–11pm 2/6d

7 Denby Road W11
All welcome to workshop every Friday 8pm organised by Carlyle Reedy.

OWL, Guerilla poets' magazine. Contributions for first edition to Kate Sanders, 17 Vardene Road, SW11
(223 5616) Sæ for return of mss.

Theatre Clubs

AMBIANCE, 1 Queensway, W2 (BAY 0990)
Lunchtime plays; subscription 5/- p.a.
Closed 10 Aug–mid Sept
Affiliated to Theatrescope.

ARTS, Gt. Newport St., W1 (836 3334)
Membership 1gn (full 3gn)
To 16 Aug 'The Rasputin Show' by
Michael Almaz. Tues-Fri 7.30pm.

GROUP THEATRE, Grange St., N1.
(CUN 9235) Closed to Sept 3

HAMPSTEAD, 98 Avenue Road, NW3
(PRI 9301) Membership 21/-, Students
7/6d, Camden Library members free.
19-24 Aug 'The Proud Roots'. Mixed race
cast in play based on incident during the
slave uprising in Haiti.
Closed 25 Aug-4 Sept.

LITTLE, Garrick Yard, WC2 (COV 0660)
Student membership 10/6, others 31/-
To 25 Aug 'Chain of Command' 3/6 members,
guests 5/-.

MERCURY, 2 Ladbroke Road, WC11.
(402 6926) International Theatre Club
closed to mid-Sept.

MOUNTVIEW, 104 Crouch Hill, Hornsey, N8.
(340 5885) Membership 7/6
15, 16 Aug (8pm), 17 (9.45), 'The Diary of
Anne Frank'. Then closed to Sept 16.

OPEN SPACE, 32, Tottenham Court Rd., W1.
(580 4970) Membership 42/-, Students 10/-,
Visitors (3 months) 10/-
To Aug 25 'Fortune and Men's Eyes' by John
Herbert. 8pm Tues-Sun.

QUESTORS, Mattock Lane, W5
(567 0011) To Sept 21 closed. Re-opening
with 'The Homecoming'.

STUDIO, Oval House, Kennington Oval, SE11
(735 2786) Re-opening mid-Sept. Membership 5/-, usually no entrance.

THEATRESCOPE, St. Martin's Lane, W1.
Lunchtime plays again end Sept.

TOWER, Canonbury Place, N1. (226 5111)
Closed for rennovation until Oct 11.

UNITY, 1 Goldington St., NW1 (EUS 8647)
To Aug 30 closed. Re-opens with Ted Roszak's
'The Rent' concerning the rootcauses of
violence in the USA. 10/-, 7/6 and 5/-
Associate membership 7/6d.

Puppets

LITTLE ANGEL MARRIONETTE THEATRE,
14 Dagmar Passage, N1 (CAN 1787)
To 30 Aug 'Briar Rose', the story of Sleeping
Beauty. 3pm each day.
4/6d children, 6/- adults.
11am Sat childrens' special show

CHILDRENS' PLAYGROUND, KENSINGTON
GARDENS Puppet shows. Free daily 11am
and 3pm.
August
5–10 Sugar Loaf Puppets
12–17 Melville Thomson
19–24 Pex puppets

LITTLE ANGEL PUPPET THEATRE
15-17 Aug Queen Elizabeth Hall
Stravinsky 'The Soldier's Tale'
Debussy 'La Boite a Joujoux'
Narrator Michael Flanders
Conductor Daniel Barenboim

Exhibitions

'ART AND MENTAL HEALTH' 9 Aug–1 Sept. Free.
Commonwealth Institute, High St. Kensington. (937 8252)

'200 YEARS OF JIGSAW PUZZLES', London Museum, Kensington Palace, W8.
(937 9816) To Nov 17

THE DESIGN CENTRE, 28 Haymarket, SW1 (TRA 8000) Free to Sept 14
'Shopping in Britain', 'Costume Jewellery'.

JEAN STRAKER'S PHOTONUDES, Academy of Visual Arts, 12, Soho Square, W1. 10/-

MODERN JEWELLERY, Ewan Phillips Gallery, 22a Maddox St., W1.

'CYBERNETIC SEREPENDIPITY', ICA Gallery, Nash House, The Mall, SW1 (WHI 6393)
To Oct 20. Entrance 8/-, members 4/-. Major international exhibition exploring and demonstrating realtionships between the arts and technology.

'PRIMARY SCHOOLS EXHIBITION', Camden Arts Centre, Arkwright Road, NW3
(435 2643). To Aug 18. Closed Mondays.

MASTERPIECES OF BRITISH GLASS', British Museum, Gt Russell St., WC1 (636 1555)
To Sept 29

'ENGLISH GLASS' 1575–1830, Victoria and Albert Museum, SW7 Until 31 Aug.

'THE GRAPHIC WORK OF ANTHONY GROSS', Victoria and Albert. Until 28 Sept.

FACSIMILES OF WORKS BY WILLIAM BLAKE (1757–1827)
To 31 Aug. Forty Hall, Forty Hill, Enfield

THE ITALIAN RENAISSANCE, Assmore Edwards Museum, Romford Road, E15
A Victoria and Albert Loan exhibition. Free, to 29 Sept

'OP' GRAPHICS, Works by Bridget Riley, Peter Sedgley, Cruz–Diezl, Heinz Mack,
J.R.Soto, Le Parc and others. Earlsfield Library, Magdalen Road SW18

CONTEMPORARY AFRICAN ARTS, 38 King St., WC1. Sculpture, Painting, fashion,
jewellery etc

Theatre

For FULL West End list see daily or evening
newspapers.

ALDWYCH, (Royal Shakespeare Co.)
The Strand, WC2 (TEM 6404)
Stalls and Dress Circles 32/6 25/- 17/6 12/6,
Upper Circle 12/6 7/6, Seats at 12/6, Box (for 4)
£5.

RSC Club Performance
13, 14 Aug		7.20
'The Relapse'		
15 Aug (begins)		7.30
16		7.30
17	2.00	7.30
20		7.30
21	2.00	(Mat)
' The Merry Wives of Windsor'		
19 Aug		7.30
24	2.00	(Mat)
'Indians' (World Premier)		
22 Aug		7.30
23		7.30

STRATFORD-UPON-AVON, Royal Shakespeare
Theatre Comapny
(Stratford 2271) Stalls and Drecs Circle 35/- 25/-
20/- 12/6
Balcony 9/-, Standing 5/-, Box (for4) £5.

'King Lear'		
12 Aug		7.30
13		7.30
17	2.00	(Mat)
22		7.30
29	2.00	(Mat)
'Troilus and Cressida'		
14 Aug		7.30
15	2.00	(Mat)
17		7.30
22		7.30
31		7.30
'Doctor Faustus'		
15 Aug		7.30
21		7.30
23		7.30
27		7.30
31	2.00	(Mat)
'As You Like It'		
16 Aug		7.30
19		7.30
24	2.00	(Mat)
29		7.30
30		7.30
Poetry Recital		
25 Aug		8.00

Trains from Paddington
(enquiries 262 6767)
Cheap day Return 32/-
The Journey takes approximately 2½hrs. No
trains back after evening performances.

STUDIO 68, 68 Broadwalk Court W8
14–15 & 21 Aug 'The TrojanWomen' by
Euripides. Set in Vietnam today, to be followed
by
'Love Me or I'll Kill You' (free 1st week in
September) by Daniel Harden Clark of La Mama.
The Panel Room, University College of London
Union, Gordon Street WC1

JEANETTA COCHRANE, Southampton Row WC1
(242 7040)
19 Aug 'The Apprentices' by Peter Terson, National
Youth Theatre. To Sept 10.

TOYNBEE, 28 Commercial Street, Aldgate E1
(247 6788)
Closed to 21 Sept. Reopening with Czech
theatre groups musical 'The Bridegrooms'
at 7.30pm. Tickets on sale a fortnight before.

Paintings - Sculpture

ART IN PARKS, on site of corner Cheyne Walk and Oakley ST., Chelsea. The arts of
100 odd artists in Pavilions—experimental films, poetry, music, sculpture painting,
experiments with lights etc. Runs until Oct 30.

CAMDEN ARTS CENTRE, Arkwright Road, NW3 (435 2643)
To Sept 1 'Preview London', an exhibition of contemporary paintings and sculpture.
19 Aug Above exhibition featured on Thames TV (1Hour)

GIMPEL FILS, 20 South Moulton St., W1 (HYD 2488)
To 24 Aug, sculpture by Isamu Noguchi

HAYWARD GALLERY, South Bank, Nr Festival Hall.
To 8 Sept 'Matisse' 10.30–7pm, sun 10—6pm

HANOVER GALLERY, 32a, George St., W1 (MAY 0296)
To 31 Aug, sculpture by 'Magritte'

LUMLEY CAZALET, 24 Davies St., W1 (499 5058)
Lithographs and aqua-tints by 'Matisse' 4 Sept Miro

MARLBOROUGH FINE ART, 39 Old Bond St., W1 (May 5161)
To 7 Sept Modern masters

OBELISK, 15 Crawford St., W1 (HUN 9821)
Continuous exhibition of young contemporaries and Surrealist masters. Until Sept.

TATE, Millbank (TAT 4444)
To 22 Sept, Henry Moore 70th birthday exhibition

TOOTH'S, 31 Bruton St., W1 (GRO6741)
French paintings include some by Boudin, Gaugin, Lebourg, Luce, Marquet, Moret,
Segonzac, Utrillo, Vlaminck. Ends Sept 28

HAMPSTEAD OPEN AIR EXHIBITION, Whitestone Pond, Heath St., Hampstead
Every Sat and Sun to 25 Aug

CENTRAL LIBRARY, Swiss Cottage
'Pablo Picasso', retrospective of reproductions from period 1900–1956 Ends 17 Aug.
'Edgar Degas' oils and pastels reproductions from period 1865–1898

Lectures

LECTURES ON ART
BM   BRITISH MUSEUM, Gt. Russell St., WC1 (636 1555)
NG   NATIONAL GALLERY, Trafalgar Sq. (WHI 7618)
TG   TATE GALLERY, Millbank. TAT 4444)
VA   VICTORIA AND ALBERT, SW7 (589 6371)

August
12 'Orcanagna' BM 1pm
13 'Cubism' TG 1pm
14 'Massacio' NG 1pm
    'Imperial Neo Classicism' VA 1.15pm
    'Callot' BM 3pm
15 'Fra Angellico' NG 1pm
    'Moves towards Abstraction' TG 1pm
    'Pioneers of Abstract Art' TG 3pm
    'Canaletto' BM 11.30am
17 'Dada, Surrealism and Its Role in C20 Art' TG 1pm
19 'Piero della Francesca' NG 1pm TG 3pm
20 'Some 'Expressionist' painters' TG 1pm
21 'C15 Masterpieces' NG 1pm
    'Romantic Style 1' VA 1.15pm
    'Persian Painting' BM 11.30pm
22 'Botticelli' NG 1pm
    'L. S. Lowry' TG 1pm
    'Chinese Porcelain' BM 11.30am
    'Goya' BM 3pm
23 'Rembrandt' BM 1pm
26 'Uccello' NG 1pm
    'Egyptian Sculpture' BM 11.30 am
27 'Degas' BM 6pm
    'Modern English Romantics' Tg 1pm
28 'Romantic Style 11' VA 1.15pm
29 'Phillippono Lippi' NG 1pm
    'Art and Technicology'
    'European Art in the 1950's' TG 3pm
31 'Contemporary English and USA Painting
    /Sculpture'
    'Chinese Painting' BM 1pm TG 3pm

NATURAL HISTORY MUSEUM, SW7 (589 6323)
17 Aug 'The Age of Dinosaurs'. Lecture with films.

CYBERNETIC SERENDIPITY (art and technology),
Lectures at the ICA, Nash House, The Mall, W1 (WHI 6393) 8pm. Non-members 7/6d,
members 5/-.
August
13   'Composer's input outputs music'
15   'Museums without labels'
20   'Who was Martin Marprelate?'
27   'Sleeping and Dreaming'

'The Snail' (Cybernetic Serendipity.)

W 14
Th 15
F 16
Sa 17
Su 18
M 19
Tu 20
W 21
Th 22
F 23
Sa 24
Su 25
M 26
Tu 27
W 28
Th 29

INTRODUCTION

London in numbers

Population of Greater London
7.69 million in 1968
7.45 million in 1971
6.83 million in 1992
7.36 million today
8.1 million predicted by 2016

£401m
Theatre box office receipts in 2006

6,000
Estimated number of restaurants, 22 per cent of the total number in the UK

3,800
Estimated number of pubs

29 drug-related offences per 100,000 Londoners, 1991
346 drug-related offences per 100,000 Londoners, 1999

Average house price
£319,000 today
£177,867 in 2000
£77,697 in 1988
£7,588 in 1969

£2,618
Average annual income of London home owners in 1969 (£31,038 in today's money)

20.5kg per week
Household waste produced by the average home

21,140
Households officially homeless in 2005

43 minutes
Average journey time to get to work, 2008

2,282 miles
Average distance per person travelled on public transport across inner London in a year

£8
Typical weekly room rental, 1968

30%
Percentage of the London population that is from non-white groups (43 per cent of the UK non-white total)

£29,000
A Londoner's average annual contribution to the economy, compared with £19,100 for inhabitants of the UK as a whole

£150
Typical weekly room rental, 2008

Currently licensed
2.5 million cars
21,000 black cabs

one and eightpence
Price of a pint, 1968

30%
Proportion of London that is open space, including 147 parks and gardens and 8 royal parks

INTRODUCTION

HEDONISM INTRODUCTION
SEX **CITYSCAPE** FASHION
SOCIETY SHOPPING COMEDY
DRAMA PROTEST & POLITICS
VISUAL ARTS PERFORMANCE
LITERATURE GANGS OPINION
COCKNEYS BARS ON SCREEN
DANCE MUSIC TELEVISION
BUILDINGS CLUBS NIGHTLIFE
SPORT & FITNESS MEMORIES
STYLE FOOD & DRINK GIGS
CONSUME RIOTS REFERENCE

Inventing the modern
metropolis

In the late '60s, a new generation of architects was turning its back on brutalism and dreaming of fun palaces, cities on legs and streets in the sky. Since then, London has abandoned its industrial territories, built upwards and established a new metropolis on the Isle of Dogs. But just how radical did the millennial city turn out to be?

By Piers Gough

Nineteen sixty-eight was a brilliant year for me. I was having my year out from college between sections of my architecture degree, and rather than work for another architect, I and my now partners found work privately through rag-trade connections. Fashion was red-hot in '68, it was Mary Quant, Biba, Carnaby Street, King's Road dolly birds, short skirts, Twiggy… We did a boutique in South Molton Street for a designer from Croydon called Mary Farrin who made angora wool dresses and skirts and tops. Somehow angora summed up the '60s – it was fluffy, fun, foolish and completely impractical.

I was studying at the Architectural Association in Bedford Square where the expectation of architects was untrammelled optimism, not only about your career prospects but also about the possibilities of architecture. We were tutored by Archigram (the avant-garde pop architecture theorists of Plug-in City), Stirling and Gowan had built the eclectic Leicester engineering block, Richard Seifert's Centre Point and the Post Office Tower had gone up, and there was a feeling that you could build just about anything. We felt like kings of the earth already, even though we were just students. Built architecture wasn't swinging by any stretch of the imagination, but the AA made you believe it would spread to architecture.

The high style of architecture in the 1960s was brutalism. The Barbican and the South Bank Centre were just finished. Unfortunately, they were only really liked by other architects and cognoscenti.

But at architecture schools we were talking about new, hopefully more popular, approaches – high-tech, colour, pop, inflatables, lightweight buildings and three-dimensional cities. In the early '60s, Cedric Price published his Fun Palace project with Joan Littlewood: a venue for dancing, music, drama and fireworks in Leicester Square. The idea of architects being involved in the naughty side of London rather than just building hospitals and schools was a turn-on. Our issues were about ramping up the excitement of the city.

In 1975 we (myself, Nicholas Campbell, Roger Zogolovitch and Rex Wilkinson) started CZWG, not to realise any particular architectural principles that we held, but simply because it

was better to work for ourselves. We were capricious people and the least philosophical. Our whole ethos was based on opposition to worthiness and the ugly architecture of the '60s. Though we liked the South Bank as a heroic thing, we wanted to avoid doing it ourselves. We wanted to move architecture on to something more popularist and thought our sort of pop approach was more likely to find public favour.

From the war right up until the 1970s there was quite a cavalier attitude to knocking down things that today we definitely wouldn't. Covent Garden had a close shave when the GLC proposed demolishing it and building a six-lane highway along Maiden Lane. Members of Save Britain's Heritage started locking themselves in buildings in Spitalfields to protect them from demolition. We also liked saving old buildings because we saw it as being against the old architectural ethos, which was to demolish everything.

The massive campaign to save Covent Garden, through an odd alliance of far-left and right, pushed everyone towards thinking about preserving many more old buildings – but eventually the heritage lobby got too powerful and started to oppose everything. Now, things have gone so far that the trend has completely reversed out to an obsession with saving everything, though, to be fair, trees are considered even more sacred than buildings.

Docklands dreams

The most radical change to London's physical geography has been in Docklands. The devastation resulting from the docks closing in the '70s was cataclysmic. The main employer for all the communities along this stretch of the Thames disappeared almost overnight when containerisation moved to Tilbury, leaving a huge, derelict vacuum. Commentators would go down to the deserted docks and write atmospheric poems to the rusting steel.

All the local authorities that were adjacent to the river were left-wing – Tower Hamlets, Newham, Southwark, Greenwich, Lewisham – and as such felt that the empty properties must be used to provide replacement blue-collar jobs. Where all of

A shining 21st-century city as seen from above Waterloo station.

these new employers would come from nobody didn't know, but they couldn't bring themselves to allow the vacant land to become white-collar or residential.

It took the right-wing radicalism of Margaret Thatcher and her environment secretary, Michael Heseltine, to break the logjam and open up the Docklands as a planning free-for-all. Setting up the London Docklands Development Corporation (LDDC) in 1981, they seized control of all former dockland in Wapping, Limehouse, Bermondsey, Rotherhithe, the Isle of Dogs and the Royal Docks, relieving the local authorities of their planning powers, much to their chagrin. In its 17 years of existence, the LDDC helped create more than 23,400 new homes, 2.3 million square metres of commercial floorspace, and boosted employment from 27,200 to 82,000 (though not necessarily with jobs for the local community). The local authorities, meanwhile, continued to oppose every planning application that was made, right to the end.

For an architect, the LDDC was wonderful. It didn't have the planning restrictions one was normally subject to (although their approach to historic buildings was controlling and exemplary). It was a committee of people who weren't elected. You simply went to the planners with what you wanted to do, and more often than not it would be passed, usually against the wishes of the local community. But that, of course, was the point: to bypass nimbyism in favour of regeneration.

In spite of the central Isle of Dogs also being heavily oiled with tax breaks, to start with the LDDC got the potential of the area completely wrong. Many of the planning officers had come from the new town of Milton Keynes, and what they created at first was Milton Keynes-on-Thames – a lot of low-rise tin sheds with saw-toothed roofs and a yellow brick road – so that Cascades, the 20-storey apartment block CZWG did in 1988, was a big surprise. You wouldn't have been allowed to build that anywhere else in London at the time, as it smacked too much of reviled council blocks.

Then a developer with the unlikely name of G Ware Travelstead turned up, and in 1985 convinced the LDDC that what it needed was a £1.5bn financial centre, to be called 'Star Wars', right in the middle of the Isle of Dogs. As it turned out, Mr Gee Whizz was just a mouth and not much money, so the LDDC approached Canadian company Olympia & York, owned by the Reichmann brothers. The myth is that by flying them

Clockwise from left: Bermondsey's swanky Jam Factory flats; Canary Wharf reaches for the sky; the Barbican causes waves; the suits move in to Docklands; and the Lloyd's Building sends out a frisson of excitement.

over the site in a helicopter they convinced the Reichmanns that the Docklands was merely an extension of the City. The scheme, rechristened Canary Wharf, began construction in May 1988 and the first occupants moved into the tower in 1991. The following year, Olympia & York, along with several of the area's other main developers, went bust in what was to be a particularly harsh recession for the construction industry.

The second phase of Docklands development over the past ten years has seen the area transform from Milton Keynes to Chicago, demolishing many of the unambitious earlier buildings and throwing up a succession of high-rises that have created a new skyline on the Isle of Dogs. It looks as if a Felliniesque flotilla has steamed across from America and just moored there.

Po-mo a gogo

Back in the centre of town, post-modernism became the rampant architectural style of the 1980s and early '90s. On the whole it was pretty gruesome. American architect Robert Venturi's 1971 book

Complexity and Contradiction in Architecture had inspired many British architects to get eclectic and mix up idioms. The problem was everyone wasn't as clever as Venturi (and even he came a bit unstuck at the National Gallery). Architects had spent the whole period having the media knock the hell out of them, but they already regretted the '60s and didn't need to be told that they had been bad boys. The profession became so denigrated that it lost confidence. The result was a lot of post-modern buildings that were desperate to please.

One exception was Terry Farrell and his prominent buildings of the '80s; his Charing Cross development, Embankment Place, is a pretty impressive office building. The most exhilarating one of the time was the Lloyd's Building, Richard Rogers' spectacular Piranesian lesson on the

anatomy of a building's guts. But it was an exception: the rising London stars (Foster, Rogers and Stirling) were building ground-breaking buildings internationally, but, at the time, not here.

Elsewhere, along the river and canals, warehouse living pioneered in Shad Thames and Wapping was catching on. Industry had migrated from central London to the M25, completed in 1986, leaving plenty of empty industrial buildings. The recession that was bad for Canary Wharf was good for lofts. In Clerkenwell, Harry Handelsman's company Manhattan Lofts had bought an old printing inks factory with huge windows and asked CZWG to convert it. Boroughs such as Camden caved in and started allowing residential conversions when they realised light industry was never going to return.

The genius of Manhattan Lofts, also at Soho and Bankside Lofts and their contemporaries, was to sell people a lifestyle. There was a huge financial slump, but instead of saying 'we need to batten down the hatches', they said 'cheer up, look at all this space you could have'. And because the property business is incredibly copycat, it wasn't long before everybody was doing it – Alaska (a former sealskin factory), the Jam factory (formerly Hartley's) in Bermondsey, and King's Cross Central.

Brilliant Broadgate

Stuart Lipton, working for the developer Greycoat, brought in the idea at Broadgate that, instead of going to commercial architects for off-the-peg office blocks, you could hire fine ones such as Arup or SOM, who would create something unique and classy. That idea has culminated in Norman Foster's Gherkin, the first high-rise the public has liked from the off, with the possibility to come of Renzo Piano's 'Shard', Richard Rogers' 'Cheesegrater', Rafael Viñoly's 'Walkie Talkie', and Jean Nouvel's 'Cloud'.

Unfortunately, these big names of high-tech are being wheeled out by every copycat developer around (Foster alone has a dozen city buildings). However, this architectural style is now way past its sell-by date. And it's almost as passé to turn to the more baroque next generation of Will Alsop, Zaha Hadid and Rem Koolhas, or the modern

Herzog & de Meuron's Laban centre (below) and Foster & Partners' Canary Wharf station have rekindled the public's passion for architecture.

rococo of Foreign Office and Herzog & de Meuron, or else undisputed kings of cool such as Eric Parry and David Chipperfield.

Architects' confidence had returned generally with the lottery and the millennium, the closest London has come to that unbridled optimism we felt as students. This time the public seemed excited too. Television shows did wonders, while the lottery ensured money for architectural delight on public buildings and infrastructure (which had stalled completely under Thatcher). Perversely, instead of projects akin to Danny Libeskind's Imperial War Museum of the North, London ended up with a lot of conversions: the converted Royal Opera House, the converted Tate Modern, ditto Royal Court, ditto Serpentine Gallery, extended National Portrait Gallery… only Herzog & de Meuron's small Laban Centre stands out as an inspiring new lottery-funded building.

The Millennium Dome, on the other hand, was bombastic. By basing it on 12 masts, it immediately predetermined how you had to lay the building out. It was so un-free, it was so lacking in grace; you had to put an arena in the middle and you had to

put things equally plonked around it. Everyone blames what they put into it, but it was the building that was also a killer.

The most interesting buildings now in London are in the urban inner suburbs – mixed use, very green and with a high proportion of affordable housing – designed by firms with chunky initials, AHMM, dRMM, DSDHA, not to mention FAT, MUF and so on. The next tranche of interest will be in the relative comfort of the well-connected suburban outer suburbs, rather than the disconnected swamps of the Thames Gateway. The architects to watch out for will no doubt be called >*/} and <%#.

In spite of all this, although London's Docklands and the central skyline are inventions of the past 40 years, fundamentally the capital remains physically unchanged. We've taken down buildings and put new ones up, but open an *A-Z* from 1908 and it would show all the main streets in all the same places. The only areas an Edwardian would get lost in are Canary Wharf, the Barbican and the South Bank. Otherwise, London is still a city of Victorian streets, squares and parks, with modern buildings standing in them.

Regrettably, the outlandish ideas of our youth and the utopian promise of a multi-level city that was started around the Barbican and London Wall, eventually came to naught. For all our caprice, architects haven't reinvented London, so much as redecorated it. We've painted the walls and put in some fancy furniture, but essentially the capital still remains a glammed-up Victorian dwelling with dodgy plumbing (that we are only now starting to put right).

Piers Gough is one of the founding architects of London practice CZWG.

TIMELINE

1968
Hayward Gallery completes the set of brutalist concrete buildings that make up Southbank Centre.

1969
The Queen officially opens London Underground's Victoria line.

1979
The Jubilee line takes its first passengers. It is London's newest line, but serves stations that first opened more than 100 years ago.

1980
The NatWest Tower is built. At 600 feet, it's the tallest building in Europe until it is topped by Canary Wharf Tower in 1991.

1981
The London Docklands Development Corporation is formed to regenerate the 7.5-mile stretch of dockland from London Bridge to Beckton.

1983
Battersea Power Station ceases to generate electricity and, over successive decades, falls into a state of dereliction as over-the-top proposals for its conversion amount to nothing.

1986
The high-tech Lloyd's Building is met with ambiguity from the public. The building, by Richard Rogers, was innovative for London in having services such as staircases, lifts and water pipes on the outside.

The M25 opens and is quickly branded 'the world's biggest car park'.

1987
The Docklands Light Rail (DLR) takes its first passengers. Great excitement at the driverless trains.

Flights start at London City Airport in the Royal Docks.

1991
Cesar Pelli's One Canada Square, the UK's tallest building at 774 feet, opens at Canary Wharf. By 2012 it will have been superseded by Renzo Piano's 'Shard' at London Bridge.

1992
Canary Wharf developers Olympia & York go into administration during one of the construction industry's worst recessions.

1995
Architects Herzog & de Meuron appointed to convert an ex-power station at Bankside into an additional London gallery for the Tate.

2000
Trams reintroduced to Croydon.

A raft of Lottery-funded architectural landmarks herald the new millennium, including the Millennium Bridge, the Dome, the London Eye and the glass-roofed Great Court at the British Museum, claimed to be the largest covered square in Europe.

2002
Laban dance centre, by Herzog & de Meuron, opens in Deptford. It is noticeable for its exterior made from translucent multi-colored layered plastic.

The Greater London Authority moves into its purpose-built new home, City Hall, designed by Foster & Partners. A rooftop gallery and visible debating chamber aim to promote the values of 'open government'.

2004
30 St Mary Axe, more commonly known as the Gherkin, becomes one of London's most distinctive, and popular, skyscrapers.

2007
A £5.8bn high-speed rail link opens from St Pancras to Ebbsfleet and the Channel Tunnel, the first major rail project in Britain for more than a century.

England Under-21s play Italy in the first football match at the new Wembley stadium.

2008
Heathrow Terminal 5 opens. Mayhem soon follows.

Save Covent Garden

In 1968, the GLC published its draft plan for the removal of Covent Garden's fruit and vegetable market to a new site near Vauxhall, and a radical remodelling of the area. The ambitious scheme proposed hotels, conference centres and a three-lane highway straight through Seven Dials. *Time Out* urged its readers to support the Covent Garden Community group in protesting against the plans.

Covent Garden is a community about to lose its heart. In 1973, literally overnight, the famous fruit and vegetable market will be parceled up, loaded on to trucks (the very trucks whose increasing size is strangling the market on its present site) and driven across the river to reopen the next morning at Nine Elms in Battersea. It is a transplant, say the GLC, from which the Garden as a whole can never recover. Accordingly, they have used the space created by the market's departure – 12-15 acres – as a reason to redevelop the whole 60 acres from Charing Cross to Kingsway and from Holborn to the Strand.

The draft plan in 1968 described Covent Garden as it is with great sensitivity. It underlined the unique quality of the area, both physically and in terms of the variety of activities it is home to. It found Covent Garden occupied by a stable,

low-income population with a high proportion of old people and very few car owners. Eighty-four per cent of the people wanted to stay in the area 'in spite of existing housing conditions'.

Employment depended only partly on the market – there were numerous small offices and industries like publishing and theatrical supply. Both people and jobs could stay in the area only if their rents remained at the present low levels. Finally, Covent Garden's traffic problem was mainly due to the market and the lack of parking controls.

Having so intelligently analysed the Garden and paid tribute to the need to conserve its character, the plan will utterly destroy it. New housing, for example – 'fair rent' housing. For some the new rents will be acceptable, others will be eligible for rebates. But past experience shows that the majority will have to move out.

Manifesto

Covent Garden is a community of about 3,000 people, the majority of them poor and without property, many of them old and dependent on the State. It is a community without facilities – without recreation areas, adequate educational services, community centres or parks. The only thing about Covent Garden that makes it different is its location – sitting on one of the most valuable pieces of real estate in Britain. And real estate that, until recently, has been undervalued because the market, like an octopus, strangled Covent Garden and made redevelopment impossible. Now the market is moving. The dam has burst. The GLC, attempting to ride the wave of private development, has

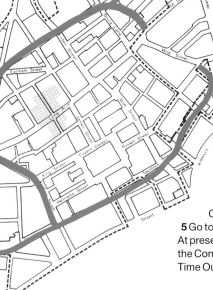

simply been swept under. Only the people of Covent Garden can save themselves. But they need everyone's help – everyone, that is, who cares about London and doesn't want to see it turn into another concrete jungle.

What you can do

1 Sign the Covent Garden Petition
2 Write to or phone the Covent Garden Planning Team. They say they want to hear your views – make sure they do.
3 Help the Covent Garden Community with money. It's going to cost money to put the objections to the Plan in proper legal form for th public enquiry.
4 Support the public meetings of the Covent Garden Community.
5 Go to the public enquiry and protest there. At present it's scheduled for 7 July, although the Community are fighting to have it put back. Time Out will have details. DO IT!

CITYSCAPE

Free speech
Interviews with local workers

Street sweeper with Westminster Council cart
It's not a bad idea that it's being moved – it's the modern age now, and this market is too small, and you can't move with all these big trucks comin' in from Spain and France. I been working here for five years – it's a better atmosphere than workin' on the road. You get a bit o' beer money and a bit o' fruit to take home and everything. The pubs open at five and you can always get a drink.

Old woman, Rules restaurant, Maiden Lane
I've been working here since 1931, and I still can't see why they want to pull this street down. They want to put a wider road through, but it won't make any difference because all the traffic will still go into the bottleneck in Fleet Street. We've put in an official objection and so have Moss Bros up the road. Rules is the oldest restaurant in London – it was built in 1780.

Old Porter, market square
I've worked here 50-odd years. I'm not interested in the change, 'cos I'm not going with it. When I first come here it was a 3d ride return from my home; now I spend six shillings a day for my fare. If I go to whatsisname it'll be more, and I won't be able to get there in time anyway. Most of the porters who live out of London won't be able to get there to start at six o'clock. When I started, you couldn't get oranges all year round – we only had 'em at Xmas and then they was 12 a penny. This market used to be more vegetables, now we sell mostly fruit. That came

in during the war, when you couldn't get the sugar for sweets. I remember an old woman who used to make toffee carrots during the war.

Fat cabbie
We come into the market square for lunch – the grub's lousy but it's handy to park. The beadles won't let you in here in the morning, but it's all right after about two. A lot of tourists ask you to bring them here – they've seen the market in My Fair Lady. It'd be a shame to change it, though – you see a lot of the old London disappearing. I don't like to see all these concrete blocks jumbled in.

Old woman picking up damaged or surplus fruit after the trucks have gone
Yes, we got some forms in to say that they're rebuilding the market – they're going to knock it down and put up flats and offices and that. They're keeping the opera house, though. I've lived here 35 years and I'm really sorry to see it going. Do you know the reason I keep walking around here is that it's the only real breath of country that you get in London – the lovely green smell of the vegetables all fresh.

Following popular protest, the GLC's plans were overturned. Some 250 buildings in Covent Garden were given listed status and the old central market buildings were restored, opening in 1980 as a shopping arcade and tourist attraction. The fruit and veg market moved to 'New Covent Garden' on 11 November 1974, and now accommodates more than 250 traders.

The campaign to save Covent Garden brought together local residents, businesses, heritage activists and left-leaning media. The map (left) shows the GLC's clumsy plan to drive a three-lane highway through the area's historic streets.

The death of Little Britain

'Over there,' says Beryl Williams, pointing at the elegant, empty terrace, 'that was a little firm that made stockings and garters, then a café; the grey doors, that was an auction room, then a bank – a beautiful building – down on the corner.' She pauses, smiling wistfully as the memories of her past neighbours come flooding back. 'There was an office equipment firm, a furrier's, a bric-a-brac shop, a shop that made buttons and ribbons and lace, a carpenter's, a cutler's, a fancy goods maker – he was a wholesaler, old Bill's café, the violin maker…'

Between St Paul's and Smithfield in the heart of the City, the area known as Little Britain is steeped in history. The narrow, winding street, named after the Dukes of Brittany who had a house there, was in existence well before the 16th century. During Stuart times, it was the haunt of booksellers. Milton had lodgings there, as did Benjamin Franklin and the young Samuel Johnson. John Wesley preached there, and Dickens made it the location for the dismal offices of Mr Jaggers, the lawyer in *Great Expectations*.

The miracle of Little Britain is that it has survived; the crime is that this week it will be hammered to dust. Although it has escaped the ravages of time, Little Britain has proved no match for the City Corporation.

Little Britain's fate was sealed on 6 December last year, when Secretary of State for the Environment Patrick Jenkin approved a Corporation-backed plan for a massive Wimpey office tower block, equalling the neighbouring Barbican in height and ugliness. It was the end of a five-year battle between the residents and traders of Little Britain, conservationists and the City of London. It is a battle that has transcended the local issue of whether Little Britain lives or dies, and has become a cause célèbre that calls into question the very existence of the City Corporation and its unique and controversial role as a 'property company that can, in effect, write its own planning permissions.'

The City of London Corporation is Britain's last 'rotten borough'. Its elected representatives often have huge financial interests – albeit declared – in projects the Corporation undertakes. It is a boast of all associated with the Corporation that 'it is a local authority without politics', to use the words of the City's Surveyor Richard Luff.

The end for Little Britain began in 1973, when Jafton Properties Ltd began to buy up half the buildings in the area. The other half had already come under the control of the Corporation itself, which had earmarked Little Britain as 'a comprehensive redevelopment area' through which a two-lane highway was to be built. Like a stack of cards, the properties fell, one by one, under threat of a compulsory purchase order.

'We lost our business, our home, our neighbourhood, everything,' recalls Beryl Williams. 'So did everybody else. They were picked off by the Corporation one by one. The place just deteriorated around us until it became a ghost town.'

By 1977, Jafton's interests had been taken over by Viewcourse, a subsidiary of Wimpey Property Holdings Ltd, which submitted a plan for outline planning permission. Its scale surprised even some City councillors: the road was indeed to be built, but it was to run beneath a massive, pyramid-shaped office block, the proceeds from which were to be shared by Wimpey and the Corporation.

The failure to save Little Britain came about through a number of circumstances. There was no single building – Covent Garden's market, for

> 'Little Britain has become a cause célèbre that calls into question the very existence of the City Corporation.'

example – to rally the press. There was no large residential population – unlike in Soho – to lobby for a stay of execution.

'I am a planner, not an aesthete,' says City Surveyor Richard Luff. 'I have to have a hard commercial nose. It's my job to maximise revenue where I possibly can.' Indeed, Luff's words are a perfect summary of Corporation policy, and bode ill for the parts of London's skyline considered 'ripe for redevelopment'. They hold particular menace for London's market sites: the 'ripest' redevelopment areas the '80s will see. Already, Billingsgate Market, which the Corporation sought to tear down to make way for another massive office block bearing a plaque with the words: 'Here Stood Billingsgate Fish Market, 1875-1982', has escaped destruction by the merest of threads.

There were two reasons why the City wanted to raze Billingsgate: the stone was so permeated with fish smells it would take a decade to clear; and Thames Street, another of the City's 'road improvement' schemes, meant that porters had to cross the road in the rush-hour. SAVE, the conservationist group formed to preserve Billingsgate, drew up an alternative scheme.

The City Corporation fought tooth and nail to press on with demolition. 'Quite frankly, we

The Barbican

By 1976, the City of London, unjustly regarded as a cultural desert, will boast London's most important cultural centre. Two weeks after a record five-hour session, the City Corporation's 'Court of Common Council' gave the green light for the Barbican Arts Centre. It will put under one roof a 1,200-seat theatre for the Royal Shakespeare Company, a 2,000-seat concert hall for the London Symphony Orchestra, a new Guildhall School of Music and Drama, a new library and an art gallery.

It is 15 years since Duncan Sandys sold the City Corporation the idea of creating a 'genuine residential neighbourhood on a 35-acre Blitzed site between Moorgate and Aldersgate Street; 15 years which have not yet proved, one way or the other, if the City can be revived as a residential area, but which have destroyed, in the interim, the whole economic basis of the attempt.

When the scheme was first discussed in 1956, a City Alderman who opposed it accused the City of 'using the most valuable land in Europe as subsidised homes for the well-to-do'. Though Barbican tenants pay from £9 a week for a bedsitter to £40 a week for a town house, they are among the most heavily subsidised in Europe. The Barbican does nothing to solve London's housing problem. Without the Arts Centre, it would be of no benefit to the 400,000 office workers who troop into the City each morning, and out again every night.

wanted to bulldoze the the place,' said Christopher Rauston, chairman of the Billingsgate Market Committee during the crucial year of 1980. 'We regarded it as a derelict old piece of Victorian ironwork destined for the scrap heap. Why save it?'

What ultimately sabotaged the City's destructive plans for Billingsgate was a secret visit by Michael Heseltine, then Environment Minister, which resulted in the building being listed. 'It was one of his famous instant environmental decisions,' says a disappointed Luff.

The City's reckless, profit-mongering behaviour at Billingsgate now overshadows the future of Smithfield Market, where the pressure for redevelopment has grown as the business of the famous meat market has fallen off. Trade has decreased substantially over the last two decades, caused in the main by big supermarket chains like Sainsbury's setting up their own 'bulk-breaking depots', thus obviating the need to buy from Smithfield, with its age-old 'restrictive practices' where 'pitchers, pullers-back and bummaries' have separately chargeable handling roles.

London's fourth market, Spitalfields, comprising 12 acres of extremely valuable land between Bishopsgate and Commercial Street, is also owned by the Corporation, although under the jurisdiction of Tower Hamlets planning authority. One of London's poorest boroughs, Tower Hamlets appears keen for the market to move to Docklands and the land to be sold for office use, to inject much needed capital into the rate fund.

At present, the City would seem to be sitting on the fence: three years ago, Greycoates, one of London's most avaricious property companies, considered a major redevelopment scheme for the area, but City Surveyor Luff says the Corporation is uncommitted: 'I don't believe anybody wants to see a thundering great office block coming out of the ground at Spitalfields.'

At any rate, one conclusion is irresistible: there will be no more Covent Garden-style developments in London if the City has anything to do with it.

Down the street from Little Britain, in Bartholomew Close, a small furrier's run by 71-year-old George Shawyer and his son Ray for the past 30 years also awaits its sentence of death. 'We've survived several arsonists, burglaries and the Blitz,' says Ray. 'But we're no match for the City. The letter turfing us out could drop through the door any day now.' *Paul Charman*

Billingsgate was remodelled by Richard Rogers in 1988, Spitalfields has been partially encroached on by developers, and Smithfield is still under threat.

CITYSCAPE

Seminal structures

The key buildings that have transformed the capital's streets since 1968.

Thamesmead

Thamesmead

GLC architects

1968

Massive overcrowding in the inner city and East End was a predominent concern of the early '60s. While some Londoners were moved out to satellite New Towns such as Harlow and Hatfield, the GLC embarked on London's own new town on 130 acres of marshland by the Thames at Abbey Wood. A mix of high- and low-rise buildings was constructed, and artificial lakes were created to drain the land.

Unfortunately, Thamesmead's promise of a vibrant new commmunity within easy reach of London never really materialised, and instead the estates became better known as the location for films *A Clockwork Orange* and *Beautiful Thing*.

Westway

Motorway Development Trust

Paddington–Western Avenue,1964-70

This 2.5-mile dual carriageway was the largest continuous concrete structure in Britain when it was opened. Planned as part of a far more ambitious network of high-speed roads around and out of London (most of which were ditched in 1973), the Westway was the subject of vociferous local protest.

Trellick Tower

Ernö Goldfinger

North Kensington, 1973

One of west London's most memorable landmarks, visible from the nearby Westway, and dominating streets around. The thin tower contains the lifts, with deck access every third floor to the residential block. Though once considered a troubled estate, security improvements and enthusiastic uptake under the 1980s Right to Buy initiative made it a sought-after address for the architecturally minded. A lesser-known twin, Balfron Tower, stands in east London.

Barbican

Chamberlin, Powell & Bon

The City, 1979

After the area was obliterated during the Blitz, it took until the mid 1950s for Chamberlin, Powell & Bon's residential replacement to be approved. The masterplan was led by the then popular notion of the podium (where pedestrians navigate the area at first-floor level), with low-rise residential blocks set out around lakes and squares, and three 43- and 44-storey tower blocks acting as a beacon. The arts centre followed in 1982.

Tower 42

Richard Seifert

The City, 1980

'The Colonel', as he was known, had already created controversial Centre Point, which had dominated the east end of Oxford Street since 1963 and been the cause of much bad feeling about the unlet office space inside. His Nat West Tower (since rechristened Tower 42), was by contrast a sleek, pin-striped symbol of a burgeoning financial centre. At 47 storeys,it was the City's first skyscraper, and for a time the tallest buiding in Europe. It said to the world that London was open for business.

Thames Barrier

Rendel, Palmer & Tritton, for the GLC

Charlton, 1984

London's defence against storm surges down the Thames, such as the catastrophic flood in 1953 that killed 307 people, cost £534m to build (with additional £100m river defences) and opened on 8 May 1984. The iconic steel hulls, like silver fish swimming down the Thames, house reversible hydraulic rams that rotate the floodgates. The world's second largest flood barrier, it has been called into action more than 100 times, and twice on 9 November 2007, when a surge was detected comparable to that of 1953.

As part of ongoing redevelopment of the Royal Docks, a modern landscaped park opened beside the barrier in 2000, using very un-British hard lines, a deep gash and fountains that came straight out of the ground (now ubiquitous).

National Gallery extension

Ahrends Burton Koralek

Trafalgar Square, unbuilt

The original 'carbuncle on the face of a much loved and elegant friend', as it was described by Prince Charles in his famous speech to the RIBA at Hampton Court in 1984. ABK had won the open competition to design an extension to the National Gallery, but Prince Charles's outburst caused planning permission to be refused and the public to turn against 'modern architecture' for at least a decade.

The design that the National Gallery ended up with, by American

NatWest Media Centre

Lord's
Media
Centre

postmodernists Denise Scott Brown and Robert Venturi (1991), attempts to be inconspicuously inoffensive, but is ultimately unheroic.

Lord's
Various architects
St John's Wood, 1985-98
A series of architecturally innovative commissions challenged the MCC's fusty image, among them Michael Hopkins' canopied Mound Stand (1987), Nicholas Grimshaw's Grand Stand (1998), and David Morley's cricket school (1995). But most daring was Future System's

Trellick Tower

Media Centre (1999), a smooth aluminium monocoque built in a boatyard and hoisted up on site.

Lloyd's of London
Richard Rogers Partnership
The City, 1986

The Lloyd's Building's extraordinarily progressive form – steel skin, and the services, famously, on the outside – was like nothing London had seen before. It made the world sit up and take notice. 'The British are coming,' it cried.

Coin Street/ Gabriel's Wharf
Lifshutz Davidson/ Haworth Tompkins
South Bank, 1984-
A testament to the power of the little people. A residents' group calling itself Coin Street Community Builders formed in 1984 to fight office development in the area. Since then, the group has turned the

Though homegrown talent such as Richard Rogers, Norman Foster, and Will Alsop spent the 1980s and '90s designing major public buildings around the world, it was still rare for such forward-thinking talents to be commissioned in our own capital.

13-acre site into a showcase of modern, low-rent housing and independent shops, with a community spirt and popular annual festival. Redevelopment of the neighbouring Oxo Tower, upped the ante, but plans for a 43-storey tower were rejected in 2007.

FT Printworks
Nicholas Grimshaw & Partners
Wapping, 1988
Architect Nicholas Grimshaw's brand of soft high tech was particularly prolific in London during the early '90s, and included influential buildings such as Camden's metallic Sainsbury's (1990), Waterloo International Terminal (1993) and Lord's Grand Stan (1998). Though now decommissioned, his FT Printworks lit up late-night journeys along the A13 throughout the '90s, its huge glazed wall giving full view of the state-of-the-art presses as they rolled out the next day's paper.

One Canada Square
Cesar Pelli
Docklands, 1991
For many, One Canada Square is Canary Wharf. Designed by an American architect, it reflected the Manhattan ethos that was coming to the Isle of Dogs. Trumping Tower 42 (then called the NatWest Tower) to become Europe's tallest building when completed, it is one of the first things visible on the skyline as you approach London. Though it was a decade before it was joined by any comparable structures on the island, leaving it looking exposed and faintly ridiculous, it has since come into its own as the linchpin of a new high-rise skyline.

Shri Swaminarayan Mandir
CB Sompura/Triad
Neasden, 1995
Neasden's marble and limestone *mandir* (temple) and adjoining

CITYSCAPE

British Library

wooden *haveli* (courtyard house and community centre) were the first to be built outside the Indian subcontinent. Materials were shipped from European quarries to India for carving, then back to England, and much of the construction and fundraising was carried out by local volunteers. In the *mandir* itself, virtually every milky white marble surface is decorated with intricate reliefs depicting flora, fauna and tales of the gods. Not only a creation of breathtaking beauty and remarkable craftsmanship, but a symbol of London's growing multiculturalism.

British Library
Colin St John Wilson
St Pancras, 1998

The new British Library was started in 1978 and completed in 1998. The long construction became a running joke. and by the time it was finished, the Library looked out of date. Good craftsmanship helped it gain a positive reception, though some academics could not get over their nostalgia for the old Reading Room previously housed in the library, now the focus of the British Museum's Great Court (Norman Foster, 2000)

Vauxhall Cross
Terry Farrell & Co
Vauxhall, 1993

Possibly the word's least discreet secret service HQ, Terry Farrell's over-elaborate block on the south side of Vauxhall Bridge houses MI6.

It was even used in a James Bond film. One of the most vulgar examples of London's craze for postmodernism – a period that ended mercifully quickly, but not before it had blighted our urban landscape.

V&A Spiral
Daniel Libeskind
South Kensington, unbuilt

The most exciting architectural proposal of the 1990s, the V&A's spiral was to be London's Guggenheim, but sadly was never built. An intellectual exercise as much as an architectural one, the building's deconstructed exterior of crashing surfaces and boxes made it impossible to tell from the outside how the building was organised inside. A similar scheme has since been proposed by Herzog & de Meuron for Tate Modern.

No. 1 Poultry
Stirling Wilford Associates
The City, 1998

The last building by Sir James Stirling, the larger-than-life London architect whose name lives on in the country's leading architecture prize. More remarkable than the building itself was the public battle it provoked between traditionalists, who wanted to keep the Victorian-gothic Mappin & Webb building (Prince Charles, City planners, the general public), and the modernisers (the architectural press, developer Peter Palumbo, architects).

An earlier proposal for a glass and steel tower by Ludwig Mies van der Rohe was rejected, but Stirling's postmodern confection, likened by Prince Charles to a '1930s wireless', finally won.

Peckham Library
Alsop & Störmer
Peckham, 1999

Will Alsop and the good people of Peckham decided to show the rest of London that municipal buildings could be fun. Wonky legs, turquoise cladding and a jaunty orange beret brightened up the skyline and won prizes. It was one of many landmark buildings introduced to Southwark during the time of its refreshingly adventurous chief planner Fred Manson, making the borough the envy of the capital for a time.

Jubilee Line Extension
Various architects
1999

Although other worthy transport schemes (viz Crossrail, or an East London River Crossing) have been on the agenda for decades,

Mrs Thatcher made sure she kept her promise to investors in Canary Wharf to link them to the tube network. Politics aside, it made stations sexy once again, allowing a series of youthful practices to enjoy themselves. Alsop Lyall & Störmer's deep blue shaft at North Greenwich, Foster & Partners' concrete cathedral at Canary Wharf and Chris Wilkinson's glass and steel wave at Stratford stand out.

Dome/O₂
Richard Rogers
Greenwich Peninsula, 1999

An elegant piece of engineering mired by politics. A 'Sorry Meniscus', wrote dissenter Iain Sinclair. Working with engineers Buro Happold, Rogers created a structure that was light, simple and dramatic – an engineering triumph at 1,197ft diameter and 164ft high. Hype, some vicious back-biting politics and a exhibition designed by committee spun such negativity around the Dome that it became synonymous with budget excess, pointlessness and

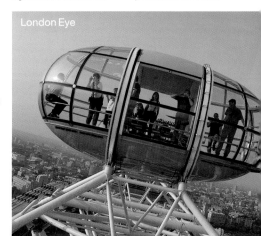
London Eye

Millennium Bridge

throughout the day. The colour scheme was devised by artist Michael Craig Martin, who was also responsible for some vibrant murals inside the building.

BedZED

Bill Dunster

Sutton, 2002

The Beddington Zero Energy Development is the UK's first carbon-neutral community, set up as a housing experiment with the Peabody Trust. All 82 homes are constructed from natural, recycled or reclaimed materials, have a high thermal mass and are well insulated, to keep temperatures stable and reduce energy consumption. Energy is supplied by photovoltaic panels and external renewable sources. Other green measures include water recycling and a car share scheme.

millennial ennui. The few Londoners who actually went to the Millennium Exhibition, however, maintain that they had a great time.

Exacerbating its poor reputation, the Dome sat empty for years after the 2000 exhibition closed, but its 2007 reinvention as a concert venue, with high-end chain restaurants and seasonal family attractions such as a beach and an ice rink, has been a quiet hit.

London Eye

Marks Barfield, with Ove Arup & Partners

South Bank, 2000

The best illustration of the free-thinking spirit that the new millennium was hoping to foster. Its pods-on-a-bicycle-wheel design allowed for a pure, unencumbered form with the emphasis on the smooth, perfect circle. The big wheel was an instant hit, and though it was originally only given planning permission for five years, it was instantly adopted as a symbol of the brave new 21st-century London. Already, it would be difficult to conceive of the skyline without it.

Serpentine Summer Pavilions

Various architects

Kensington Gardens, since 2000

While developers and planners have been nervous to commission the sort of cutting-edge architecture being built in other cities around the world, the Serpentine Gallery took it upon itself to invite leading international architects, previously unbuilt in London, to create a series of temporary summer pavilions. In this way the capital has thrilled to one-off outings from premier-league names such as Zaha Hadid, Daniel Libeskind, Rem Koolhaas, Toyo Ito and Frank Gehry.

Millennium Bridge

Foster & Partners, with Ove Arup & Partners and Sir Anthony Caro

Bankside–St Paul's, 2000

Nicknamed the 'wobbly bridge', due to the fact that when it opened it had the unnerving habit of oscillating to the tune of users' footsteps. It was quickly closed, and didn't reopen until February 2002. At 1,148ft long and 13ft wide, it is a light, elegant structure that Foster imagined as a 'blade of light'. Its most important contribution to the capital has been to change its geography, opening up a new pedestrian connection between Bankside and St Paul's that brings the City and the South Bank closer together.

Laban

Herzog & de Meuron

Deptford, 2002

Riding high after their Tate Modern success, Swiss architects Herzog & de Meuron brought colour, class and the world's media to Deptford Creek. A home for revered dance school Laban, it features a semi-transparent polycarbonate façade that changes colour

BedZED

Norman Foster

CITYSCAPE

From the Gherkin to the Great Court, Canary Wharf Underground station to Wembley Stadium, Trafalgar Square to the Millennium Bridge, Norman Foster, it seems, has built London. Today, Foster can claim to have built more London buildings than Christopher Wren (35 at a rough count). Seventy this year, he is one of architecture's few superstars, in demand all round the world. He was brought up in working-class Manchester, but is now worth a reputed £100m.

He was knighted in 1990 and ennobled in 1997. He flies his own plane to meetings on the Continent, spends a month each year at his St Moritz bolt-hole training for the annual Engadin Valley cross-country skiing marathon, and lives in a glazed riverside penthouse above his practice's Battersea offices (in a building he designed himself). He is married to Elena Ochoa, his third wife, a Spanish TV sexologist 25 years his junior, with whom he has two young children, Paola (six) and Eduardo (three). But unlike Britain's other famous architect, twinkly grandfather of eight, Richard Rogers, whom Foster worked with as Team 4 in the 1960s, he rarely socialises and is widely regarded by peers as a cold-blooded control freak.

I wanted to talk to Foster about London, his city. We met at his practice. It's an impressive place, a glass box entered via a grand staircase, at the top of which an officious receptionist sits at a glass and steel Foster-designed table, fielding calls in a succession of European languages, while Foster employees sip cappuccinos and leaf through that day's international press at the in-house coffee bar. The 500-plus staff, including Foster himself, work at long tables in the airy, double-height studio overlooking the river. It's a sophisticated space, everything in black, white, grey and silver – including the employees – with models of famous and current projects displayed in glass cases.

Lord Foster of Thames Bank strides in and whips off his charcoal grey corduroy jacket, revealing a flash of pink lining.

'Just Norman,' he says shaking hands with the photographer. He's just back from taking his kids to school, and has an important client meeting at 10am, but he's all ours for an hour.

Foster is not known for his small talk, so our discussion of London borders on the academic, with talk of 'sustainability' (good), ''high-density housing solutions' (also good),

'public domain' (one of his major concerns), balancing acts (old versus new, history versus modernity), CO_2 emissions (to be minimised) and 'energy consumption' (the most important factor in the architecture of the future). Yes, it's dry stuff, but his passion for the capital does eventually seep through.

So does London work? 'Yes, I think it does. It's an incredible city. I think the point I would make about any city is that quality of life is about the infrastructure. If you think of any city that you work in, live in or visit, the chances are that your impression is going to be much more about how you travelled to work or how you've gone shopping in other words, the experience of the streets, the bridges, the connections, the public transport, or the absence of it.

'If you asked me the pluses and minuses, I'd say that London is a fantastic city in terms of the variety that it offers, and I suppose that extraordinary character has come out of the fact that those were individual places, and as London has grown, they have all become absorbed but somehow kept their own character. And although it's a very dense city, it has an extraordinary amount of greenery. If you look at the destinations on buses – Blackheath, Islington Green, Shepherd's Bush, Hampstead Heath, Clapham Common, Hyde Park – it is all about green space.

'The downside of London is the public transport.' He thinks the best areas are those with a high density of people, well served by public transport and with a mixture of uses: Belgravia, Chelsea, Kensington, Notting Hill, areas of Georgian or Edwardian terraces with squares in the middle and mews behind.

In the current trend for improving the spaces between buildings, Foster's Millennium Bridge, despite initial wobbles, has created a popular new route between Bankside and the City, bringing prosperity (and tourists) to the top corner of Southwark. And it was his verve and drive behind the pedestrianisation of Trafalgar Square – an idea eventually adopted by Ken Livingstone, and one that, now the roadworks have gone, has even won over many sceptical Londoners.

He is currently involved with improvements to Parliament Square: 'One of the main things that makes a city desirable is the quality of its public spaces, and I would say that any public space could benefit from some degree of taking away the clutter, improving the quality of signage, improving the quality of greenery, improving connections.' Foster would also like to see London using more art to enliven public places, and engaging more fully with the river.

The current word on Foster is that his work is softening. Curvaceous new buildings such as music centre the Sage Gateshead, the Gherkin, Albion Riverside in Battersea, and City Hall suggest, say some critics, the emergence of a feminine side. But it is more than the lines of his buildings that is softening. A family man for the second time around (he already has three grown-up children and a son in his late teens), he talks of the joys of the school run and has pictures of his wife and kids on his mobile phone. He describes a recent try-out of a Smart car as 'really fun' (though it's hard to visualise) and is working on designing meters where electric cars could be recharged.

Having reinvented the office, the skyscraper, the factory, the airport, the metro station and the arts complex, he says, for him, 'the next big thing is housing', and can't wait to sink his teeth into London's social housing provision.

Foster sees public projects such as Trafalgar Square, the Millennium Bridge, the Great Court and Wembley (a great public venue beyond the celebration of football) as his most important projects, though is proud of Swiss Re because it proves that 'a tall building doesn't have to be a boring box. It can have more variety, more life.' While no one wants a city of 'boring boxes', nor does anyone want one of undulating icons. Too many Sages and Albions, even Gherkins, would be hard to live with. Just as it doesn't really matter whether or not he turns up to architectural soirées, not every building has to be a landmark. In a city not short on socialites or soundbites, but desperately in need of bold vision, Norman Foster is one of the few people we can trust to shape modern London.

Original interview conducted by Jessica Cargill Thompson.

Probably the most famous London building by Foster & Partners: 30 St Mary Axe, aka the Gherkin.

Get around, round, round, we get around

From the death of the Routemaster to the troubles of the tube, no topic animates Londoners as much as their transport system.

By Lisa Mullen

When the Queen unveiled a plaque at Victoria tube station in March 1969, declaring the new Victoria line officially open, she was also unwittingly marking an important end point in the history of London Underground: it was the last time any part of our tube system could claim to be state of the art.

The smart silver train which then whisked the royal personage, clutching her 5d ticket, to Green Park, was equipped with the latest technology: an Automatic Train Operation system enabled the whole line to be computer-controlled from a central hub – the driver's job was (and still is) mainly to operate the doors and reassure the public. Begun in 1962, the line was intended to serve as an advertisement for British engineering, but it also came to symbolise the nation's economic decline. By the time the first section was completed in 1968, Harold Wilson's famous 'white heat of technology' had gone chilly in the face of currency devaluation and other fiscal woes: sharp budget cuts meant

Above: pristine Northern Line tube stock c1973.

that the final stage of the project, the fit-out of the stations, was done on a shoestring. Soon they were falling apart as the cheap bathroom-quality tiles peeled off the walls; only four decades later is the line finally getting a makeover.

It's a sad story, but one that sums up the extraordinarily low status given to transport. A long tradition of underfunding the network has produced a visibly crumbling tube system that struggles to move ten million people around the capital every day (compared to just over two million in 1970). Recently, Transport for London has secured a deal that will bring in £10bn over five years, but, as it acknowledges, reversing decades of decline won't be a quick or easy process.

Other new lines did eventually follow: the Jubilee Line in 1979, though not at first with automated trains, and, another 20 years later, its architecturally-celebrated extension to Stratford (mothballed in the early '80s due to cost). The elevated Docklands Light Railway opened in 1987, and was an essential part of the regeneration of the area; but despite its efficiency, as an off-the-peg system imported from Germany and dressed in garish livery, it has never been a source of national pride in the way the Victoria Line was.

38 Time Out London Calling

Crossrail, first mooted in 1974 and exhumed sporadically since, is getting closer to becoming a reality. Gordon Brown gave an official green light in 2007, with completion set for 2017. Whether this will, strictly speaking, benefit Londoners is a moot point: the main purpose of the line will be to whisk suburban commuters non-stop into the City, rather than to connect new areas of London to the network. Meanwhile, long-promised developments that really would be meaningful, such as the underground Chelsea-Hackney line (first proposed in 1901), seem unlikely ever to appear on the tube map.

This history of governmental foot-dragging is odd, since transport has always been seen as a vote-winner. Ken Livingstone's socialist GLC made subsidised Underground fares a central plank of its policy agenda in 1981 (though the tube-less Bromley Council saw to it that 'Fares Fair' was outlawed before the year was out), and later fought the 2000 mayoral election with a manifesto that proposed the revolutionary Congestion Charge as the answer to the capital's gridlock and pollution, its roads unable to cope with the 100,000 cars entering central London every morning. Though far from popular, its success has inspired a number of other cities to consider it as a potential solution for their own traffic troubles.

Of course, London's roads were already heavily congested by 1968 – but the favoured solution back then, a complex of motorways known as Ringway 1, which would encircle inner London, was perhaps one of the worst ideas ever to occur to the city's planners. The first phase of the scheme, the elevated motorway that came to be known as the Westway, opened in 1970, but the process of carving a path for it through west London caused

Above: Holborn's Piccadilly Line platform, refreshingly empty in 1973. Above right: the No.9 rounds Piccadilly Circus. Along with the 15, it is one of only two 'heritage' routes to be maintained since the Routemaster fleet was taken out of service at the end of 2005.

such devastation and public protest that the rest of the plan was shelved in 1973.

No transport battle has been more bitterly fought – and lost – by Londoners than the one to save the Routemaster. Screen star (*Summer Holiday*, *On the Busses*, *The Double Deckers*) and design icon (the first hop-on, hop-off RT model was created in 1939 by Albert Arthur Molteno Durrent using his experience of aircraft production), London's red buses were recognised around the world. Their absence from the city's streets, save for a couple of select tourist routes, is still keenly felt. Despite Livingstone's 2000 campaign pledge that 'only a dehumanised moron would get rid of the Routemaster', he wasn't long in office before he was persuaded that they had to go, having been deemed inefficient and, with their open back platforms, a health and safety nightmare. The introduction of the hated 'bendy bus' in 2003 was the harbinger of the Routemaster's final demise in 2005.

In fact, the Routemaster fleet had been scaled back from the 1970s onwards, when cheaper front-entry, driver-only buses began to be imported from abroad; and even now the bendy buses, reviled as insufficiently agile for London's streets (and susceptible to fare-dodging to boot), only make up five per cent of the capital's bus fleet. But that didn't stop Boris Johnson from making the return of the Routemaster one of his most popular campaign pledges during the 2008 mayoral race.

Whether a revival will materialise remains to be seen, but two things are certain. One is that London's transport system will always be a pawn in a political game. And the other is that, while they have breath in their carbon monoxide-choked, tube-suffocated lungs, Londoners will continue to moan about it.

Hail to the tarmac tourniquet

Iain Sinclair's homage to the M25, London's 'mad highway'.

CITYSCAPE

Prime Minister Margaret Thatcher opens the final stretch of the M25 in 1986.

Why the M25? Why walk around it? That was my project. I had to find out where London gave up the ghost. Motorway as storm-fence, holding in the rubbish of the city. Holding the voices of the poor and dispossessed who ended their days in suburban asylums, now being sold, asset-stripped, converted into flats and housing units with pretentious titles.

The mad highway, when it was opened by Margaret Thatcher on 29 October 1986 (ribbon slashed with terrifying scissor-sweep), was already posthumous. It belonged in a luridly coloured *Look at Life*, back in the '60s, when white-hot technology was still on the menu. The M25 (Old Tory) was the precise contrary of New Labour's Millennium Dome: it was much, much more popular than it was supposed to be. Popular to the point of gridlock. The first car broke down at 11.16am, one minute after opening time. The M25 had a terrible, fetishistic fascination for Londoners, now trapped (though they didn't realise it) within the choking embrace of a tarmac tourniquet.

Highways Agency officials debate the precise length of the road. Somewhere, sticking to the middle lane, between 117 and 124 miles. Walking, detouring, doubling back, dodging foot-and-mouth prohibitions, is another matter. I travelled, in company with an old Hackney friend, the painter Renchi Bicknell, to find out – in the words of Bill Drummond's manic associate Gimpo – 'where the M25 leads'. This Gimpo, as Drummond reported, led a seasonal charge (at the spring equinox), 24 hours on the road, round and round. Starting at South Mimms.

Nothing defines the quadrants of the M25 like the quality of the service stations. The planners hoped to provide one for each cardinal point of the compass. South Mimms, close to the spot where Thatcher cut the ribbon, on the north. Thurrock, a satellite of the Lakeside retail swamp, in the east. Rustificated Clacket Lane, with its fountains and shards of Roman pottery, in the south. Heathrow Airport is the missing service station in the west. Wait four hours for a delayed flight and get a free cup of coffee.

The great Kentish shopping city of Bluewater, part *Star Wars* set, part oil revenue oasis, is the destination of choice for all M25 voyagers. Bluewater balances Heathrow, offering the full terminal experience – multiple-choice coffee stops, mindless retail browsing, panic attacks – *without having to get on a plane*. No deep-vein thrombosis, no recycled air, no terrorists. This, after September 11, is the alternate America. Shopping, as a displacement activity, substitutes for everything: art, television, seaside excursions, adultery. Visiting Bluewater is like joining the Mormons. You are inducted into the Elect. As many compensatory, wife-substitute/lover-substitute toys as you like. A soft pornography of display, overlit, Muzak-coshed, weatherless.

Our walk through London's liminal strip – boarding kennels, golf courses, converted asylums – also demonstrated that there was no countryside left. A pattern of erasure and memory-trashing evasion. A choked orbital highway duplicating the conditions of the inner city, Old Street roundabout, Trafalgar Square.

The M25 experience might be the final democracy, where all are equal, all suffer. All except royalty. Thatcher, cutting the ribbon, left the road immediately, a speeding cavalcade through north London. The only time most royals will have any dealings with the vulgar circuit that links Essex swamp-life with Surrey suburbia is when the funeral cortege passes through the wonderfully complex Junction 15, or along the Colnbrook bypass on the way to Windsor.

Iain Sinclair's record of his walk around the M25, *London Orbital*, was published by Granta in 2002.

London's recent economic prominence can be attributed to its ambitious redevelopment of the Docklands. Now, with pressure on housing and amenities, the city is poised for further expansion down the Thames estuary.
By Peter Murray

The city marches east

The eerie marshlands of the Thames Estuary are earmarked for 160,000 new homes, part of Europe's largest regeneration project.

London owes a lot to G Ware Travelstead. Without Travelstead, London might not have become the financial capital of the world, not have experienced ten years of sustained economic growth, and not be growing at an unprecedented rate with an extra 80,000 people a year (well, it was until the credit crunch).

'Gee Whizz', as he was known, was a charismatic American developer who, in 1984, came up with the idea of Canary Wharf. Until then, the general plan was that London's empty docklands would be turned into low-rent industrial sheds and low-rise business parks. Travelstead worked as property advisor to the bankers Credit Suisse First Boston (CSFB), and realised in a eureka moment that if one bank could move there, so would others. He persuaded the London Docklands Development Corporation and, most importantly, Margaret Thatcher, that a ten million square foot financial

services district in West India Docks would work. After the creation of the London Docklands Development Corporation in 1981, the area was designated an Enterprise Zone (between 1961 and 1971, almost 83,000 jobs were lost in the Docklands area) that gave developers substantial tax breaks and rate rebates. This allowed Canary Wharf to attract companies at really low cost – in the 1980s you could rent space in 1 Canada Square for £6 a square foot, whereas City rents were more than five times the price.

Meanwhile, a new strategy was being cooked up to help East London and beyond. In 1991, Environment Secretary Michael Heseltine decided that the route of the Channel Tunnel Rail Link should run from St Pancras, through Stratford, past Thurrock down to Maidstone, Ashford and Folkestone. It was clear that this would have an economic and physical impact on the area. The Government commissioned the East London Corridor Study, which looked at the benefits of bringing together a massive and disparate area that stretches from Tower Hamlets to Southend and to Medway to create Europe's largest regeneration project. The working title of 'East London Corridor' was rebranded as 'Thames Gateway', and found a willing champion in John Prescott when he was deputy prime minister.

It's hard to comprehend Thames Gateway as any sort of real place. What has Rochester got in common with Barking? Or Swale with Greenwich? What they have in common is economics. They are linked together by the impact of their geographic relationship with Europe. Like routes throughout history, High Speed 1 (the new rail link between Stratford and Ebbsfleet), will attract trade, investment and people. Some 160,000 new houses are planned; places like Ebbsfleet – potentially the site of Mark Wallinger's White Horse sculpture – will have 9,500 new houses; Stratford City, which was being developed before the area was chosen as the site for the Olympics, will have 5,000 new homes, as well as a regional shopping centre and offices; the Dubai-owned London Gateway port will be one of Europe's largest, at a cost of more than £1.5bn.

Architect Terry Farrell has been pressing the government for some time to turn chunks of TG into a national park. While government ministers struggled to describe a 'vision' for the Gateway, Farrell, working off his own bat and unpaid, produced designs that started to smack of a coherent plan. He has now been appointed Thames Gateway Parklands Design Champion, and, in 2008, Housing & Planning Minister Caroline Flint promised £35m to help implement Farrell's strategies.

The centre of gravity of London is moving inexorably eastwards. The docks have gone, the factories and gasworks have gone, and in their place are shopping centres, apartment blocks, offices and the O2. The expanding DLR and the Jubilee line makes it easier to get there; one day CrossRail will make it even easier. The Olympics will generate investment, as well a major shift in perceptions of the East End.

Will the Olympics and its legacy conquer East London's heritage of poverty? How will it create a proper social mix? The wealthy bankers of Canary Wharf are happy to live in apartments in the east when childless, but move to Chelsea or the Home Counties when they have families. What high-end residential developer will start building top-end houses in Barking or Canning Town? Will the area that journalist Jonathan Glancey described as 'Cockney Siberia' become a ghetto of affordable housing? Most importantly, whether it gets developed at all in the foreseeable future depends on the London economy.

Which brings us back to G Ware Travelstead. In the '90s, it was touch and go whether the financial capital of Europe would end up being Paris, Frankfurt or London. The City of London was constrained in the amount and size of offices it could build; the big banks and financial houses needed football-pitch-sized trading floors in which to operate. It was Canary Wharf that provided the right space at the right time. It allowed the financial sector of London to expand. Without the right space in which to work, the big banks would have located elsewhere, and the story of Livingstone's London – and of the East End – would have been very different.

Peter Murray is the director of New London Architecture (www.newlondonarchitecture.com).

Map showing the extent of the Thames Gateway development, from east London to the Isle of Sheppey.

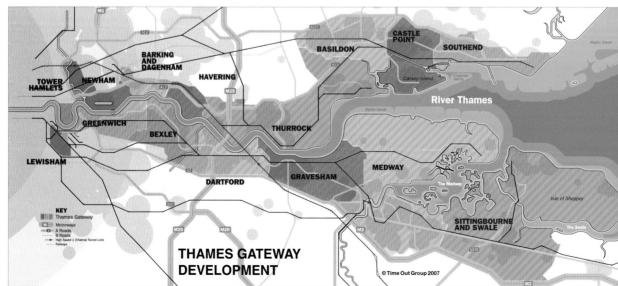

KEY
Thames Gateway
Motorways
A Roads
B Roads
High Speed 1 (Channel Tunnel Link)
Railways

THAMES GATEWAY DEVELOPMENT

© Time Out Group 2007

HEDONISM INTRODUCTION
SEX CITYSCAPE FASHION
SOCIETY SHOPPING COMEDY
DRAMA PROTEST & POLITICS
VISUAL ARTS PERFORMANCE
LITERATURE GANGS OPINION
COCKNEYS BARS ON SCREEN
DANCE MUSIC TELEVISION
BUILDINGS CLUBS NIGHTLIFE
SPORT & FITNESS MEMORIES
STYLE FOOD & DRINK GIGS
CONSUME RIOTS REFERENCE

Welcome to
Banglatown

Asian youths in east London, 1980.

The impact of Brick Lane's Bangladeshi community has been huge, and its triumphs and conflicts reflect the experiences of many of London's immigrant communities as the city becomes ever more multicultural.

By Kate Gavron

Tower Hamlets, the core of London's East End, has for centuries been the arrival and dispersal point for hundreds of thousands of immigrants to the capital, arriving via the docks. It has also been a place where many thousands of immigrants settled permanently, from French Huguenots to Irish railway construction workers, from Jews escaping pogroms to those later fleeing fascism, from imperial subjects from the Caribbean and South Asia to refugees from African war zones. Though London was already a fairly multicultural city in 1968, it has been the arrival of Bangladeshi families, coming in the '70s to join their menfolk who had been working here since the '50s, that has had one of the most defining impacts, not just on the local culture, but on the city as a whole.

Like most migrant communities, the Bangladeshis only began to be noticed once the women and children arrived. The fathers and husbands had been largely out of sight of most of the neighbourhood, living and working in closed, Bengali-speaking environments. Many of them spoke little or no English, and initially planned to return to Bangladesh once they had earned enough money to help them and their families to prosper at home. A number of factors changed their minds: the devastating cyclone of 1970; anxiety about political instability following the War of Independence, which created the new state of Bangladesh in 1971; and, above all, the legislation restricting immigration to Britain that was brought in from 1962 onwards.

In 1968, the East End was, by historical standards, underpopulated and relatively homogenous. The last major migrant community to settle there, the Jews, had largely moved to other parts of London by the end of the war, and a slum clearance programme had stripped out some of the worst housing, leaving a population smaller than at any time for more than a century. In 1911, the population of the area covered by Tower Hamlets was well over half a million. By 1971, it had dropped by two-thirds to under 164,000, and by 1981 to approximately 140,000. With the arrival of the Bangladeshis it started to rise again, against trends in the rest of inner London. By 1991, the population was 168,000, and it would continue to rise, to 196,000 in 2001.

The rate of the Bangladeshi influx over the past 40 years is remarkable. Between 1971 and 2001, the number of Bangladeshis in Tower Hamlets rose from an estimated 4,000 to just under 66,000; or, to put it another way, from just over two per cent of the borough's population to just over a third – the largest concentration of a single minority ethnic group in any borough in Britain. Furthermore, by 2001 well over 50 per cent of the school population of the borough was of Bangladeshi origin. This means, of course, that Tower Hamlets is in fact *less* multicultural than many other parts of London.

HEART SWEET

Competition and conflict

As far back as the 17th century, immigrants to London were bitterly resented for being prepared to work for lower pay and in worse conditions than those above them in the labour hierarchy. As historian Walter Thornberry wrote in 1873, the arrival of Irish competition as early as the late 18th century had antagonised Huguenot textile workers, sending 'these turbulent workmen in[to] a state of violent effervescence'. There was always competition for housing too. Jews arriving in the late 19th century had to find places in which to live in the private rental market, usually squalid and overcrowded. After World War II, Bangladeshi men found housing and work through their compatriots already settled in London; it was not until their wives and children arrived that the local authorities became involved. Peaking in the mid '80s, just as the introduction of right-to-buy legislation was draining local social housing stock, immigration caused housing waiting lists to grow exponentially, fuelling resentment and local hostility.

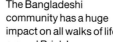
The Bangladeshi community has a huge impact on all walks of life around Brick Lane.

Meanwhile, the East End was also coping with the closure and redevelopment of London's docks. Thousands of well-paid jobs were being created, but few of them went to those living in the East End. Swathes of desirable Georgian and Victorian housing in Spitalfields and Victoria Park became the subject of gentrification, again with a deleterious effect on the housing supply.

Consequently, it was not hard for supporters of the National Front (NF), and later the British National Party (BNP), to fan the flames of hostility towards new arrivals. (This has happened more recently in other parts of London that are experiencing mass immigration for the first time.) It was no coincidence that the first ever BNP local councillor was elected in Tower Hamlets, in 1993, after a decade of lengthening housing queues. There was very little local councillors could do to alleviate the problem, either for ill-housed or homeless new arrivals, or for the adult children of long-term residents who wished to continue living in the area where they had been brought up.

SOCIETY

'Since the mid '70s, Brick Lane has seen a spectacular growth of the Bangladeshi niche business par excellence: the "Indian" restaurant.'

Indeed, just as the East End is known for its immigrant communities, so it has also been infamous for the activities of extremist parties. Oswald Mosley's British Union of Fascists recruited there in the 1930s, espousing a viciously anti-Semitic message; London dockers marched through Tower Hamlets in support of Enoch Powell in 1968; and the NF and BNP have targeted the same streets in more recent decades. In Tower Hamlets, electoral success for these Far Right groups has only involved a six-month period with a BNP councillor, but other districts going through extensive demographic changes recently have been more susceptible to their arguments.

Settling in an area where there are already large numbers of immigrants from a single ethnic group has obvious advantages: help with finding housing and work; language; companionship; even finding marriage partners. But there are also disadvantages. Beatrice Potter, later Beatrice Webb, the co-founder of the London School of Economics, wrote in 1902 of the East End Jews: 'The inner life of the small Hebrew communities bound together by common suffering and mutual helpfulness has developed other qualities, but has also tended in its own way to destroy all friendly and honourable intercourse with surrounding peoples.' Much the same has been said about the Bangladeshis.

The 'mutual helpfulness' that Potter described can be one of the best consolations of settlement in a new home, but it may also delay the process of integration with other communities. It is often left to children to start the process, through their interaction with other children at school. There is

Memory bank

Ansar Ahmed Ullah remembers Brick Lane

I arrived from Bangladesh to live in Britain in 1980, when I was 21. I lived in Luton, but visited Brick Lane regularly with friends. It was the place in which to find anything and everything to do with Bangladesh.

I was really into Bengali film music, such as Adam Khan, one of the first Bengali rock singers. We used to go the cinema (where Café Naz stands now) and see Bengali films, and then go next door to buy the music in Milfa cassette shop. Further along, we could buy Bengali magazines and newspapers. So it was a whole day out to a 'mini Bangladesh'. You never saw any white people there at all.

I moved to Brick Lane in 1982, first living on top of the police station and then moving to Heneage Street, off the Lane, where I lived for almost 15 years. Back then, the whole street was geared up to serving the Bengali community. These days, you've got 50-odd restaurants serving tandoori chicken and tikka masala, and locals would never step in the door.

When I lived there, garment and leather sweatshops and factories lined the street. I worked in a factory gluing down shirt sleeve seams and pressing them. It was piecework and could pay up to £10 a piece, so you could end up with £100 a day if you worked hard;

we began at 8am and finished at 8pm. Today, there's not a single factory left.

In 1998, I joined Tower Hamlet's regeneration department. It was on the cusp of big changes in the area. With council assistance, the street was cleaned up; it had been run-down, but now it started to look like the West End, and became a magnet for white City workers who wanted a quick curry lunch, as well as those visiting the clubs on the weekend.

Today, although Bengalis are less visible on the streets, they have stayed here – many of them on the poor estates surrounding the Lane. Some businesses are being forced out by high rates, but I think the changes have made the place more attractive to visitors and put Brick Lane on the map. We have some fantastic

festivals ,such as the Brick Lane Festival, and the area is the centre for Bengali satellite TV stations and newspapers, as well as travel agencies, accountants and some restaurants that still cater to the community.

When I first lived here, the National Front sold their papers at the top of the street. There were incidents every day where Bengalis were beaten up. It was a warlike situation. That racist violence has almost completely disappeared.

Another big change is that Bengalis are opening up some clubs and bars, which is a real break with tradition. Brick Lane will remain a focal point for Bengalis for years to come.

Ansar Ahmed Ullah is a community activist in Brick Lane.

---

also a risk that new arrivals may be exploited by members of their own community in a way that is hard for outsiders to notice or insiders to communicate, especially if there is a language gap.

The Jews who arrived in the East End in the two decades either side of the beginning of the 20th century were more numerous than any other community to implant itself in the area before or since. However, the Bangladeshis have arguably had just as much of an impact on the area, principally because of their access to public resources, particularly housing. In both cases, the majority of incomers arrived over a relatively short period of time – approximately 20 years – and each succeeded in transforming the local environment, economically as well as culturally.

Forty years ago, most Bangladeshi men living in the East End worked in the rag trade, often for Jewish employers, and in other locally based light industries. Since the mid '70s, however, Brick Lane and the streets around it have seen a spectacular growth of the Bangladeshi niche business par excellence, the 'Indian' restaurant. This has developed to such an extent that the Brick Lane area, in the heart of western Tower Hamlets, is known today as 'Banglatown'. One advantage of a

'niche' activity like specialist catering is that it can easily accommodate low-paid, inexperienced new arrivals, just as new Jewish immigrants were hired as street traders or in the rag trade a century earlier.

Rich mix

What does the arrival and settlement of Bangladeshis in Tower Hamlets tell us about recent immigration to London? First, that at an individual level, relations between immigrants and the host community are usually friendly and mutually tolerant. It is worth making the point that, despite the enormous population changes of the past 20 years, there has been no major violent uprising; the riots of 2001 in northern cities involving youths of South Asian origin were not replicated in London. Nor has the violence of the 1970s, when the National Front fought with anti-fascists – allied with Bangladeshis – on a regular basis, been repeated. Certainly, there are still violent incidents, racist and otherwise, but these are relatively rare. Local leadership, including at borough council level, has by and large succeeded in keeping the temperature of community relations low, despite accusations of favouritism on both sides.

SOCIETY

Today, hostility to immigrants or, more accurately, immigration itself, seems to take the form of a perception that it is too easy for immigrants to get access to public resources, especially social housing and places in good schools: these are the areas where competition has been fierce. The apparently over-generous disbursement of state benefits is also a bone of contention for older, white, working-class East Enders, many of whom feel betrayed by local and national government, and believe that the security and comfort that was promised to them after World War II, when the area suffered so grievously, has not been delivered.

It's easy to forget that politicians trod the streets of the East End during the Blitz promising postwar rewards to the beleaguered members of this heroic community. Consequently, locals felt that the expanded welfare state was created with them in mind, and the symbolism of the first new benefits of the postwar era being paid out in the post offices of the East End did nothing to disabuse them of this. As they now see it, they are being asked to share their hard-earned gains with outsiders, newcomers, who have not made the same sacrifices and contributions.

Much of this sense of frustrated entitlement is based on misconceptions and malicious hearsay, of course. Yet whether or not white East Enders' sense of grievance stands up to close scrutiny, it has always been the case that the impact of immigration varies from class to class. The better-off, for instance, have usually gained from immigration, whether as employers or consumers, whereas the poor have always had to compete for scarce resources with new arrivals who are often prepared to work for less, with a consequent downward pressure on already inadequate wages. This is especially the case in places where work is casual and disorganised, or part of the informal economy.

If governments (of whatever stripe) want to reduce the influence of Far Right parties, they must 'invest' in immigration by mitigating the effects on the people it most affects. The challenge, therefore, is to help immigrants to settle without neglecting the concerns of poor, working-class whites, whose plight needs to be recognised along with that of marginalised minority ethnic and migrant groups.

London is rightly thought of as a successful and tolerant city, a model of diversity. Indeed, this was one of the main arguments used in the campaign to win the right to stage the 2012 Olympic Games in the East End. Migrants, national and international, have made the capital what it is, and its history and geography mean that, compared with other large cities, it remains comparatively unsegregated, economically and ethnically. It is a true melting pot, and all that is required of its politicians is that it be kept simmering nicely.

Kate Gavron is the co-author, with Michael Young and Geoff Dench, of *The New East End* (2006).

TIMELINE

1968

Greater London's population is 7.69 million, but there are only 20 public sports centres in the capital.

John Lennon is fined £150 (equivalent of £1,875 today) for possession of cannabis.

1969

The Kray twins, Ronnie and Reggie, infamous East End gangsters, are sentenced to life imprisonment.

Rupert Murdoch, aged 37, buys the *News of the World*, his first Fleet Street newspaper.

1971

Oz, the hippie periodical, provokes the longest obscenity trial in British history when schoolkids edit an issue featuring Rupert Bear with an erection.

1974

From January to March, power cuts and the three-day working week become the norm.

1975

One million are unemployed for the first time since World War II.

1976

Hundreds are left injured after riots break out at the end of the Notting Hill Carnival.

The Scarman report cites the 'racial disadvantage that is a fact of British life' as the main cause of the Brixton riots.

1982

Unemployment peaks at more than three million. Approximately one in seven of the working population are unable to find jobs.

1983

AIDS is still not taken seriously as Jasper Carrott announces on his show: 'I thought AIDS was a biscuit.'

1986

'Big Bang' in the City as the London Stock Exchange deregulates, and markets boom.

1987

Margaret Thatcher opines: 'There is no such thing as society. There are individual men and women, and there are families.'

Thirty-one people are killed in a fire at King's Cross tube station. Safety improvements, such as the removal of wooden escalators, are subsequently instigated throughout the network.

Winds reach 94mph as the south-east is battered by the worst storm since 1703. Trees are uprooted, roofs blown off and blackouts experienced.

1988

Second Summer of Love as youth culture enjoys a revival of raves and free parties.

1991

The *Big Issue* is founded by John Bird and Gordon Roddick as a way to help the large numbers of homeless people sleeping rough in London.

1992

'Black Wednesday' in the City as the UK quits the ERM.

1993

Time Out reports that students' average annual debt is £1,000. In 2007, graduates' average debt is £17,500.

Stephen Lawrence is murdered. In 1999, the Macpherson report concludes that the police had been 'institutionally racist' in their investigations.

1999

Thirty-one people die in the Paddington train crash.

2004

The Civil Partnership Act gives same-sex couples equal rights and responsibilities to those in opposite-sex marriages.

2007

A smoking ban in enclosed public places sees a ten per cent drop in business at London's pubs.

2008

New Tory Mayor of London Boris Johnson bans alcohol consumption on the tube, buses and DLR.

SOCIETY

London lives

Since 2005, *Time Out* has profiled individual Londoners from
a multitude of different nations and cultures. Here are just a few.

SOCIETY

The Polish migrant

Forget talk of 'bogus asylum seekers': most
immigrants arrive legally in Britain, from
countries that have employment treaties
with the UK. In 2005, *Time Out* joined two young
Poles on the long journey from Warsaw to discover
the reality of starting a new life in London.

2 March

11am, Warsaw bus terminal The Warsaw to
London bus is about to leave. Every day, hundreds
of Poles make the 26-hour bus journey to London
in search of work. Since Poland joined the EU
last May, 20,000 have arrived in the country. It's
estimated there are 250,000 Poles living in London.

Wiola Andrzejewska (22), from Konin, three
hours from Warsaw, boards the bus with her
brother Slawek (20): 'This is the first time I have
left Poland,' she says. 'I thought about coming to
London about a year ago. I wanted to come for a
sense of adventure. But also, the fact is, Polish
people can legally work in Britain and bring
money home. Compared to what we can make in
Poland, it's good for us to come to Britain.

'We just booked our tickets a week ago and said
to our family: "We are leaving." They think it's a
good thing. It's a matter of being in this little town,
Konin, and thinking, well, what can you do?

3 March

3.30pm, Victoria coach station Wiola arrives in
London with Slawek. 'I didn't sleep much on the
coach. The most stressful thing has been arriving
in London. We are very surprised because we didn't
imagine London being so big. We don't have a map
and don't know where to go.

'Eventually, we decided to go to the Polish
Cultural Centre in Hammersmith that we had
heard about. There, my brother ended up meeting
a guy, Jarek, and asked him if he knew where we
could stay. Jarek said we could stay for the night
at the rented house he shared with other Poles.
We got a bus and got off a few stops before
Heathrow airport. We stayed in our sleeping bags!
I was so grateful for his kindness.'

4 March

11am, the Wailing Wall, Hammersmith The
Sciana Placzu ('Wailing Wall') is a little cornershop
more famous in Poland than in Britain. The shop
window is crammed with fliers, notes advertising

Wiola Andrzejewska
(left) and friends.

job vacancies and accommodation, and notes to
friends and relatives. Every kind of work is offered
here, from catering and cleaning to pizza and
newspaper delivery. Most make no mention of pay.

'Jarek suggested we go to the Wailing Wall to look
for work,' says Wiola, 'but masses of people were
crowded up against the window when we got there,
so we decided to go back later. We have another
lead for work, from when we were on the bus
going to Jarek's house the night before. By chance,
Jarek met an elderly Polish woman. She told him
that she needed some girls to work in a place in
Hammersmith and gave us the address. When
we turned up, it was a dry-cleaner. It's run by
Indians who don't speak English, but luckily,
there was a Polish woman working there who
could translate, and she told us to come back again
on Sunday morning.'

5 March

8pm, Hotel Crimea, Ealing 'Last night we also
found somewhere to stay. My brother bumped
into some Poles on the street and they told him
about this place, the Hotel Crimea. We don't have
to pay a deposit. It's £65 per week. I share the room
with my brother.'

At the end of her first year in London, Wiola had
found decent accommodation as well as regular
employment and babysitting work. She has
decided to stay.

The Ghanaian doctor

Kitted out in formal Victorian top hat and tails, Dr John Ferrel Easmon stares out from a black and white photo that shows his graduation from University College Hospital, Bloomsbury, in 1879. There is nothing unusual about this photo – apart from the fact Dr Easmon is black. 'We think he was probably the first black doctor at UCH,' says 45-year-old Charlie Easmon, Ferrel Easmon's great-grandson, and himself a doctor in Harley Street, where he set up his own practice in 2002.

Born in Sekondi in Ghana in 1961, Easmon now lives in Clapham with his Scottish wife and six-year-old son Byron. Although his efforts are concentrated on his Harley Street practice, Easmon is keen to retain his Ghanaian roots. 'We'd like Byron to be aware of both sides of his heritage. I'd like to take him to visit Ghana one day.'

The Afghan waiter

Nasser Abdul arrived in Britain in 1998, claiming asylum from war-torn Afghanistan with a fake passport he bought in Kabul for £6,000. 'I'm telling you all this, so you have an idea of what most Afghanis go through. To get a visa to

Sergei Kolushev

Britain, you need power or money. Most Afghanis have neither. Once we are here, our asylum details can be properly processed,' says Abdul.

Abdul, 28, now works in an Afghani restaurant, Masa, in Harrow, but his story is typical of many of the 30,000 Afghans thought to live in London, most of whom fled the country after the Taliban came to power in 1996.

Abdul has great affection for his adopted city. 'I really like London. It's an old city, and makes you feel attached to it. I recently went on my first holiday in six years, but when I got there, I missed London so much I ended up changing my flight for an earlier ticket back.'

The Russian entrepreneur

In his neat grey suit, entrepreneur 39-year-old Sergei Kolushev is the consummate businessman. Kolushev is the managing director of Eventica, a Canary Wharf-based company that organises such business and cultural events as the Russian Economic Forum and the annual Russian Winter Festival. Splitting his time between Moscow and London, he perfectly represents the new batch of Russian entrepreneurs steadily making the capital their home.

Kolushev's wife, whom he met here, is also Russian: 'There's nothing wrong with American, French or English women, but, the Russian man needs to be spoiled by the Russian woman,' he says. He also wants his two-year-old son, Nikita Patrick, to be proud of his heritage. 'We speak Russian all the time to him and have a Russian nanny.'

The Australian dancer

Antipodeans have been hitting the backpacker trail to London since the 1960s, but 28-year-old dancer Mandy Liddell is part of a growing number of foreign professionals coming to work in London, staying and making it their home. While there are still plenty of backpackers paying their way by pulling pints in pubs across London, around 30 per cent of Aussies working here now are in banking, finance and other high-salaried professional jobs. These days it's Shepherd's Bush, or the more upmarket Fulham or Putney, where Liddell

Mandy Liddell

lives, that are hosting the new generation of Australians, rather than the seedy backpacker hotels of Earl's Court.

Her first few weeks in the capital read like the archetypal Aussie-in-London experience. 'I was staying in Bayswater in an awful house-share with a lot of my fellow countrymen. There were three rooms, with ten people in each room, and one bathroom.

God, the dirt! The place was full of people working in pubs. We spent all our money on beer in theme pubs that I don't go to any more.'

Australians are also becoming a cultural force in London; there are antipodeans at the helm of the South Bank Centre and Sadler's Wells, as well as the Royal Ballet School and London Philharmonic Orchestra. And these days, fashion from down under doesn't just mean surf gear. Alannah Hill, Wayne Cooper and other top designers are stocked at Austique on the King's Road and have a strong following here.

'I don't have any desire to go back,' says Liddell.

'Sydney is amazing, but I don't miss it. Last Australia Day, I was in the Walkabout in Covent Garden. I ended up having an argument with another Australian. He was complaining about the weather and slagging off everything about Britain and I got so angry. OK it's cold, but go home if you don't like it.'

All reports by Rebecca Taylor.

Nasser Abdul

SOCIETY

The strange death of the COCKNEY

It was the closure of Goddard's that did it. When Greenwich's venerable pie and mash shop, opened in 1890, was turned into an upmarket burger joint earlier this year, it appeared to be another boot into the battered body of the cockney. His language was being usurped, his pubs, cafés and markets closed, his culture mocked or ignored; even the sparrow had forsaken him. So, is the cockney dead? Has 150 years of tradition and culture gone to the great pie shop in the sky?

But first, what is a cockney? The most popular theory is that it's from 'cock's egg' – 'an unnatural object, a freak of nature', as Peter Ackroyd points out – and the term was originally used as an insult to distinguish the effete city dweller from his hardened country cousin. The label soon turned from slight to proclamation, and the defiant, self-reliant, confident cockney was born. Cathy Ross of the Museum in Docklands explains: 'In the 19th century there had been a lot of fear of the working class, but then he was reinvented as the cockney, standing very much for empire and almost part of the establishment. He became allied with the chauvinism of the Edwardian era and was the acceptable face of the British urban working class.'

VS Pritchett believed the cockney had the 'hard-chinned look of indomitable character', while Roy Porter expands the theme in *London: A Social History*. 'The true cockney was smart, wearing flash attire, perhaps a battered silk hat… bright, sharp, never-say-die, streetwise, sturdy optimism in his unwavering determination not only to make the best of things as they are, but to make them seem actually better than they are by adapting his moods to the exigencies of the occasion and in his supreme disdain of all outside influences.'

Michael Collins, author of *The Likes of Us*, a social history of the Walworth working class, sees cockney simply as 'a localised culture based around market and pub and the cockney language that came out of the costermonger culture', but the best definition is that you know one when you see one. And you don't see them as often as you used to.

You can't miss Jimmy Jukes, though. The pearly king of Camberwell, Jukes is 'proud to be a pearly, proud to be a Londoner, proud to be a cockney', but his kids have no interest in following the tradition – 'They're embarrassed by it all' – and he doesn't expect to pass on the suit when he retires. 'It's gone down the drain,' he laments. 'It's very rare you'll find a young pearly. I was over in Spitalfields and a kid there – about 35, from Mile End – saw me in my suit and had no idea what I was about. If your own people can't understand your culture, why should anyone else?'

'It's hard to live in London now. All my family

> ""If your own people can't understand your culture, why should anyone else?" Jimmy Jukes, pearly king.'

have moved out and I always thought I wouldn't, but it's got to the point where, financially and mentally, I've got to. It's a 100mph city and you don't want to live like that. It's hard to find a pearly king who lives in his borough now. The pearly king of Hornsey lives in Shepherd's Bush, the pearly king of King's Cross lives in Arnos Grove, the pearly king of Peckham lives in Epsom and the pearly queen of Newham lives in Jersey!'

Demographic changes are also having a huge and increasingly documented impact on the traditional cockney accent of 'whining vowels and ruined consonants' (Pritchett). Cockney speech has always assimilated – 'From Dutch and Spanish, Arabic and Italian, French and German; the cant of thieves and argot of prisons,' according to Ackroyd in a particularly rich chapter of his *London: The Biography* – but the latest borrowings are of inflection as much as vocabulary, and as such are almost unrecognisable as cockney.

A survey of London accents among teenagers by Queen Mary College in 2005 found: 'It is certainly different to the traditional cockney model, and it is an accent that seems to be influenced by Jamaican, Indian subcontinent and West African English.' While some of the words lifted from Caribbean

and Bengali patois chime happily with rhyming slang's numerous borrowings, the real difference comes when the long vowels of cockney become shortened – 'face' was 'faice' but is now 'fehs' – creating what some have imaginatively dubbed 'multicultural London English'.

'Kids have their new street talk; it's a form of what we had, but it's not rhyming slang,' says Jukes, resigned but not resentful. 'People who move here have their own culture, so they're not interested in ours and nobody bothers to teach it in schools. It's dying.'

Cathy Ross of the Museum in Docklands claims that the most thriving cockney tradition is the extravagant funeral, 'a status symbol among established cockney families, especially since the Krays died. I would have said cockney was dead about five years ago, but not so much now. There's a sort of postmodern ironic cockneyness coming back. You've got the latest White Stripes album with them in pearly costumes, Bethnal Green Working Men's Club is very trendy, and Alexander McQueen had a pearly collection. It might not be real, but it adds value.'

This is a familiar pattern. Kill a culture and then sell it back in antiseptic form. Mockney itself isn't anything new; George Melly has spoken about flapper-era mockneys, while Mick Jagger and Jamie Oliver represent not so much faux cockney as an entirely legitimate suburban strand, the result of the postwar diaspora and social mobility. Mockney, though, is little more than an accent, while this recent flowering of pearly and music-hall fashion suggests something more involved, borrowing from cockney and selling it to the hip and the rich, where it will be a fun fad for five minutes before fizzling out. Its impact on the urban working class it takes from is likely to be minimal.

Whether this counts as cockney, Collins doesn't know and isn't even sure it's important. 'If you talk about any characteristics that define a culture, you are left with clichés. People denigrate pie and mash while talking up the Carnival, but there's not much difference. People criticised cockney culture for years and said it had no colour but, if it had been regarded as any stronger, the crossover into what is called multiculturalism would have been much more difficult.'

So where does this leave the cockney? Suspended like an eel in jelly; slowly suffocating as he fights for his own slice of multicultural London and the right to be represented among a thousand other voices? Retired in Dartford, having served his 150 years as the face of London?

Or happily evolved into something new, that's still finding its voice in Lady Sovereign, Lily Allen and Gautam Malkani? Either way, the result is inevitable.

Admit it, you'll miss him when he's gone.

Original article by Peter Watts.

SOCIETY

Roof justice

Jim, 62, has been fighting for squatters' rights since the 1970s.

Originally I'm from Clydebank and Leeds, and I came to London when I was 16. I worked in office jobs and was even employed as a trainee reporter on the *Telegraph*, but as the 1960s and '70s went on, I began to find it difficult to afford accommodation. In 1975, I was living in a bedsit in Stratford and simply couldn't pay the rent – it was more than half my income. Squatting was the sensible answer.

I started off in a squat in Turner Road, Tower Hamlets. It was a very different scene from today. There were lots of pan-London squatting activities, including the annual London Squatting Festival and a Squatting Action Council, which helped with legal matters. There were squatters' football leagues; the Battersea Squatting Association boasted a very good team.

Whole streets and blocks of flats were given over to squatters: Frestonia (a triangle of squats in Notting Hill, which declared themselves a republic, set up their own council, newspaper, flag and theatre company and, in 1977, attempted to secede from the United Kingdom) was one of the best. The squatted streets were particularly well organised, and many were able to resist eviction.

Most of us were under 40 and the emphasis was on communal living. We had house meetings and ate and cooked together, but it certainly wasn't based on living a hippy idyll – people squatted because they couldn't afford to live elsewhere.

In 1977, the GLC offered a 'squatting amnesty'. Squatters were given the chance to take up short-life leases for six months, or to be rehoused. Huntley Street was given a short-life-lease – which actually ended up lasting for the next 26 years. I ended up in a squat in Hackney, where I eventually worked out a lease with the council and have remained to this day.

In the early 1980s, squatting went through another phase. It was buzzing with new people and ideas. Social centres were the big thing: places such as a squat on on Rosebery Avenue that was a meeting hub and had great cooking evenings, where everyone donated £1 and cooked a feast. The Ramparts was another social centre in Hackney that had its own particular character.

These days, the lack of council housing has created an even greater need for squatting, and

The police (and their state-of-the-art patrol car) keep a watchful eye on a house full of squatters, 1970.

it affects all ages. It is far more precarious. There is a lot of money in redevelopment, and landlords are employing more aggressive means to retain their properties. Evictions have got very violent. We've seen an increase in Polish and eastern European squatters. They come to work here under the new EU employment legislation, but can't afford the rents once they're here.

There has also been a spate of arty-farty squatting, where artists are setting up galleries in empty buildings. That's great, but at the end of the day, it's about getting a roof over your head.

Jim is an activist with the Squatters Advisory Service (www.squatter.org.uk).

The view from the street
Brian Bleasdale, 74, homeless since 1983

I've been homeless on and off over the last 25 years. I'm from Rochdale, but came down to London in the 1950s. My marriage broke up. I had a long-term girlfriend, but she booted me on to the street after I'd been in hospital with angina.

I started sleeping in doorways along the Strand. There were lots of men my age, in their 50s: we all knew each other. There was a lot of drink and you had to be hard to survive, be able to fight to defend yourself.

I went to a day-care centre in St-Martin-in-the Fields on Monday, hand my clothes over to the laundry and have a shower. On Wednesday, I'd pick up the clothes and have another shower. I was always smart and shaved and wore fresh clothes from the second-hand racks at the day centre.

I also slept in St James' Park. We always cleaned up our patches behind us when we got up, not like today where rough sleepers leave a mess behind them. There are so many teenagers on the streets these days, and their behaviour is unpleasant. There's more drugs around. It's also much harder to get council housing – and getting your head around the different papers to get benefits is a nightmare.

In the park, we got soup and bread pudding from the Salvation Army, and the 'Chocolate Man' used to hand out Mars bars and sweets. A van came round with clothing, and another with curry. But we were constantly moved on by the police. My sleeping bag has been all over London, it's done good service.

The Bullring underground precinct at Waterloo was another patch. That was so organised that the local postman used to drop off our mail there: we'd engrave a number on the walls above our patches so he'd know where to leave it. I had a carpet, full-size mattress, wireless and a stove to brew tea on. It was quite comfortable.

Later, I got a place in a hostel in Hackney, but there was an off-licence next door and the place was full of booze. I've also been in rented council digs, and since 2005 I've been at a St Mungo's hostel in Royal Oak. I have my own room and we're responsible for cleaning the communal bathrooms and kitchens. I've found it hard to get used to sleeping in a bed, and when I was first here often ended up sleeping on the floor. I still disappear back on to the streets for a bit.

On Monday, I go to the local market and do t'ai chi. On Tuesday, I go to a day centre where there's a lonely hearts club – just what the doctor ordered. My life is much more comfortable now. I have some quiet and peace of mind.

Coming up

Starting in the late 1960s, previously down-at-heel neighbourhoods of inner London have been transformed by the unstoppable force of gentrification.

SOCIETY

The term gentrification was coined in 1964 by the sociologist Ruth Glass, to describe the 'invasion' of working-class quarters of London by the middle classes. She saw the process at work in Islington, an inner-city borough where incomers, described by the local paper as 'new Chelseaites', had begun to turn insalubrious rooming houses back into well-appointed family homes. The architectural signature of gentrification in the late '60s and early '70s was 'knocking through', the removal of internal walls to create open-plan spaces. The 'knockers-through', as these urban pioneers were known, were satirised in Mark Boxer's weekly cartoon for the *Listener*, 'Life and Times in NW1'.

Islington

Then A survey carried out in the late '60s revealed that Islington had the highest concentration of multi-occupation houses in London. Since the Edwardian era, most of the area's grand terraces either side of Upper Street had been divided up into flats. According to the writer Jonathan Raban, a keen student of gentrification, Islington was a 'cheap place for immigrants' – especially the Irish and the Greeks – 'to get a peeling room'.
Now The 'academics, journalists of a literary turn, television directors and producers' who bought houses here during the first wave of gentrification now occupy some of the most expensive real estate in London – if they've stayed. For many have been displaced by what is sometimes called 'super-gentrification'. Today, one's Islington neighbours are more likely to be hedge-fund managers or corporate lawyers than 'cultural entrepeneurs'.

Battersea

Then In 1968, Battersea was somewhere you went if you wanted to slum it. Peter Collinson's film *Up the Junction*, released that year and starring Suzy Kendall and Dennis Waterman, captures perfectly the atmosphere of what was then a grimy, semi-industrialised working-class suburb.
Now In his classic 1974 portrait of urban life, *Soft City*, Jonathan Raban describes the knockers-through moving south of the Thames in a 'pincer movement… through New Cross, Camberwell, Clapham and Battersea.' However, gentrification really took off here in the 1980s, during the Lawson boom, turning shabby Northcote Road, for instance, into a bourgeois wet-dream of a traditional high street.

Notting Hill

Then The novelist Colin MacInnes described Notting Hill in the late '50s as a 'rotting slum of sharp, horrible vivacity'. Ten years later, not much had changed – the stucco was still hanging off the substantial early Victorian villas – though the denizens of London's nascent counterculture had begun to move in, among the West Indian and Irish immigrants. Donald Cammell and Nicolas Roeg's 1970 film *Performance*, in which Mick Jagger played a reclusive rock star holed up in a house in Powis Square, is a deeply unsettling record of this transitional moment in the history of the area.
Now Today, the hippies and immigrants (the poor ones at least) have mostly left, replaced by some of London's wealthiest residents, who have turned Notting Hill's resplendent crescents and private gardens into a kind of exclusive playground.

Northcote Road: once grotty, now gentrified.

Gangland capital

The Triads do not steal car radios. The Yardies do not mug old ladies. The Colombian drug cartels are not accomplished cat burglars and Russian mafiosi are hopeless at picking pockets on the Underground.

However, according to Scotland Yard, MI5 and the National Criminal Intelligence Service, London has been penetrated from top to bottom by international organised crime. Every major gang, from the Mafia to the Japanese Yakuza, now has operatives in London.

It affects our lives in countless ways: the desperate heroin addict who burgles or mugs to pay for his next fix, which is supplied, albeit indirectly, by a major Turkish underworld syndicate; the neighbour who seemed so nice and quiet, wouldn't hurt a fly, who turns out to be an international drugs baron; the fight in your local pub or restaurant, that settles underworld scores. Once you start digging, it's remarkable how many lice crawl out of London's woodwork.

In September 1993, a local London newspaper carried a one-paragraph report about an air ambulance landing in the High Street following a fight in a pub. There was nothing to indicate that anything out of the ordinary had occurred and even the landlord, who does not wish to be named, can add only a few vague details: a fight broke out in the toilet, a man was stabbed, a few customers ran to his aid and then everyone ran away before the police arrived.

In the legitimate world, the story is seen as another example of our violent society. In the underworld, however, the story has assumed folklore status and perfectly demonstrates how the two worlds interact.

'Colin called me up at 10am that morning to ask if I could get a few lads together,' says Roy, a well-known south London 'face'. 'He didn't give me the full SP, he just said that he'd arrange to meet up with a bloke he owed money to, and wanted some back-up in case there was trouble.'

The truth, as Roy later discovered, was that Colin had stolen almost two kilos of cocaine from a senior member of a Scottish crime family, and then fled to London. He'd planned to start his own little enterprise, but had been rumbled within a few days. The Scots had sent down a delegation to get their money or drugs back.

'Of course, Colin didn't die,' says Roy. 'He used to be a normal bloke, but now he's like that,' he says, holding up his little finger. 'He must weigh all of six stone, but he's happy to be alive.'

The image of the villain as a moronic thug, too stupid to do anything except rob banks or beat up people, is out of date. Even the Hell's Angels, recently described by Interpol as the 'fastest growing criminal organisation in Europe', learned long ago that the only way to progress in organised crime is to blend in.

When conducting 'business' (drug trafficking, protection and the like), '90s Angels are more likely to be wearing suits and driving Audis than wearing cut-down leathers and riding Harley Davidsons.

And what the Angels are doing today, others have been perfecting for decades.

For example, no one suspected that Patrick Thomas was anything other that Mr Average. 'He was really nice,' said a neighbour from the Turnham Road estate in Brockley. 'Not flashy or loud – not one of those lads that think they're really tough or bad. Just a decent bloke.'

Thomas did little to attract attention. He shared a flat with his step-sister, her husband and daughter, worked periodically as a barman and car dealer, drove around in a ten-year-old BMW and drifted from day to day with no obvious plans or ambitions.

In the early hours of 29 December 1991, he was found dead in his hallway from a single gunshot wound. Soon after, police discovered more than £150,000 in various bank and building society accounts, many of which he had opened in false names. Behind the quiet façade, Thomas was a career criminal, specialising in armed robbery and drug-dealing.

The Goldsworthy family also managed to fool everyone. Occasionally they had friends round to their Fulham home and in the summer sometimes lounged around in their garden, but for the most part, their neighbours barely noticed them.

In December 1988, a few months after her husband Keith had taken a job in America, Claudia Goldsworthy and her young daughter disappeared. When the police came looking they found a domestic Mary Celeste: furnishings and clothes all in place, food in the fridge, schoolbooks on the kitchen table and every creature comfort left behind.

Neighbourhood concern rapidly turned to astonishment when those who had lived close by learned they had been fed a string of lies. Keith hadn't gone to work abroad: he'd been sentenced to 22 years for his part in a multi-million-dollar cocaine ring. As for Colombian-born Claudia, she had vanished six days before she was due to appear at Knightsbridge Crown Court on a charge of laundering millions of pounds of her husband's drug profits.

And far from being a quiet family, the Goldsworthys were incredibly busy – paving the way for a major narcotics revolution. When the pair arrived in England in 1985, cocaine wasn't

considered much of a threat. Average seizures for each year of the previous decade were just 17kg and the total haul for 1984 was just 35kg.

Heroin, on the other hand, was the number one scourge. A massive 312kg had been seized, and government statistics, notoriously understated, pointed to some 50,000 addicts, leading to a flurry of magazine and newspaper articles on the 'heroin crisis'. By the time of Claudia Goldsworthy's midnight flit, British seizures of cocaine had increased ten fold to 362kg, overtaking heroin for the first time.

At the time, the two events seemed entirely unconnected, and no one thought of Claudia as

GANG STAR

A who's who of the toughest teams on the capital's turf

Name	Russian Mafia	Triads
Membership London Worldwide	45 3 million	5,000 80,000
Structure	Arranged into separate gangs, but will co-operate for particular jobs	Separate gangs include Wo Sing Wo, Wo On Lok, 14K and San Yee On
Strongholds	No set base, but have supposedly purchased property in Mayfair and Knightsbridge	Soho, Queensway
Core activities	Money laundering, racketeering, drug trafficking	Protection and extortion, some drug trafficking, illegal immigration rackets
UK murders since 1980	3	4 (40-plus attempts)
Annual UK earnings	£5m	£10m
Associates	Turks, Italians and Colombians are all on friendly terms	Keep themselves to themselves, but regular in-fighting among rival gangs
Future threat rating	Much vaunted, but size of threat is somewhat overstated as they have little interest in the UK	Longest established criminal gang in the world. Fears that they could expand in UK following the handing back of Hong Kong in 1997

SOCIETY

Yardies	Turkish Mafia	Colombian drug cartels
40-80	300-plus	10
3,600	23,000	1,600
Loose-knit coalitions of illegal immigrants	Close-knit gangs based around illegal gambling dens	Close-knit cells, each headed by representative of major drug trafficking family
Brixton, Harlesden, Clapham, Stoke Newington	Manor House, Stoke Newington, Hackney and Haringey	Extremely mobile. Initial base in Fulham, but now move around regularly
Crack dealing, small-scale drug smuggling, some prostitution	Drug smuggling, extortion, protection, and transport of illegal immigrants	Cocaine trafficking, though now moving into heroin. Some money laundering
57	6	6, indirectly
£2m	£300m	£300m
Colombians sometimes supply coke, but generally distrusted by other gangs	Close co-operation with Sicilian Mafia, but bitter in-fighting among rival UK-based gangs	Strong alliances with the Sicilian Mafia, Japanese Yakuza and new Russian Mafia
Overhyped, but undoubtedly over here. Reputation way out of proportion, but responsible for police being increasingly issued with firearms and body armour	The NBT – Next Big Thing – in criminal circles. Have taken over the running of 40 per cent of the heroin trade in Europe in just five years. Second only to the Sicilian Mafia	Skilled at marketing. Invented crack and now pushing heroin as the new 'in' drug. Undoubtedly the most dangerous gang of all

The membership comes from the highest criminal class in the capital. The men and women who make up its ranks rarely commit crimes themselves, but use their contacts and influence to organise everything from bank robberies and drug deals to fraud and money-laundering. Most of them lead lives of luxury: so skilled are they at distancing themselves from prosecution that only a minority have any convictions.

Co-operation between international criminal gangs is growing all the time.

In the last five years, a number of inter-gang summits have been held across Europe and in London. The Russian mafia, the Triads, the Mafia and Colombian drug cartels have all attended at one time or another to discuss ways of working together. The Japanese Yakuza were expected to attend in 1993, but the meeting was aborted after the deputy head of Japan's largest gang was arrested in Paris while en route to London.

Even the Hell's Angels make the most of their international links, particularly those with the Commonwealth. In 1985, a Canadian Angel wanted on a murder charge was found hiding with a group of his British counterparts in a flat in south London. In February 1995, two more Canadian Hell's Angels were jailed for 14 years following a massive cocaine swoop the previous year. The two men, Pierre Rodrigue and David Rouleau, had been arrested in a plush suite in the Hilton hotel last summer. They had been in contact with British Angels during their time here, and were thought to be helping to draw up plans to open up new cocaine routes in Britain.

What is of greatest concern to the law enforcement authorities is that all this activity is tied up with increasing levels of co-operation between home-grown British and foreign criminal gangs. The learning curve is a sharp one, with the heirs to the Krays and those that followed them learning from the mistakes of groups like the Mafia and Triads, who have been involved in organised crime for hundreds of years.

Meetings between supposedly rival British groups to carve out new territories and combine resources can only be a few years away. Ruthless, able to travel worldwide with ease, backed up by the latest technology and willing to kill to maintain the status quo, this fledging British mafia may yet turn out to be a major force in international organised crime.

As Albert Pacey, Director General of the National Criminal Intelligence Service, told the Home Affairs Select Committee inquiry into organised crime during an oral evidence session in July 1994: 'There is no one Mr Big, but there are plenty of Mr Big-Enoughs.'

anything more than a typical gangster's moll. This could not have been further from the truth. Claudia had not arrived in Britain by chance – she had been handpicked and sent to London by her cousin, one Jorge Luis Ochoa, who, along with his chum Pablo Escobar, hoped to develop the British end of what quickly became the largest and most profitable criminal conspiracy in the world, the Medellin Cartel.

Home-grown villains are just as elusive. A wine bar in the City of London, set back a discreet distance from the main road, is the favoured meeting place of a group of individuals known simply as 'the syndicate'.

Original article and chart by Tony Thompson, author of Gangland Britain.

When the red lights go out

Though the brothels have given way to cosmopolitan coffee bars, and the gangsters to website designers, Soho's naughty nature will never completely die.

By Felix Dennis

'New' Soho, London

Old Soho waits, revamped, new-lamped,
For bouncer's dusk to fall – grown proud
Of her new horde:
Fresh meat shipped in to scan the crowd
In search of what has long decamped.

Skin deep – her plastic surgery
Has served to hide the old whore's limp;
The sluttish fraud
Now plies her trade sans bruise, sans pimp,
Grown fat on gloss and perjury.

Those fools who crow: 'The ghost is laid!'
Should save their breath to sniff her sheets
Still neatly stored.
For forty years I've walked these streets:
Old Soho waits – new paint will fade.
Felix Dennis

And so she does, and so it will, although not many realise it. For those few of us who have lived for three or four decades in the heart of Soho, the transformation of the old whore via the claims of property developers and City Hall spin-doctors into a shiny new neighbourhood is a wonder to behold. And for a simple reason: we know what nonsense such claims are.

Names have been changed (where did 'West Soho' come from?). Bricks have been steam-cleaned. New facades erected. Seedy sex shops refitted within an inch of their 17th-century lives. Carnaby Street rents have quadrupled. Ikea chairs and tables wobble precariously on pavements in a desperate attempt to persuade us that we are part of a sophisticated European café culture. Bijou shopping malls have reared their Prada-like heads where once, and not so very long ago, illegal immigrants bowed heads in grimy sweatshops sewing trousers and waistcoats for Savile Row.

The working girls who once roamed the alleys and streets like herds of nervous gazelles have long been chased to King's Cross. Gorillas in smart blazers stand beside the velvet ropes of club entrances, expertly selecting midnight wannabes from the gonnabes. Michelin-starred restaurants now charge more for a meal or a bottle of wine than I used to earn in a week

(or a month!) 30 years ago. Tourists are thronging back. Soho has come of age – again.

All has changed. All is safe. All is deodorised. Except, perhaps, for a little uncouth shouting and urinating and car door slamming when the clubs turn out. Welcome to modern Soho!

And yet, beneath this manicured veneer, Old Soho waits. The rats still lurk inches below your feet – literally, in some locations. Secret tunnels built by the fearful Huguenots and others still connect building to square and basement to sewer. The back rooms, basements and garrets of many bland Soho facades are still safe harbours for certain activities – mostly involving gambling and paid sex – that would give the lie to advertising copywriters and idle compilers of London guidebooks.

Not only has Old Soho never gone away, from my own perspective it is flourishing and likely to continue to do so. But what was it like, back then?

Forty years ago, I acquired, through blind luck and adolescent gall, an unfurnished top-floor flat in a Soho backstreet, previously tenanted by four Scottish prostitutes. They had come together down to London to make their fortune, and had sworn a blood oath to stick together, to eschew pimps and to only entertain their 'clients' in the safety of the flat, never on the street. (A flat, by the way, then owned by Her Majesty the Queen through the offices of the Crown Commissioners. Not that I am suggesting for a moment, you understand, that their landlords were in any way aware of their activities – despite the red light in the window, the discreet card pinned by the front door bell and the incessant parade of seedy old farts puffing and wheezing their way up three floors of rickety stairs for an 'appointment'.)

For three years these Scottish ladies had successfully plied their trade to the damp-macintosh brigade of central London, and were now, by some miracle, all returning to Edinburgh together. And in Edinburgh, as far as I know, they still reside today, quite probably as highly respectable grandmothers and great-grandmothers.

My negotiations with them to acquire the flat, which took place around their kitchen table, were businesslike, but somewhat protracted, as one or another of them hurriedly left the room to minister to yet another client. Eventually, we settled on a payment of the enormous sum of £2,500 for

The Pigalle cinema, famous for showing uncensored sex films, in 1977.

'I quickly discovered my new flat was situated above two clubs – one a "gentleman's club" that charged £35 for a bottle of champagne, the other a late-night haunt for gangsters and villains.'

a few miserable 'fixtures and fittings' – a common dodge used in those days to avoid the illegal payment of 'key money'.

The flat was enormous, but in a parlous state – and not just from its recent use as a brothel. The street windows were cracked, some of them broken and patched with brown tape. The floor joists had gone in two of the rooms, and a white line had been painted around their centre with an ominous warning: 'Do Not Walk Here: Joist Broken!' The roof leaked, the walls were covered in blotchy mildew, the bathroom was situated outside on a half-landing on the stairs, there was no hot water, and the only heating was supplied by two-bar electric radiators.

But it was perfect for a 20-year-old idiot. I quickly discovered that my new flat was situated above two clubs – a 'gentleman's club' that charged £35 for a bottle of champagne and the company of skimpily dressed 'hostesses', and a late-night haunt for gangsters and villains. Although I was permitted a 'discount' (providing I wore a jacket and tie) in the 'gentleman's club', the latter was by far the more dangerous establishment – with subterranean log fires illegally sending smoke up the brick chimneys, much of which permeated its way through the rest of the building.

It was also common for CID police officers from West End Central nick to station themselves on the roof above my head, leaning precariously over the parapet while they made notes on the comings and goings of this club's clientele. Occasionally, I took pity on them and handed them cups of tea across the fire escape.

Some years later, those cups of tea were repaid handsomely. I was approached by two hard-boiled Maltese pimps who had identified my flat, quite correctly, as the perfect location for a new brothel. When I refused their offer of a thousand quid to 'scarper or take the consequence', they made it clear what those consequences were likely to be by killing a local cat and posting its body through my letter box. Only a 'quiet word in their shell-like' from the CID persuaded them to look elsewhere. The close relationship between police and villains in London, then as now, would surprise many members of the chattering classes.

I loved Soho 40 years ago – and I love it now. I love the food, the market, the music, the street, the roofscape, the congestion, the pubs, the history, the mixture of Babylon-on-baked-beans and the knowledge that somewhere, far closer than you might think, certain things are taking place that perhaps ought not to be.

And I know this: that no matter how many coats of paint are applied, or how many Starbucks coffees are served, or how many cobbles are laid in newly pedestrianised streets and courtyards, Old Soho waits. Its return is preordained. The vagaries of fashion in real estate will prevail, and eventually, just as it has so many times before, Soho will return to its disreputable roots.

You can kill the flower of a stinging nettle, but its roots are a different matter. In Soho, those roots are secretly alive and well, thank you very much.

And long may it be so.

SOCIETY

Felix Dennis still lives, as a tenant under the 1969 Rent Act, in the same top-floor Soho flat. His latest collection of poetry, *Homeless in My Heart*, is published by Ebury Press.

Green shoots

By Jonathon Porritt

Time Out and modern environmentalism in the UK are almost as old as each other. Although organisations like the RSPB, the Ramblers and the Council for the Protection of Rural England have been around for much longer, it wasn't until the *Torrey Canyon* came to grief on the Isles of Scilly in March 1967 [leaking 31 million gallons of oil along the south coast of Britain and the Normandy beaches], that a broader-based environmental awareness began to emerge.

The late '60s and early '70s were a time when the 'never had it so good' generation began to take account of the costs as well as the benefits of modern industrialism. Landmark publications such as the Club of Rome's 'Limit to Growth' and the 'Blueprint for Survival' (which led to the founding of the Ecology Party as the first specifically green political party in Europe) were hugely influential, disseminating a brand of upmarket doom and gloom that seemed to be wholly vindicated by the massive increases in the price of oil caused by OPEC's 1973 blitzkrieg on the world economy.

A new generation of environmental organisations was born at that time, including Friends of the Earth and Greenpeace. Radical, irreverent and imaginative, they rapidly gained widespread support from people who wanted to see the earth-bashers confronted and complacent politicians put on the spot.

It was an exciting time. But it proved to be a false dawn. The political ferment of the late '60s remained wholly untouched by the early stirrings of green politics; it was not the environment that drew students to the barricades, and it wasn't until the late '70s that people like Rudi Dutschke began to see a little green. The genuinely radical impulses of the hippy movement were neutralised by too many people simultaneously opting out and turning in on themselves.

The spasm of ecological awareness caused by the oil trauma of 1973 was rapidly shaken off as international capitalism came bouncing back with a vengeance. Environmentalists found themselves once again beyond the pale, prophets unloved in their own land.

But they hung in there undeterred. The turnaround began in the early '80s. A series of shocks to the industrial system (Three Mile Island, Bhopal, Seveso) came and went, but the groundswell of apprehension and dissent grew apace. Though environmental memories are short (even Chernobyl has been absorbed as an unfortunate, one-off accident, and in a few years' time few will remember the *Karin B* and

its lethal cargo of toxic waste), the message continues to spread inexorably.

The eruption on to the scene of *die Grünen*, quickly followed by the emergence of successful green parties in many other European countries, rattled politicians of left and right. There are now ten western European countries in which a green parliamentary presence has begun to breathe some life into the political system.

At long last, some sense of this dynamism and vitality is being reflected through the media, particularly TV. A diet of breathtakingly beautiful but politically naive nature films has now been enriched by a wide range of first-class documentaries and environmental magazine programmes. The armchair ecologists are at last being exhorted to stir themselves into action.

Such programmes will almost certainly have a bigger impact on ordinary people than the weighty environmental reports that have punctuated the last 20 years, including President Carter's 'Global 2000 Report', the 1980 'World Conservation Strategy', and last year's 'Our Common Future', the report of the United Nations Commission on Environment and Development. But combined with the huge advances in our scientific knowledge about the state of the Earth, and our impact on it, such reports do serve to strengthen the hand of determined civil servants and that small band of far-sighted politicians.

There are, in fact, few today who can deny the compelling logic of the Greens' case: that on a finite planet, a permanent expansion of human numbers and industrial production is literally unsustainable. The ecologists of the early '70s may have been a little premature in their predictions about oil shortages, but they are right about ozone depletion, soil erosion, chemical pollution, deforestation, the greenhouse effect and a host of other environmental issues that are now coming home to roost.

Twenty years is a relatively long time for any publishing venture, but in evolutionary or geological terms, it is but a split second. It is a sobering process to take stock of the irreversible damage we have already done to the Earth and ourselves during that time, and were it not for the vision of green ideas and the onward march of green organisations, there would be little cause for optimism. It's not too late – the solutions are there. But let's hope it doesn't take another 20 years to seize hold of them.

Jonathon Porritt was a prominent member of the Ecology Party, and Director of Friends of the Earth.

SOCIETY

High society

From LSD to H, E and K, *Time Out* does drugs.

By Michael Hodges

The cover of *Time Out* 25-31 October 1974 features a black and white photograph of a human nose. Beneath the nostrils and above the top lip, one word, rendered in black type, proclaims the issue's main concern: Coke.

There are more lines below, but rather than bemoan the drug's influence (cocaine was cutting a swathe of misery through thousands of London lives and fuelling narco-militias of unbending viciousness in Latin America), the lines are jaunty, telling us cocaine 'made Sigmund Freud randy' and 'helped Sherlock Holmes in his sleuthing.'

If the tone seems reprehensible, more suited to a 1990s lads' mag than a campaigning journal, we might remember that the then editors had little idea that London was about to embark on a 30-year drug binge. In the late '60s and early '70s, drugs were, alongside feminism and listening to very loud rock music, part of the radical agenda. Left-leaning publications such as *Time Out* carried the numbers of lawyers to call if you had been busted, and, in May 1974, complained of 'Prices of £16 an ounce for mediocre Moroccan up to an outrageous £25 an ounce demanded and got for good Afghani or bona fide Nep and Kasmiri.'

Public pressure for the legalisation of cannabis continued throughout the 1980s. After his wife Linda was caught with cannabis at Heathrow airport in 1984, Paul McCartney wrote an article for *Time Out* advocating dope as a 'relaxant'.

'It seems,' said the former Beatle, 'the main problem is legality. Hitler was completely legal, so was slavery', thus putting himself alongside Churchill and Wilberforce as a moral campaigner.

Ultimately, McCartney got his wish. In October 2001, Home Secretary David Blunkett reclassified cannabis from a class B drug to a class C. Blunkett had little choice: since July 2001, the Met had effectively abandoned the persecution of dope users, an initiative pioneered by Lambeth police commander Brian Paddick and informed by the fact that cannabis cases cost the Met 74,000 man-hours a year, and gun and knife crime were, as Brixton DJ Devon Clarke told *Time Out*, 'out of control in the area.'

By then, young Londoners weren't smoking Afghani or Nep, but skunk, a particularly venomous form of grass, grown under hydroponic systems in London attics and similar to LSD in its ability to remove the user from normality. Five years later, effects of the declassification coupled with skunk were clear: a generation of young men dead-eyed and incapable of clarity of thought or action, effectively stoned all the time.

There was nothing new in young people rendering themselves senseless in the capital. In 1982, *Time Out* reported from the Mozart Estate in Kilburn, where teenage boys listened to Madness and sniffed up to a pint of glue a day – though, as one pointed out, 'Bostik's no good: it burns through the bag.' The same report carried more ominous news:

Uppers and downers: London's been there, and everywhere in between.

'Ecstasy didn't give you a rush;
it picked you up and threw you at
the ceiling, from where you
declared your love for the world
and, indeed, the ceiling.'

SOCIETY

'In some London comprehensives it [glue] has been rendered largely obsolete in the senior forms by the schoolkid-sized deals of heroin that are now easily obtainable.'

Heroin had been the drug of London's rock aristocracy; now it seeped into the housing estates. In 1980, *Time Out* reported 'an unprecedented increase in the supply of cheap, good quality heroin in London.' The consequences soon became apparent. 'Every drug dependency clinic we talked to, in each major hospital area,' the report continued, 'said their new registrations were rising.' In the 1980s, addicts sharing needles in squalid flats was seen as a driving force behind the HIV epidemic – but not all users were poor and desperate. Toby, a professional who regularly smoked heroin, told *Time Out* in September 2001, 'I like it, and I'm not going to apologise to people who believe all the crap they read.'

Heroin and cannabis were staying-at-home drugs, but London is a city where people go out,

if largely tedious, house music. But if 'loved-up' culture made drug use seem safe, other arrivals would maintain narcotics' dark reputation. The cocaine derivative crack came to London in the 1990s, and extracted a high price from London's Afro-Caribbean community, as crack turf wars fed spiralling gun crime.

By the time crystal meth arrived at the end of the 1990s (it too, had a variety of names – crank, crystal, meth – but whatever you called it, the effect of the super-charged amphetamine was the same), London was the world's recreational drugs laboratory, offering a full panoply of highs, be it goths crammed into Camden Lock to buy legal unprocessed magic mushrooms or old Ethiopian and Somali men chewing khat, a twig that released a mild amphetamine.

Khat did not progress much beyond its own community, although there was the occasional middle-class user like Jeremy, who told *Time Out* in 2001, 'I tried making tea with it, and even gave it

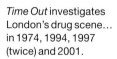

Time Out investigates London's drug scene… in 1974, 1994, 1997 (twice) and 2001.

and drug trends have been closely linked with the city's music scene. Although Johnny Rotten declared, 'Anger is an energy', punk actually relied on the amphetamine habit it had inherited from mods and soul boys for its drive. Speed was a necessary stimulant, and remained so into the mid 1980s, when a new pill started to appear in venues like the Wag Club or the Mud Club. It didn't give you a rush; it picked you up and threw you at the ceiling, from where you declared your love for the world and, indeed, the ceiling. Ecstasy had arrived.

Ecstasy (or MDMA, or simply E) was the first drug to unite all social classes – bringing Londoners together in clubs that appeared to be barns full of waving lunatics listening to hypnotic,

out at my house-warming party, but my guests weren't particularly impressed.'

At the risk of being as flippant as the 1974 coke issue, it is Jeremy's example rather than wasted teenagers on estates or gurning ravers that remains the happiest face of London drug use. Despite the return of cannabis to class B status, there is still, when it comes to the search for a high, a spirit of derring-do in London, the spirit that leads a man to make tea with a small shrub. This is, after all, the city that gave the world the Camberwell Carrot. A joint, in the words of its inventor Danny, in Bruce Robinson's 1987 film *Withnail and I*, 'that can utilise up to 12 skins' and 'will tend to make you very high.'

HEDONISM INTRODUCTION
SEX CITYSCAPE FASHION
SOCIETY SHOPPING COMEDY
DRAMA **PROTEST & POLITICS**
VISUAL ARTS PERFORMANCE
LITERATURE GANGS OPINION
COCKNEYS BARS ON SCREEN
DANCE MUSIC TELEVISION
BUILDINGS CLUBS NIGHTLIFE
SPORT & FITNESS MEMORIES
STYLE FOOD & DRINK GIGS
CONSUME RIOTS REFERENCE

Street fighting

years

L ondon may not have a tradition of revolutionary street theatre to match that of Paris, say, but, as befits the centre of political power and influence, the UK capital has seen its fair share of mass protest and dissent. In the mythology of radical revolt, there are certain key dates, not least 1968, the global 'year of the barricades', on which London played its part. The confrontation that year between police and demonstrators in Grosvenor Square shocked observers with its ferocity, such as hadn't been seen since the anti-fascist battles of the 1930s.

Grosvenor Square
17 March 1968

One historian of the New Left has described the British student movement of the late 1960s as a 'puny specimen' in comparison with its American, French and German counterparts. Certainly, students in Britain didn't manage to bring the government to the brink of collapse, as their comrades in France did during the *événements* of May 1968. Nevertheless, Whitehall officials were sufficiently worried by radicalism in British universities to predict, in that same month, that there would be a 'shallow but destructive explosion in the fairly near future'.

A report presented to the Cabinet by the Foreign Office's information research department described local student groups as 'frighteningly radical' but 'badly lacking in theory' (in this, as in other respects, they lagged behind the Europeans and Americans, who went into battle with the 'pigs' hopped up on Marcuse, Althusser and Marx). But the report warned that what these homegrown radicals lacked in ideological sophistication, they made up for in their enthusiasm for violence: 'Under the influence of Trotskyists and Syndicalists, the Radical Student Alliance was involved with the Vietnam Solidarity Campaign in the violent demonstrations against the American embassy in March.'

Those 'violent demonstrations' in Grosvenor Square on 17 March 1968 were the culmination of a march that began in Trafalgar Square and was organised by the Vietnam Solidarity Campaign (VSC). The VSC had been founded two years earlier by members of a Far Left groupuscule called the International Group (later the International Marxist Group). And although it had initially received financial assistance from the Bertrand

Poll tax riots, Trafalgar Square, 1990.

London isn't just the centre of power in this country. It's also been the stage for mass protest and political theatre – from Grosvenor Square to Hyde Park, from Victoria Park to Wapping.

By Jonathan Derbyshire

Russell Peace Foundation, the VSC wasn't in any sense a 'peace' movement: rather, it campaigned for an American defeat in Indochina.

To the sound of chants borrowed from the American student movement ('Hey, hey, LBJ, how many kids have you killed today?'; 'Ho, Ho, Ho Chi Minh'), the march set off from Trafalgar Square in the direction of the US Embassy. It was led by Tariq Ali, the Pakistan-born and Oxford-educated public face of the VSC, who was candid about the organisation's aims. 'I often thought,' he wrote later, 'about the possibilities of organising international brigades from Europe, the Americas and South Asia, which would enable some of us to fight side by side with the Vietnamese.'

Ali never managed to recreate Spain by the South China Sea, of course, but his cadres did set off the most violent confrontation between demonstrators and police seen in London since the Battle of Cable Street in 1936. When the march reached Grosvenor Square, the American Embassy was surrounded by hundreds of police. A battle ensued, as marchers broke through the police lines on to the Embassy lawn. Mounted police responded to missiles and smoke bombs by charging the crowd with batons raised. There were more than 200 arrests, and 86 people were treated for injuries, including 25 police officers.

The VSC called another huge march in October of that year, in the run-up to which the *Times* made lurid predictions of even more serious

violence. The 'Thunderer' thundered: 'A small army of militant extremists plans to seize control of certain highly sensitive installations and buildings in central London.' Nothing of the sort happened, and the march, which was 100,000-strong, passed off largely without incident.

During the seven months separating these two demonstrations, the global student movement suffered a series of defeats: in Paris, Chicago and in Berlin, where an attempt was made to assassinate the student leader Rudi Dutschke. In retrospect, the Battle of Grosvenor Square looks more like the end of something than a glorious beginning.

Victoria Park
30 April 1978

What did begin in 1968 was the rise of the racist Right in Britain: Enoch Powell gave his notorious and incendiary 'Rivers of Blood' speech in April of that year, which was followed shortly afterwards by a demonstration of London dockers in support of the maverick Tory's stance on immigration.

The National Front, founded in 1967, prospered in the climate created by Powell's intervention, and exploited popular disquiet at the influx into Britain of Asians fleeing Kenya and Uganda. By the second general election of 1974, it was able to field 90 parliamentary candidates, who garnered more than 113,000 votes. In 1977, the NF polled

Demonstration against the Vietnam War, Grosvenor Square, 1968.

more than that number of votes in the May local elections in London alone.

Until then, opposition to the Far Right had been largely inchoate. However, these startling electoral successes convinced many on the Left that organised resistance to the Front, physical as well as political, was essential. And in May 1977, the Anti-Nazi League (ANL) was formed, with members of the Socialist Workers Party (SWP) occupying many of the key posts in the leadership (rather as the IMG had used the VSC as a front a decade earlier). The first test of the SWP's avowed intention to run the NF off the streets came in Lewisham on 13 August 1977.

An 'anti-mugging' march by the NF from New Cross to Lewisham was met by thousands of anti-Front demonstrators. Hand-to-hand fighting between the two sides, and between anti-fascists and the police (many of whom weren't shy of advertising their NF sympathies), was vicious and sustained. And at the height of the battle, riot shields were used for the first time by police on the British mainland. (The previous year, at the Notting Hill Carnival, the men of the Met had tried to protect themselves from missiles with hastily commandeered dustbin lids.)

Victoria Park in the spring of 1978 would not be another Lewisham, however. Nor, despite the best efforts of the SWP, was it a grimly sectarian affair. Instead it was, as the *New Musical Express* described it, the 'biggest public celebration of human solidarity since [NF leader] Martin Webster and his buddies slipped off their jackboots to softshoe their way to the polls.'

Organised by the ANL and Rock Against the Racism, the event began with a rally in Trafalgar Square, before a caravan of floats and marchers set off for the East End, with two enormous papier mâché effigies of Webster and his fascist *confrère* John Tyndall (designed by Peter Fluck and Roger Law of *Spitting Image* fame) leading the way down the Strand and through the City.

By the time the end of the cavalcade reached Victoria Park, more than 80,000 people were waiting on the greensward to hear X-Ray Spex, the Tom Robinson Band, Steel Pulse and the Clash. The raucous performance by Strummer and co was captured in Jack Hazan and David Mingay's film *Rude Boy*, and was marred only by a guest appearance from Jimmy Pursey, absurdly dressed, Marcel Marceau-style, in voluminous Oxford bags, braces and a striped T-shirt.

The general election the following year saw a dramatic reduction in the NF's share of the vote, though the ANL can't take all the credit. It was Margaret Thatcher who drained (or rather creamed off) much of the Front's support when, in an interview with the BBC, she alluded to fears that Britain was being 'swamped by people of a different culture'.

Wapping
24 January 1987

If race was one of the defining political issues of the 1970s, especially in the capital, another was trade union power. With the Winter of Discontent, during which multiple strikes paralysed public services, fresh in the memories of many voters, Thatcher entered Downing Street in 1979 promising to bring the unions to heel.

By 1986, successive pieces of employment legislation, not to mention the débâcle of the miners' strike of 1984-85, had drastically circumscribed the unions' bargaining power and deprived them of the right to secondary picketing. However, one last redoubt of old-style union strength remained – in Fleet Street. Buttressed by an array of so-called 'Spanish practices' (including automatic overtime pay and zealous demarcation), the print unions set their face against the introduction of new technology. Rupert Murdoch, whose News International

Memory bank

Lee Hurst joins the printworkers dispute at News International in 1986

I was 23, unemployed. I thought it was morally justifiable to join a demonstration to save jobs. It was on my patch. I'd lived in Tower Hamlets all my life. Also, I was a young man and it was exciting.

Out on the Highway, near Tower Bridge, I found myself at the front of the picket line. People were grabbing the metal crowd barriers and holding them together to jam the police horses in and stop them getting to us. Suddenly, off to my left, the mounted police broke through, with the riot squad following after them. In front of me was this old fella, he must

have been about 60. He had a copper in riot gear heading straight for him, so I pulled him behind me. And there was his assailant, in front of me. I could see the eyes, but I couldn't see the face, because his visor had steamed up.

When he charged at me, truncheon raised, I grabbed a metal barrier and hurled it under his feet. He fell over it. There were half a dozen coppers behind

him, heading for me. I decided to run, but there was nothing but piles of barriers all over the road, blocking any escape. Two of them grabbed me. I made a mental note that I'd fight back only if they laid into me. They didn't. I was led off, a policeman on each arm, like a really bad date, through the lines to the print plant itself. At that point, I got hit on the top of my forehead by a chunk

of brick. Blood was pouring down my face. Of course, it had been thrown from our side.

I was bound over for 12 months to keep the peace. The dispute ended in February 1987, but it had a big impact on me. I got quite heavily involved in picketing after that.

Comedian Lee Hurst set up and ran the Backyard Comedy Club from 1998 to 2007.

Memory bank

Jeremy Hardy on sending the poll tax packing in 1990

I have been very proud of this city since I moved here from the Surrey suburbs in 1982. At that time, south London was still reeling from the Brixton riot, an event that is now lumped together with the bombings of July 2005 in an attempt to show that multiculturalism in Britain has failed. In fact, the civil disturbances of the early '80s were an explosion of anger against heavy-handed and unjust policing, and the participants were not exclusively black. And the 7/7 bombers were assimilated, chip-eating, football-loving Yorkshiremen – basically miserable Northern bastards disgruntled by our sophisticated metropolitan ways. Moreover, the poll rax riot was the biggest thing London had seen since the war, and the people who found themselves in confrontation with the police that day were mostly white.

On 31 March 1990, London had won the competition to host the end of the poll tax. Other cities had put in bids, but ours was strongest. The final battle was not in a deprived area, but, rather magnificently, in the West End. And I missed it. I missed it because I was doing topical comedy on a TV show. I marched for a bit, but when we got to Whitehall, I had to peel off to go to rehearsals in Great Windmill Street. By the time we finished the recording, London looked as though Godzilla had passed through, and Thatcher's government was in serious trouble. And I had missed it because I was busy making humorous observations about current events.

Jeremy Hardy is a socialist and comedian.

PROTEST & POLITICS

empire included the *Sun* and the *Times*, was convinced that the situation couldn't endure. Encouraged by what he saw as the readiness of the government and police to 'protect private property from the actions of massed pickets,' Murdoch laid plans to move his printing operation to a new high-tech plant in Wapping.

News International employees went on strike in January 1986 after the unions failed to settle a deal with Murdoch over the move east from Fleet Street. And for the next year, and despite the legal ban on secondary picketing, there were frequent violent clashes between police and the strikers and their supporters.

Murdoch had been right about the police: they were conspicuously assiduous in ensuring the passage of newspaper vans to and from the News International plant. The worst night of violence came near the end of the strike, on 24 January 1987. Pickets managed to overturn a lorry, and hurled three and a half tonnes of rubble at the police, who responded with such ferocity that a subsequent Police Complaints Authority report would accuse some officers of indiscriminate violence.

Trafalgar Square
31 March 1990

The violence at Wapping was effectively the death rattle of large-scale trade union militancy in Britain. Margaret Thatcher's tenure as prime minister would be ended in 1990, not, as her predecessor James Callaghan's had been, by the unions, but by the unpopularity of one of her own policies.

Having seen off the GLC in 1986, the Thatcher administration set about further reform of local government. The Tories' 1987 general election manifesto promised to replace the rates system, in which residential property owners made a payment to their local authority based on the value of their home, with a 'community charge' or 'poll tax', for which all adult residents were liable.

As implementation of the new tax loomed in 1990, a national campaign of non-payment was organised by the Anti-Poll Tax Federation, in which members of the Militant Tendency played a leading role. The Federation called a demonstration in London for 31 March. That day dawned unseasonably warm and sunny, encouraging a crowd of around 100,000 to assemble in the morning in Kennington Park for the march to Trafalgar Square.

In mid afternoon, the procession ground to a halt in Whitehall, close to Downing Street. Fighting soon broke out between police and a phalanx of

Protest against the Iraq war, 2003.

anarchists, who objected to some heavy-handed arrests. The confrontations then spread to Trafalgar Square, where the head of the march had already gathered. Mounted police repeatedly charged demonstrators, who responded with missiles of all kinds. Scaffolding was dismantled and hurled at police, cars set on fire, and shops in the West End ransacked and looted.

The following week, the *New Statesman* argued that the riot showed the redundancy of conventional politics. Not even Tony Benn, it declared, could speak 'to the young people who ran amok last Saturday'.

Hyde Park
15 February 2003

Tony Blair's poll tax moment – the point at which he was revealed as a political mortal – was his decision to follow the US into Iraq in 2003. It was his display of 'conviction' and moral certainty, rather than tuition fees or public sector reform, that fatally drained Blair's political capital and began the slow, protracted agony of his leaving.

Popular opposition to the Iraq war coalesced around the Stop the War Coalition, which organised the mass demonstration in central London on 15 February 2003 that brought an unprecedented number of people (estimated to be somewhere in the region of two million) on to the streets, and ended with a rally in Hyde Park.

Like the VSC and ANL before it, Stop the War had the appearance of a mass movement, but was, in fact, tightly controlled by a cabal of full-time officials of the SWP. The anti-war movement turned out to be the testing ground for the Trotskyist party's new political strategy, which dictated a tactical alliance with the Muslim Association of Britain, co-sponsors of the 15 February demonstration and an organisation with close links to the radical Islamist Muslim Brotherhood.

The architect of that strategy was the SWP's chief ideologue Chris Harman. In 1969, Harman had enraged many on the Left, especially those in the VSC, when, at a memorial meeting in Conway Hall for the late Ho Chi Minh, he denounced the murder of Vietnamese Trotskyists in 1945. Thirty-five years later, he and his comrades showed themselves much less fastidious when it came to explaining the actions of the Iraqi 'resistance'.

There's a description of the march in Ian McEwan's novel *Saturday*, the action of which takes place on 15 February. The protagonist Henry Perowne watches the marchers gather in Gower Street. Their placards and slogans catch his eye. Some belong to the Islamist group that helped organise the march, an outfit, Perowne remembers, which believes that apostasy from Islam is an 'offence punishable by death.'

TIMELINE

1968
Some 30,000 gather in Trafalgar Square to protest against British support for the US in the Vietnam War. Rioting and arrests follow outside the American Embassy in Grosvenor Square.

1972
The first UK Gay Pride march takes place in London, with about 2,000 participating. In 2006, Europride in the city draws 600,000.

1978
The 'Winter of Discontent' follows national strikes by trade unions campaigning for pay rises.

1979
Anti-Nazi League member Blair Peach dies, allegedly after being beaten by the police during violent protests against a National Front meeting in Southall.

1980
Linton Kwesi Johnson publishes his book of poems, *Inglan is a Bitch*.

1981
Some 5,000 people are involved in the first of the Brixton riots. Further riots occur in 1985 and 1995.

1984
The miners' strike begins after the announcement that 20 uneconomic pits are to close down, putting 20,000 miners out of work.

Free Nelson Mandela by the Special AKA reaches No.9 in the UK charts. The 24-hour anti-apartheid vigil outside South Africa House continues through the '80s.

1985
The death of Cynthia Jarrett triggers the Broadwater Farm riots in which PC Keith Blakelock is killed.

1986
Police use riot shields during the industrial dispute outside the News International printing plant in Wapping. More than 1,200 are arrested.

1988
Salman Rushdie's novel *The Satanic Verses* is published. The book is burned in Bolton and Bradford at the instigation of the Islamic Cultural Centre at Regent's Park mosque.

1990
Violent clashes with police at the poll tax riots in Trafalgar Square leave more than 100 injured.

1992
A bomb planted by the IRA at the Baltic Exchange in the City kills three people.

1993
Environmental protesters are evicted from a 250-year-old chestnut tree in Wanstead.

1999
Anti-capitalist riots in the City of London leave 42 injured.

2000
Running as an independent, Ken Livingstone is elected the first Mayor of London, heading up the new Greater London Assembly.

2001
Brian Haw begins his anti-war vigil in Parliament Square. Police confiscate his banners in 2006, but his protest continues.

2003
Around one million people march through London to demonstrate against the 'war on terror' in Iraq.

2005
George Galloway is elected MP for Bow & Bethnal Green, drawing on Muslim support for his stand against the war in Iraq.

2007
Brian Haw's protest is reconstructed by artist Mark Wallinger for his work *State Britain*, which goes on to win the Turner Prize.

2008
Pro-Tibet protesters gather in London to disrupt the parade of the Olympic torch through the capital.

Mark Thomas and McDemos

PROTEST & POLITICS

The first and last time I demonstrated about anything was just before the invasion of Iraq in February 2003. I took to the streets with my mate Steve and about a million other people. It felt great. We were standing up and being counted – obviously the police only counted about a third of us, but that wasn't the point.

As we all know, just days after that, Tony Blair had a rethink about this unjustified and unwinnable conflict, decided to tell George Bush to shove it, and we all lived happily ever after in a safer and more tolerant world. After such a successful inaugural demonstration, I more or less retired from public disobedience until I caught up with comedian and activist Mark Thomas. For the past 18 months he's been campaigning against the Serious Organised Crime & Police Act 2005, which, among other things, restricts our right to protest anywhere near Parliament without asking for written permission from the police. His main tool in this struggle has been a huge amount of approved demonstrations.

'Free speech is the cornerstone to every right we have,' says Thomas. 'The demos are a legal way of using this law's stupidity against itself. The demos can be whatever people want: fun, silly, serious, inane, clever. That's the point of free speech. We should do one together.'

I warn him that after my previous triumph I'm slightly afraid of my almost preternatural ability to influence Westminster. He takes this to mean that I'm actually too lazy to bother filling in the forms and printing up a placard. 'It's OK, that's why we set up our protesting company, McDemos. It's the easy way to demonstrate. You book your demo with our trained team of expert and experienced demonstrating staff, and we do all the work. So you can sit back in the hot tub with your choice of cocktail, while we create world peace on your behalf.'

But what would I demonstrate about? 'It could be about anything you want.' Thomas's enthusiasm is infectious. Could I protest against you?

'That would be brilliant. And I'll do a counter demo against you.' Deal. McDemos is remarkably easy.

I visit mcdemos.com, send off some personal details, a nominal fee and Bob's your uncle. So at 8.30am on a freezing, wintry morning four

days later, I find myself trudging down Horse Guards Parade to meet a very smiley Thomas and a police escort.

'All right, Tim, have you got your two forms of ID?' PC Paul McInally asks. I nod, suddenly a little nervous. 'Let's see your poster, then.' He reads the sign I'm somewhat sheepishly holding and smiles, gently shaking his head. 'Come on then.'

McDemos is nothing if not thorough. I'm given a choice of two slogans. One reads 'I don't want to write about Mark Thomas' and the other, which I end up choosing, says 'Make God smile – kill a comedian'. It's funny, if a little harsh. I only really chose it to impress Thomas. His simply states 'Cull critics not badgers'.

'The demonstrations can be whatever people want: fun, silly, serious, inane, clever. That's the point of free speech.'

As we make our way through the security gates I become a little anxious. Why exactly are we doing this again? 'To ridicule and challenge this law. If the police decide that the law is more of a burden than a boon, then they will work with us to change it.'

What would be the ideal outcome? 'To get rid of the Act and strengthen our right to protest and free speech. Oh, and bring about the downfall of international capitalism.' A serious-looking policeman with a gun walks past and reads my sign. 'That shouldn't say comedians, it should say politicians.'

We take up our positions about ten yards from the Prime Minister's front door. What do these police officers make of Thomas? 'I have had quite a bit of support from some of them. I really like PC Paul McInally and PC Gary West; in fact, I get on well with all the folk at Charing Cross Special Events.'

After we complete our brief vigil, we prepare to go our separate ways. Obviously, now I've been involved it'll be all be over by Christmas, and Thomas can move on to something new. In the past, he has led campaigns against Coca-Cola, the arms trade, hydroelectric dams and many other public evils. How does he choose what's next?

'I have a small Thai boy who dresses me, and every year I let him pick what campaign I am going to work on. It saves me having to worry about it, and, bless him, it makes him feel involved in the struggle for global liberation.'

Of course, always the gentleman.

Comedian Mark Thomas (on the right) and *Time Out*'s Tim Arthur make a stand for free speech.

Interview by Tim Arthur.

Brian Haw, peace campaigner

A fixture of Parliament Square, Brian Haw's round-the-clock peace camp was threatened with eviction from Parliament Square under the 2005 Serious Organised Crime & Police Act. This was his response:

'I came here on 2 June 2001 and I'm still here today. I've got a wife and seven children who are more precious to me than life itself. I want to go back to my own kids and look them in the face again, knowing that I've done all I can to try and save the children of Iraq. I'm quite tired, but not half as tired as the people of Iraq.

'I came here to say stop the genocide. I've had five court cases and five vindications. I've been put in hospital three times; I've had three broken noses; I've been threatened; I've been fitted up and completely exonerated twice. They passed the Serious Organised Crime Act to get the mafia, but Mr Jack-in-the-Box Blunkett came after me with it. I'm their first target. But I've been here for four years and I came because my neighbour's kid is as precious as mine.'

Interview by Peter Watts, 29.6.2005. Haw's vigil continues, but most of his banners and placards have been confiscated by the police.

PROTEST & POLITICS

A is for anarchy

This is a selection from *Time Out*'s second 'Red Pages' agitprop guide, which listed more than 800 radical organisations based in the capital.

PROTEST & POLITICS

Anarchy Collective
We are revolutionary, non-pacifist anarchists, who, through the medium of *Anarchy* magazine, aim to provoke anarchist thought, discussion and action. Collectively we are not aligned to any anarchist groupings.

Association of Communist Workers
Fighting revisionism, Trotskyism, Social Democracy and all opportunism in the working-class movement, to build the vanguard party of the Proletariat.

Belt & Braces Roadshow Company
Providing articulate and entertaining theatre for, and about, issues fundamental to working-class people in their daily struggle against capitalist society.

Black Liberation Front
Black community self-help organisation advocating the need for black unity and support for the struggles in Africa, Asia and the Caribbean.

Camden Men Against Sexism
Group of men, Marxist-oriented, discussing sexism in our society. What is a non-sexist society and how do we achieve it?

Catonsville Roadrunner Collective
Radical Christian group. Slogan: Not power, but the revolutionary dynamic of transforming love.

Directory of Social Change
Agency disseminating, through publications and seminars, ideas for social change.

Earth Exchange Centre
Craft information and marketing; natural foods and kitchen crafts shop; vegetarian soup and salad bar; mutual help exchange.

East End Abbreviated Soapbox
Community theatre providing educational, political, music hall and street theatre in Newham.

Finchley Women's Centre
A place where women can come to find out who they are, where they are and what they want.

Friends of China
Promotes true friendship between British and Chinese people. Disseminates Mao Tse-tung Thought and supports all revolutionary struggles.

Gay Liberation Front
Gay people are oppressed because we undermine the sexist foundation of the family by living outside the gender role system. GLF works to strengthen Gay Pride, which will help topple patriarchy.

History Workshop
Journal of peoples/socialist history aiming to reach active socialists, trade unionists, libertarians, community-based cultural workers and radical historians.

Humpty Dumpty
Magazine trying to criticise the various areas (eg prisons, industry, sexism, mental disorder) where psychologists operate, and to suggest alternative, more socialist ways of looking at these issues.

International Communist League
Trotskyist organisation formed December 1975 by fusion of Workers' Fight and Workers' Power. No Fourth International exists in the tradition of Trotsky. Our task is ideological regeneration and organisational reconstruction.

International Sparticist Tendency
International Trotskyist tendency, we aim to build the world party of proletarian revolution. For the rebirth of the Fourth International.

Justice for George Davis Campaign
Campaigning for George Davis. Support and solidarity for Peter Chappell and others in working-class communities who protest against police. OK.

Kartoon Klowns
Socialist theatre group that performs agitprop plays mainly for Labour Movement audiences, both at the workplace and in local communities.

Knuckle
Community paper. Spreads views of linked struggles of workplace and home. Relates the fights of wageless to those of waged workers. Reflects oppression and strength of women.

Librarians for Social Change
Radical librarians aiming to widen the context of information work and to evolve a social responsibility in librarianship and related work.

London Gay Medics & Dentals Group
Educating ourselves and professional colleagues about gay people. Working towards eradication of concept of homosexuality as clinical entity.

Mental Patients Union
Mental Patients Unions are unions of patients and ex-patients formed to fight for human rights for society's so-called 'mental patients'.

Monstrous Regiment
Theatre group dissatisfied with the opportunities offered to women working in the theatre, and with a desire to create and perform material specifically geared to a company that will never contain more women than men.

National Abortion Campaign
Opposes restrictions on abortion on demand in law and in practice as woman's right to choose.

Omega Hunger
Not aiming at any definite analysis of, or response to, hunger.

Other Cinema
Alternative film distributors and exhibitors collective, specialising in social and political films with emphasis on British independents, women's films, campaign films and Third World.

Paedophile Information Exchange
National organisation for adults sexually attracted to children. Hoping to change negative social attitudes and give help to those in trouble.

Persons With a Disability Liberation Front
We aim to be for persons with a disability what the Black, Women's and Gay Liberation Movements have been for them.

Radical Alternatives to Prison
Pressure and information group working towards the abolition of prison and an equal and unoppressive society.

Radical Philosophy Group
Criticise the current shape of philosophy, ecnourages philosophical discussions on the left and develops socialist theory in general.

See Red Women's Workshop
Seven women opposing images of the model woman used by capitalist ideology to keep women subservient, by putting forward a positive image of women through posters, illustrations etc.

Teaching London Kids
Exploring practice and dilemmas of socialist teachers in state schools, impact of 'progressive' teaching methods on education of working-class children and the power structure of society as it affects organisation of schools.

That Tea Room
Non-profit making community café providing vegetarian wholefood.

Undercurrents
Basically anarchist-libertarian magazine publishing radical features, news and reviews on science and alternative technology.

Urban Struggle
Marxist analysis of urban developments and conflicts, aiming at unified class analysis and actions on physical/social environment.

Voice Newspapers
Independent socialist newspapers supporting the struggle for socialism wherever it takes place. Socialism can only result from the self-activity of the workers and not from the activity of any elite.

Women's Liberation Front
To end sexual discrimination, social oppression and exploitation and domestic slavery; and for achieving women's liberation. WLF organises and unites women for an all-round social revolution.

Young Communist League
To win young people for the ideas of socialism and communism. To unite youth in the fight for socialism. To fight for better and more democratic conditions at school and work.

Nuclear paranoia

The fear of nuclear war that hung like cold fog over the cultural landscape of the 1980s seems almost quaint in a post-9/11 world. Yet it was real, and nourished by a widespread belief in the inevitability and imminence of annihilation.

A 1981 Gallup poll showed that 39 per cent of British adults expected a nuclear war to occur in their lifetime. *Time Out*'s follow-up cover story spoke of Londoners suffering 'graphic imaginings of a post-holocaust world, while simultaneously knowing it is unimaginable'. Rose Shapiro interviewed women who were experiencing waking nightmares in which they were forced to kill their own panicking children; families who were planning to move to New Zealand, where they believed they would be safe; and one Roger Williams, who ran a company called FACS (Fallout and Chemical Shelters) Ltd from his Dulwich home. Williams built his shelters above ground so that they would have a peacetime utility. They cost £15,000 a pop. He expected to have installed 500 of them by the end of 1984.

What stoked this doomsday mentality? Fear of the Soviet Union and, on the domestic front, a new political order that favoured brinkmanship and escalation. In 1979, Margaret Thatcher allowed American Cruise and Pershing missiles to be deployed in the UK, at the same time as Moscow was deploying its new SS-20 missiles in Eastern Europe. The following year, she agreed to buy the US-manufactured Trident missile as part of a £5bn programme to replace the Royal Navy's Polaris submarine force. From this point on, her government was locked in a permanent PR battle with peace groups, especially CND, Cruise Watch and the Greenham Common protesters. (CND was considered a real threat: in March 1983, Defence Secretary Michael Heseltine set up a special unit, DS19, to counter its 'propaganda' on unilateral disarmament.)

Thatcher also had big ideas about UK civil defence, a subject to which no one had paid much attention since plans for the country to be governed from below ground by a 300,000-strong Civil Defence Corps were scrapped in the late 1960s.

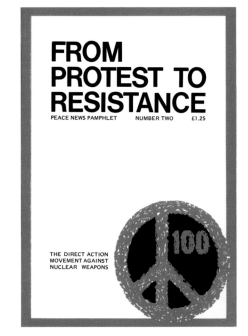

FROM PROTEST TO RESISTANCE
PEACE NEWS PAMPHLET   NUMBER TWO   £1.25

THE DIRECT ACTION MOVEMENT AGAINST NUCLEAR WEAPONS

What a Nuclear Attack Really Means

LONDON AFTER THE BOMB

The first of these was the publication in May 1980 of the *Protect and Survive* booklet, which suggested, wonderfully, that a nuclear attack could be survived by bricking up windows and building a fallout room in your house: 'Because of the threat of radiation, you and your family may need to live in this room for 14 days after an attack, almost without leaving it at all,' it advised. The second, that September, was Square Leg – an exercise that aimed to assess the effects of what was felt to be a realistic attack scenario: 131 nuclear weapons falling on Britain with a total yield of 205 megatons.

London had five nuclear bunkers, or Group Controls, from which the city would be ruled in the aftermath of an attack: one at the barracks in Mill Hill, others in Wanstead, Gipsy Hill, Southall and Cheam, plus the London Flood Control Centre in Southampton Row, Holborn, one of London's most mythologised subterranean spaces – even if all it amounted to was, in *Time Out*'s words, 'a couple of Portakabins in a tram tunnel'.

As Square Leg's grim conclusions filtered into the public domain, the gulf between the reality of a nuclear attack and the *Protect and Survive* fantasy became glaringly apparent. The document, and its accompanying films narrated by the actor Patrick Allen, came in for ferocious mockery (see *The Young Ones* episode 'Bomb') and had hardened into cliché by the time Frankie Goes to Hollywood used an Allen soundalike on the 12-inch of 'Two Tribes' in 1984, the year the BBC broadcast Barry Hines' hard-hitting drama about a nuclear attack on Sheffield, *Threads*.

London After the Bomb, a book co-authored by five scientists, suggested the Home Office casualty estimate was hopelessly optimistic. It used Square Leg projections to determine the effects on the Greater London Council area of a one megaton bomb exploded at 6,000 feet over Trafalgar Square – a so-called 'air burst', much more damaging than a 'ground burst' where buildings and hills limited radiation emission. The authors estimated that the initial blast alone would kill 16 per cent of London's population and injure 36 per cent, and leave the city an unrecognisable, contaminated wasteland: 'Richmond, Kew and Chiswick Bridges are down and the elevated section of the M4 near Brentford is blown away. Kew Gardens is now a blackened, charred landscape.'

'On hearing the all-clear, you may resume normal activities,' stated the official advice. But the government knew very well this was nonsense.
John O'Connell

Memory bank

Omid Djalili on the storming of the Iranian Embassy in 1980

April 1980. Living in Kensington near the Albert Hall, and being Iranian, I was very aware of the Iranian Embassy siege going only 200 yards up the road. I was 13. In a break during the world snooker final on TV, I decided to go for a kickabout with friends in Hyde Park, near the Albert Memorial. A group of foreigners passing by joined in. We had a relatively intense seven-a-side.

It came to halt when a massive explosion drew us up to the crossroads by Exhibition Road, where a police cordon had been set up. We could hear screams and machine-gun fire as the SAS stormed the embassy. Plumes of smoke billowed from the building. A second explosion made us flinch and run back for a few seconds, but then we returned, mesmerised. Then we heard shouts of 'Him!' and 'There!', followed by two shots. The police, who had been relaxed up to then, told us all to disperse. I went home and watched the rest of the snooker. Alex Higgins won. The silence and the screaming and the two shots played in my mind for weeks after.

Even with a population of ten million, London really is a small world. It was a good 22 years later that I found out my kid's karate teacher, Robin Horsefall, was an ex-SAS man and he'd been involved that day. When I told him about my experience, he said three things. 1) You'd never get that close to a terrorist event as a spectator these days. 2) The shouting was commotion coming from inside the building as a terrorist was identified by the hostages trying to escape in the smoke. 3) It was Robin himself who took him out with two shots to the head.

Omid Djalili is an actor and comedian.

Gentlemen terrorists?

IRA bomb attacks were part of urban life in the 1970s and '80s. Is today's terrorist threat any different?

By Patrick West

After the attacks on the World Trade Center in New York in 2001, many Londoners feared, correctly as it turned out, that it would only be a matter of time before they were next. Radical Islamists often refer to the UK as 'Little Satan' to the USA's 'Great Satan', so it was perhaps inevitable that our capital, one of the world's economic powerhouses, would become a target. The only question was how Londoners would respond to this inevitability.

In a way, we should not have been frightened. We knew how to deal with such a threat. Bombs in London were not a new phenomenon, after all. The IRA had bombed the capital for three decades during the Troubles. However, with today's scares about Islamist attacks and the very visible policemen in body armour on the Underground, not to mention the perpetual requests to 'report any suspect packages' on public transport, it is

easy to forget the extent to which the threat of IRA bombs concentrated Londoners' minds during the 1970s and '80s.

The IRA's decision to take its 'war' to the British mainland, and to London in particular, was taken on the assumption that the British government and people cared little, and understood even less, about Northern Ireland. Ulster was regarded by Londoners as a colony, rather than as an integral part of the United Kingdom, and it was treated as such by Westminster.

There was an element of irony about the Provisional IRA's plan to bomb London, which it first did in March 1972, attacking the Old Bailey and Whitehall. Its chief of staff at the time was Sean MacStiofain. 'The British needed a short, sharp shock,' he later said of the 1972 campaign. MacStiofain was not from the Six Counties, however. Like the 7/7 bombers, he was a

The aftermath of an IRA bomb on a train outside Cannon Street station, 4 March 1976. The carriage was empty, but eight passengers on a passing train were injured in the blast.

disaffected, home-grown terrorist. His real name was John Stephenson: he was a Londoner from Leytonstone, with a solitary Irish grandparent, who harboured delusions of Irishness.

Although some of the IRA's most appalling atrocities on the mainland took place outside the capital – in Guildford, Birmingham, Aldershot and Brighton – the years that followed did see 'Belfast come to London', as tabloid headline writers were fond of putting it. In July 1974, an explosion in the Tower of London injured 41 and killed one. Eight years later, two bombs were detonated in Hyde Park, killing 11 soldiers and killing and maiming a number of their horses. A year after that, a car bomb exploded outside Harrods, taking six lives. Towards the end of the Troubles, Bishopsgate, the Baltic Exchange, Canary Wharf, Downing Street and Hammersmith Bridge were all hit by IRA bombs.

London became a target because the IRA knew that Britain would listen if it was hit at its financial centre. And this is why IRA attacks on London were generally designed to destroy infrastructure rather than to take lives. The IRA's activities in Belfast, in contrast, were often aimed at people and motivated by sectarianism. Their aim on the mainland was deliberately, and literally, to 'terrorise' Londoners. Bomb threats were part of the background noise while I was growing up in the capital in the 1970s and '80s: unattended packages became an automatic source of suspicion, litter bins were removed from the streets and the Underground, and the City of London became a virtual citadel.

This is not to say that the IRA were 'honourable' terrorists. They may have given warnings, but often such warnings were vague, or too late – sometimes deliberately so. Yet, in retrospect, it is understandable that today's terror threat is regarded as far more pernicious than that of the IRA; and, also, why there's a temptation to regard the IRA as 'gentlemen terrorists'.

'At least the IRA gave warnings', I heard a man say to anti-war demonstrators when I witnessed a march in Dublin in 2003. It is a phrase I have heard on many occasions since. As the *Times* defence correspondent, Michael Evans, wrote in December 2002: 'This country is already blessed with almost unrivalled expertise, because of decades of having to deal with Provisional IRA terrorist acts. But the IRA gave warnings, it was not an organisation committed to creating mass casualties, and its so-called active service units always devised an escape route. Suicide was not for them.'

Evans seemed to be implying that, presented with a choice, we'd prefer to have the IRA back, rather than have to deal with the jihadists. Admittedly, the Provisionals had their own cult of martyrdom, as witnessed in the eulogies that followed the deaths of Bobby Sands and the other hunger strikers in 1981. But that's nothing compared to the terrifying cult of death that grips

Islamist terrorists today, a pathology that glories in suicide and the negation of life itself.

Whether they were of Unionist or Republican persuasion, Londoners at least understood that the IRA had a legitimate political objective: a united Ireland. But what makes Islamist terrorism so unsettling is that its goals are either unfathomable or utterly unrealistic. We could deal with the IRA because we knew what they wanted. But you can't negotiate with people who call for the destruction of Israel or, indeed, of western civilisation itself.

Anyone who has heard an IRA bomb go off – as I have: in Manchester in 1996 and in Hammersmith in 2000 – may well find nostalgia for 'gentlemen terrorists' a little galling. But I can't say I'd blame Londoners if they felt that way.

Patrick West is an author and television critic.

LONDON'S YEAR OF BOMBS

1973

8 March Four car bombs in London, including one at the Old Bailey.
11 April Letter bombs at the Ministry of Defence, Royal British Legion, Union Jack Club, Old Bailey, Stock Exchange and Downing Street. Four explode.
18 August 14 incendiary bombs in West End stores.
20 August Carrier-bag bomb in a shopping arcade in Hampstead.
24 August Bomb at Baker Street tube station.
31 August Bomb at Marble Arch.
8 September Bomb at Victoria railway station; five hurt.
10 September Bomb at King's Cross and Euston stations; 13 hurt.
12 September Bomb at Comm and O Association, Lower Sloane Street; five hurt. Bomb in Oxford Street offices of Prudential Assurance Company.
20 September Bomb at Duke of York Barracks, King's Road; five hurt.

28 September Bomb at West London Air Terminal; eight injured.
1 October Bomb at Westminster offices of security firm Allen International.
5 October Bomb at Army Careers Office, Surbiton.
23 October Three fire bombs in shops in Wembley.
27 October Bomb near Moorgate tube station.
17 December Two letter bombs at London post offices; six hurt.
18 December Car bomb outside Home Office building, Westminster; 54 hurt. Car bomb outside Pentonville Prison; five hurt.
19 December Parcel bomb at Oxford Street post office.
20 December Carrier-bag bomb at French Embassy.
21 December Two bombs at, and near, the Hilton Hotel.
22 December Three bombs in the West End (one in Leicester Square, two near Charing Cross). Three bombs in London

cinemas (Swiss Centre, Cinecenta, Jacey). Letter bomb at Shooters Hill police station; one policeman injured.
23 December Bomb at a pub near Centre Point. Bomb at Kensington police station. Bomb at Wimpey offices in Hammersmith.
24 December Two bombs at Swiss Cottage.
26 December Bomb at a pub in Victoria. Bomb at Sloane Square tube station.

1974

5 January Bomb at Madame Tussaud's.
6 January Bomb at Chelsea home of Major General Ward.
10 January Two fire bombs at Heal's.
24 January Bomb at Chelsea home of Tory MP Oscar Murton.
23 October Three fire bombs in Wembley shops.
1 February Home Secretary Reginald Maudling receives a letter bomb.
4 February Letter bomb at *Daily Express* offices; security guard injured.

PROTEST & POLITICS

The Angry Brigade

The beginning, in May 1970, was inauspicious. A small package found on the site of a new police station in Paddington turned out to be an unexploded bomb. It was made of two cartridges of French explosive unobtainable in Britain, a continental detonator and – the British connection – a gas lighter head for the ignition system. But the discovery didn't warrant a line in the press. It was the Angry Brigade's first action.

Three months later, their technique had improved. The offices of the Spanish airline Iberia were lightly damaged by a half-pound device. Then, within ten days, two substantial explosions – hushed up in the interests of the state – testified to the growing expertise of the bombers, and brought home to the authorities that an armed conspiracy had begun.

Even as the Brigade was planning its next action, the police were beginning to make forensic connections between the unexploded Paddington bomb and an earlier one found aboard an Iberia plane at Heathrow. The two devices were identical. The Heathrow bomb, police believed, had been planted by the First of May Group, a Spanish anarchist outfit responsible for a series of attacks on the Franco regime's overseas arms.

Attacks on the homes of 'establishment targets' convinced the police that the First of May Group was providing the expertise for the Angry Brigade, fighting back, as it said, against the the encroachments of the 'new corporate state'. And one name leaped out of Special Branch files, bridging the two guerrilla groups: Stuart Christie, a young Scottish anarchist previously jailed in Spain for attempting to blow up Franco, and with known links to the First of May Group.

On 19 November 1970, four ounces of TNT exploded under an empty BBC transmission van at the Miss World contest. And early on 4 December, a car slewed through Belgrave Square and machine gun fire hit the Spanish Embassy. A communiqué, delivered to the offices of *International Times*, claimed responsibility for the Angry Brigade, the first in a series of idiosyncratic messages that would accompany subsequent attacks.

The Special Branch, used to cohesive groups with clear leadership and lines of communication, were sure that Christie was organising the campaign. (Later, it would emerge that a diverse, chaotic group – some of which have never been caught – carried out the actions.) Events were now moving so quickly that within a month of the first Angry Brigade communiqué, Britain was to get its first anti-urban guerrilla force, the Bomb Squad.

In May 1971, the Brigade tried to blow up the police computer at Tintagel House on the Embankment. 'Bureaucracy and technology [are] used against the people,' read the message. 'Police computers cannot tell the truth. They just record our crimes. The AB is the man or woman sitting next to you. They have guns in their pockets and anger in their minds.'

In the meantime, Chief Superintendent Habershon of the Bomb Squad, together with Scotland Yard's political expert Roy Cremer, had stumbled upon a crucial link to the Angry Brigade. Jake Prescott, who had a record as a petty criminal and had become radicalised in prison, was picked up, allegedly drunk. Stolen cheque books and an address book were found in his possession. It was to be a petty fraud scheme that would lead to the arrest of a substantial part of the Angry Brigade.

A police informer sharing a cell with Prescott claimed that he had heard him speak of the bombing of the Barnet home of Robert Carr, the Home Secretary. Habershon decided to release Prescott on bail and have him followed. Prescott, and the man to whom he went, Ian Purdie, were arrested and charged with the Barnet bombing.

In July, four friends of Prescott's and Purdie's, 'wanted for questioning' – Anna Mendelson, John Barker, Hilary Creek and Jim Greenfield – moved into a flat in Amhurst Road, Stoke Newington. Habershon and Special Branch were raiding the homes of every dissident and radical they could cull from the files, but the four AB members at Amhurst Road continued to elude them.

But then luck and another informer turned up. A friend of Mendelson's parents discovered her whereabouts and called the police. On 20 August, a day after Barker and Creek returned from Paris with a consignment of gelignite, the police raided the flat and found a treasure trove of weaponry, including 33 sticks of gelignite and the 1938 submachine gun used on the Spanish Embassy.

The next day, as police were examining the flat, Stuart Christie walked through the door and was immediately arrested. At the subsequent trial, Christie was the only one of the five to walk free (three other accused were also found not guilty). In all, the Angry Brigade had been responsible for 19 bombings, a further six devices that failed to go off, and four more explosions after the arrests of the eight alleged AB members. No member of the public had been injured.

Original feature by Ron McKay.

Angry Brigade
demonstration
outside the Old
Bailey in 1972.

Red Ken

Through five years at the helm of the GLC, eight years as Mayor of London, and a stint as MP for Brent East, Ken Livingstone has been one of the capital's most controversial, outspoken, influential and entertaining politicians.

By Michael Hodges

A month before the 2008 London Mayoral elections, *Time Out* ran a hustings for the four major candidates at the University of London (though the Conservative, Boris Johnson, declined the invitation). Ken Livingstone arrived 20 minutes late and immediately downed a glass of wine. He looked tired, sweaty and slightly dishevelled, but seemed extremely confident. When he went on stage, he held an audience of 300 in the palm of his hand for an hour, and his words, at times, were greeted with wild applause.

A month later he was defeated by Johnson and out of power in London.

Ken had been there before, when he was effectively ousted from the leadership of the GLC by Margaret Thatcher in 1986. Livingstone's GLC regime was the epitome of attention-grabbing, radical local politics: it stood for republicanism, full employment and cheap fares, and against racism, police brutality and the Conservative Party. Surely *Time Out*, a radical organ at the time, would have been solidly behind Livingstone? Well, not quite. A look back at the Red Ken years suggests the magazine wasn't that impressed at all.

The rise to power

At the 1979 general election, Livingstone stands for Labour in the then marginal seat of Hampstead. When news comes through of his defeat, *Time Out* reports that Livingstone 'turned to colleagues at Labour Party HQ and said, "Don't worry, I'm not het up about losing. Now we [meaning the left] must win control of the GLC."'

Livingstone's plan is simple: to stand in the 1981 GLC elections and ensure that enough of his left-wing allies also stand, so that, after a Labour victory, they can remove the Labour leader on the GLC, right-winger Andrew McIntosh, and hand control of the capital to Livingstone. Livingstone approaches left-wingers like Val Wise and encourages them to stand as candidates. Usually, according to *Time Out*, 'over a drink.'

This didn't blur Livingstone's ability to think clearly, however: 'By election day he had worked out a detailed chart, inked in coloured pens, predicting both the seats to be won by Labour and those returned who would vote for him against McIntosh. He was right in every seat but one, and there he erred on the side of caution.'

'Livingstone may be untouchable in the GLC, but he is about to be undone by his nemesis, Margaret Thatcher.'

On the morning of the GLC election, the *Daily Express* hectors its readers: 'Remember this Red Threat when you go to vote today'. Labour duly wins the election, and in May 1981, McIntosh is deposed by 30 votes to 20. He claims he has been 'the victim of a plot organised by an elite, secretive caucus'. He has, though Livingstone's campaign is, superficially at least, open to public scrutiny. In a classic application of the 'give them enough rope' principle, Livingstone offers a platform to McIntosh in the left-wing newspaper, *London Labour Briefing*. *Time Out* says of Livingstone's campaign that, 'in it, the style, indeed the genius, of Livingstone as a political operator was plainly displayed.'

The reins of power

After dispatching McIntosh, Livingstone moves to consolidate his control. Soon *Time Out* notes 'the extraordinary psychological domination that Livingstone has now built up at County Hall. His name is on everyone's lips, all the time: he has become the first point of reference in the discussion of any subject remotely connected with London politics. Even the walls of Horace Cutler's office are decorated with cartoon originals of him.'

Livingstone launches himself as a national figure and, in a direct challenge to Margaret Thatcher's Conservative government, London's rising unemployment figures are displayed on the walls of County Hall, clearly visible from the terrace of the House of Commons on the riverbank opposite.

When the Law Lords declare Livingstone's 'Fares fair' cheap public transport policy – funded from the rates – illegal in December 1981, Livingstone and 24 left-wing Labour councillors vote to defy them. Livingstone knows he is in no danger of winning, and faces possible surcharge, contempt of court and dismissal from office, as the Tories, Alliance and the right wing of the Labour party will vote against him. *Time Out* calls the threat 'a

feint, rooted in purely political objectives: to appear the bold left-wing martyr risking everything… Meetings, rows, lobbies and debates, all striving to create the impression that Livingstone really was about to lead the GLC in a revolutionary struggle against the Law Lords. But from start to finish the process was a sham.' For on the day after the judgement, London Transport had quietly begun to make plans to double fares. 'The simple, brutal truth of the affair was almost totally obscured: that the Law Lords had made cheap fares illegal…'

In December 1982, Livingstone invites Sinn Féin leaders (and alleged IRA commanders) Gerry Adams and Danny Morrison to London. When they are refused entry, Livingstone travels to Ulster. Following widespread public outrage, a vote of censure is passed against Livingstone on the GLC, with the support of right-wing Labour councillors. The *Sun* calls him 'the most odious man in Britain'. *Time Out* sees the Ulster trip as a carefully planned stunt designed to protect him from a leadership challenge.

As the Livingstone regime becomes ever more radical, the *Daily Telegraph* calls him 'a left-wing loony', and the *London Evening Standard* acknowledges, as it will have cause to do again in the future, that 'we don't much like Mr Livingstone.' But, as *Time Out* argues, 'the extremist coverage… has done him nothing but good, exaggerating his importance and granting him a position on the left that he would not otherwise have achieved.' Nonetheless, Livingstone is so disarming in person that right-wing newspapers are obliged to instruct their journalists not to become friendly with him.

In January 1983, *Time Out* journalist David Rose has dinner with Livingstone and Labour Party apparatchiks near County Hall. Livingstone drinks several bottles of wine. 'By the end of the evening, he will be mildly but distinctly tipsy.'

Eviction from County Hall

In 1983, Livingstone is apparently at the height of his power. *Time Out* observes that 'Ken Livingstone is on a star trip. As he lollops along the corridors with his distinctive, apelike stride, he is permanently surrounded by an entourage of aides, hacks and sycophants.' Livingstone may be untouchable in the GLC, but he is about to be undone by his nemesis: Margaret Thatcher.

The Conservatives win the 1983 general election, pledging to abolish the GLC. Livingstone mounts a PR campaign and a series of free concerts in response. When these fail to create a popular outcry, Livingstone and three other left-wingers resign their seats to fight by-elections on the anti-abolition ticket. Turnout actually drops and, in 1986, the GLC is finally laid to rest.

Will Livingstone be back? *Time Out* seems to think so. 'For all his amiability, Ken the politician never sleeps. That is why he is so good.'

There's a riot going on

Race relations deteriorated dramatically in the early 1980s, with major riots in Brixton and Tottenham. While black people tried to organise politically, a renascent Far Right stoked white fears of a racial apocalypse.

Mayall and Railton Roads last Saturday were choked with smoke, as youths hurled missiles at the police. It wasn't the place for dialogue. During those hours and around those streets, reporters were under constant pressure from police and rioters. The youth of Mayall Road wasted little time explaining why they were there. 'We hate the police, they arrest us for nothing.' The police had beaten their friends. The police insulted them on the streets. If the police caught anyone now, they would beat them half to death.

Crouching against a wall, I edged towards Railton Road. I was within five yards of the police before I could make out through the smoke the uniformed figures huddled behind perspex shields. They looked at me, but no one seemed willing to move.

The light from a blazing plumber's shop made the police easy targets for the barrage of half bricks and broken paving stones coming from both ends of Railton Road. At the junction with Effra Parade, Chaucer Road and Leeson Road, the rioters pressed a relentless attack, making a mockery of an inspector's exhortation to 'Hold the line.'

The police could hardly spare men to deal with the wounded. The limp and bloody forms of officers, some of them half-conscious from head

This week, the New Cross Fire inquest was due to conclude. Three weeks ago, there was Brixton. At the beginning of March, thousands of black people demonstrated in central London against that fire, and against public indifference to it.

Black politics is on the mainstream political agenda, triggered by those events, and by moves like the Conservative government's Nationality Bill. But the sea change in black politics took place earlier, in 1980, with the Bristol disturbances, large-scale campaigns against immigration raids, the 'sus' laws, and the use against the black community of the Special Patrol Group. In the wake of those events came, in June, the Black People's Convention in London, which led to the formation of the Afro-Asian Alliance.

Though it received a great deal of media coverage at the time, little has been heard of the Alliance since. But the reality was that black politics had been flourishing for a long time. This dates back to the 1960s, before and during the establishment of the Community Relations Commission, the forerunner of the Commission for Racial Equality.

By the early 1970s, the black movement in this country had split into two main tendencies. One insisted on the importance of an autonomous black working-class organisation. The other moved towards pan-African ideas derived from Marcus Garvey, the 'Back to Africa' advocate of the early years of the century.

What is frequently described as the fragmentation of black politics is partly a working out of the tension between these two tendencies. But, after a decade, it is now clear that a broad pattern of consolidation has taken place as a result of the activities of both groups.

On the pan-African side, there was the setting up of Vince Hines' black self-help hostel and, in Islington, Brother Herman's Harambee. These were signals for a switch of emphasis by the 'nationalists', who promptly set up a number of similar projects and began fighting the welfare system for the resources that would give them control of property and services.

By 1980 it had become apparent that such small-scale efforts were inadequate, and mass campaigns were emerging. Yet the projects had given the black organisations a firm base. The recent moves of blacks and Asians into the Labour Party is the culmination of a tradition of struggle between black groups and local political establishments.

Their inevitable concern with issues like housing and unemployment has led to accusations, on the left, of insufficient radicalism. But in a society where racism permeates all institutions, everything that impinges on black people becomes a radical concern.

Brixton residents survey the devastation after a second night of rioting, April 1981.

and face wounds, lay in Chaucer Road and Effra Parade. Then, suddenly, there was another attack, this time with Molotov cocktails. Two bottles soared through the air, to land with a barely audible tinkle of glass, before the whumph! whumph! of exploding petrol and two blinding balls of fire.

As the police line wavered, the charge was upon them, a hail of rocks at point-blank range. Five youths came right on top of the shield line. They were wielding any weapon they could get hold of. One youth, bare chested except for a few rags of a torn T-shirt, ran straight through the flames.

A young policeman born and brought up in Brixton, and visibly upset, told me: 'I never thought it would come to this, but I feel it's only the beginning.' He was one of a minority of officers who, by Sunday afternoon, were actually talking to blacks in Railton Road. But the opinion of the local community was ominously similar: this is not the climax, but the start of a frightening new era in Brixton – and probably elsewhere in London too.

Eyewitness report by Colin McGhee.

Report by Mike Phillips.

PROTEST & POLITICS

Handsworth, Brixton, Toxteth, Peckham and now Tottenham. Any pretence that these are outbreaks of mass crime must begin to strike even Jeffrey Archer as a ludicrous reading of what has been taking place on British streets during the summer and autumn of 1985. The stirrings of a *war* between sections of both black and white youth and the police would seem a more apt interpretation.

'I've just come back from South Africa,' said a journalist working for a French news agency, 'and the similarities are just amazing.' A freelance photographer noted that whereas in Handsworth you could show a press card and get what you wanted from the police, tonight you might as well have shown them a set of piranha teeth. And at the epicentre of the battle – the Broadwater Farm estate – an officer clad in black riot gear looked out from his ranks at the smouldering battleground. 'Brixton was nothing like this. This place is like a fortress. There's just no way in and they know it. They've got us over a barrel.'

Earlier, I'd watched as 100 youths strode down Woodville Gardens. Bricks, milk crates and other missiles were hurled through shop windows. Some bounced off comically. A blazing rubbish bin was shoved towards the door of a tobacconist, but this was removed a couple of minutes later by another clique. A couple of hundred yards away we saw what looked to be a house in flames.

Spectators melted into 'rioters' as all concerned assumed a no-guilt posture.

Then came the black-clad police. A score of them rushed down the hill, voices and batons raised. Round the corner in the High Road were dozens more. Vans patrolled up and down, despositing fresh contingents for a mop-up of the cluttered streets.

They shouted for cliques to 'Move!' or 'RUN!', but then frequently gave chase and clubbed the victims to the ground for obeying. People were cowering in corners trying to interpret what the police wanted of them. Many officers seemed not only out of formation, but out of their minds. 'I told you already to move, you fucking lefty cunts!' a quickly advancing officer shouted at photographer Andrew Moore and myself. In fact, he'd told us no such thing, and protestations that we were 'press' brought more abuse and threats.

Further along the High Road were swarms of bobbies in PC Dixon gear. One told us bitterly that if it was an interesting picture we wanted, we should cross the road where a man, stabbed by a black rioter, was bleeding to death. We crossed and found a white man in his late twenties, blood pouring from a head wound that his friends told us was delivered by a police truncheon. No, they insisted, he hadn't been part of the fracas.

Clashes between police and rioters were often bitter and bloody affairs.

Report by Andrew Tyler.

PROTEST & POLITICS

'Richard Edmonds is the name. I'm calling on behalf of the British National Party. We say: Put the British people first. Why not? It's our country. Or supposed to be. Let's put an end to all the violence, the baby-slashing and coppers getting knifed. Shouldn't be like that. Didn't used to be like that. Briefly, love, I'm selling our party newspaper. Maybe you'd like to have a read?'

A young mother with two toddlers at her skirt glances at the headline 'Thatcher Caves in to Black Violence' and reaches for her purse.

'Young mothers are our best customers,' remarks Edmonds, first-class graduate engineer and leading BNP activist. (The BNP, formerly the New National Front, is a breakaway faction of the National Front, led by self-proclaimed Nazi John Tyndall.) 'Mothers have most to worry about; they know we're right. Look at New York – it's a hell-hole and 100 per cent of the violence there is committed by blacks. Here it's about 95 per cent, but there'd be *no* crime under the BNP.'

We were in the East End, preparing the ground in an area where the BNP hope to field a candidate in the forthcoming local elections. Both the NF and the BNP plan a return to the ballot box in 1986. Not, at this stage, in the hope of winning seats, but of 'raising' the level of debate and, most importantly, spreading the word.

Both parties are eager to stress that their official guidelines urge supporters to vent their anger on

Neo-fascist movements were on the rise in the late '70s and early '80s.

the 'race traitors' in Parliament, rather than the blacks on the streets. The Front is self-conscious about public opinion. Edmonds is honest about his reasons. 'It's a waste of time if one of our blokes goes down for assault. It's of no direct use to our cause if a few whatsits get slashed across the face.'

Although there is no evidence to suggest that violent attacks are carried out on orders from on high, there are nevertheless 18 Nationalists currently charged under section 5A of the Race Relations Act (incitement to racial hatred), including BNP leader Tyndall, who is charged with publishing racist material. NF Youth Organiser Joe Pearce received a 12-month sentence in December.

And the Nationalists are not fussy whose anger they marshall. As to any revolutionary, chaos is a welcome gift, and the BNP and NF were much cheered by last summer's spate of rioting. They have interpreted the situation as lending credence to their assertion that the only alternatives facing Britain are race war or compulsory repatriation.

Encouraged by such a 'good year', Edmonds is increasingly urgent about the need for Nationalists to unite, and has made clear his willingness to respond to any overture from the Front. 'Then we can really make the electorate sit up and listen, and they will understand that our solution is the only solution.'

Report by Miranda Ingram.

Women's liberation

In 1973, my life was totally bound up in women's liberation, socialism and community politics. Ah, what heady days, when everything seemed possible. Charting that year from still existing magazines (*Spare Rib*), from a now defunct journal (*Red Rag*), clues in books about 'the movement' enable me to remember events and the way certain groups and individuals were thinking. But they miss the intimacy of the politics I was wrapped up in back then; they can't convey the way so many of us woke up thinking about women's liberation, and went to sleep at night with it still tumbling around in our heads.

I was 32, married, an ambivalent, no-waged work mother of two boys born in 1968 and 1970. Like many other London women, I'd been in a consciousness-raising group since 1969. I think I saw myself as a grass-roots girl, growing very slowly, gaining confidence, spurred on by the isolation of motherhood, wanting something different, better. Women's liberation created in me and many others a kind of headiness, a belief that through the difficulties and contradictions, and out of pure necessity, we would forge a way of doing, relating, rebelling, which would knit together a politics that spoke the realities of 'daily life' (one of the early '70s buzzwords).

But by 1973, the different 'currents' (Trotskyist buzzword) were certainly present. As a movement, we were five-year-olds – plenty of time to start the process of attacking each other and defining our own interests. There were socialist feminists, radical feminists, separatists, mothers and non-mothers, working-class and middle-class splits.

The 'we' I was part of spoke often enough of women outside the movement, and, to be fair, did try to make links (a big 1973 word). There were marches in support of Marion and Delores Prize, the two IRA women serving a sentence in a men's prison in England, who were on hunger strike, solidarity meetings about Mozambique…

In 1973, I was in one of many Marxist study groups around town, where we read and talked passionately, making more links between feminism and socialism. I read and sent news and opinions to the weekly London women's liberation newsletter, went eagerly to *Red Rag* collective meetings, spent time each week at a local women's centre.

Early that year saw the first women's liberation and socialism conference, and then the second at Conway Hall in the autumn, as well as a big national women's liberation conference in Bristol in the summer. The usual frustrations of conferences existed, but these were also occasions for incredible

Road rage: this graffiti appeared on Farringdon Road in 1979.

highs. Questions of structure, content and style often dominated, but issues and ideas were included – like wages for housework, threats to the Family Allowance, abortion, sexuality and lesbianism.

They were social times for hundreds of women too. During the Bristol conference evening social and dance, a friend of mine argued heatedly that turning down the lights encouraged an aping of heterosexual couples, which oppressed her, and for a while a battle of lights on, lights off was waged in the large hall of women. (Women with men in tow remained in a smaller adjoining room.) It was the heyday for women-only conference bops, where heterosexual women probably outnumbered the growing number of lesbians, and were among the first to throw off their shirts and dance bare-breasted in loose circles of hippyish abandon.

A funny year for me, with peculiar juxtapositions of memories: little kids, going mad as a mother, Ireland coming home to roost in IRA bombings, flares, anti-fashion, but where to find the dungarees insiders were wearing? Were men the enemy, or did it all rest on capitalism's dominance? Heterosexuality reigning but tottering. Looking through old *Spare Rib*s, I spotted a classified ad: 'Anyone who responded to Commune Ad in May issue, please phone 445 8307. Profound apologies. Tom McHugh.' It amused me.

Sue O'Sullivan was involved in the early women's liberation movement, and was a member of the *Spare Rib*, *Red Rag* and *Feminist Review* publishing collectives.

Pink is the colour

A personal history of gay London.

By Paul Burston

PROTEST & POLITICS

I came to London in 1984, fresh out of south Wales and under the pretext of furthering my education, but with a secret, burning need to get as far away from my home town as possible. Then, and only then, could I be myself. I was 19 and firmly in the closet. I didn't know anyone who was gay, I hadn't told anyone I was gay, and I had never been to a gay bar or club. I didn't know London, but I was familiar with the sleazy Soho scene celebrated in the songs of Soft Cell, and I knew that Frankie Goes To Hollywood had filmed the video for 'Relax' at a gay club called Heaven.

In those days, Heaven could lay claim to being the most famous gay club in the world. It was the only gay club I'd ever heard of, and the only one I could find. I stood outside for over an hour, smoking furiously. And when I finally plucked up the courage to walk in, I was overwhelmed by the smell of amyl nitrate and the sweat of 2,000 men. I remember the moustaches, the flannel shirts, the faded Levis and the fan dancers. And I remember one man sweeping past me and shouting out: 'So many men, so little time.' These were the words to a popular dance tune at the time. None of us knew then how prophetic those words would be.

London in 1984 was a very different city from the one we know today. It was the year people wore T-shirts saying 'Frankie Says Relax'. It was the year Soft Cell finally fell apart with an album called *This Last Night In Sodom*. It was also the year Rock Hudson first appeared on *Dynasty* and rumours spread that he was dying of AIDS. Soon the British tabloids would be full of scare stories

Held annually, Gay Pride is both a celebration and an affirmation of gay life.

about the 'gay plague', and the country would experience the biggest homophobic backlash since the 1950s. You could forgive me for thinking that I'd arrived after the party had ended.

There was no gay café culture in London in 1984. There were no gay couples holding hands on Old Compton Street, no glass-fronted bars packed with people happy to be seen in venues frequented by 'known homosexuals'. Gay bars had blacked-out windows. Gay clubs were underground. Gay life was tucked away in areas like Earl's Court, and it happened after dark. Despite years of gay activism by the Gay Liberation Front, there was still the sense that homosexuality was something to be hidden. When newspapers referred to 'the twilight world of the homosexual' or spoke of someone's 'gay shame', they weren't being ironic. Basement bars like the Brief Encounter on St Martin's Lane were full of married men sneaking off for a queer encounter before catching the last train back to suburbia. All the more reason why we needed Gay Pride.

I attended my first Gay Pride march in June 1985. I'd never seen so many gay people in one place, or in broad daylight. The march began in Hyde Park and ended in Jubilee Gardens. In those days there was a separate march for women called Lesbian Strength. I couldn't see the sense in lesbian separatism, but I could understand why lesbians were so angry. I was angry too. Luckily for me, some of my fellow marchers had devised a way to express this anger with a chant we could all gaily sing along to. It began with: 'Give me a G!' and ended with: 'What else is gay? Angry!'

What were we so angry about? Where do I start? An unequal age of consent (brought home to me by Bronski Beat and their 1984 album *The Age of Consent*). Police harassment (there were no openly gay policemen in those days, though there were plenty of 'pretty policemen' who spent their time hanging around public toilets). Queerbashing (I'd been assaulted on three occasions at this point, and further attacks would follow). And that's before you take into account the lack of employment or partnership rights, or the specifically gay 'crime' of 'gross indecency', for which Oscar Wilde was imprisoned almost a century before.

Contrary to popular belief, the Sexual Offences Act of 1967 didn't make male homosexuality legal. It decriminalised homosexual acts between consenting adults in private. The legal definition of private meant that public displays of gay affection could and did lead to prosecution. Straight couples had 'lovers' lanes'. We had 'homosexual haunts', and anyone caught with their trousers down faced a stiff sentence. Even a kiss could land you in trouble. And since the age of consent for gay men was enshrined in law at 21, at 19 I was under age and compelled to break the law on a regular basis. Plus of course, I was still in the process of coming out, risking rejection from my friends and family. For me, Pride wasn't merely a celebration. It was an affirmation.

There were no social networking sites for gay teenagers in the mid 1980s. There were no gay characters on *Coronation Street*, no *Queer As Folk*

> 'Gay bars had blacked-out windows. Gay clubs were underground. Gay life was tucked away in areas like Earl's Court, and everything happened after dark.'

and no John Barrowman sizing up potential Josephs on prime time. The best television could offer was Mr Humphries on *Are You Being Served?* Frankly, I didn't think my needs as a gay viewer were being served. So that was one more thing to be angry about.

And there was far worse to come. As Manchester's chief of police James Anderton spoke of 'homosexuals swirling in a cesspit of their own creation', and tabloids called for gay men to be rounded up and quarantined, the horrors of AIDS struck home. Then Margaret Thatcher went to war on local councils, and Clause 28 reared its ugly head. Between them, AIDS and Clause 28 (later Section 28) made homosexuality more visible, and gay men and women angrier than ever before. Numbers at Gay Pride swelled. A group of lesbians abseiled into the House of Lords, and stormed the BBC's *Six O'Clock News* studio, chaining themselves to Sue Lawley's desk and prompting her classic comment: 'I'm sorry, we do rather seem to have been invaded.' The age of queer activism was upon us.

A dozen ACT-UP activists, including Paul (wearing cap), bring traffic to a halt on Westminster Bridge in 1991, before the police move in with bolt cutters.

ACT-UP storms the *Daily Mail* in response to its vicious coverage of gay issues, 1990. Paul (left) and pop star Jimmy Somerville (centre).

Like many people, I was moved to join ACT-UP by the death of a friend. And then another. And another. By the late '80s, the funerals blurred into one. I was still in my early 20s, and I'd seen more death than people three times my age. Meanwhile, the rest of the (straight) world carried on as normal. There was some ad with an iceberg and the occasional mention of AIDS in Africa, but for those of us living through the epidemic, it was like being in the middle of a war zone. By the time I was 25, I'd buried half my friends.

AIDS activism was as much about finding an outlet for all that grief as it was about raising public awareness. Not that ACT-UP didn't try. In two short years we catapulted condoms over the walls of Pentonville Prison, stormed the offices of the *Daily Mail* and the Australian Embassy, and blocked traffic by lying down in the road. We did that a lot. Our battle cry could have been 'ACT-UP London, lie down!'

On one occasion, a dozen of us handcuffed ourselves to an enormous pink anchor chain, padlocked across Westminster Bridge. The police came with bolt cutters and reeled us in like fish on a line. We were held in the cells for four hours, cautioned and released. Returning to the London Lesbian & Gay Centre in Cowcross Street for a debriefing, I and another male activist were refused entry by the lesbian on the door. The remains of the handcuffs dangling from our wrists were deemed 'a celebration of sadomasochism' and therefore offensive to women.

Out of ACT-UP came OutRage: same tactics, different agenda. OutRage was about gay rights,

pure and simple. The dying days of ACT-UP were fraught with arguments over outreach work and forming alliances with other AIDS organisations. I remember meeting with a woman from a support group for drug users with HIV, and being told in no uncertain terms that many of her clients were homophobic and that I should simply accept this. I didn't, but the energy wasted trying to talk her round was energy that could have been spent elsewhere, and it was no surprise to anyone when ACT-UP burned out a few months later.

'I was overwhelmed by the smell of amyl nitrate and the sweat of 2,000 men.'

OutRage avoided making the same mistakes. Not that it didn't divide opinion. Soon the gay world was split in two: supporters of the direct action group led by the controversial Peter Tatchell, and supporters of the polite lobbying group Stonewall and that nice Ian McKellen. The irony, of course, is that the Stonewall group took its name from the riots that first sparked the modern gay rights movement, yet it was OutRage that best embodied the true spirit of Stonewall. As one T-shirt slogan put it, 'Stonewall was a riot'. When OutRage supporter Derek Jarman publicly criticised McKellen for taking tea with John Major and accepting a knighthood from a homophobic

Tory government, the battle lines were drawn. To some extent, they remain to this day. OutRage still pursues its course of non-violent direct action, and Stonewall still politely lobbies MPs.

Jarman died in 1994, a few days before MPs voted to lower the gay age of consent. The night of the vote, there was a candlelit vigil outside the Houses of Parliament. It began peacefully, but when it was announced that MPs had voted against equality at 16, a riot broke out and people stormed the building. The following morning's papers talked of 'gays on the rampage'. These weren't the headlines we wanted to see, but at least we weren't taking it lying down.

'For those of us living through the AIDS epidemic, it was like being in the middle of a war zone. By the time I was 25, I'd buried half my friends.'

It would take another 12 years, a change of government and a lot of pressure from Europe before gay men and women would see the headlines we really wanted. Tony Blair made a lot of promises to gay voters when he swept into power in 1997. Getting him to honour those promises wasn't as easy as some people hoped, but better late than never. It's now over 40 years since the partial decriminalisation of 1967, and, finally, the vast majority of the legal battles have been won.

We have an equal age of consent, gay employment rights, even 'gay marriage' in the form of civil partnerships. Section 28 has been repealed, and relationships that were once described in law as 'pretended family relationships' are now legally sanctioned and celebrated all across the country. I don't think it's a coincidence that in the last few years, numbers at Gay Pride have dwindled. For many people, there's an overwhelming sense that we don't really need it anymore. Rightly or wrongly, it's assumed that all those years of activism have served their purpose.

In September 2007, my partner and I held our civil partnership ceremony on Tower Bridge, a short distance from the centre of government. I like to joke that we'd have chosen Parliament Square if we could, but the truth is that we simply liked the venue. It was only on the day itself that the significance of the location became apparent.

After the ceremony, the photographer thought it would be a good idea if the entire wedding party went out on to the bridge and stood in the middle of the road for a group photo. So there we were, surrounded by our friends and family, blocking the traffic on one of London's busiest historic bridges. Nobody came to arrest us, and nobody yelled abuse. If someone had told me 20 years ago that my mother would have that photo on her wall, I'd have laughed in their face.

Paul Burston is an award-winning novelist, and has been Gay Editor of *Time Out* since 1992.

From civil disobedience to civil partnership: Paul celebrates on another of London's busiest bridges, 2007.

HEDONISM INTRODUCTION
SEX CITYSCAPE FASHION
SOCIETY SHOPPING COMEDY
DRAMA PROTEST & POLITICS
VISUAL ARTS PERFORMANCE
LITERATURE GANGS OPINION
COCKNEYS BARS ON SCREEN
DANCE MUSIC TELEVISION
BUILDINGS CLUBS NIGHTLIFE
SPORT & FITNESS MEMORIES
STYLE FOOD & DRINK GIGS
CONSUME RIOTS REFERENCE

The Merry-go-round

From Swinging London to the YBAs and Frieze Art Fair, the capital's artistic energy has grabbed the attention of the world. In between, London has been studded with periods of recession that have pushed more radical ideas through from the margins, constantly rejuvenating the scene with new technologies, philosophies and geographies.

By Sarah Kent

London top for culture', announces a headline in *thelondonpaper*. 'London has been named the world's most culturally vibrant city,' says the article. According to a report by the Development Agency, 'The capital [is] ahead of New York, Paris, Shanghai and Tokyo in virtually all categories, with more museums, musical performances and venues, public art galleries and major theatres.'

This upbeat claim provokes in me a serious attack of déjà vu – it is so similar to the assertions made back in 1965 by Diana Vreeland, editor of *Vogue* magazine, who wrote: 'London is the most swinging city in the world at the moment.' Have things really come full circle in the 40 or so years since then, and if so, what happened in the intervening decades?

The answer is both 'yes' and 'no'. There are huge differences between now and the '60s; the last few

years, in particular, have seen exponential growth in the scale of London's cultural sector.

Tate Modern is the embodiment of London's art world success. It attracted five million visitors in 2007, making it the most popular contemporary art museum in the world. Art is a major tourist draw, then; but it is also big business. In the 1960s, we had virtually no collectors, and the handful of dealers showing contemporary art had to rely on Americans for sales. Now buying art has become fashionable and a new breed of collectors has sprung up here and abroad; the market has gone global, and London has become an international centre for contemporary art.

Galleries have mushroomed all over the capital and major international dealers like Gagosian have set up shop beside home-grown enterprises like White Cube, which have matured into significant players on the world scene. Since it was launched

Left to right: Gianni Motti's (living) *Yogic Policeman* at Frieze 2007; Rachel Whiteread's *House*; St Katharine Docks pioneer Bridget Riley; Marcus Harvey's controversial painting of Myra Hindley that brought protest to Sensation; sculpture by David Altmejd at Frieze 2007.

in Regent's Park in 2003, the Frieze Art Fair has established a huge international reputation, attracting plane-loads of wealthy collectors from America, Europe, Russia, and Japan. And prices for modern and contemporary art are soaring into the stratosphere; in February 2008, Christie's sold Francis Bacon's *Triptych 1974-77* for £26.3m, a new record for post-war art. The anonymous buyer was rumoured to be Roman Abramovich, Russian billionaire and owner of Chelsea FC.

London 'swings'

Back in the '60s, though, Robert Fraser was one of the few dealers showing young artists. Based on a newspaper photograph, Richard Hamilton's *Swingeing London '67* shows him and Mick Jagger being arrested on drugs charges. The pair personify the '60s love affair between Pop art and pop music; the most famous examples were John Lennon and Yoko Ono, who collaborated on films, music and performances, like the *Bed-In* of 1969, a between-the-sheets plea for world peace.

Their political naivety was in sharp contrast to the seriousness of the student rebellion that erupted the previous year at the Sorbonne in Paris, and quickly spread to Berlin and London, where student sit-ins took place at the London School of

Economics and art schools such as Hornsey (now Middlesex University). Then, youth culture was not just a style statement, but a genuine attempt to challenge the status quo and shatter a class system that stifled creativity.

Time Out was launched that year, from a desire to support the groundswell of alternative culture. Politicised by the student rebellion, young artists were turning their backs on the marketplace and the hedonism of Pop. Having led the Hornsey sit-in, Stuart Brisley developed a provocative kind of performance art. To dramatise his rejection of establishment values, he lay for hours in a bath of offal and hung naked from a scaffolding structure outside the Hayward Gallery. The Hayward had opened in '68, the year the Institute of Contemporary Art (ICA) moved to the Mall from nearby Dover Street, where it began life as an artists' meeting place.

Artists began taking the initiative in numerous ways. An artists' union was set up, and, as a first step in what was to be a long battle for recognition, a women's branch was established. Artists Bridget Riley, Peter Sedgley and Peter Townsend set up Space, turning disused buildings in St Katharine Docks into studios. The occupants soon began opening their studios to the public; floating on the water, a huge inflatable by Graham Stevens

advertised the first of many such shows. Over the river, meanwhile, artist and film-maker Derek Jarman shared the fifth floor of Butler's Wharf with Andrew Logan, who lived inside the Alternative Tower of London, a plaster castle bought from Biba, the famous clothing store. The castle yard became the venue for the annual Alternative Miss World Competition compèred by Logan in a garment that was half dinner jacket, half evening gown. Most of the contestants were men dressed in costumes so flamboyant that they soon attracted media attention.

In 1970, Edward Heath came to power amid galloping inflation and high unemployment. The optimism of the swinging '60s had long since faded and, as far as art was concerned, we were in for a schizophrenic decade. The art market had stalled and artists were opting for ephemeral art forms such as installations, performances and photographs that were difficult to exhibit and impossible to sell. Students at St Martin's School of Art led the way: Richard Long walked a line through the daisies in the name of art, and Barry Flanagan beamed a light across sacks full of sand. Gilbert and George painted their hands and faces bronze and posed for eight-hour stretches as 'living sculptures'.

This generation was to change the face of contemporary art. The current climate – in which artists use film, video, photography, writing, installations or performance, as well as traditional media, to engage with personal, social or political topics – stems directly from initiatives taken in the early '70s. The public responded with hostility, though. The BBC television series *Art and Technology* broadcast artists' videos for the first time; anticipating viewers' incomprehension, the producer introduced them with the warning: 'Do not adjust your sets'.

The atmosphere was so negative that, in 1974, after seeing the Hayward's British Painting '74, I declared in *Time Out*, 'Britain is a cultural backwater. The sooner we admit it, the sooner something can be done.' And when Hestor van Royen opened a small gallery in the newly trendy Covent Garden, I wrote, 'There is a standing joke in the London art world that to open a gallery here is the quickest route to bankruptcy.'

A crisis was in the offing. In 1976, the press launched a campaign designed to censor art by attacking the galleries that supported it. A reporter discovered that the Tate had bought a sculpture by Carl Andre consisting of a stack of fire bricks, and demanded that no further public money be spent on such worthless nonsense. The 'Tate bricks', or *Equivalent VIII*, to give them their official title, soon became a symbol of the idiocy of modern art and the gullibility of institutions professing to believe in it.

With only a handful of dealers supporting new names, young artists were reliant on museums

and public galleries like the ICA, Whitechapel, Serpentine and Hayward; but these were dependent on government and local authority funding (business sponsorship, as yet, being unheard of) and were vulnerable to attack from people whipping up controversy.

A few months later, the ICA exhibited Mary Kelly's *Post-Partum Document*, a study of her relationship with her baby son that included his nappies. The show was pilloried by the press and 'dirty nappies' soon supplanted the Tate Bricks as an emblem of absurdity. Two months later, Genesis P-Orridge and Cosey Fanni Tutti of COUM Transmission staged Prostitution, an exhibition likening the art market to the sex industry. A Tory MP went on the attack and demanded 'that the Arts Council be scrapped'. The newspaper report went on, 'Questions were asked in the Commons last night about why taxpayers' money was being squandered on such exhibitions.' When ICA director Ted Little refused to close the exhibition, the Arts Council suspended its grant and pushed the gallery to the brink of bankruptcy. A national campaign called 'Arts in Danger' was launched, and I urged people to write to their MP in support, saying '1977 will be the year when Britain decides whether the arts are a vital part of national life or a luxury that can be axed.'

Saatchi, sharks and the YBAs

Under Margaret Thatcher, the economy rallied and large bonuses soon gave City slickers enough cash to lavish on luxury items. Buying contemporary art became the daring new fashion and galleries sprang up to satisfy their appetite for figurative painting. Over the next few years, the commercial sector was the most vibrant part of London's art scene and impressed observers with the money being made; colour supplements began publishing articles about artists and their dealers.

The art market was small, parochial and vulnerable, though. On 19 October 1987, 'Black Monday' saw a huge fall on the stock market, and five years later came 'Black Wednesday', when the pound fell to a record low. Dozens of commercial galleries folded as prices plummeted and collective cynicism returned; contemporary art was perceived as a con foisted on the public by dealers, critics and curators.

Nevertheless, the first seeds of London's current success were sown during this volatile decade. To generate interest in contemporary art, the Patrons of New Art launched the Turner Prize in 1984. The annual event really got off the ground seven years later, when Channel 4 became sponsors, guaranteeing media coverage.

But the main catalyst for change was a private collector. In 1985, Charles Saatchi opened a gallery on Boundary Road in St John's Wood. Housed in a former paint factory, it was the most beautiful

Artist and filmmaker Derek Jarman and the Bankside Crew (from left: Jarman, Peter Logan, Luciana Martinez) at his legendary art squat in the 1970s. The squat occupied a whole floor of the old warehouse building and hosted many outrageous parties.

Awareness. Classes Mon-Sat, 6.30 pm and Tues, Thurs, Sat, Sun 10.30 am at 34A St Stephen's Gardens, W2. 229 0555. Also Thurs 6.30 at 45 Atkins Road, SW12. Free feast and holy songs at St Stephen's Gardens every Sunday at noon.

● **Cheapest Van Moves.** Large and small. Ned Ludd. 889 5715.

● **Grecian Urn Health Studio** for men, Sauna, massage, sun ray etc. Wives or friends welcome. 25-27 Rupert Street, W1.

● **Low Cost Jet Flights:** To USA, Canada, East Africa, South Africa, India, Far East, Australia. Contact G. S. Enterprises. 580 3298, 637 1971.

● **Chippy!** Carpentry, joinery, shop-fitting, practical interior design and decoration. Phone 858 3625.

● **Very cheap,** efficient, Auto servicing and repairs. Phone 603 3658.

● **India for £75.** By subsidiary companies of Air India and BOAC (some flights subject to Govt. approval). India Bound, Triumph House, 189 Regent St, W1. 734 3598.

● **Qualified masseur.** Chinese and Swedish methods. Exprerienced instructor in using Ti Chi Chuan for relaxation. Daytime visiting to heterosexual clients only. Box 85/1.

● **Typewriting Services.** Cheap rates. Phone Laurence 229 0395, Flat 2.

● **Gentle Ghost Service;** anything you need. 603 8581.

● **Profesional guitarist/saxophonist,** American, offering lessons. All styles. 274 5440.

● **English Lessons given.** Phone Laurence 229 0395, Flat 2.

● **Gentle Ghost Removals** 603 8581.

● **Reichian Therapeutic Massage** by Esalen masseuse. 9-12 and 4-7 Mon to Fri. 458 1367.

● **Portuguese Lessons** given. Phone Klinger 229 0395, Flat 2.

● **Gentle Ghost** 603 8581.

● **Expose yourself for £5.** Brilliant photographer will photograph absolutely anything from £5. 272 8033.

● **Friendly Van Moves Anywhere.** 603 8581.

Jobs Offered

● **Fleet Street** magazine publisher requires young attractive girls with good figures for nude modelling. Advertising, promotion, and film extra work also available. Payment £10 to £20 per session. Free composites on completion of work. All work according to existing British laws. Phone Miss Shipley 583 0912.

● **Part-time work available** during the day for young people 18 and over to do housework, baby-sitting, help at parties, etc. About 32½p per hour. Tel: Problem Ltd, 353 8281 10 am-5 pm for details.

● **Nude models wanted,** £5 per hour, for magazine illustrations. 935 3879.

● **Professional touring theatre group** wants to share its poverty and happiness with another actor/actress. Ability to work in small group situation important. Exeprience with children a help. Please send short life history with s.a.e. to Chamelon Thettre Group, Grove Farm, Hedge End, Southampton.

● **Do you want financial independence** from part-time work? If you're free any evening ring 300 3141 9.30 am to 12 noon for appointment.

● **Gentle Ghost** need vans big and small, and people to answer our phone. 603 8581.

● **Friendly girl** needed to help me in the afternoon with my new home and two children (18 & 4 months). Please ring Juliette at 727 1332.

● **Girls, 17-21,** long blonde hair, tanned, lean, primitive, wanted for low budget movie—little bread. Ring 928 1047 office hours before 5.30 pm Wed, 6 Oct. Genuine.

Flats Wanted

● **Young spiritualist organisation** desperately need house. Should be central London. Will renovate. Ring 229 0555.

● **Chick (26 and guy (27)** seek space in commune or commune-to-be group of down-to-earth people in London. 348 1621.

● **Two girls,** early twenties, want own rooms in mixed house/flat North London preferred. Day 549 0063 ext 41, Anna. After 6.30, 359 0865, Clare.

● **Composer** requires (semi-) detached house/flat £7,000 limit within 6 miles West End. 997 0662 evenings.

● **£50 reward offered** for anyone finding Time Out writer nice (and perhaps spacious) flat or room in Hampstead/ Parliament Hill area, to rent at reasonable price. Ring John Howkins at 278 5481.

● **Large room/small flat** for journalist and loud stereo. Congenial location and space/garage for 2 mo'sickles essential. Pay f & f, premium or bribe if necessary. Mark Williams. 730 0344 (days).

● **Macro guy,** at present living in room, needs to share flat with other macro. people. Interested in opening restaurant. Write Dave, 26 Nether St, Tally Ho, Finchley, or call after 6 pm.

● **Poet** (22½) seeks own room in poetic/ folky flat. Phone Mike: 834 6912, ext 141 (day); 226 0905, rm 14 (evening).

Flats/Rooms

● **Bed and Breakfast** £1 per night. 722 1005.

● **Couple/two** wanted for semi-communal house Streatham. Ring 764 2419.

● **Unattached girl** wanted to share mad flat in N22. Own room, £4 p.w. 889 6135.

● **onely guy** (24) seeks attractive and understanding chick to share experiences and pad in Holland Park (rent £5 p.w.) Box 85/7.

● **Fourth girl** wanted to share room in s/c W11 flat. £4.50 per week. 229 2322—ask for Flat 65.

● **Community living** in Blackheath area. Couples interested in joint purchase large house please phone 852 9675.

● **Graduate** wanted own room to share large c.h. flat overlooking Ealing Common. 567 9625.

● **Two intelligent chicks** wanted to share room (£5 each) in large mixed flat, High St, Kensiington—Church St. Ring Joe 370 2961 10 am-4 pm or 30 Campden Grove, W8 after 7.

● **Single room** in West Hampstead flat. £6 p.w. Phone 328 4936 after 7 pm.

● **Male, 25-30,** for mixed house East London, on District Line. Own room. Colour TV. £20 p.m. 552 8544 evenings.

● **Fresh-painted room** in hip writer's friendly Blackheath home for happy simple living person. £5 inclusive. Call 858 9412, 7-11 pm, mornings 858 0049.

● **Due to an unscheduled departure of wife,** Pete has spare rooms in W1 flat to share with interesting person/s. 636 8529.

● **Two girls** to share flat with two students. Own room, share expenses, Chiswick. About £3.50 each. Ring 994 2066 (evenings) John or Martin.

● **Two girls** wanted to share c/h Ealing flat—own rooms. £18 monthly. Phone 567 7110 evenings.

Jobs Wanted

● **London male,** 18, Sats, Suns, any work. Box 85/2.

● **Gent** requires part-time work, anything very interested at all considered. Box 85/3.

● **Work wanted:** Painting, decorating, carpentry, house repairs, etc. Box 85/4.

● **Young couple** want to make bread. Anything considered. Box 85/6.

Articles for Sale

● **The Young male nude.** Highly illustrated brochure/penfriend magazine. Fantastic value at 50p. Don Busby Studios, 10 Dryden Chambers, 119 Oxford Street, London, W1R 1PA.

● **Mo'sickle;** 1971 BSA 250cc Street Scrambler. Works maintained. Taxed, low mileage and bloody immaculate. Must sell hence £270 ono (HP poss). Mark Williams 730 0344 (Days).

● **Essenses**—Dresses made to measure 20's, 30's clothes and jewellery bought and sold. Antiquarius Market, 135 King's Road, Chelsea. Stall N8 Essenses.

● **1967 Honda CD175 Motorbike.** Good condition. MOT June 1972. £100. Ring Paul 883 5256.

● **Quad** 33+303 stereo pre-amp and power amp. Perfect condition. £80 cash. Ring Chris at Time Out 278 5481.

● **BSA Gold Star 350 cc.** Trials/Road Bike. Engine just rebuilt, not yet run-in. V fast. £150 ono. Details from Isobel at 278 5481.

● **Large Buxom Girls** fully untouched nude photos for the adult artist. £1 samples or s.a.e. for lists. Miss Maxzine, 466a Hoe Street, Leyton, London, E17.

● **Uninhibited Erotica.** Books, films. magazines. Samples and lists 25p. Private Swedish Book Service, 60 Knightsbridge, SW1.

● **Girls Together':** 10" x 8" unretouched photos; Ten for £2; PO only to Box 84/3.

● **Four snow tyres** for sale. Ring Colin at 352 5857.

A quantity of decorated Victorian organ pipes, some over 6 ft high. 485 9021.

● **Gay, gay, gay magazines/films.** Send today for free brochure. Ariel Trading (Ref T6), Post Box 8, 2900 Hellerup, Denmark.

● **For Sale,** the Revolution of Everyday Life (Part 1) by Raoul Vaneigem, p & p, 25p. Blank postal order to 7 Queensgate Villas, London, E9.

● **Increase** your pleasure by reading 'Ejaculation Control Techniques' (£1) Plain Cover. From Robin Saxon, PO Box 722, W2.

● **Erotic-Danish Magazines and Films.** All types available. Send today for free brochure or send £1 (uncrossed PO's) for sample offer. Ariel Trading (Ref T6), Post Box 8, 2900 Hellerup, Denmark.

Personal

● **Contacts Unlimited** 437 7121. See Services column.

● **Educated gentleman** (42) offers home to one or two slim girls. Possibly one child. Box 83/10.

● **Personal massage** for men by women. 734 0246.

● **Time Out?** Then drop in to London's latest Health Bar. Madam Fish, 244 Gt Portland Street, W1 (opp Station) 10.00 am-7.30 pm.

● **Beautiful man** (for women) early thirties. Am I the last crazy one on this astonishing earth? Box 84/7.

● **Contacts Unlimited** 437 7121. See Services Column.

● **Sex Manuals,** photo-books, films, way-out erotica. Illustrated lists. 25p. Private Swedish Book Service, 69 Knightsbridge, SW1.

● **Intelligent,** open and unconventional woman would like to meet interesting, sensual and understanding man, for friendship with mutual respect and freedom. Colour, age, appearance, background, all unimportant, any area. Box 85/8.

● **Young man,** 24 and mobile, seeks attractive young lady 19-29 living West London, Surrey, Middx. Box 85/9.

● **Efficiency and reliability** are not qualities looked down upon by bachelor, 27, graduate. Interests: electronics, science fiction, classical music, ESP. Seeks intelligent, educated single girl, not fat; no ties, for faithful reliable friendship leading to marriage. Dislikes: crowds, cities, journeys. (Herts.) Box 85/10.

● **Chick** to partner with swinging couples. Box 85/11.

● **Mickeybliss and Scrunt.** Attendance requested at Party HQ. Oct 2nd.

● **Swinging couple** seeks other couple, early 20's. Box 85/6.

● **Successful Seduction Techniques!** Author publishing new book seeks personal experiences/opinions. Confidence guaranteed. Usual fees. Box 85/12.

● **Refined Secretary,** musical, varied intellectual interests, seeks friendships (30-40) London. Box 85/13.

● **Would tall black guy** who approached shy redhead for light Gloucester Road station 20/9 around 9 pm thence Notting Hill please contact Box 85/14.

● **Rawhide.** New issue physique magazine of teenagers. Send now for your copy, 50p Fulham Studios (Photographic), 494 Fulham Road, SW6 5NH.

● **Young male masseur** offers private services to ladies. Box 85/15.

● **Lonely gent** wishes to meet couple to exchange ideas. Box 85/16.

● **Danish Male Nude Magazines** £1. John, BM/FBGH, WC1.

● **Attractive couple** seeks others, and single males and females, for mutual enjoyment. Box 85/17.

● **Meet your perfect match** with the Operation Match computer. Free literature: Operation Match (TOB2), 70 Pembroke Road, London, W8. 937 2517.

Miscellaneous

● **Upsurge** Room 5, 14 Queensberry Place, SW7. Encounter meetings each Tuesday 7.30 pm. £1.

● **Nudist Club, Kent,** welcomes you. Year-round activities. Details free from 'T.T.', 50 Marling Way, Gravesend. or ring 0474 64207 or 74418.

● **£39 to India** by Budget Bus. Leaves Sept. 24, Nov. 20. 445 8608 (evenings).

● **Shiatsu Japanese Massage** by **Minoru Kanetsuka,** London Aiki-Kai, Greater London Sports Club, 994 2182 evenings Monday-Friday or messages 458 2632 8 am-9 am. Private Visits.

● **Massage Service** for Gentlemen by appointment. 242 3096.

● **Time Out's Messenger** desperately needs big old bike—little or no bread—can repair (esp Norton 650's). Ring Chris at Time Out 278 5481.

● **Kabul Afghanistan.** Minibus leaving Mid Oct. £45. 852 8717. (Rod after 7 pm).

● **'Stimulus'** is the New, Exciting Monthly Magazine for YOU (whatever your interests). SAE for details without obligation to: 'Specialist Mail-services', 41 Livingstone Road, Bath, Somerset.

● **India Overland** with Indigo—£69. Departures 18th Oct-13th Nov. Phone 834 5545.

● **Uncensored gay books,** magazines, new, incognito. 80p. Illustrated lists 5p. Swedish Books, 69 Knightsbridge, SW1.

● **Carpet,** nice and free or very cheap needed for BIT Information Service office. Roughly five yards square. Telephone 229 8219.

● **Presentable flats and houses** in the London area wanted on a £1 per hour hire basis for International Photographer. 935 3879.

● **Wanted Mobylette** or similar bike about 50 cc. Must be in good condition and with two seats. Ring Lindsey at 278 5481 day.

● **Found:** One International Student? Identity Card, no name; who wants it? 229 7251.

● **Come alive** with Bodymind Training Encounter Group: s.a.e. to 10 Steele's Mews South, NW3 4SJ: 529 8864 except 3-8 pm.

● **Hung Up?** Depressed? Problems with drugs, etc? Ring 242 0010 or visit New Horizon Youth Centre, 1 Macklin Street, WC2. Open Monday-Friday 10-10 pm. Weekends 10-6 pm.

● **Vibrations corrected.** Radionic Broadcast. Explain your problem. Send specimen of hair and £1.50. Law. Box 85/18.

● **Nepal, India**—hitching companion for male, 24. Leave 3rd week Oct. Phone 265 3333, ext 235, ask for Subhash.

● **Can you help a struggling drama student** in desperate need of £530 for fees, having been refused a grant. Already done one year very successfully. References available foom college. Any suggestions? Box 85/19.

● **Interested in working week-ends on organic farms?** Send s.a.e. to Box 85/20.

● **Artist-architect** (London) seeks mixed company for 4-day car trip in Loire Valley, end-October; churches, chat, chateaux, and Chateaubriand! Bringing back good wines cheaply. Box 85/21.

● **Verses for Stag Occasions.** Box 85/22.

● **Encounter Groups and the New Therapies.** A series of lecture-demonstrations by Jerome J. Liss, MD.
Monday, October 11th, 7.30 pm. General Introduction: Encounter Groups and the New Therapies.
Monday, October 18th, 7.30 pm. The New Individual Therapies (Lowen Expressive Neo-Reichian Touch and Primal Scream).
Monday, October 25th, 7.30 pm. The New Group Therapies (Encounter, Gestalt, psychodrama, Bioenergetics).
Monday, November 1st, 7.30 pm. Body Expression and the Physiology of Emotional Release.
Monday, November 8th, 7.30 pm. Co-operative Help (A Method of Mutual Help for Untrained People).
Monday, November 15th, 7.30 pm. Couple, Family and Network Therapy
Fee: £1 per evening.
For details write to Jerome J. Liss, MD, 6/8 Cornwall Crescent, London, W11.

● **King Rat** wants super mouse to travel to Afganistan, Goa, Kathmandu? Beautiful Minnies only. Ring 229 7251.

● **Week-end Seminar with your Self,** 9/10th October. Participate with Centre Community in personality feedback based on self-discovery techniques: meditation, colour and yoga. Phone 727 3865.

● **Wanted.** Amateur models willing to pose in own home surroundings for pin money for keen amateur photographer. Send description or snap to Box 85/23.

● **American, 23,** would like companion to travel around Europe. Sharon 837 4583.

exhibition space in London. At the time, the capital had no museum of modern art; the Tate (now Tate Britain) had to perform two roles, as a museum of British and modern art; there wasn't enough room for the permanent collection, let alone major touring shows. Meanwhile, in one splendid exhibition after another, Saatchi demonstrated a level of commitment to contemporary art that put our institutions to shame. New York Art Now featured young Americans like Jeff Koons and Robert Gober; the scale and ambition of the work was a revelation to the students who were soon to become known as the Young British Artists (YBAs).

Ironically, the recession kick-started another important trend. With commercial galleries folding and public spaces short of funds, graduates had little chance of being offered a show; empty factories, warehouses and shops were there for the asking, though. In 1988 Damien Hirst found

in an abandoned Docklands factory. He showed *A Thousand Years*, two glass chambers containing a swarm of bluebottles, a work both elegant and repellent. Charles Saatchi bought the sculpture and switched his allegiance from American to British art; over the next decade, his support for artists such as Sarah Lucas, Marc Quinn and Rachel Whiteread was vital to their survival.

He commissioned Hirst's famous pickled shark, *The Physical Impossibility of Death in the Mind of Someone Living*. Swimming in a tank of formaldehyde, jaws open as though about to bite your head off, it formed the centrepiece of Young British Artists I, the exhibition that was to give the YBAs their name. Over the next five years, Saatchi staged five more shows of YBA work, and used his flair as an ad man to attract media attention. In 1993, Jay Jopling, who had become Hirst's agent, opened White Cube in Duke Street, St James's, round the corner from Christie's and

VISUAL ARTS

a derelict building in Docklands to launch himself and 13 fellow Goldsmith's graduates on to the scene. Freeze has since acquired mythic status, but hardly anyone went to see the exhibition. Undaunted, Hirst sent taxis to fetch Nicholas Serota, director of the Tate, and Norman Rosenthal of the Royal Academy.

Exhibitions curated by artists were nothing new. In 1979, Robin Klassnik began inviting friends to show in his studio in London Fields, and financed the exhibitions by teaching. Most memorable was *20:50*, an installation by Richard Wilson that was later bought by Charles Saatchi. Flooded with sump oil, the space was magically doubled by the foul liquid whose black surface acted as a mirror.

Tate Modern arrives

The most exciting and most memorable decade for British art, the '90s saw the rise and rise of the YBA generation. In 1990, Hirst helped organise two more shows, Modern Medicine and Gambler,

The Saatchi empire before the move to Chelsea: the original gallery at Boundary Road (left) and grander premises at County Hall (right).

Sotheby's – perfectly placed for introducing Hirst, Tracey Emin, Gavin Turk and other YBAs to foreign collectors and curators who would spread the news abroad.

But the commercial sector was dormant compared with the alternative scene that continued to grow. By '93, roughly a third of galleries were run by artists. Little by little, public perceptions changed. Hostility and scorn grudgingly gave way to admiration, then to genuine respect. The climax came in 1997 when the Royal Academy mounted Sensation, a survey of YBA art from the Saatchi Collection. After a decade on the fringe, the YBAs had finally been embraced by the establishment and 300,000 people flocked to see the show, which subsequently travelled to Berlin and New York, where Mayor Giuliani tried to close it down on the grounds of blasphemy.

London's transformation from cultural backwater to market leader came about gradually, then; the opening of Tate Modern in May 2000 was the culmination of a process that had begun

over a decade earlier as a grass-roots phenomenon without which the scale and ambition of the Tate project would have been unthinkable. At the opening, a friend summed up the seismic shift in attitudes represented by the museum when she said, 'I have to keep reminding myself that we're in England'.

Tate Modern had an immediate impact. Visitors to the Saatchi Gallery dwindled to a trickle, and it soon closed. Saatchi later relocated to County Hall and installed his YBA collection in the wood-panelled rooms of the former local authority offices. A disastrous warehouse fire destroyed many pieces from his collection, including Tracey Emin's tent *Everyone I Have Ever Slept With 1963-1995* and, repudiating YBA art, Saatchi sold most of his art, including the famous shark. He abandoned County Hall for a new gallery in Chelsea.

Tate Modern's location in Southwark encouraged commercial galleries to quit the West End and join the many alternative spaces in east London. Jay Jopling endorsed the trend by opening White Cube 2 in Hoxton Square in 2000; a further cluster opened in nearby Bethnal Green, and American collectors were soon cruising East End streets in hired limos. But once the novelty wore off, they became reluctant to traipse eastwards and in 2006 Jopling built a new White Cube round the corner from his first gallery in St James's. Others are consolidating their presence in the West End by opening smart new premises in Soho and Mayfair. The influx of money has also transformed the alternative sector: instead of disregarding the market, many fledgling gallerists now aspire to be the next Jay Jopling.

Public venues are thriving, however. Lottery funding and corporate sponsorship allow them to upgrade their premises and stage first-class shows. The Whitechapel Gallery is expanding into the library next door, and the Royal Academy has acquired the former Museum of Mankind. Tate Modern is planning an extension that will open in 2012. Designed by Herzog & de Meuron, the Swiss architects responsible for the original conversion, the 11-storey-glass pyramid will expand the

Left to right: The Whitechapel Gallery in its early days; Tate Modern's dramatic Turbine Hall; Jay Jopling's White Cube, which caught the Hoxton wave.

gallery's space by 60 per cent, at a cost of £215m.

But the market now dominates the scene. When, in 2000, Damien Hirst sold *Hymn*, a bronze enlargement of an anatomical toy, to Charles Saatchi for £1m, the sale hit the headlines, but compared with today's prices, that figure seems modest. At White Cube last year, Hirst exhibited a human skull encrusted with diamonds, *For the Love of God*, which sold for £50m to an investment group whose members include the artist. He is obsessed with death and claims that the glittering bauble mocks the Grim Reaper; but it also embodies the glamour and superficiality of a scene in which taste is dictated by money.

The noughties have seen the transformation of London into one of the world's leading centres for exhibiting and selling contemporary art, but as the commercial sector and the establishment assert

TIMELINE

1968
Hayward Gallery opens.

1969
St Katharine Docks closes, and artists begin to squat the empty warehouses.

1969
Gilbert and George perform *The Singing Sculpture* and become living works of art.

1971
The Photographers' Gallery opens.

1976
Outrage over the Tate's purchase of Carl Andre's conceptual piece *Equivalent VIII*, described by critics and the baffled public as 'a pile of bricks'.

1981
The V&A and the Conran Foundation open the Boilerhouse project, dedicated to industrial design. It closes in 1986.

1984
The Turner Prize is launched, and quickly becomes an annual festival of outrageous behaviour, outrageous art, and general public outrage.

1985
Advertising supremo Charles Saatchi opens a gallery in St John's Wood to display his private collection.

Artangel is founded, going on to fill London's disused buildings and unassuming public spaces with unusual happenings.

1988
Damien Hirst and other Goldsmiths students host Freeze in Surrey Docks.

1989
Terence Conran opens the Design Museum at Butler's Wharf, the world's first museum dedicated to contemporary design.

1993
Rachel Whiteread creates *House*, a concrete cast of the interior of a Victorian house, in Mile End. Thousands sign a petition against its demolition. They fail.

1997
Sensation exhibition, at the unlikely venue of the Royal Academy, raises the profile of YBAs and causes excitement and controversy over works such as a portrait of Myra Hindley, deformed children, and animals in formaldehyde.

2000
Annual Becks Futures prize, to support new talent, launched at the ICA.

Tate Modern opens.

Jay Jopling opens White Cube 2 in Hoxton

Square, building on the success of his Duke Street gallery.

Victoria Miro moves her gallery eastwards, from Cork Street to Wharf Road, N1.

The Serpentine Gallery commissions Zaha Hadid to design a temporary summer pavilion. It becomes a popular annual event, with a different architect designing each year's pavilion.

2003
First Frieze Art Fair held in Regent's Park in a marquee designed by architect David Adjaye.

2004
Art turns to ashes as an east London warehouse rented by Momart burns down. Hundreds of works by leading British artists, including many YBAs, are destroyed.

2007
Gilbert and George become the first living British artists to be given a retrospective at Tate Modern.

2008
Mayor Boris Johnson considers ditching the changing displays on Trafalgar Square's Fourth Plinth and replacing them with a permanent statue of another war hero.

their control, the alternative scene is dying. The injection of energy from grass-roots activities has been replaced by a growing passivity; assuming that dealers will come to them, young artists see no need for action. And, no longer able to afford the inflated prices commanded by contemporary art, museums are now reliant on private collectors for gifts and loans.

Money leads and everyone else follows. As I write, the American economy is in trouble, and London dealer Benjamin Rhodes tells me that, although his lease soon runs out, he is making no plans in case the art market collapses. If this does happen, I will have witnessed the London art scene go from boom to bust three times over.

Sarah Kent was Visual Arts Editor of *Time Out* from 1976 to 2006.

Tracey Emin

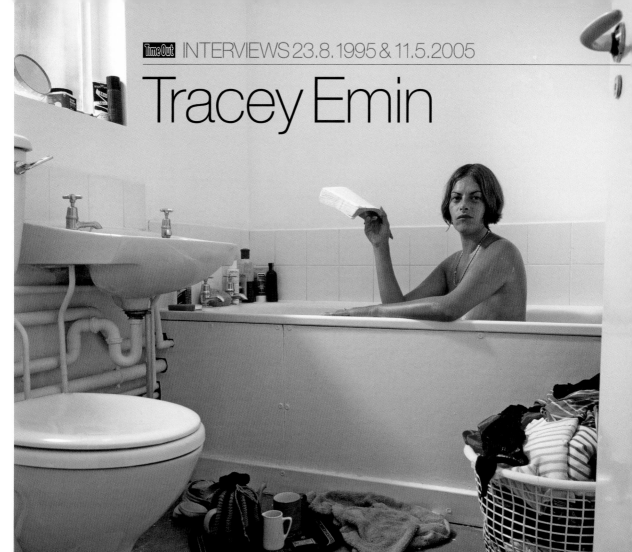

VISUAL ARTS

I imagined that if ever I had my portrait taken, it would be in the bath,' says Tracey Emin, 'because it's intimate and personal – naked without being naked.' Emin is keen to share intimate moments with the public. She planned a month-long, round-the-clock exhibition in which anyone could join her at home – eating, sleeping, watching TV. Like all her work, it would be a living autobiography. 'When I'm dead,' she says, 'my work won't be half so good.' Now she is planning a modified version in an old cab office on Waterloo Road, SE1, which she intends to open every day for a year. 'It will be an Emin museum, where I'll present myself and my work – every moment of creativity can be shared, everything I think or make will be on view.'

It doesn't occur to her that her willingness to expose herself could encourage rapists, murderers and nutters of all sorts to wander in, intent on doing her harm. Her innocence is surprising, since she has had the usual dismal experiences of a young woman with an appetite for life. But it's this openness that makes her special. 'I don't want to hide behind a screen – the work,' she says. 'Being an artist is a 24-hour thing; it isn't a veneer.' It's the directness of her work, the lack of evident artifice, that makes it so affecting. People end up in tears, sharing their own stories with her.

This Sunday she will read from her new book of short stories (also autobiographical) at the Royal Festival Hall. You'll have to turn up early, because although she has only had one solo show in London – at the White Cube Gallery in November '93 – Emin has a cult following.

People got to know her when she ran a shop in Bethnal Green Road for six months in 1993, with fellow artist Sarah Lucas. On Saturdays they stayed open all night and the shop became the place at which to hang out and buy weird things made by the artists, such as Emin's 'Rothko Comfort Blankets, for Private Views and State Occasions': pieces cut from a favourite childhood blanket, fringed in yellow blanket stitch and cornered with a comforting piece of satin. 'The shop was like my family, doing it meant so much,' recalls Emin. 'We didn't get any sleep and lived on Guinness and Indian takeaways.'

Through the shop she met Jay Jopling, Damien Hirst's dealer, who invited her to show at the White Cube. She had six weeks to prepare what she ironically called 'My Major Retrospective', assuming that it would be her one and only show.

Emin is a hoarder; she opened the cardboard boxes gathering dust under her bed, sorted the trolls, the teapots, the diaries, letters and family snaps, put them into frames and installed them as a wall of memorabilia. The death of her uncle Colin, decapitated in a car crash, was recorded with the newspaper story, family snaps of him and his midnight blue E-type Jaguar, and the pack of B&H that he had, screwed up in his hand, when he died. The cabinet commemorating her abortion made some people cry.

Ten years ago we photographed Tracey Emin in the tub, book in hand, coffee mugs on the floor and clothes piled in a plastic laundry basket. Since then Emin has spent a decade baring her soul (and more) in her work, but also, less willingly, in the tabloids. So we asked her to repeat the performance.

Then, she was an aspiring young artist doing her first interview; now she is a household name hounded by media hacks. A decade ago she lived in a council flat in Waterloo, which was so cramped that photographer Magda Segal had to crouch in the hallway; now she owns a beautiful, five-storey Georgian townhouse just off Brick Lane, with a spacious, wood-panelled bathroom.

As it happened, when we spoke a decade ago, change was only days away. The week my article was published, Emin did a reading at the Royal Festival Hall as part of a show called *Whistling Women*. A room large enough for 50 people was booked, but 500 turned up and a larger space had to be rapidly improvised. A few weeks later she opened her 'museum', a former minicab office in Waterloo Road, which she used as a studio.

'The museum was about communication,' Emin recalls, 'and from that point of view it worked well. But too many people came, and I spent all day talking – about thinking, breathing, seeing, feeling, making art – and I came home exhausted. There was no fun in my life.'

'Being an artist is a 24-hour thing,' she insisted then; now she has to protect herself from the public. 'I couldn't do the museum again – it would be too dangerous. I forgot how well known I am. The other day a complete stranger came up and hugged me in the street. I was terrified. I thought I was going to be stabbed. It's a balance, though – you should see me when I want a table at the Ivy.'

Her next exhibition, at White Cube, will include four large blankets, textured with appliquéd embroidery patches. One reads 'Stupid drunk bitch', but with 'stupid' crossed out and replaced by 'super'.

'The work is getting closer to my phobias. I drink too much and the effect is unpredictable. Last time I got drunk in the Golden Heart, I ended up pulling pints for people and dancing with Sandra [the pub's landlady]. This show is about drawing a line under things, especially drinking.'

'Before I was an artist, I was perceived as a bit of a nutter. Now I've a place for my thoughts to exist, I'm perceived as a successful artist. If I didn't have art as a release, I'd spontaneously combust. The pressure builds; it's like a slow candle burning within, or a boil that'll burst.'

Inspired by her Margate childhood, previous sculptures have included a beach hut, a helter-skelter and a pier. This show will feature a rollercoaster made from scrap wood, which undulates in height from four to 16 feet and, according to the sketches, is shaped like a woman's leg. Nothing will be travelling round the model railway track, though; this is a mental piece inspired by a dream. 'I dreamt I was on a rollercoaster ride in Margate when it got stuck,' says Emin. 'Next to me was a 30-foot penis made of real flesh; I was tiny and it was too big to hug, so I clambered down it by clinging on to the veins. It saved my life.'

During the last ten years, there have been times when Emin has been so immersed in her celebrity status that I didn't want to speak to her, let alone do an interview. Now she seems to have come out the other side – just as thoughtful, but wiser. And listening to her, I realise that fundamentally she hasn't changed; she is still the person I like and admire – direct, gutsy, honest and self-questioning.

Both interviews were conducted by Sarah Kent.

For her first ever press interview, Tracey Emin was photographed by Magda Segal for *Time Out* in the bath of her council flat (left). When she reprised the pose ten years later for photographer Hugo Glendinning, she had become a successful artist and her surroundings considerably more glamorous.

VISUAL ARTS

Damien Hirst

It's five years since the shark swam into view at the Saatchi Gallery, in the gallery's first exhibition of Young British Artists (YBAs). It attracted phenomenal publicity, and immediately became a symbol of the radical new art. Hirst was cast in the role of the bad boy whom everyone loves to hate; but he is not just a figurehead. 'I'm still hanging on to being an enfant terrible,' he says. 'Later I can be an adulte terrible – for ever; that's what art's about. Secretly, though, I'm a traditionalist without being establishment.'

Beneath the morbid, wild boy façade, Hirst is a romantic. 'Everything I do is celebration… I'm really obsessed with life, and death is the point where life stops… Art's about life and it can't really be about anything else… There isn't anything else.' When presented with the Turner Prize in 1995, he declared his best artwork to be Connor, his newborn son.

'The steel and glass cases came from a fear of everything in life being so fragile,' says Hirst. 'I wanted to make a sculpture where the fragility was enclosed. We get put into boxes when we die because it's clean. We get put in a box when we are born. We live in boxes.'

The glass containers have hit a nerve in the national psyche, inspiring cartoons and even adverts. The Ford company sliced a saloon car in half and displayed it in a Hirst-style vitrine – so you know that it's art.

Life and death co-exist in Hirst's work. In his first West End show – in an empty shop off Oxford Street, in 1991 – gorgeous Malaysian butterflies hatched from pupae attached to canvases, and spent their lives in the simulated climate of a tropical rainforest, sipping sugar water, mating, laying eggs and dying. Downstairs, though, butterflies were embedded in the gloss of monochrome paintings as though they had got stuck and slowly died. Hirst understands the power of empathy. 'You have to find universal triggers; everyone's frightened of glass, everyone's frightened of sharks, everyone loves butterflies.'

Hirst has become a standard-bearer of the generation he has done so much to promote and publicise. Having assiduously cultivated his image, he has gained the kind of media attention usually reserved for pop stars. In the past two years, Hirst has made a clichéd pop video for Blur's single 'Country House', and an appalling,

'You have to find universal triggers; everyone's frightened of glass, everyone's frightened of sharks, everyone loves butterflies.'

sub-Peter Greenaway film. Later this year he is opening a restaurant in Notting Hill Gate called Pharmacy, featuring waiters dressed in lab coats.

But he is immune to criticism. 'I've learned that you must never compromise; you must get on with it, and have a laugh. I'm working on a car crash. There'll be no bodies, but I want that feeling of absolute horror, just after a crash – the wheels turning, personal possessions spilling out, the radio on, the horn going. I'm using a red car and a corporation grey car and calling it *Composition in Red and Corporation Grey*. I'm a traditional colourist at heart!

'I'll stop when I'm bored or when I'm barking like a dog in the gutter on my hands and knees…'

From an interview by Sarah Kent.

Full list of YBAs exhibited at Sensation, Royal Academy, 1997

Darren Almond	Martin Maloney
Richard Billingham	Jason Martin
Glenn Brown	Alain Miller
Simon Callery	Ron Mueck
Jake & Dinos Chapman	Chris Ofili
Adam Chodzko	Hadrian Pigott
Mat Collishaw	Marc Quinn
Keith Coventry	Jonathan Parsons
Peter Davies	Richard Patterson
Tracey Emin	Simon Patterson
Paul Finnegan	Fiona Rae
Mark Francis	James Rielly
Alex Hartley	Jenny Saville
Marcus Harvey	Yinka Shonibare
Mona Hatoum	Jane Simpson
Damien Hirst	Sam Taylor-Wood
Gary Hume	Gavin Turk
Michael Landy	Mark Wallinger
Abigail Lane	Gillian Wearing
Langlands & Bell	Rachel Whiteread
Sarah Lucas	Cerith Wyn Evans

Plinth charming

London is one big outdoor art gallery. There are works by (among others) Rodin, Henry Moore, Barbara Hepworth, Eduardo Paolozzi, Antony Gormley and Anthony Caro, as well as a tree made out of traffic lights (Isle of Dogs) and a giant black cat (Catford).

Public sculptures are commissioned for a number of reasons: to mark an event; to celebrate a public figure; or to create a visual identity for a new area (witness the extensive public art programme undertaken by the London Docklands Development Corporation in the late 1980s and 1990s).

Sculptural artworks in public places not only have to relate to the landscape and architecture around them, but also to the people who will encounter them. It's easy to get it wrong. Turner Prize nominee Vong Phaophanit's huge illuminated glass wall lined with ash and silk may have been beautiful, but installed in a public park in Greenwich in 1993 it couldn't survive the local youth lobbing stones at it and was dismantled three years later.

More sturdy works have fared little better. Built after the rejection of a design by acclaimed artist Anish Kapoor, the Princess of Wales Memorial Fountain, designed by Kathryn Gustafson, has been beset by problems since it opened in 2004. Blocked pumps, slippery algae and hairline cracks all contributed to a £2m cost overrun and an ongoing annual maintenance bill of £250,000. And Rachel Whiteread's concrete cast of an East End terraced house may have won her the Turner Prize in 1993, but it couldn't win over Tower Hamlets' councillors, who demolished it months later.

Security is another issue. The 2005 theft of Henry Moore's large-scale bronze reclining figure (worth £3m) from Perry Green in Hertfordshire, and the removal of part of Lynn Chadwick's £600,000 bronze, *The Watchers*, from the grounds of Roehampton University in 2006 demonstrates that size and weight are no deterrent to sculpture thieves. Despite a reward of up to £100,000 for the recovery of the Moore, neither has been found.

The success of projects like the Fourth Plinth in Trafalgar Square show that, when executed thoughtfully, public sculpture can still stimulate and (even if disliked) provoke valid debate. Although only life-size, Mark Wallinger's humble marble Christ figure, *Ecce Homo*, dominated its surroundings during its tenure on the plinth in 1999. Likewise, Marc Quinn's sculpture of the disabled artist Alison Lapper, eight months pregnant, challenged how we judge what a public sculpture is and should be. *Helen Sumpter*

VISUAL ARTS

Tate Modern

With its iconic façade of brick (4.2 million of them) and soaring chimney, Tate Modern has quickly become a symbol of 21st-century London. Opened on 12 May 2000, it is now one of the capital's most visited locations, attracting over two million visitors in its first 100 days, and over five million in 2007. At the same time, it has been central to the transformation of a once run-down hinterland into one of London's most vibrant and popular cultural spots.

Tate Modern was originally built as Bankside Power Station, designed by Sir Giles Gilbert Scott, architect of the Battersea Power Station and designer of the red telephone box. After it was decommissioned in 1981, the plan was to either knock it down or, as MP Kate Hoey proposed in 1994, to use the 325-foot chimney as a practice point for mountain climbers and convert the interior into a national ice-skating centre. These plans were rejected.

Instead, the redundant building proved an astonishing discovery for the Tate. Swiss architects Herzog & de Meuron respected the integrity of the original industrial architecture, marrying it with modern interventions such as the glass box, or 'lightbeam', that runs along the length of the roof. The 115-foot high Turbine Hall, kept as an open space, forms a dramatic entrance and public piazza. Artists have risen to the challenge of its extreme dimensions, filling it with giant slides (Carsten Höller), a radiant indoor sun (Olafur Eliasson), a monstrous spider (Louise Bourgeois) and thousands of white polyethylene boxes (Rachel Whiteread) .

An 11-storey glass annex, due to be completed by 2012, has been designed by Herzog & de Meuron. It will increase the exhibition space by 60 per cent, to allow more of the Tate's collection to be displayed. *John Sunyer*

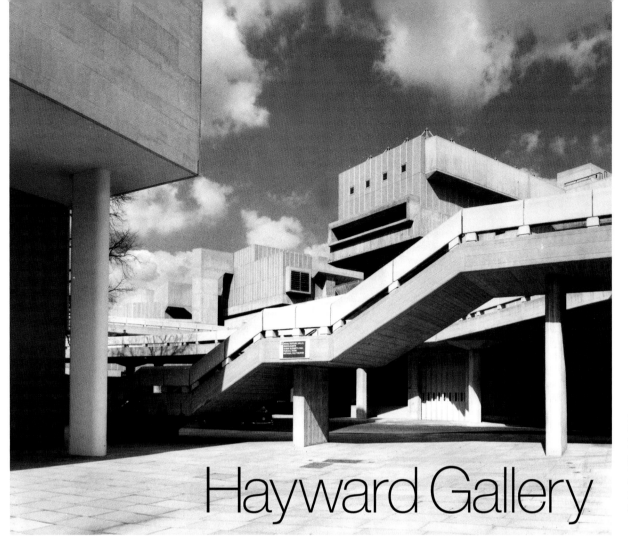

Hayward Gallery

Although the Hayward Gallery was built by the Greater London Council, it was the Arts Council, where I worked, which ran the exhibition programme. They didn't appoint a director in those days. There was a man on site who was an administrator, but he had no control over the artistic policy.

It was a great idea to open the Hayward with a Matisse blockbuster, which the Arts Council had for a long time wanted to do. And it *was* a blockbuster. Marguerite Matisse, Matisse's daughter, came. She stayed at the Savoy hotel across the river. And it was very well attended. The opening was a great occasion: it was said that if a bomb had landed on the Hayward Gallery that day, the arts world would have been totally depleted.

When she went round the gallery, Her Majesty looked extremely serious; she was most interested in it. Her manner rather nicely contrasted with Madame Matisse, this rather volatile, rather splendid French woman.

I remember that the lighting was terribly controversial. Henry Moore, at an Arts Council meeting, had said, 'You mean to say there's no God's daylight in this new gallery?' It was very carefully controlled, filtered light, so that you could keep the same lighting regardless of what was going on in the sky outside. But, interestingly enough, Madame Matisse really liked the lighting. Some thought it was a little bit dead, but she thought it was really great.

The gallery doesn't suit all exhibitions. The Matisses were such strong works of art, it was great for them, but for other exhibitions you had to do things to the gallery to make them work. It was quite an expensive gallery to run, I think.

People have rather accepted the Hayward now, but at the time a lot of people thought it was Brutalist architecture, but a bit after its time. It was nicknamed Alcatraz because it looked like a prison. But gradually it has become more human. I think there's a very good atmosphere now. There's a sense of occasion. The whole riverbank is so vital and lively now.

It was a little bit out of date when it was built, but, 40 years on, who cares?

Mark Glazebrook is an art critic and curator. He wrote the speech given by the Queen at the opening of the Hayward Gallery in 1968.

INNER LONDON PROBATION AND AFTER-CARE SERVICE

require Full-time secretaries for offices in Arlington Road, NW1 and Frederick Street, WC1. Interesting work in a social work setting. Salary according to ability and experience on a scale £4322-£4748 pa. 36 hour week Monday to Friday, one day off in every four weeks in addition to 19 days annual leave. Superannuable posts.
Applicants should have 80 wpm shorthand and 40 wpm typing. Also required Telephonist/Receptionist for office in Arlington Road, NW1.
Salary on a scale £3926-£4610 pa. Superannuable post.
Apply to Personnel Department, 73 Great Peter Street, SW1P 2BN (tel: 222 5656) or for Arlington Road vacancy ring 267 9231/8 or Frederick Street vacancy ring 278 7733.

LONDON COMMUNITY WORK SERVICE SECRETARY/TYPIST

Friendly informal office in Euston concerned with community work needs person with competence, common sense, and good typing speeds. Admin and usual office jobs.
Salary on scale £3322 to £4102 (under review) + £726 London weighting. Five weeks holiday per year pension scheme LVs. Further details from Lewis Donnelly or Fiona Sandilands, Community Work Service, London Voluntary Service Council, 68 Chalton Street, NW1 1JR.
01-388 0241.

SECRETARIAL ASSISTANT
Centre for Adolescents

Reliable person wanted to assist in running office of organisation concerned with adolescent mental health. Audio essential, shorthand an advantage. Age over 25. £4030 pa. Good holidays.
Tel: 328 4216
Brent Consultation Centre,
51 Winchester Avenue, NW6.

PATHFINDERS

The specialists in permanent, temporary secretarial and general office jobs in
MUSIC, TV, FILMS
ADVERTISING AND DESIGN
'Nobody will look after you the way we do!'
PATHFINDERS
Personnel Services Ltd.
(1 min. Oxford Circus Tube)
TELEPHONE 629 3132

ADVERTISING DIRECTOR
requires
SECRETARY

with shorthand to become involved in the business. SW1. £5300.
Phone Christine Pearce,
Woodhouse Appointments, 01-404 4646.

SECRETARY

required for Hammersmith fashion company. Must be able to work under pressure. Travel opportunities. Shorthand required. £5000.
Phone Christine Pearce, Woodhouse Appointments, 01-404 4646.

● **CHAIRWOMAN** of Brook Advisory Centres needs intelligent, experienced secretary. Salary £4038. Telephone Caroline Woodroffe 580 3424.
● **PART-TIME** secretarial help required by music business solicitor. NW6. Approx 15 + hours weekly. Rate negotiable. Box J158.
● **CREATIVE CAREERS**. Superb openings in Publishing, The Arts, Current Affairs, Politics, Education and the Business World, for 'A' Level and Graduate Secretaries and Typists. Appointments welcome. COVENT GARDEN BUREAU, 53 Fleet Street, EC4. 01-353 7696.
● **AUDIO TYPIST REQUIRED** for Human Rights Organization. Pleasant office near Oval. Salary and hours negotiable. 18 months contract. Telephone 582 4040.
● **SOUTH MOLTON STREET**. Part-time book-keeper required for friendly, expanding Video Company. Ability to work quickly and efficiently more important than previous book-keeping experience: Approx. 10 hours per week to suit applicant. Phone Bill on 493 0515.
● **AUDIO TYPIST** required for Human Rights Organization. Pleasant office near Oval. Hours and salary negotiable. Telephone 582 4040

Domestic Jobs

AU PAIR WANTED

urgently to look after 10 year old child and dog. Finchley area.
Call 346 8022 (evenings).

CASH DAILY

People living NW/Central, required cleaning AM/Full days.
Lee Stevens Agency
624 9774

IF YOU NEED WORK WE NEED YOU

£5.00 + fares for 4-hour sessions, morning or afternoon. Central or North-West London.
'Spick 'n' Span'
Domestic Agency
580 1949.

● **DAY BABYSITTING** and light domestic work at highest available rates for nurses or similar. Childminders: 01-487 4578.
● **TWO PEOPLE** needed to love and generally care for 3 boys, 8, 4, 20 months, dog and house near Banbury, while mother studies dance in London during week. Cooking, driving, coping till father gets home. Most weekends free. Live as family though accommodation is s/c cottage. Start August. Tel 0295 811 247.
● **£1.40 p.hour + FARES** Part time home-helps required. Reliable people. Refs. London Domestics Ltd., SW3. Ring now 584 0161.
● **YOGA TEACHERS** with young family need reliable household help 9.30-5.00pm weekdays; £35 pw plus free classes. Suit yoga student ideal). Highgate 348 1284.
● **GIRL AU PAIR** required in France July/Augst. Please write: Camping de la Chapelette, 13310 St. Martin de Crav, France.
● **GIRL/AU PAIR** required June, look after happy infant. Own room, money. 677 3260.

Computer Staff

COMPUTER PROGRAMMERS

Zeus-Hermes Ltd is an energetic software house and consultancy situated in Tottenham Court Road. We do minicomputer software, real-time and microprocessor work, and we are now looking for assembly code programmers with ambition to achieve results. Name your right starting figure, then go up with us.

Maureen Chapman, Zeus-Hermes, 01-388 2393.

ZEUS-HERMES

Theatreboard

ASSOCIATE DIRECTOR, DOGG'S TROUPE.

Dogg's Troupe, Inter-Action's children's/community theatre company, are looking for an associate director to work with a small resident company. A large proportion of the work is in schools, playgroups and playgrounds, with emphasis on participation. Reply in writing for application form and job description to
Catherine Smith,
Inter-Action,
15 Wilkin St., London NW5 3NG.

● **THE WOMEN'S THEATRE GROUP** NEED a musician to work on a musical for young people on nuclear power starting 22nd September. Phone 251 0202.
● **JOIN IN A THEATRE WORKSHOP** for 16-25 yrs on Tues & Thursdays 8 pm at The Centre, 12 Adelaide Street, WC2. Ring 930 2561 for details.
● **REHEARSAL PIANIST** teaches singing, coaches for auditions, musicals, rock, jazz. London University Graduate. 267 2598.

7:84 THEATRE COMPANIES ENGLAND & SCOTLAND

being theatre companies touring the best in socialist entertainment require:
1. ENGLAND: TECHNICAL MANAGER
Must drive, have experience of some/all technical areas of theatre, have some knowledge of maintenance of equipment and organisation of technical side of shows, and be willing to tour. Salary negotiable.
2. ENGLAND: ASSISTANT ADMINISTRATOR
To run office, deal with book-keeping, organise day-to-day working of company and generally assist administrator. Some experience helpful. Salary negotiable.
3. SCOTLAND: ADMINISTRATIVE DIRECTOR
To take charge of financial and office organisation, administer company on the road, supervise production budgets, and assist Artistic Director in all areas. Must be prepared to live in Scotland. Salary under review.
Replies by Friday, June 13th to:
7:84 Theatre Company,
31 Clerkenwell Close, London EC1 or
7:84 Theatre Company,
58 Queen Street, Edinburgh.

● **OVAL HOUSE REQUIRES A THEATRE CO-ORDINATOR** to join a Staff Team of nine full-time workers. The Theatre Co-ordinator is responsible for programming the theatre space, liaising with incoming theatre groups and for liaison with the Arts Council on financial and policy matters. The Theatre Co-ordinator shares with the Staff Team the policy making, planning and programming of activities as well as the day to day running of this lively arts/community centre. Applicants are expected to be able to work closely with people of different ages from varied cultural and theatrical backgrounds. Salary £5,000 pa. Closing date June 30th 1980. Applications to the Staff Team, Oval House, 54 Kennington Oval, SE11. Tel: 735 2786.
● **AWARD WINNING PLAY** seeks company and director for Edinburgh Festival. Box H863.
● **DEDICATED GIRL DRUMMER** and GIRL electric GUITARIST with singing ability to complete band. All original material. Ring 995 2156.

● **SCRIPTS WANTED** new production company all read and returned. Francis Brown, 45 Finborough Road, London SW10.
● **IF** you want to develop socialist theatre, despite financial hindrances, are hard-working, can go to Edinburgh Festival, write to BITE, 12 Castle Road, NW1.
● **MIME WEEKEND** with Robert Williams of Intriplicate Mime Co. 21st-22nd June 10am-5pm. £14 to register. Send deposit, 66 Ridge Road, N8. Enquiries 348 9714.
● **JAZZ DANCE CLASS** – Professional teacher. Beginners welcome. Saturdays 4.45. Chiswick, Details 01 736 2619.
● **PEOPLE NEEDED** for experimental movement group Tuesdays 7pm Intergalactic Art, 31 Morcombe St., SE17 Jo 508 1266.
● **ACROBATICS** Wednesday 6-7.30pm Ring 930 2561. Thursday 1.45-3.45 Ring 677 9673. Helen Crocker.

Jobs Wanted

● **EXTRA CASH – BIG MONEY** Self-employed man, 27, car, living near Bromley, wants propositions – ideas. Box H901.
● **FRENCH GIRL SEEKS JOB** CINEMA, TV, THEATRE, TOURISM, TUITION. SERIOUS. Box H922.

● **MALE UNDERGRADUATE (20)**, seeks well-paid position, driving, anything legal. Excellent references. Zaf 01-946 1318.
● **INVENTIVE** graduate (22), needs £600 urgently. Absolutely anything legal considered. Motor bike/car and couple of friends also available. Box J241.
● **INTELLIGENT**, attractive young woman requires £2,500 + immediately. Genuine (Legal). Box J329.
● **MALE**, 24, into new skills, preferably free hand, drives, (August test), worked with horses, books, wants occupation, interesting, enjoys physical work, (USA visa) Box J348.
● **ARE YOU** looking for an intelligent mature responsible person for part-time work? I am a Fine Art graduate with the above qualities, ex-PA to Managing Director of large international company. Looking for employment max 30 hrs a week at min. £3 per hour. Box J336.
● **POLISH PERSON**, also speaks fluent Russian, English, German, seeks summer work. Enquiries to 01-515 5021.
● **ANYTHING LEGAL** considered. Female design student, 20, seeks summer employment. Box J234.
● **PSYCHOLOGY GRADUATE** female, 25, seeks interesting work. Anything legal considered. Box J297.
● **BLACK WOMAN**, 28, needs £1000 urgently. Evenings, weekends only. Anything legal. Box J153.
● **ANYWHERE**. ATTRACTIVE GAY ORIENTAL (22), PHOTOGRAPHY STUDENT, PERSONABLE AND HARDWORKING, SEEKS SUMMER EMPLOYMENT, PREFERABLY AS PHOTOGRAPHER'S ASSISTANT. Box H915.

Flats Wanted

TIME OUT'S AD MANAGER

requires s/c flat/studio flat. Preferably centralish but would consider most places in London postal area.
To £35pw. 379 6997 10.30-5.30 Mon-Fri.

WANTED—URGENTLY

2-bed s/c apartment for two young professional gentlemen, up to £50 pw. Please write Mr S Connolly, 14 Sleaford House, Blackthorn Street, London E3, or phone (after 7.00pm) 515 9862

GAY GUY

twenties, spiritualist, requires own room preferably north London. Will furnish if necessary. All replies answered Box J229

MOTHER AND CHILD

(coloured) need accommodation ASAP Box J299

DRAMA TEACHER

M.31. needs room modest rent pref. S/W London
Telephone 788 1375

WOMAN, 30

wants QUIET room N London/Wood Green. Working full time and studying. Independence essential. Will decorate/furnish Phone Rowan 272 2778 after 9pm

● **E2 FLAT** suit 3, G.C/H newly furnished available Sept. £180 pcm exc. electricity, gas. Box J307.
● **ADAM INTERNATIONAL** urgently requires accommodation for waiting gay clients. Free service to landlords! 01-437 0703.
● **YOUNG CIVIL ENGINEER** seeks o/r flat/house west London. Tel. 023-57-2102 evenings.
● **A ROOM IN A FRIENDLY FLAT** Pref. NW London where are you? Please contact Jane day 935 0020 eve 435 4274.
● **FEMALE SOCIAL WORKER** 28, requires own room West London from mid-June. Box H906.
● **MUSIC FIEND** 26 friendly, intelligent, needs room in shared house/flat. North London. Nigel 388 1962 ext. 28 (work) 267 1599 (home).
● **NIGERIAN MALE** student accountant (30) seeks room north or west London 328 0723.
● **GIRL 23 SEEKS OWN ROOM** in shared flat central London. Phone 445 6775 after 6.30pm.
● **2 GAY GUYS** need un/furnished flat, B/S from July 0224 631158.
● **HETBOY 21** Humorist artcook bed. space to work SW 670 6298

Photographers' Gallery

Sue Davies recalls the early years of the Photographers' Gallery, the first publicly funded photography gallery in the world.

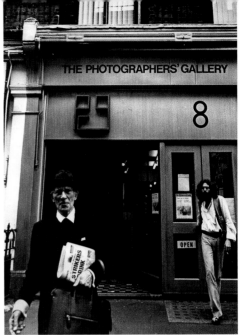

I got to know the area around Great Newport Street because it was near Charing Cross Road, which was where the bookshops were. At 77 Charing Cross Road there was Doug Dobell's jazz record shop, and 8 Great Newport Street used to be an old Lyons tea shop. My husband is a jazz musician, so on a Saturday morning everybody would buy their records at Doug's, then go round to the Lyons and boast to each other about what they'd got.

When I was looking for space, I thought it needed to be near Charing Cross Road, because books were where you saw photographs – no one bought them as objects in those days. Of the other places on that street, the Porcupine pub is still there, the bookshop opposite is still there, and the Spaghetti House is still there. In between, there were the *Oz* magazine offices and a late-night drinking club, the Kismet. The Arts Theatre was there, rather run-down. It was far more louche than it is now.

Before starting the gallery, I was working at the ICA, and after the Spectrum show, photographers came in hoping to show their work there. But the ICA wasn't interested in more photography, and there were no commercial galleries for them. The Royal Photographic Society was considered rather stuffy by professional photographers. There was the Kodak Galley in Holborn, but it focused on amateurs and was full of kittens and that kind of thing. Even the National Portrait Gallery had hardly any photography. I realised I was going to have to set up something myself.

I had to hunt for money from people like Kodak, bankers and newspapers. I was helped by a couple of photographers, Bill Jay and Bryn Campbell, who put me in touch with influential people such as Tom Hopkinson, who had edited *Picture Post* and became the first chairman of our trustees.

Great Newport Street became my patch. You knew everybody. Chinatown was just beginning, and there were still whores in Newport Court. Little Newport Street had lots of drinking clubs. Nick Hart-Williams, who used to do the films at the ICA and went on to establish the Other Cinema, let me share his office on Little Newport Street; and Spare Rib (which published its first issue in 1972) let me use their Roneo machine for our begging letters. It's a myth that I mortgaged our house (I just got into debt), but the story of people sleeping in the gallery has some basis – we had those big '70s floor cushions to which they added sleeping bags.

Photographers were really grateful to have a place to exhibit in. One of our first shows was Jacques-Henri Lartigue – he came over from France specially. Later we had André Kertész, who Henri Cartier-Bresson always credited as his greatest influence. Lester Bookbinder, then a very successful advertising photographer, thought it so important that he wanted to buy the whole show to circulate round colleges. Unfortunately, the $75-per-print turned out to be too expensive, although now I think they're all worth four or five grand.

David Puttnam, whose father had been a photographer, was a great help. At the time he was the agent for David Bailey, Brian Duffy and Terence Donovan, and as the years went by the 'creatives' from ad agencies started to buy photographic prints – partly as inspiration. The first degree course in photography also started in 1971 at the Regent Street Poly with Margaret Harker, so we got people coming out of college thinking that they were artists rather than just going to work in the trade. And, indeed, they were artists.

What I wanted to do was to show good prints in frames, and make people think about photography in a different way. Modern art had got to a point where everybody was frightened that people would think they were stupid because they didn't understand Carl Andre's bricks. Whereas with photography people came in happily and said exactly what they thought. Art for the people!

Sue Davies started the Photographers' Gallery in 1971 at 8 Great Newport Street, WC2. In 1980 it expanded into No.5. It is due to move into a purpose-built new home in Soho in 2011.

VISUAL ARTS

Way out East

VISUAL ARTS

It can be hard to spot an East End art gallery. An unassuming door with a small silver plaque above a buzzer is sometimes the only indication that an old shopfront or some rusty garage doors could actually be hiding a veritable cocoon of contemporary creation. For much of the week, the lights stay off while the proprietors of the more shoestring operations work their other thankless day jobs, but at weekends and on opening nights, these out-of-the-way venues come to life.

All great art capitals need incubators in which creativity can flourish and, arguably, artists first populated the postcodes of EC1 and N1, now Clerkenwell and Shoreditch, over 300 years ago. The medieval parish of St Giles-without-Cripplegate, for example, housed craftsmen belonging to artistic guilds or livery companies, and only members of the Painter-Stainers' Company could pursue employment as 'Face Painters [portraitists], History Painters, Arms [heraldic] Painters or House Painters [domestic decorators]'.

But fast-forward to modern times, and it was two abstract painters, Peter Sedgley and the now world-famous Bridget Riley, who set up the legendary SPACE studios in disused riverside warehouses by St Katharine Docks in 1968. This was apparently in response to the billboard-sized paintings by Americans such as Jackson Pollock and Mark Rothko that were beginning to filter across the Atlantic (first shown at Aldgate's venerable Whitechapel Gallery around 1960), which prompted British artists to start thinking bigger and beyond the easel.

The giant warehouses and light industrial buildings that sprang up in the voids left by the Blitz provided the perfect raw architectural environment for the scale and aesthetic of the work by a new generation of Young British Artists, whose leader-elect, Damien Hirst, staged their first landmark show, Freeze, in Docklands in 1988. There was no shortage of affordable live/work spaces in the East End at the time, and it was the settlement of artists such as Gilbert and George in Fournier Street and Helen Chadwick in the

Clockwise from above: the Whitechapel Gallery, with Faces in the Crowd (2004) and Jackson Pollock (1958); Vyner Street Studios. Plus a patient dog outside the White Cube.

colony of old workers' cottages in Beck Road that really cemented the area's artistic reputation.

It wasn't until the early 1990s that Hoxton Square became the focus of the growing East End art scene after one of the YBAs, painter Gary Hume, bought up some property alongside the studio of an unknown fashion designer, Alexander McQueen. In 1993, a brilliant young curator Joshua Compston (who died three years later aged just 25) staged the first annual 'Fête Worse Than Death' in a massive marquee on the grass there, with entertainment including a Beijing Opera, a pubic hair exchange and Tracey Emin reading palms. Since the YBA's favoured dealer Jay Jopling opened his gleaming White Cube emporium on the square in 2000, this historically lowly, crime-ridden square – originally known as Hogsdon in Domesday times, on account of the pigs kept there – has become achingly cool and the centre of more than just the art scene.

Now a new hub has emerged on Vyner Street in Bethnal Green, previously home to Huguenot weavers, Jewish refugees and now Pakistani, Bangladeshi and Bengali communities. The ever-changing clutch of galleries and studios on Vyner Street feels less like a district of commercial showrooms and more like a collective of art laboratories.

However, what's there today won't necessarily be there tomorrow, and there is a very real danger that none of London's art will still be made or exhibited in the area, say, in 25 years time, given how the capital's Orient is booming. In fact, the current popularity of east London and the influx of media businesses, estate agents and Olympic stadia that is threatening to drive out the artistic community is largely the fault of those avant-garde artists and pioneering galleries that colonised the boroughs of Hackney, Islington and Tower Hamlets in the first place. Wherever artists fear to tread, property developers will soon follow.

For now, the spirit of cooperation and camaraderie you encounter in every gallery feels like the East End art scene of old. You just have to get past the door. *Ossian Ward*

ART BY NUMBERS
£50m – cash!
For the Love of God, a diamond-encrusted skull by Damien Hirst. The artist's claim of the sale is disputed by some commentators.

£288,000
Paid for Banksy's *Space Girl and Bird*, 2007.

£45m
Raised in a single sale of contemporary art at Sotheby's, 2007.

68,000
Number of visitors to Frieze, 2007, including 151 of the world's leading galleries from 28 countries.

55.3%
Rise in value of contemporary art on the Hiscox Art Market Research Index.

Cash flow

The art merry-go-round used to be so simple, so quaint. The Old Masters and Impressionists were the most-valuable art assets one could dream of, but were available only to a very select group of highly knowledgeable and rich collectors, while a mere handful of contemporary galleries made their livings by selling the few big names. In the public sector, the government funded our venerable national museums handsomely enough, and everyone lived happily ever after.

That was the fairytale, because after a few cuts in National Lottery grants here and a funding nip and tuck there, the London art scene was starting to look starved of its divine cultural mandate to buy and exhibit works of art for the nation. This is where the much-vaunted 'Third Way' stepped in.

An early exponent of what could be deemed the steady privatisation of art was Charles Saatchi, the most serious and voracious collector of British art since Sir John Paul Getty. Throughout the 1990s, a rotating display at Saatchi's eponymous gallery showcased his 1,500-strong collection of young British (and German and American) art, while the pre-Modern Tate was realising that museums could not keep up with the private buyers.

After Saatchi and the YBA boom, London's art scene grew rapidly, but there had to be demand to meet this increase in supply. A breed of younger, more contemporary art-oriented collectors duly came from abroad and from the cash-rich City. Where money goes, the market follows, so as soon as London grabbed second place behind New York in terms of global art sales (with revenue in excess of £500m being mooted), the publishers of *Frieze* magazine decided it was time for an international art fair to complement the growing popularity of the capital as an art-buying mecca, and launched the first Frieze Art Fair in October 2003.

While all this was going on, auction records above the old glass ceiling of £1,000,000 for work by British artists, especially Damien Hirst, Lucian Freud and Francis Bacon, were constantly being smashed at Christie's and Sotheby's. Other collectors then opened their own art mausoleums in London, including Anita Zabludowicz's 176 Project Space, Canadian publisher Louise MacBain's LTB Institute and Ziba de Weck's Parasol Unit.

For the cash-strapped old art institutions the obvious answer was to follow the American model of private and corporate sponsorship. Huge deals between Tate and UBS or between the Frieze Art Fair and Deutsche Bank give hope that our museums will be fit to fight another day, but so far the trickle-down to the average art school graduate is negligible. *Ossian Ward*

VISUAL ARTS

John Lennon & Yoko Ono

By Tony Elliott

Grapefruit is the Yoko Ono paperback just published by Sphere Books. To launch the book, the publicity-conscious John and Yoko were interviewed by virtually every newspaper in the country. (The press officer called to say did we want to interview Yoko Ono? 'John Lennon's wife, you know?' He promised John would be there if we wanted to go.) The interview was done two weeks ago at the Lennons' Ascot home as just one of a tightly scheduled day of similar encounters with the media.

John: We've had tons of shit thrown at us over the last two years. I'm getting sick of it. It's just like I'm some guy who got lucky and won the pools and that's me Hawaiian prize! So anyone who's met her before, like you, won't have that attitude about her being a Hawaiian actress etc!

Yoko: *Grapefruit* is being published five or six years after the first printing, and I was afraid that it would be kind of dated, so I read it again. I saw that things like my Touch Poems have been translated into the Esslen psychiatric thing. But there are still loads of things that have not been picked up at all.

I think *Grapefruit* is still relevant because it's like a frame of mind, and once you get into it it's easy for anyone to be an artist. Everyone could start thinking like that and start doing creative things. People would then forget about being violent, because it's a form of resentment, a way of showing to people that they are not communicating. Violence is the saddest form of communication because it's the kind that doesn't make it at all. The best way to communicate is to open up your mind and show what you're thinking.

John: [Reading through a previous interview with Yoko] So you were quite intelligent before I met you, love!

Yoko: You've got a very good deal, and well you know it. What I'm doing is to use a way of communication, and if everyone picks it up it could promote peace.

Time Out: The forms have changed, though, from the earlier years. Are you still doing the sculpture pieces and things like the dance cards?

Yoko: Yes. 'War Is Over If You Want It' posters was my idea. I would have done that before, if I had had the money. It was possible because John was on my side. It's still like the dance thing, but on a larger scale.

Time Out: So you are conscious that, financially, you have the opportunity to achieve more than most people can?

Yoko: Yes. But it still isn't really very different. I want *Grapefruit* to be pushed and I came back specially from New York to do so.

John: It's a beautiful book that's more relevant than the I Ching or the fucking Bible.

Yoko: I was poor and doing things like earning bread at the time of writing *Grapefruit*. Instead of getting a job where I would have to work eight hours a day, I would get a janitor's job or something, so that I could spend my time writing. I used my head like that. In this society, if you relieve yourself from thinking properly then you can do things better. People inhibit themselves and every day spend energy and time killing themselves as human beings. John and I have a lot of energy because we don't kill ourselves and spend our energies.

John: The only thing we make money on is records. I can't help that and I'm not going to throw it down the drain now it's happening. The peace poster cost us £30,000. We subsidise ourselves like people used to subsidise classical music. We give relatively large sums of money away. It used to be to relatives, but now it's to people like Gypsies. I try to get it or somehow cheat it from Apple Films or some angle. Once you get money, people know it and charge you twice for everything. We think that's a fair people's tax!

Yoko: It means I can't make films cheaply any more, which was my pride and joy. So many things I used to get a kick out of I can't do any more, like I tried to live on nothing and tried to outdo the establishment by living like that.

John: I certainly don't agree with the philosophy that you can't be left-wing because you're rich. I just happen to be rich by a rather dubious process called showbusiness. We're artists, so we're revolutionaries too. The other revolutionaries we meet, whether it's Jerry Rubin, Abbie Hoffman or Tariq Ali, agree that our place is as artists. We're revolutionary artists. All we're doing is exactly the same as when we met, only instead of me being another poor artist, I'm a rich artist. I was reading this other interview to see how she's changed, but she hasn't. We might get some museum shows for her in New York in the fall. She has plenty more ideas and concept shows to put on. It was hard to get them to do anything before she was Mrs Lennon.

The bed event was the result of us lying in bed together for a few months. When we first met we didn't get out of bed and we wanted to find something we could do together. She wanted me to go down to Trafalgar Square and stand there in a black bag, like she used to. I said if I go down there, I'll get killed, and said let's go and do the most comfy thing. What we really like is being in bed, so we'll develop from things like that.

Yoko: We have to make money every day, let's face it, because we live in a society where money counts. But gradually we're doing various things. Everybody can be an artist, there's no necessary specialisation. The way we live here is exactly like I've always lived, except that there's more people here and the place is larger.

John: It's a very large council house. It's got three bedrooms! Yoko hasn't changed at all. Here she is putting out *Grapefruit* with the Dance Events in again. In the Syracuse exhibition, apart from some brand-new ideas, there'll be a section with her past work from the Indica shows etc. I don't think the money will have changed her development as an artist.

Yoko: You know the art world is very snobbish. For instance, I tried to do a show at the ICA. We went there and they were so snobbish! We said, please give me a show exactly as you would another artist who you think is good. I made that point clear. But they had to go round saying that John was offering them some money so I could get into the ICA! *World in Action* asked John to do a programme. I said why don't you include me and push my work, because I felt it was important. They said how could she have the nerve! The whole atmosphere was terrible in those days – you know 'Yoko trying to use John's name' etc. I would have used any other circumstances.

John: Or any other lover… I'm her favourite husband, you know.

Yoko: Even Sphere Books said, are we going to get John Lennon as well for the autographing session? It's like sometimes I am just a way to get to him. Unless John goes to the toilet or something, no one speaks to me.

John: I turned on to rock and she turned me on to avant-garde, or whatever you call it. In the early days, she would be sitting in the Beatles sessions and would say, 'Why is everything always four in the bar?' I would say that that was what we liked. To get there, she had to do it intellectually. You know – a form of art that's a heartbeat, heartbeat is primitive, primitive means it's OK, that's great. She really turned me on to filmmaking. I was just messing around with 8mm, but she made me do it properly. I love it. I want to have them on at the Odeon.

Yoko: We concentrate our minds in trying to free ourselves to do whatever we want, and for that we need some money. It's like having a baby. It's a great drag for a woman, taking nine months, and after eight you just count the days to go! Similarly, some of the most beautiful things that happen take a slow time to work, and most impatient people just try and use violence instead of being patient and doing it like a woman has a baby. Do it gradually, and then the whole world would really be peaceful.

John: It's got to be like natural law, Mother Nature or whatever. Our duty is to keep the balance rather that let it go the other way. The main problem today is to keep the balance.

Yoko: The next generation is going to be better, just an inch better. I know my generation is better than my mother's. *Grapefruit* could help indirectly in the way my Touch Poems and concerts may have helped people to communicate better. If I've turned one person on, then I'm happy. John and I have turned each other on, and that's enough in a way.

Time Out: Do you follow through completely? Like 'Cold Turkey' was about drug addiction, so have you done anything to help junkies?

John: I'm not here to help junkies. Don't you see I have my own problems? I can't go around setting up schools for junkies, I have my own day-to-day problems with that scene. Singing 'Cold Turkey' is my contribution to junkies. I'm not telling people not to do it. All I'm saying is that it hurts. That's my contribution. I'm an artist – I'm not anything else, so I sing about the pain I had with that situation. I can't give any more than art. Setting up a rehabilitation centre would be like sending a bag of rice to India.

Yoko: We're not that rich and the money we can give is relatively small. We give more in our songs and our work.

John: We have to go. How about just one more question?

Time Out: Why don't you ask me one for a change?

Yoko: Well, what are you going to write about *Grapefruit*? How much space do you think you'll give it?

Lisson Gallery

I set up Lisson Gallery in 1967 while I was at the Slade. In some respects, it would never have happened without the enthusiasm of Derek Jarman (who was an older postgraduate student), or without my anxiety that I would soon be out in the big world as a practising artist, along with 15,000 others. It was clear through my art history studies and my observations of artists' careers that the chances of being able to make a living and simultaneously stay sane were pretty remote. I also realised that there were almost no spaces for younger artists to show work in. The Cork Street galleries seemed very provincial and backward as I eagerly read the first issues of *Artforum* and *Studio International*.

London was in the last throes of the Swinging Sixties and the hippy generation. People went to the Roundhouse to see John 'Hoppy' Hopkins and Suzie Creamcheese, stayed up late, and did acid and dope. I was interested in this scene, but not an integral part of it. I became interested in the concrete poetry movement, and then the emerging thoughtfulness and debate with the minimal artists and the emerging conceptualists. Many were five or ten years older than me at the time – I was only 20 when the gallery started.

I soon became aware that there was a much bigger, more exciting art world outside London, outside Britain – in Germany and France and, in particular, New York. There was also an enormous hunger here to see and meet the artists that people had been reading about in the international art press.

I mugged up as much as I could and went and spent time in those countries, and made contact with artists such as Dan Graham, Dan Flavin, Carl Andre, Robert Ryman, Hans Haacke and Sol LeWitt. They were surprised that someone had actually come from London and sought them out; I was among the first to express interest. Lisson was really the first gallery to maintain a coherent international programme in London.

There were only two really switched-on collectors in London at that time: Ted Power and his son, Alan. Ted had a brilliant collection from Brancusi to Barnett Newman; he was a great mentor and supporter of Lisson in the early days. The gallery gathered respectful support from European and American collectors and museums.

Over a few years in the late 1960s and early '70s, other independent galleries came and went. There was Nigel Greenwood at Glebe Place, Situation in Horseshoe Yard, and others. The Mayfair Gallery in Bond Street, which was run by Ira Gale and Robert Self (ex-partner of the Situation Gallery), was backed by Princess Miriam of Jahore. We were all very envious and admiring of their resources, though she ended up withdrawing her support and became disenchanted with the art world. That was the history of a lot of galleries – it was very fragile.

Lisson, from the early '70s onwards, mounted the first London exhibitions of many of the most significant international artists of the time: Art & Language, Richard Long, Donald Judd, Dan Flavin, Jo Baer, Hans Haacke, Carl Andre, Robert Ryman, Robert Mangold, Dan Graham, Michael Asher, Sol LeWitt, John Latham, Giulio Paolini, Peter Joseph, On Kawara and Daniel Buren.

This was the first major phase of the gallery. The next generation of British sculptors was the next logical step – beginning with Tony Cragg in the late '70s, followed by Bill Woodrow, Richard Deacon, Anish Kapoor, Shirazeh Houshiary and, a little later, the younger Julian Opie. This became a defining moment in the growth of Lisson, as these were all British artists who benefited greatly from being launched internationally with the gallery's existing reputation and connections.

Remaining in Bell Street, regardless of fashion, has given Lisson an unusual and mysterious stability. When I started, the area was much the same as it is now, perhaps a bit scruffier. The artists liked it because it wasn't trying to pretend to be anything. Now the gallery is in a stable and mature phase. We continue to give our full support to the historical artists we continue to work with, the middle generation and the emerging artists that we find interesting, in the same spirit as the earlier days. It is quite remarkable how London, which was on the periphery, has now become centre stage.

Nicholas Logsdail founded Lisson Gallery in 1967. He remains its director. Lisson Gallery is at 29 & 52-54 Bell Street, NW1.

David Hockney

Whitechapel
18 April 1970

Paintings and drawings and the complete prints 1960-70. The opportunity of seeing several years of work raises Hockney's stature way above that of being just a 'Pop' artist. It's particularly interesting to see his recent work entering the area of 'photographic realism' that is becoming widespread in the States, but has not been much in evidence over here yet. Hockney cites the influence of Edward Hopper, who is one of the forefathers of this tendency, in the interview in the expensive but informative catalogue.

Angela Flowers Gallery

D'Arblay Street
10 December 1971

In a field where more businesses go bust than new ones open, it is interesting when the unlikely survive. Angela Flowers first opened her gallery two years ago above the AIA on Lisle Street. The rooms were so small they seemed like the art world's answer to Matchbox cars.

Since September, she has moved to larger premises on D'Arblay Street. The new gallery, with one large room given to exhibition space, and another, almost as large, used as a kitchen, office and meeting space, retains some of the personal atmosphere of a home and a kind of aura of sensible, middle-class respectability that Angela Flowers epitomises.

Saatchi Collection

Saatchi Gallery
25 April 1985

The collection, to be shown in parts at three- to four-monthly intervals, begins with Warhol, including his famous Campbell's soup can, his media personalities like Chairman Mao, Marilyn and Elvis, and the horrifying Electric Chair and Disaster series. Plus Cy Twombly's tasteful graffiti, Donald Judd's ultra-cool minimalism, and Brice Marden's geometric exactitude. *Sarah Kent*

Turner Prize

Tate
10 November 1993

This year the K Foundation (formerly the KLF) intend to turn up and give £40,000 to the 'worst' artist of the four, according to votes sent in by 'the people'. To this end they have placed ads , with ballot papers printed on them, in magazines and newspapers. 'Let the people choose,' they say. 'Who is the worst of them all?' *David Lillington*

Tight Roaring Circle

Roundhouse
9 April 1997

The principal feature of the Roundhouse's re-animation is a huge bouncy castle, on which visitors are encouraged to bounce. In the darkened space, the luminous white inflatable is floodlit. This, and musician Joel Ryan's computer-generated soundtrack booming from giant speakers, increases the sense of being an extra in a theatrical event.

Certainly the positioning of a bouncy castle here is nonsensical, although combining gothic turrets and crenellations with a classic Victorian industrial building of cast iron and timber has more than a hint of some aspects of po-mo architectural practice.

As a spectacle, Tight Roaring Circle is funny and an unexpected chance for exercise. But to pretend it is anything other than that really is nonsense. And I'm not sure that £4.50 represents good value for admission to a bouncy castle in Camden. *Mark Currah*

Monet, Royal Academy, 1999

Sensation

Royal Academy
24 September 1997

On the walls of these august chambers have hung pictures by Titian and Tiepolo, Turner and Constable, Picasso and Braque. Would the Young British Artists (YBAs) be up to the test, or would their work prove to be high on shock value and low on enduring qualities, as hostile critics have claimed?

How would installations such as Jake and Dinos Chapman's *Tragic Anatomies* survive these smartened circumstances? Cruising through such salubrious spaces, would Damien Hirst's shark seem more of a tiddler than a ravening predator?

I needn't have worried: the work occupies the galleries magnificently, and holds its own against the art of the past. The show demonstrates without a shadow of a doubt that, although only in their 30s, most of these artists are world class.

Hung so that you see it through a series of doorways, Marcus Harvey's portrait of Myra Hindley also gains its mesmeric ferocity through the juxtaposition of opposites – evil and innocence, small and large, touch and vision, the immediate and the mythic. Had Harvey made an ordinary portrait of the Moors murderer, I doubt a single eyebrow would have been raised. But by using the cast of a child's hand to make a giant painting of the familiar police mug shot, he invests the image with almost unbearable pathos. The mask-like face becomes a huge icon of evil.

The frenzy of outrage whipped up by the press is as savage as it is ritualistic. The resulting attack on the portrait last Thursday, first with red and blue ink, then with egg, caused such damage that over the

VISUAL ARTS

weekend it was removed for specialist restoration. *Sarah Kent*

Monet in the 20th Century
Royal Academy
27 January 1999
Seeing the Monet exhibition will be a problem. With advance bookings numbering 150,000, buying a ticket will be the first hurdle; once inside the show, getting a reasonable view of the pictures will be the second.

I envisage processions of people trooping round the galleries a few feet from the walls. At that distance you'll only see the surfaces – the blobs, smudges, dabs and squiggles that are layered into dense meshes of colour. But the marks themselves are not important; the trick of appreciating Monet is to look through rather than at the surface of his paintings. Given the expected hordes, I suggest going late in the evening or waiting until the promised 24-hour opening and booking for two in the morning. It will be worth it. *Sarah Kent*

Eighteen Turns
Serpentine Pavilion
4 July 2001
Commissioned by the Serpentine Gallery as the second in an excellent series designed to bring innovative architecture to public view, Daniel Libeskind's structure is like a sequence of angular bridges that

intersect to create a space that feels like a room, yet is not enclosed. The raised level and the nifty overlay of planes that provide the walls and ceiling ensure that those inside remain dry even in heavy rain. The pavilion is more like a sculpture than a building; with the skin and supporting structure made from a single material – aluminium – it has a degree of coherence normally impossible in an architectural space. *Sarah Kent*

Chris Ofili
Victoria Miro
3 July 2002
Upstairs, you are in for a big surprise. The architect David Adjaye has built a room that eliminates daylight. This chapel-like chamber houses Ofili's *Last Supper*: lining the walls are 12 paintings spotlit so that they glow like stained glass. Each disciple occupies his own picture and, seen in profile, each faces the smiling image of Christ

who dominates the scene from the end wall. Wait for it, though – they are all monkeys.

With each panel differently coloured, the gathering seems like a rainbow of spiritual potential. *Sarah Kent*

Gilbert & George
Tate Modern
21 February 2007
Are they irreverent or reverent, are they serious or joking? You may not be any the wiser having left Gilbert & George's Major Exhibition, which flits schizophrenically between godly and sinful, and from innocence to torment, but you will have made two pensioners very happy indeed.

Some of the difficulty in pinning down these sprightly artistes lies in their ability to tap into public opinion at just the right time: the racial tensions of the late '70s morph into issues of sexuality and AIDS in the '80s, which spiral into the paranoid noise of the politically-correct

'90s and then come back full circle to the religious and racial uncertainties of today. Given that this is no mean achievement, their idiosyncratic ruminations on the world justify the unprecedented scale of this exhibition – a whole level of Tate Modern had never been given over to one living artist before.

They might have seemed odd and wilfully obtuse before their time, but after spitting, shitting and spunking their way through a 30-year career they now stand as the eternally youthful (or, at least, youth-obsessed), predictably perverse Peter Pans of the London art world.

Nevertheless, the 1977 *Dirty Words Pictures* are destined to remain their real triumphs, not only in composition and content, but in their keen depiction of social dysfunction as well. One of these lyrical but tough works even went as far as answering the ensuing decades' worth of critics who denounced their scandalous affronts against art and accused

them of courting controversy, in one simple bit of graffito: 'Are you angry or are you boring?' *Ossian Ward*

Event Horizon
Hayward
22 May 2007
There is a charming series of children's books called 'Where's Wally?' in which the aim is to spot the tall, gangly-framed cartoon fellow, smiling behind round glasses amid a crowd of people on a beach, at a fairground or in a bustling museum. Many passers-by on Waterloo Bridge have already been playing 'Where's Gormley?' by picking out some of the 31 body-casts of Antony Gormley dotted around the busy skyline surrounding the Southbank Centre.

Gormley's vision of our place within the built environment is, however, unremittingly grim. All the harsh, grey, robotic avatars of Event Horizon look despondent and hunched, as if being layered and cast in plaster repeatedly was a gruelling performance for Gormley himself.

He suffers for his art, and, to some extent, so do we – the feeling of being alone in our bodies and in space is one we can all understand.

Perhaps the 'Where's Gormley?' game alleviates some of this coldness. One Londoner has already softened Event Horizon, by slinging a white T-shirt over a figure on an adjacent office block. *Ossian Ward*

Event Horizon, Hayward, 2007

VISUAL ARTS

Graffiti 2.0

Vandalism, social protest or museum pieces? How 'graffiti' became art.

By Ossian Ward

Graffiti has always been a dirty word for a dirty form of mark-making that blights our city's walls and trains. Night after night, indecipherable tags and secret codes are scrawled on railway sidings and pedestrian bridges, and dripping silver spraypaint smears every other high-street shopfront. Most passers-by are immune to its messages; others are confused, or angered by the visual intrusion into their daily commute.

Yet, all of a sudden, London is now embracing its disenfranchised *plein-air* daubers, and they aren't being derided as criminals or delinquents any longer. Graffiti has gained a newly acceptable face, alternatively called 'street art', 'urban art' or even 'post-graffiti'. Much of this is still close to original graffiti's brash and bold aesthetic, but now hangs in galleries on canvas or on paper, selling for high prices and adorning the mantelpieces of admiring collectors. So how did this once lowly act of vandalism gain such credence almost overnight?

First came the word – which is why graffiti culture relies on the use of language to disseminate its message – and, in London at least, the tradition of scrawling words on walls is more established than one might think. From desperate records of dwindling existence etched into the cells of the Tower of London in the 1650s and even older examples of public toilet humour, all the way up to the kind of political sloganeering that helped free a wrongly convicted man in 1976 ('G Davis is innocent'), graffiti has always been a way to leave a mark on the world and convey a message that otherwise would not be heard.

The city around us not only influences but hems us in and keeps us in our place, so graffiti is a release from that, a burst of colour or resistance in a grey world. It was the disenfranchised youth of gangland America who progressed beyond simply marking their territory to painting 'pieces' (from the word masterpieces) in the early '1970s; their style and attitude were exported to London along with hip hop music. It took hold in the mid '80s in inner-city areas such as Brixton and Westbourne Grove, with small brigades of writers 'tagging' their names all over town. Pseudonyms such as Robbo and Drax (after James Bond's enemy in *Moonraker*) were near ubiquitous on the tube, but the most famous of all was Mode 2, who set up the first renowned graffiti crew, the Chrome Angelz.

VISUAL ARTS

POLLARD STREET

Banksy's witty, instantly recognisable stencils have brought graffiti off the street and into the gallery, where his work commands huge prices.

Soon, designated 'halls of fame' for graffiti sprang up in housing estates and train yards from Neasden to Hammersmith.

However, after waves of bad publicity and the first graf-related death of a young 'bomber' named Evil in 1987, the British Transport Police (better known as the dreaded BTP) launched a fully-fledged graffiti squad to keep pace with the rampant crews, whose in-fighting escalated from merely 'lining' through or 'dogging' rival pieces to all-out violence and wanton criminal damage. The famous London crews – World Domination (WD), the Subway Saints (SBS) and Drop the Bomb

Coming to a street near you? New-wave graffiti courtesy of Adam Neate (top) and D-Face (below).

(DTB) – began to fracture and splinter. Many of those pioneering writers, including Eine and Astek, went on to paint legal commissions, and are at the heart of today's scene, but that doesn't quite explain why Graffiti 2.0 has reached such heights of popularity and acceptance.

Since 2000, newspapers began to run stories, seemingly from a parallel universe, in which ignorant councils were accused of whitewashing over treasured murals and masterpieces painted by hooded men under cover of darkness. It was clear that attitudes had changed. The media frenzy initially centred on one man, the graffiti world's very own Scarlet Pimpernel, the bearded thirtysomething from Bristol called Robert Banks or just Banksy (he could also be tall or short, fat or skinny and black or Asian, depending on who you believe).

While his chosen medium of sprayed-on stencils was nothing new (recalling as it did the anarchic ad campaigns and 'subvertising' of punk bands such as Crass, who covered the Underground with their feminist, anti-consumerist slogans in the early '80s), Banksy's signature images of kissing coppers, flower-chucking terrorists and mischievous rats on doorways and side streets were immediately consumable, and soon became highly sought after – and ludicrously expensive.

In spite of a glut of pseudo-Banksy copycats looking to cash in on his forced anonymity (although prosecution for his years of paint-inflicted property damage would probably cause a public outcry), a whole street art industry has now formed in London, with young galleries and artists selling prints and unique pieces of accessible graffiti. So although the boom may have begun with Banksy, his witty one-liners will certainly not be the last word in street art, especially now that

there's an emerging generation of artists like D-Face and Pure Evil, who are less concerned with painting illicit and illegible pieces for the benefit of their tiny community than they are with attaining a wider fame and bigger audiences.

Also, artists such as Adam Neate and CutUp are no longer constrained by the medium of spraypaint on walls, and are now incorporating all kinds of street furniture – from signage to statuary – into ad hoc installations, impulsive public interventions and increasingly political statements. Either way, the widening of the term graffiti has led to an explosion in buying and selling this previously unobtainable commodity.

If history is repeating itself, the London graffiti scene will crash and burn as it did in New York after the '80s art boom. In this scenario, only a few devotees will continue to make serious work, and graffiti will go back underground, where there will always be a steady stream of restless teenage boys who feel compelled to spray their immature artistic seed on any available vertical surface. However, the sophistication of today's artists suggest that graffiti, street art, or whatever it's called, will be around for many years to come, perhaps even crossing over into the museum collections and art history books as well.

Ossian Ward is Visual Arts Editor of *Time Out*.

HEDONISM INTRODUCTION
SEX CITYSCAPE FASHION
SOCIETY SHOPPING COMEDY
DRAMA PROTEST & POLITICS
VISUAL ARTS **PERFORMANCE**
LITERATURE GANGS OPINION
COCKNEYS BARS ON SCREEN
DANCE MUSIC TELEVISION
BUILDINGS CLUBS NIGHTLIFE
SPORT & FITNESS MEMORIES
STYLE FOOD & DRINK GIGS
CONSUME RIOTS REFERENCE

Fringe
benefits

The abolition of censorship in 1968 allowed London's underground theatre to blossom, but since then fringe has grown into a garden of many and varied delights.

By Jane Edwardes

The theatre critic, Kenneth Tynan, called him the 'Royal Smut-Hound'. Others knew him by the quaint title of Lord Chamberlain, and before 1968 his office was responsible for vetting every new play before it could be staged. Powers that had existed since 1737 were disastrously toughened in 1843, effectively allowing the Chamberlain to object to anything he – and it was always a he – found offensive. References to religion, living politicians, the royal family, sex, bad language and defecation could all be contentious. Quite often the Chamberlain saw filth where it was never intended.

For years he laid a dead hand on British theatre, until his powers were finally abolished by Harold Wilson's government in 1968. Immediately, the American musical *Hair* opened at the Shaftesbury Theatre, a celebration of free love, nudity and smoking dope that also attacked American involvement in the Vietnam War.

As censorship bowed out, fringe, otherwise known as underground theatre, blossomed, making the most of the new-found freedom, although it is unlikely that playwrights such as Howard Brenton and Snoo Wilson would have meekly trooped off with their script and ten-guinea fee in hand to ask for their plays to be censored. In fact, many shows were never written down, and the proliferation of venues round the country would have made it hard for the Lord Chamberlain to keep pace with the refuseniks whose work he would surely have objected to.

The word fringe was borrowed from the Edinburgh Festival and acknowledged the fact that the movement existed outside of the hierarchical structures of mainstream theatre.

Fringe companies played gigs, not shows, reflecting an affinity with rock musicians rather than with those who worked in the West End. Theatre was hip and the Roundhouse, in particular, promoted fringe companies – such as Steven Berkoff's London Theatre Group – alongside its rock stars. Some companies, influenced by events in Paris, wanted to change the world. Others were fascinated by the French playwright Antonin Artaud and his fondness for ritual and what he described as 'Theatre of Cruelty'.

At a time when so many believed in the power of the imagination, theatre was a cheap and accessible way to be creative, boosted by the ease with which one could claim the dole, as well as the energy of a number of Americans who settled in Britain at the time, including Jim Haynes (Arts Lab), Nancy Meckler (Freehold and Shared Experience), Dan Crawford (King's Head), Charles Marowitz (Open Space) and Ed Berman (Arts Theatre). There were seminal visits from companies such as Café La Mama, Joe Chaikin's Open Theatre and the Living Theatre, whose members lived as a commune and specialised in an aggressive combination of nudity, politics and audience participation.

It was also helpful that *Time Out* was launched in 1968, in that it provided free advertising for cash-strapped companies and acted as a noticeboard for those who worked in the field.

In London, the Arts Lab in Drury Lane was the home of counter-culture for music and films as well as theatre, where the smell of dope wafted in the air. It was as exclusive in its own way as the often derided Royal Opera House. 1968 also saw the launch of Charles Marowitz's Open Space in a

Posters for assorted productions at the Roundhouse in the 1960s and '70s.

Tottenham Court Road cellar, where he attracted the assistance of a performer called Thelma Holt, nowadays a well-known West End producer. The Oval House, a youth club in Kennington, was a popular place to play, and was run by Peter Oliver before he ran away to join a company himself. Lunchtime theatre was, strangely, considered to be a radical option – presumably because of the opportunity to attract a different audience. Fred Proud and Verity Bargate set up the Soho Theatre and Ed Berman launched the Almost Free Theatre club just off Piccadilly Circus, where seat prices lived up to its name: members of the audience were free to decide how much they would put in the pot.

The major touring companies were Portable, Freehold, the People Show, and Pip Simmons. Portable Theatre, founded by David Hare and Tony Bicat, was unusual in that it stuck to new writing, attracting the talents of Howard Brenton, Chris Wilkinson and Snoo Wilson, and staging plays that were obsessed with violence, corruption and decay. The titles say it all: *Plays for Rubber Go Go Girls*, *Hitler Dances* and *Blow Job*. Nancy Meckler's Freehold, in contrast, was more interested in ritual and movement, making its name with a version of *Antigone* in which all references to 'The Gods' were changed to 'Love'.

The long-lasting, highly influential People Show produced anarchic, lyrical shows that dazzled the imagination. Pip Simmons's devised pieces – such as the *George Jackson Black and White Minstrel Show* – were vaudeville attacks on liberal complacency, combining the anger of Portable with the physicality of Freehold.

The '70s and beyond

The death of fringe theatre was first declared as early as 1973, confirming director Peter Hall's belief that every new theatrical movement has a five-year life span. By then it was clear that the revolution wasn't going to happen. Poor pay and uncomfortable touring in unreliable vans eventually took its toll. People fell out with each other. Freehold folded in 1972, the year that Portable went bankrupt, leaving those involved to abandon the fringe and seek out a wider, more challenging audience at the Nottingham Playhouse and the National Theatre. Although he later retracted, Pip Simmons announced his retirement to *Time Out* in 1973, declaring that 'The circuit has revealed itself as being totally empty except as a means to earn a living. It's just a lot of small arts theatres and university centres full of intelligent people. The scene is supposedly left, but these left-wing people have no struggle. There's no real politics in England.'

If the war had been lost, there was still the possibility of winning a number of smaller skirmishes and the early '70s saw a growth in companies that gave voice to sections of the community that had been pushed to the sidelines

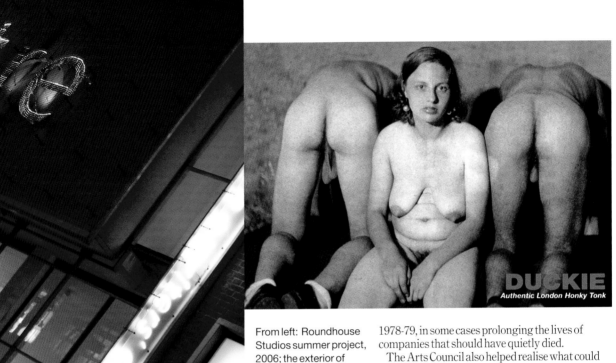

DUCKIE
Authentic London Honky Tonk

From left: Roundhouse Studios summer project, 2006; the exterior of Soho Theatre; and a flyer for Duckie's 'event culture' at the Royal Vauxhall Tavern.

or even oppressed. Admittedly, the work could be simplistic and usually performed to their own interest groups, but these companies filled the gaps that the bigger theatres shamefully avoided.

The Dark and Light Theatre, Temba, Brixton Arts and many others presented the black experience on stage. Jatinder Verma at Tara Arts gave the classics an Indian spin, as he still does today. The Women's Theatre Group was set up in 1973, and initially discomfited its host venues with its female roadies and technicians. It still tours today under the name of Sphinx. Monstrous Regiment set out in 1975 to discover and encourage new women writers. Gay Sweatshop began life at the Almost Free the same year, its actors bringing comfort and courage to isolated and/or closeted gays round the country. Graeae, a company for disabled people, started in 1980 under the charismatic Nabil Shaban.

Inevitably, the Arts Council was a bête noir from the beginning, constantly berated by fringe companies who delighted in trotting off to demonstrate outside its offices, then in Piccadilly. But in fact, the Council was a benign supporter of fringe in the '70s, dramatically increasing its funding from £15,000 in 1969-70 to over £1.5m in 1978-79, in some cases prolonging the lives of companies that should have quietly died.

The Arts Council also helped realise what could be called the first supergroup. Joint Stock was the idea of Max Stafford-Clark, who had been running the Traverse Theatre in Edinburgh, William Gaskill who had just left the Royal Court, and David Aukin, who had managed Freehold, organised the Fringe Festival at the Cockpit in 1971 and had recently formed Foco Novo with Roland Rees. It was, in the words of the company's historian, Rob Ritchie, 'a company that could act as a bridgehead between the small-scale studios of the fringe and the bigger stages, a company that could retain the flexible methods of the fringe yet have access to better facilities, reach a broader audience and achieve higher standards.' It did all this with such notable productions as *Fanshen*, *Cloud Nine*, *Epsom Downs* and *The Ragged Trousered Philanthropists*, playing in London at the ICA, the Royal Court and the Roundhouse.

After the plenty of the 1970s, the '80s proved difficult for theatre of all kinds, as the Conservative government looked at the success of the Andrew Lloyd Webber musicals in the West End and wondered why the arts needed subsidising at all. It began to pressurise companies into finding more and more sponsorship from the private sector. Some fringe companies lost their Arts Council grants, although the GLC was there to pick up the baton until it was abolished in 1986. Even so, it was clear that the network of fringe theatres, with or without a manifesto, was here to stay. In 1980 there were nearly 50 such places in London. Some of these, such as the Bush, the Orange Tree and Hampstead (although *Time Out* could never decide whether Hampstead was a fringe theatre or not), were sufficiently subsidised by the Arts Council to mount their own productions, and had a distinctive identity. They were also able to pay Equity rates

Punchdrunk's *The Masque of the Red Death* at BAC, 2007.

and actors were just as happy to play at these theatres as they were to traipse off to the regions, which were in decline as a result of severe Arts Council cuts. Fringe theatre was increasingly reviewed in the broadsheets, and casting agents were far more likely to take a tube to Islington – however scruffy the venue – than to head up the M1 to Sheffield.

In addition, the arrival of the Almeida and the Tricycle, both opened in 1980 and both larger than most other venues, appealed to the more established touring companies. The former played host throughout the '80s to Theatre de Complicite, and was firmly put on the map when the company played a whole season there in 1989, including *The Visit*, thus inspiring a whole generation of would-be actors to travel to Paris to study physical theatre with Jacques le Coq.

Touring companies often turned to the classics, especially when they discovered they were easier to sell to their bookers. The Almeida hosted the first appearance of Kick theatre in London, started by Deborah Warner and committed to scrupulous productions of the classics. Cheek by Jowl quickly made a name for itself by presenting an astonishing number of British premieres of European plays, from Racine's *Andromaque* to Corneille's *Le Cid*.

Despite all the difficulties, new theatres continually appeared, including the Old Red Lion, the Man in the Moon, the Etcetera and the Finborough. In the '70s, many had suggested that publicans should be paying the companies who played in their old function rooms for bringing in extra business. That proved a fantasy by the end of the '80s, when the pubs were charging higher and higher rents, frequently leasing the space to a young impresario who took on the task of renting out the theatre. Some concentrated on the quality of the work, taking a box office split if necessary; others set out to make as much profit as they could, presenting two or three different shows every night. The quality was variable, to say the least, and much of the work was there simply to showcase the talents of those involved – whose ultimate aim was to join the mainstream. There was no longer a sense of the fringe being an alternative to the establishment.

Once Ian McDiarmid and Jonathan Kent took over the Almeida in 1989, and Sam Mendes and Caro Newling, backed by the Ambassadors Theatre Group, moved into the Donmar Warehouse the following year, it became obvious that fringe as a term was becoming more confusing than helpful. Both theatres challenged the National Theatre and the RSC, and became famous for their high production standards, sexy, glamorous casting, and A-list audiences. They illustrated the increasing chasm between their work, along with that at the Bush, Hampstead and the Young Vic, and those unsubsidised venues presenting a play about

'Members of Living Theatre lived as a commune and specialised in an aggressive combination of nudity, politics and audience participation.'

flatmates, on a budget of £50. In 1992, *Time Out* decided that the old Fringe section should be divided into two, one part to be called Off-West End, which consisted of theatres that produced their own shows, and the other to remain as it was.

There were a few protestors, including a very small demonstration outside the *Time Out* offices, organised by Brian McDermott, who first started the Bush – he handed out leaflets dressed in a combination of Nazi uniform and fishnet stockings. But most felt that the decision was long overdue, and others quickly followed suit.

The fringe today

Fringe theatre is still an important part of London's theatre culture. The Royal Vauxhall Tavern, London's longest surviving gay venue, became home to Duckie in 1995, when it began staging what Simon Casson, the company's founder, has described as event culture. 'It's not theatre; it's not cabaret; it's not a club. It's something in between. A place where dancing girls and oompapah meet live art culture.'

Equally interesting today are companies that have shunned the often confined rooms of the fringe and created their own performing spaces, indoors and out, believing that where they perform has a profound effect on what they perform. It wasn't an entirely new trend; in 1987 Neil Bartlett presented *A Vision of Love Revealed in Sleep*, a tribute to the life of the Pre-Raphaelite artist Simeon Solomon, performing naked among the puddles of a disued warehouse in the backstreets near Tower Bridge.

In 2000, a collective called Shunt turned up in a railway vault in Bethnal Green and tapped into the zeitgeist with a show about terrorism called *Dance Bear Dance*. The audience got a shock when it discovered that an identical show was being performed simultaneously to a separate audience next door. Interestingly, Shunt weren't keen to describe what they did as fringe or theatre. Later, they moved closer to the centre of the city, to more railway vaults at London Bridge, where they now not only present their own shows but also curate other companies who feel more at home in Shunt's clubbing atmosphere than in more conventional theatres.

Punchdrunk took the idea even further. The Exeter graduates first came to London with *Sleep No More* in Kennington. But they really made their mark with *Faust*, when they took over an old office block near Tower Bridge and used the whole building as a gigantic set, creating forests, bars, a diner, church, fleapit and sleazy hotel. Audience members were given anonymous masks to wear and were free to wander round the building at will, bumping into scenes at random and creating their own story out of what they saw.

In 2007, Punchdrunk collaborated with BAC in Battersea, a place that has always welcomed people who want to explore new ideas about theatre and about the relationship between actors and audience. Punchdrunk used BAC's Victorian building, once the old town hall, to create another immersive experience, *The Masque of the Red Death*, inspired by Edgar Allan Poe.

The belief in an impending revolution may have gone, but as long as there are new young artists who want to be independent and free to realise their own vision, fringe theatre will surely survive.

Jane Edwardes is Theatre Editor of *Time Out*.

TIMELINE

1968
Theatrical censorship ends as the office of the Lord Chamberlain is abolished. The first show to take advantage of the new climate is hippy musical *Hair*, which opens in the West End.

Sadler's Wells Opera moves to the Coliseum (in 1974 it becomes English National Opera).

1970
Dan Crawford founds the King's Head Theatre at the back of a pub in Islington.

1976
Denys Lasdun's brutalist concrete home for the National Theatre opens on the South Bank.

1978
Dance Umbrella founded as a showcase for emerging choreographers.

1979
The Comedy Store opens above a strip club in Soho.

1980
Michael Bogdanov's National Theatre production of Howard

Brenton's play *The Romans in Britain* is the subject of an unsuccessful prosecution by Mary Whitehouse, who objects to a scene depicting a homosexual rape.

1982
The Barbican Arts Centre opens (though it is several years before anyone can find it).

1985
Cameron Mackintosh's production of *Les Misérables* opens at the Barbican before moving to the West End, where it has run without interruption ever since.

1988
Michael Clark collaborates with Mark E Smith of the Fall on punk ballet *I Am Curious Orange*.

1989
Darcey Bussell is promoted to principal at the Royal Ballet, the youngest ballerina to occupy the position.

1995
Sarah Kane's first play, *Blasted*, is performed upstairs at the Royal Court and immediately establishes her as an important new voice.

Harold Pinter writes her a fan letter.

1996
BBC documentary *The House* lays bare management failures at the Royal Opera House, Covent Garden.

1997
Shakespeare's Globe opens on the South Bank.

2001
The RSC announces that it will leave its home at the Barbican after nearly 20 years.

2002
The Laban centre for contemporary dance moves into stunning new premises beside a muddy creek in Deptford. The building is designed by architects Herzog & de Meuron, who also created Tate Modern.

2003
Kevin Spacey joins the Old Vic as artistic director.

2006
The Roundhouse reopens after a £30m facelift. The inaugural performance in the new space is post-industrial dance-rave spectacular *Fuerzabruta*.

●AFFECTIONATE, caring male, professional musician, 35 in relationship crisis, needs kind, understanding lady for friendship. Teledate: 0839 813389.

●COUNTRY MALE, 55, handsome, slender but not mean, with Gloucestershire house and flat in London. Seeks meaningful relationship with compatible young woman of slender means. Teledate: 0839 813391.

●ATTRACTIVE PROFESSIONAL GAY, 30, slim, boyish, smooth, seeks similar, non-scene, discreet guy, 24-35, for sincere relationship, holidays, restaurants, theatres and walks. Teledate: 0839 813397.

●PROFESSIONAL OUTGOING DYNAMIC male, 5'5", 29 years, fit, brown hair and eyes, well travelled, seeks pretty woman for partying, romance and weekends away. Teledate: 0839 813398.

●AMERICAN WRITER, 47, male seeks female. Teledate: 0839 813455.

●HANDSOME BLACK GUY, 29, honest and sincere, seeks attractive, white female, 22-29, for friendship and fun. Teledate: 0839 813458.

●SPECIAL OFFER! SPECIAL OFFER! SPECIAL OFFER! For details call 071-465 8880. Teledate: 0839 813460.

●GAY GUY, 35, tall, slim, attractive, fun loving and intelligent, seeks well adjusted, considerate guy, 21 +, for fun and perhaps more. Teledate: 0839 813483.

●TALL SLIM MAN, 42, seeks woman, late 20s to early 40s, who would equally enjoy a night of sleazy blues, swimming with wild dolphins or exploring a forest at dawn on a clear spring morning. Teledate: 0839 813484.

●WIN THE POOLS. Genuine/stylish single lady, early 30s, varied interets, seeks sincere, professional chap-good times out, maybe more. Teledate: 0839 813488.

●ADORABLE, BRIGHT, AFFECTIONATE, Jewish, blue-eyed, blond lady, late 30s, seeks a happy, spontaneous, financially secure, guy, 35-45, who loves to love and be loved. Teledate: 0839 813497.

●HOW DO FAIRY TALES BEGIN? Gay female, 39, seeks partner for romance, laughter and happy ever after. Teledate: 0839 813502.

●BLACK LESBIAN, professional, 26, strong, natural beauty — romantic, healthy, dynamic, adventurous, 5'7". Seeks similar, humorous, attractive, monogamous lover, 24-35. Teledate: 0839 813507.

●ATTRACTIVE FRIENDLY MAN, fun loving, recent initiate, 34, seeks second bite at the cherry with sensuous caring woman. Teledate: 0839 813508.

●INTELLIGENT, ATTRACTIVE female, classical musician, 39, wide interests, graduate, seeks sensitive, handsome, humorous, country loving man, 30 early 40s to share and explore all that lies ahead. Teledate: 0839 813509.

●GOOD LOOKING-STRAIGHT ACTING, professional guy, 31, seeks similar, 21 +, under 35, for nights in and out and walks in the country. Teledate: 0839 813510.

●FUN IN 92? Virgo male, 41, loves skiing, sailing, fast cars and stuff, homes UK/France, want slim, petite lady, 25-35, to join in. Teledate: 0839 813511.

●SUCCESSFUL, PROFESSIONAL, attractive lady, 38, tired of work and no play, seeks tall, slim, handsome male, 40ish for romantic relationship. Teledate: 0839 813512.

●PROFESSIONAL MALE, 40, 6ft, fit, non-smoker, varied interests, seeks tall, educated lady, 25-35 for permanent relationship. Teledate: 0839 813513.

●WORST OF THE SUN SIGNS, deep dignified, stylish gay lady, slim, attractive, feminine, middle class, professional, seeks extraordinary, passionate, attractive woman. Must enjoys good times, fascination of sexual fulfilment extended in style. I don't waste time, shall return honest calls. Only contact if truly sensual pleasures desired, being aware that together could burn the bedroom down, be brave, come through. Teledate: 0839 813514.

●AMERICAN BUSINESSMAN, 38, financially successful, good looking, easy going, fun, hot blooded, independent, reliable, seeks smooth, hasslefree, 1:1 relationship with a personable, easygoing, attractive, busty, leggy lady. Teledate: 0839 813516.

●BACK PACKING BUDDY wanted by Aussie girl for Inter-rail trip East Europe, March, urgent replies. Teledate: 0839 813520.

●GAY WOMAN, feminine, stylish, very attractive, seeks same for love. Teledate: 0839 813542.

●IF NONE OF THE MALE ADVERTISERS MATCH YOUR DREAMS PLEASE CALL 0839 81 3821 OR 0839 81 3825 OR 0839 81 3834 OR Teledate: 0839 813979.

56 LONELY HEARTS

TIME OUT LONELY HEARTS

designed for individuals wanting to meet other individuals for 1:1 relationship. We reserve the right to refuse any advertisement without explanation. Circulars, promotional literature and offensive material are not forwarded where discovered. If you received such material with your box replies please let us know.

Write enclosing the material to:
Nicky Osborne at TIME OUT.

●AMERICAN WRITER, 47, male, seeks female. Photo telephone essential. Box 37.

●CITY PROFESSIONAL, bachelor gent, 43, seeks academic, athletic, palindromic spinster. Box 172.

●HANDSOME BUSINESSMAN, 33, living in Madrid, seeking London female, up to 30, attractive, feminine, educated, independent. Wishing travels, new cultures for friendship, share residences, London-Madrid and perhaps more! Box 326.

●SCORPION Male artist, 43, seeks sensually hirsute model and aspiring authoress for collaboration in genuine work of erotica. Travelling UK luxuriously — April-September. Harmony ensuring commitment to permanent tender union. Box 251.

●SINCERE MALE, 31, seek easy going female, 18-32, with view to caring friendship and possible romance, box 365.

●SUCCESSFUL LAWYER, male, 31, good looking, charming, with wicked sense of humour, yet warm and genuine. Seeks attractive, compatible female, 20-33, for friendship and hopefully relationship. Send photo. Box 368.

●UNDERSTANDING and loving girlfriend, age 18-35, sought by gentle intelligent and very affectionate man, 32, attractive, with special need to kiss a womans hands and feet. Long-term, close and affectionate relationship desired. Telephone please. Box 382.

●AFFECTIONATE, SENSITIVE, HUMOROUS, PROFESSIONAL MAN. Vegetarian, interested in music, alternative medicine, Buddhist meditation, Green politics; likes cooking, cats and kids. Seeks tender loving relationship. Single mums welcome. Photo please. Box 385.

●GAY GUY, 33, professional, active, fit, attractive, (OK — balding). Seeks slim, (skinny even) guy, 21-28, for whatever develops. Photo essential. Box 389.

●SINCERE, CARING PARTNER, 21 +, sought by professional gay man, 50, am slim, tall, athletic, serious, humorous. You similar. Photo? Box 391.

●ATTRACTIVE, PERSONABLE GAY MAN (26), seeks similar (22-30), for dancing, film and cappuccino. Blue eyes and brutal honesty essential. Photo helps. Box 405.

●GOOD LOOKING MAN, 38, graduate, very affectionate, music lover, seeks attractive girlfriend for warmth, tenderness and lasting relationship. Box 422.

●GOOD-LOOKING GUY, 32 years, successful, stylish, wears 501's, likes going out, socialising, still has not met that special, attractive, intelligent, slim lady to share affection, warmth, sensual evenings and cuddles with. Am I just dreaming. Photo appreciated with letter. box 424.

●CREATIVE GAY MALE, 34, recedingly handsome, fit and masculine, desires cultured, muscular companion, 21-40, for interesting romantic friendship. Photos returned. Box 433.

●GAY WOMAN, 38, feminine, attractive looking, for uncomplicated, caring, affectionate, feminine woman, non-smoker to share varied interests and happiness. Box 418.

●GAY GUY, 32, writer, attractive, slim, humorous, intelligent with keen interest in South East Asia, seeks cute guy (21 +), speaking Malay, Chinese, Vietnamese or neighbouring languages. Photo appreciated. Box 434.

●GOOD LOOKING, masculine gay, 48, non-scene, bright and cuddly. Seeks intelligent, younger guy, any nationality, for close relationship. box 443.

●GRAPHIC DESIGNER, 39, 5'8", attractive, slim, own design agency. Seeks attractive, romantic, genuine woman, 25-35, for wining dining, fun holidays etc, for relationship. N S. Photo appreciated. Box 469.

●WHAT ARE YOUR FANTASIES? Petite, sexy, lonely little lady lost in London. Anxious to meet tall, professional man, 45 +, to share life's pleasures. Please be genuine. Telephone and photo. Box 479.

●CONTINENTAL BLOND BEAUTY, mid-20s, slender, charming and sexy, seeks an upmarket, successful, wealthy and generous older gentleman, who appreciates genuine beauty, sensitivity and brains to spoil her and enjoy wonderful times together. Nationality unimportant. Box 480.

●VERY ATTRACTIVE, gay guy, tall, slim, dark, sexy designer, successful, have many lifes' trappings except a lover, maybe you (21 +). Islington. Box 547.

●PASSIONATE JEWISH GUY, seeks his Valentine, a similar female (25 +), to spend cold winter days but hot winter nights together. Telephone number and photo much appreciated

LONELY HEARTS

Up to 20 words for £25.00 including Box Number

Up to 30 words for £35.00 including Box Number

●PETITE UNIVERSITY LECTURER — empathetic, well-maintained 42, seeks highly intelligent, perceptive man, medium chunky physique, for cultural and sensual occasions. Box 498.

●BEWITCHINGLY beautiful blonde female, 26, needs EXCEPTIONALLY attractive, professional, successful male for lasting loving adventure. Box 595.

●GAY GUY, straight-looking, warm, friendly, genuine, youthful, attractive, 38, usual interests, south SW London — seeks youthful, 25 +, for caring and sharing times ahead. Photo and telephone number helpful. Thanks. Box 546.

but not essential. Box 554.

●PETER still dreams of a slim, gentle woman, 21-35, to love and cherist, share life and laughs together. I'm 34, tall, attractive, intelligent and affectionate. Photo, telephone no appreciated. Box 568.

BLACK LESBIAN

Professional, 26, strong, 5'7", natural beauty. Mobile. Romantic, healthy, dynamic and adventurous. London. Seeks similar, humorous, attractive, monogamous lover friend, 24-35. Photo number appreciated. All letters answered.

Box 540

●ROLE REVERSAL? Tame domesticated man, 41, willing to do housework, seeks woman willing to take the lead in a relationship. Box 605.

●ARTIST, TEACHER, socialist entrepeneur, into equality, peace, creativity, dancing, cross-dressing (sometimes), Espana, swimming underwater and shopping. Seeks woman friend. Box 625.

●TALL, ATTRACTIVE, graduate man, 34, with wit, grace, style and passion. Seeks exciting, adventurous, original romance with sensual, sophisticated, sparkling female counterpart. If you have brains, beauty, creativity, charisma treat yourself in '92. Photo, telephone please. a.l.a. Box 639.

●ATTRACTIVE GAY WOMAN, 35. Feminine, educated, humorous, works in media. Loves film, theatre, opera, travel, art. Seeks similar romantic and live. Box 640.

●AMERICAN MALE IN NEW YORK, seeks to import British beauty. Box 504.

●GAY MALE, 35, professional, attractive, non scene, caring. Seeks romance, love, 1-1 with special person, 21 +, to share life with. Box 505.

●ASIAN FEMALE, 35, professional, interested psychology and arts, seeks n/s, intelligent male companion. Box 506.

●DEAR, WARM, friendly, professional lady (31), seeking similar male. Free tonight for meal and theatre? Write me, photo appreciated. Box 507.

●COMPATIBLE MAN, for attractive, professional woman, 55. Box 508.

●TRULY OUTSTANDING young woman, 27, 5'4", Continental, very feminine, shapely and sensuous with high standards, seeks a strong, handsome man (25-35 max). Photo please, returned. Box 509.

●GUY, 35, likes music, food, country walks, gardening. Seeks similar who is also gay, 21 +, with sense of humour, for concerts, food, walks, hopefully 1:1. Discretion essential. Box 510.

●FRENCH GAY GUY, 23, straight acting/looking. Seeks similar guy, 21 +, under 30, for fun and/or more. Photo, letter please. Box 511.

●WOMAN, 38, professional, attractive, intelligent, fit, interested in arts, tennis, mountains. Seeks relationship with gentle kind, courageous man. Box 513.

●GAY GUY, 26, tall, slim, sincere, looking for a special guy (21-28), for friendship and possible 1.2.1. Photo please. Box 514.

●GAY GUY, 49, seeks similar, 25-40, for fun and friendship. NW/W London or Middx area. Photo and telephone number please. Box 515.

●PROFESSIONAL MALE, 37, divorced. Seeks female (30-44), for sincere relationship. I am tall, slim, sports-playing. a.l.a.w.p. Box 516.

●ATTRACTIVE FEMALE, 27, needs love of good man, cuddles on waking, a shoulder to cry on, a best friend, confidant, someone to rely on. Needs reciprocated. Photo, telephone. Box 521.

●PASSIONATE BUT COOL Italophile, tall, rugged, handsome, earthy, 45, accomplished, creative, unconventional, cultured, unmarried, ready for change. Seeks sympathatic career woman, modern, trendy, literate, visual, n/s, Epicurean, BEAUTIFUL. Photo PLEASE. Box 522.

●HANDSOME, TALL, graduate, Continental, professional, 30, humorous, outgoing, affectionate, caring. Interested in good books, films, sports, music, travelling, conversation. Seeks compatible, warm, feminine female for sincere relationship. Box 517.

YOUNG JAPANESE/THAI SPEAKING WOMAN

Sought by very good looking and genuine English man, 34, financially secure, single, intelligent, adventurous and well travelled. All letters replied to.

Box 518

●UNBEATABLE BARGAIN. First time advertiser. Gorgeous girl (23), seeks marvellous man. Hurry! Offer ends soon. He who dares . . . Box 519.

●VALENTINES SPECIAL — romantic Jewish widower, 54 y/o, generous and caring, solvent, semi-retired, seeks female friend. N/s, travel, sun, fun, cinema, music. Must swim, drive, above all have style. Box 520.

●NOVELIST, 27, male, enjoys cinema, contemporary dance and music, mountain walking, climbing. Seeks independent, Camdenish woman for evenings out. Box 523.

●BOHEMIAN IN SPIRIT? Special lady seeks tall, dark, attractive man (34-45), with compelling eyes. Are you kind, witty, cultured, entrepeneur, artist or professional for 1:1 friendship?? Letter photo please. Box 524.

●HANDSOME GAY LAD, boyish, 35, muscular, romantic, requires hunk for regular passion, 21 +. Photo appreciated. Box 525.

●ANDREW, 30's, tall, cuddly, non-smoking, professional. Seeks aware woman for committed relationship. Box 526.

●TEACHER, 41, 6ft, n/s, caring nature, interests travel, homelife. Seeks younger woman — pretty and intelligent, for stable relationship. a.l.a. with photo. Surrey. Box 524.

●MALE, 51, 6'1. Reasonable table manners. Can hold doors open and books right way up. Would share offshore sailing and onshore arts with warm, thoughtful, adventurous, sometimes outrageously glossy, female. Box 528.

●OCCASIONAL TV, 26, graduate, seeks attractive, slim, understanding female, for long term relationship letter. Photo, telephone appreciated. Box 529.

●GAY LADY, very feminine, attractive, 35, energetic, loving, romantic, discreet, seeks similar female, 22-40, for friendship relationship. Photo telephone number appreciated. Box 530.

●THE DEEPEST ATTRACTION, sought between sensual, fair woman and her male complement. I've had my children. Now it's a time to live. Photo please. Box 531.

●LIVELY, ARTISTIC, socialist redhead (37), enjoys jazz, country walks, galleries and eating out. Seeks sensitive, intelligent, n/s man, for fun and romance. North London preferred. Letter/photo appreciated. Box 532.

●FRENCHMAN, 5'8½" YES, small-medium built young 33, naturally wild, often cute, charismatic, intelligent, sincere, loves ragga, jazz-rap, funk, arts, reading, fashion, cinema, drinking, laughing, dancing. Seeks groovy girl with attitude. Box 533.

●MALE, 31, secure, non-smoker, vegetarian. Seeks female for friendship and fun times. Photo appreciated. Box 537.

●PISCEAN WOMAN, 25, no longer believes she will find her intelligent, funny, caring male soulmate by chance — please send a letter and photo to prove you are out there — somewhere. Box 538.

●MALE, 22, engineering student, likes art, cinema, cycling, walks, etc. Seeks a caring female, 20 +, for a warm relationship. Box 539.

●BOLD, BALD JEWISH MALE, 34, seeks woman for fun friendship and whatever follows. Box 541.

●GAY MALE, 27, attractive, medium build, non-scene, straight-acting, loves music, cinema, theatre. Caring and sincere. Seeks similar (21 +), non-smoker, to live life to the full with!!!!! a.l.a.w.p. returned with mine. Box 542.

FOREVER LADY?

Star dancing, tree talking, surf crashing, love making, life loving, thought provoking, communicating, spirit, mind, body melding. I'm 6'1", dark, attractive, 37, very intelligent. Who are you my love?

Box 548

The Arts Lab years

The Arts Lab existed for just two and a half years, but in that time it was the hub of London's avant-garde arts community, a vibrant meeting, performance and party space whose influence endures today. Its director, Jim Haynes, remembers those incredible years.

1967

Move to Long Acre in Covent Garden. Share the flat with Jack Moore and thousands of others. We have a pay phone installed and everyone comes for tea and/or to use the telephone. More and more disappointed in the Jeanetta Cochrane Theatre and the restrictions and pressures of running a theatre company in a large conventional space. I resign in order to devote myself to *IT* [*International Times*] and to finding a warehouse in which to create an experimental space. Soon manage to acquire the perfect space – two warehouses connected to each other at 182 Drury Lane. This is the birth of the Arts Laboratory.

The Lab contains a cinema in the basement designed by Jack Moore and run by David Curtis. The entrance contains a large gallery space, and Biddy Peppin (David's girlfriend) and Pamela Zoline direct the gallery activities. The theatre is in a separate (but connected) warehouse, and is designed by Jack Moore. He and I co-direct the activities there. The upstairs space in the front contains the restaurant that is run by Susan Miles. I live in the back above the storage and dressing rooms. A number of other people live in various corners of the building.

We are everything we claim to be, and the space is an instant success. All London comes at all hours to experience the Lab.

My policy is to try never to say the word 'no', and in three years of running the Lab I almost never do. We have a number of successes, including Steven Berkoff's first production, a Kafka adaptation, Graziella Martinez and Toni-Lee Marshall's late-night dance production, Jack Moore/Jack Bond's direction of the Jane Arden musical, *Vagina Rex and the Gas Oven* (with music by Shawn Phillips), John Lennon/Yoko Ono's sculpture exhibition, Jack Moore's direction of Tutte Lemkov in Kafka's *Lecture to an Academy*, and Moma Dimic's *The Very Long Life of Tola Manolovic*.

David Bowie uses the Lab to rehearse his music. Lindsay Kemp stages many productions. So, too, the People Show.

1968

Our newspaper *IT* creates UFO, where the Pink Floyd and the Soft Machine are the house bands. Jack creates the Human Family and begins to spend more and more time touring Europe with his bus, geodesic dome and his actors. More and more of the staff and personnel in the Lab resent scarce funds being spent on him and his activities on the continent, and not on the Lab itself. Ultimately and painfully, I side with Jack. This causes a major eruption and some of the staff break away to create another Arts Lab.

At some point, I meet Lynne Tillman at Shakespeare & Co in Paris and invite her to come to London and to assist me in running the Lab. She accepts and soon is contributing her positive energies. In December, we hire the Albert Hall to organise a fund-raiser, *The Alchemical Wedding*. John Lennon and Yoko Ono participate with their bag happening. An evening to remember, but the management of the Albert Hall is not amused. I had promised Leonard Cohen. He didn't come. The event is taped with one of the first Sony video cameras.

Inspire and help Tony Elliott to launch *Time Out* in London. Party with Jay and Fran Landesman, Ronnie Laing, Christine Keeler, Mama Cass. Am invited to dine with Indira Gandhi. Meet Leonard Cohen earlier via Michael X. Leonard and I discuss starting an egghead publishing company.

1969

Squat the empty Bell Hotel next to the Lab after all attempts to rent it from the Greater London Council fail. Soon after, we are expelled by the police. Some say this is the start of the squatting movement.

Last year of the Arts Lab in London. The writing is on the wall, but one of the interesting things about the Arts Lab is the number of other Lab-like places that explode all over Britain and the continent as a result of the example the Lab's success provided. Places like the expanded ICA in London (under the direction of Michael Kustow), the Milky Way in Amsterdam (where Jack Moore is one of the founders), the Entrepôt in Paris (which Frédéric Mitterrand shows me around when it is an empty shell).

www.jim-haynes.com.

The Rocky Horror Show

There's a sign outside the Chelsea Classic Cinema in the King's Road, put there to remind passers-by that *The Rocky Horror Show* is theatre and not one of the B-movies it so successfully sends up. Unfortunately, they didn't get the sign quite right and it says 'The Rocky Horror Show. Alive on Stage.' It couldn't be a more appropriate place to have a rock musical that turned the Royal Court's Theatre Upstairs into a ghostly flea-pit, with Pat Quinn as a voluptuous but distinctly odd usherette, and the company leading everybody to their seats wearing leering plastic face masks. It did its allotted few weeks there, but by the end there was already a thriving black market in tickets. Even Mick Jagger failed to see it on the last night. The performance was cancelled because Rainer Bourton, who plays Rocky, got glitter down his silver briefs and had to have treatment. However, they did get a visit from Vincent Price.

Here's the plot: Brad and Janet, a very respectable American couple, are saving themselves for each other and are, as the song says, 'so much in love'. They have a blow-out on a lonely road near Frank's place. Frank is the full B-movie horror works, a renegade from the planet Transexual and caught up in devious sexual experiments. Assisted by his twisted butler and his two hermaphrodite cohorts, he has just created the perfect male – Rocky. It wouldn't be fair to tell you what happens to Brad and Janet.

Richard O'Brien wrote the script and the music and lyrics, and also plays Frank's hunchback assistant. Being in his own show means he doesn't think too much about having written it at all. He says the show is a collage of all the things he likes.

It's pure escapism and bound to be popular at a time when people in the theatre are finding it too tough to face up to real issues, and are taking refuge in fantasy. Its lifeline to reality is in its treatment of sexuality. 'I think people should do what they want sexually,' says O'Brien, 'but I don't mean that sexual psychopaths should be encouraged.'

It's a joyful, randy, innocent show, projecting better than any other musical I've seen the sexuality of rock music and exploiting up to the hilt the Bowiesque confusion of gender that is currently fashionable. The music is heavily sent-up '50s rock and teen scene with more modern overtures of the recent Country and Western revival. The sex part is the protein and the surface glitter is provided by O'Brien's entertaining dig at kitsch films.

Tim Curry plays the amazing Mr (or Miss) Frank-n-Furter, otherwise known as Frank. His first entrance is in corset, feather boa, black underwear and high heels. 'The shoes were very important,' he says. 'I didn't get near the part until very late in rehearsal, and I said, "I must have the shoes!" Then it all happened. I tend to work from the feet upwards.'

In this play, a lot of men in the audience turn their heads the other way when he first bounds on stage. He thinks it's because there's no strong tradition of male exhibitionism or male eroticism.

Instead of being arch and pseudo-serious as a lot of sci-fi-influenced stuff can be, this one's a guided tour of erotic situations – very funny and with some of the best rock music in town. Jonathan King has just produced an album of the musical numbers of the show sung by the present cast. The one I remember best is 'Time Warp', led by the amazing Jonathan Adams as a velvet-jacketed Lustgarten figure who acts as the straight contrast to all the kinky jinks, and narrates the show as if we were all personally responsible for the evil doings. *Dusty Hughes*

The Rocky Horror Show became one of London's longest running productions, appearing at various theatres for 2,960 performances until 1980. It was turned into a cult feature film, *The Rocky Horror Picture Show*, in 1975, and a revived stage show still tours.

ORIGINAL LONDON CAST

Usherette/Magenta
Patricia Quinn
Janet Weiss
Julie Covington
Brad Major
Christopher Malcolm
Narrator
Jonathan Adams
Riff Raff
Richard O'Brien
Columbia
Little Nell
Frank-n-Furter
Tim Curry
Rocky Horror
Rayner Bourton
Eddie/Dr Everett Scott
Paddy O'Hagan

Camden
Roundhouse

Camden's former Victorian engine shed was
one of the most exciting venues of the 1960s and
'70s alternative culture. Bought by the GLC in 1966,
it hosted the Doors, Patti Smith, Jimi Hendrix and
Pink Floyd, and was used as a theatre for Peter
Brook's experimental *The Tempest* and '70s
shocker *Oh! Calcutta!*.

Empty for much of the '80s and '90s (aside from
Artangel's memorable intervention of a giant,
white bouncy castle) the Roundhouse was
remodelled and relaunched on 1 June 2006 with
De La Guarda's anarchic assault of colour, noise,
performance and party mayhem, *Fuerzabruta*.
Subsequent bold programming, such as the
BBC's Electric Proms and an RSC history-plays
marathon, have confirmed the Roundhouse as a
venue of ongoing influence.

OH WHAT A LOVELY WAR

THE ROUNDHOUSE CHALKFARM
Monday - Saturday 7.30 | Dec. 8-13
Prices: 6/- 10/- 15/- 20/- 30/-
BOX OFFICE: 485 8073

Morrissey on Alan Bennett

Bennett's one-time Chalk Farm neighbour explains the playwright's genius.

Time Out: Were you a fan of Alan Bennett before you met him?

Morrissey: I was the dull, fat kid in spectacles sitting in a Manchester council house who caught the first transmissions of his plays in 1978-79, and I was thunderstruck, because it was the first time I'd seen what I pitifully considered to be my sense of humour on screen.

TO: Did you immediately get on?

M: Yes. This happens when both parties tend to find life inevitably disgusting.

TO: When is Bennett at his best?

M: He's so terribly funny that when he writes a line full of biting sadness it cuts through all the more. I also admire the fact that he doesn't seem to envy or even much care for other writers.

TO: Was he a good neighbour?

M: Well, he didn't turn up at the door with steaming broth or anything like that. I would call on him at two in the afternoon, and he would knock on my door at seven at night. I would ask him about the daily obituary columns. I remember one day I knocked on his door, and he opened it and I said 'Peggy Mount's dead', and he said, 'Oh, good – come in.' Either he was pleased to see me or he was relieved that Peggy Mount was dead – I don't know which it was.

TO: Did you hang out together?

M: I often tried to pull him into the Good Mixer before it became the Britpop training school. I would say, 'It's the perfect place – full of homeless men, and me', and, laconically and full of dread, he'd say, 'Oh yes, sounds ideal.'

TO: Do think Bennett voices a particular type of Northern-ness?

M: Yes, it's largely the sodden gloom of the North – the walled-in lack-of-choice North that, really, he loves. The family is a battleground and every character trembles on the edge of confession. Sex is on everybody's mind, but nobody says anything. This, I think, is Alan himself.

TO: Was Bennett aware of your work before you met?

M: He knows nothing at all about pop or rock music. I gave him a copy of my *Bona Drag* CD and he placed it on the mantelpiece where it remained unshifted six months later. In the early draft of his play *The History Boys*, he used a line from 'The Headmaster Ritual', which thrilled me – but he dropped the line just prior to publication and replaced it with a Pet Shop Boys lyric, which infuriated me.

TO: Did he give you any fashion tips?

M: Only on the art of distancing oneself.

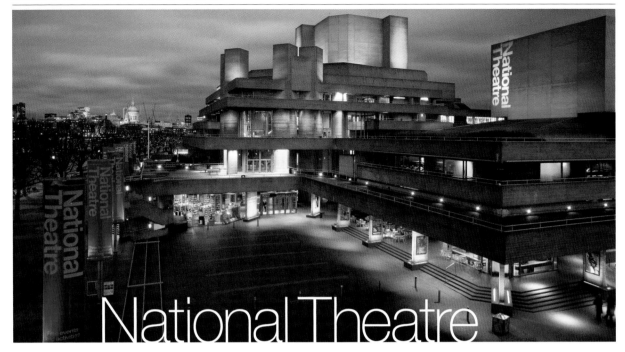

National Theatre

PERFORMANCE

In 2001, a *Radio Times* poll featured Denys Lasdun's building, uniquely, in the top five of both the most hated British buildings and the most loved. Before that, in 1988, Prince Charles declared, 'The National Theatre seems like a clever way of building a nuclear power station in the middle of London without anyone objecting.' But Lasdun was ahead of the game, creating an austere building that doesn't curry favour but, equally, won't go out of fashion. As the years have passed, his careful composition of horizontal and vertical elements has won ever more admirers, and today the National is an iconic landmark.

The first mutterings of a National Theatre were heard in 1848. In 1907, a detailed scheme was presented by Harley Granville Barker and William Archer, supported by George Bernard Shaw. But nothing happened, and it took the establishment of the Arts Council after World War II to inch the project forward. Various sites on the South Bank were mooted, and the foundation stone shunted around like a hockey puck.

In 1961 the government helpfully declared that the country couldn't afford a National Theatre, and it was left to London County Council to offer to pay half the cost of construction in addition to providing the site rent-free. The government came on board again and, in 1962, Laurence Olivier was named as the first artistic director. In 1963 the National Theatre Company moved into the Old Vic. While Olivier and his company of extraordinary actors – including Maggie Smith, Robert Stephens, Denis Quilley and Derek Jacobi – strutted their stuff on the Cut, an architect was sought.

The optimism of the '60s gave way to the strike-bound '70s, and delays made it less likely that Olivier, in deteriorating health, would be able to lead his troops into the new building. Peter Hall, who had set up the Royal Shakespeare Company, was chosen as successor, and when McAlpine, the builders, kept postponing completion, he increased the pressure by moving in gradually, starting with *Hamlet* in the Lyttleton in 1976.

It's not easy to build a theatre that is both intimate and able to seat enough people to make it viable. Lasdun spent most of his time working on the Olivier Theatre, looking at ancient Greek theatre at Epidaurus and finally coming up with the idea of putting the stage in the corner, encircled by the audience. The acoustics have always posed a problem, because, according to Richard Eyre, 'The volume of space is so huge in proportion to the number of people in the audience.' But, gradually, directors like Eyre and Nicholas Hytner discovered that it works best either with a huge set that uses the famous revolving drum, or with almost no set at all.

In 1996 work started on several major changes, some of them against Lasdun's will. A new public space, Theatre Square, is used for outdoor shows. Coloured lights have lit up the Lyttleton flytower, and in 2007 artists Heather Ackroyd and Dan Harvey were even allowed to grow grass up the building's front. The South Bank has grown more popular with the addition of Tate Modern, Shakespeare's Globe, the London Eye and the restoration of the Royal Festival Hall. The artistic quarter that Lasdun dreamt of 40 years ago has well and truly arrived. *Jane Edwardes*

NATIONAL FACTS

Opened at the Old Vic 1963; moved to South Bank 1976

First production
22 October 1963: *Hamlet*, starring Peter O'Toole and directed by Laurence Olivier

Artistic directors
Laurence Olivier (1963-73), Peter Hall (1973-88), Richard Eyre (1988-97), Trevor Nunn (1997-2003), Nicholas Hytner (2003-)

Productions staged
more than 600

Annual audience
600,000

Steps in time

The capital's dance scene has shown some fancy footwork.
By Donald Hutera

The dance scene in London over the past 40 years has been a multi-coloured kaleidoscope of people and places. It's the former ballet wunderkind Michael Clark turning bum-baring bad boy at Sadler's Wells in the early 1980s, and DV8 Physical Theatre's bone-chilling examination of male alienation and desire, *Dead Dreams of Monochrome Men*, springing out of the ICA later in the same decade. It's Matthew Bourne's gender-bending *Swan Lake* making history in the '90s as the longest-running dance show in the West End. It's Kathak-trained Akram Khan's swift ascent to superstardom, which has generated some of the loudest clamour since the noughties began, fuelled by his subsequent collaborations with Sylvie

Akram Khan in *Third Catalogue*, which premiered at the Purcell Room in 2005.

Guillem and Juliette Binoche. And it's certainly the hop-skip-and-jump that the hungry young Israeli Hofesh Shechter took between three major dance venues in six short months in 2007.

Over the decades, these key players have not only set the tone for dance in the capital but become players on the global stage. In turn, iconic artists and influential international ensembles – from godfather of modern dance, Merce Cunningham, to the Tanztheater Wuppertal of German guru Pina Bausch – have been keen to display their Terpsichorean wares in the Big Smoke.

In the late 1960s and early '70s, the scene was dominated by the Royal Ballet on one side and London Contemporary Dance Theatre (now defunct) and Rambert Dance Company (still going strong) on the other, with occasional visits by foreign troupes. Bubbling beneath was an untold number of independent operators whose smaller-scale, often experimental work was borne on the waves of the decade's so-called 'dance boom'.

Its rate of artistic success may vary, but the Royal has remained the keeper of the crown jewels of British ballet in terms of both its repertoire and its roster of extraordinary dancers. When its Covent Garden home closed for massive refurbishment in 1997, the institution plunged into a soap operatic meltdown but bounced back admirably and has since opened its polished doors to artists outside the academic vein via Deborah Bull's progressive strand of programming, ROH2.

Less grand, but no less influential, the LCDT was based at the Place, a former military drill hall near Euston station. Founded in the mid '60s by Robin Howard, an ardent admirer of Martha Graham, this was the official birthplace of modern dance in the UK. The school and the theatre attached to it rapidly became the seedbed for a generation of eager, questioning young dance-makers such as Richard Alston (its current artistic director) and Siobhan Davies (who now has her own headquarters near Elephant and Castle).

The buzz at the Place has continued unabated for 40 years, thanks in part to inspired programming by the avuncular John Ashford. His long reign has been punctuated by a series of annual seasons, including The Turning World (international contemporary dance), Resolution! (a platform for emerging artists from Britain and abroad) and Spring Loaded (emerging, but strictly UK-based).

Lording it over London's prime dance stages is the venerable but now thoroughly modernised Sadler's Wells, presided over by Alistair Spalding. Under his stewardship the Wells has been transformed into a receiving and a producing house with a string of glittering associates artists: Khan, Bourne, Guillem (refashioning herself as a contemporary performer), the prolific Wayne McGregor (also resident choreographer at the Royal), Russell Maliphant, Christopher Wheeldon, Jasmin Vardimon, George Piper Dances (aka TV's the Ballet Boyz) and hip hop dance-theatre supremo Jonzi D.

If London has become a dance mecca, it owes much of its status to the contemporary international festival Dance Umbrella, a fixture since 1978. Besides nurturing home-grown talent, founding artistic director Val Bourne sustained particularly close relationships with big American guns including Cunningham, Stephen Petronio and Mark Morris. She also supported Scottish-born trailblazer Michael Clark through thick and thin. Clark looked like an angel, but this outrageously virtuosic devil managed to inject Britain's relatively staid dance scene with a massive dose of punkish, camp energy. A Clark show had the aura

Clockwise from above: members of Ballet Rambert in the 1970s; *Yippeee!!!* by the Cholmondeleys and the Featherstonehaughs; Jonzi D; Paul-Andre Fortier performing as part of Dance Umbrella.

of rock concert; indeed, one, *O,* was staged at Brixton Academy and *I Am Curious Orange* featured the Fall playing live on stage. His later struggles with addiction and perfectionism are common knowledge. The fortysomething maverick has since matured and been taken under the Barbican's well-feathered wing.

Who or what else merits mention? Laban, for one. The south London conservatory has produced a host of gifted people, from the Broadway-worthy Matthew Bourne to Lea Anderson. The quirkily rhythmic, design-led performances Anderson concocts with her two groups – the all-female Cholmondeleys and the men-only Featherstonehaughs – have helped to define British dance culture as much as any work out there. The brainy Shobana Jeyasingh has been at it almost as long, deliberately infecting her background in the classical Indian dance style of Bharatanatyam with the complex, high-speed pulsations of modern life. Without Jeyasingh, there may not have been an Akram Khan. But isn't that how it is in any art form, one generation clearing the way for the next?

Donald Hutera has written about dance since 1977, and has contributed to *Time Out* since 1984. He was once a Featherstonehaugh – for a week.

PERFORMANCE

W hen, in 1968, that sturdily demotic slice of high culture for the people, Sadler's Wells Opera, was looking for a central London outlet for its more commercial enterprises – operetta, musicals and so on – it lit on Frank Matcham's opulent Edwardian music-hall, the Coliseum. With its magnificently blowsy mish-mash of decorative styles, it would become the seat of the newly-named English National Opera, which would soon be making headlines, getting audiences booing, cheering and even fighting in the foyer.

While the ENO has dedicated itself to staging opera in English, is family-friendly and relatively reasonably priced, its near-neighbour in Covent Garden, the Royal Opera House, has always been a glamorous magnet for the biggest international names, performing operas in the original language. Though the two aren't meant to be rivals, London critics love to take sides, and the rollercoaster fortunes of both houses in recent decades have had them taking turns in enjoying critical acclaim.

In recent years, ENO's financial woes and administrative and artistic ineptitude have coincided with Covent Garden enjoying a new lease of life under music director Antonio Pappano. London-born, American-reared and with wide experience of the European opera scene, Pappano is the best thing to have happened to the ROH in years.

But ten years ago, fortunes were reversed. The ROH was floundering, its internal organisation memorably compared (by the National Theatre's Richard Eyre) to a 'World War I battlefield'. An overdue, over-budget refurbishment was followed by a humiliating period of postponements, cancellations and operas simply grinding to a halt in the middle of a performance, as backstage staff discovered they had no idea how to use the newly installed multi-million-pound state-of-the-art-technology.

While Covent Garden was squandering its hefty public subsidy, helped by wealthy sponsors and fundraisers whose principal interests appeared to be social rather than artistic, ENO had been accruing good will with brilliant theatrical savvy. This golden age, featuring Music Director Mark Elder and David Pountney as Director of Productions, is still referred to longingly as the 'Powerhouse Years'. Pountney's overpowering, expressionistic staging of Shostakovich's *Lady Macbeth of Mtsensk* remains the greatest theatrical experience I have ever had.

Even something as apparently conventional as Humperdinck's *Hansel and Gretel* became, in Poutney's hands, unbearably moving. He modernised it as a tale of latchkey kids who spend the night in a municipal park, the dream pantomime of the original replaced by a vision of childhood longing – birthday cake, panto

Opera! Opera!

Forty years of the Coliseum versus Covent Garden.
By Martin Hoyle

London's opera giants: the Royal Opera House, above, and the ENO's Coliseum, right.

clowns, a secure home – overshadowed by the threat of abduction and abuse.

ENO's 'concept' productions – whether updated, timelessly stylised, abstract or simply outrageous – introduced continental European theatrical ideas to London long before the capital's stolid 'straight' theatre caught on, though it has to be said that this audacity has sometimes verged on exhibitionism. A particularly lurid example was Calixto Bieto's lager-swilling, blow-jobbing 2001 *Don Giovanni*, updated as a British hooligan's Costa holiday nightmare.

ENO's guest directors have come up with classic productions too. Alongside his gangster *Rigoletto* and evergreen, flapper-era *Mikado*, Jonathan Miller realised the best *Turn of the Screw* ever, proving that Britten's intimate ghost opera can dominate even the Coliseum's vast spaces, provided it is performed with sufficient intensity. Miller was also responsible for a memorable *Rosenkavalier* that transposed Baroque Vienna to the date of the work's composition, just before the outbreak of World War I. An ageing aristo, toyboy and bourgeois heiress made sense, as did the conviction that an assassin was just around the corner waiting to blow their bittersweet world to bits.

The Princess in *Rosenkavalier* was sung by Anne Evans, Bayreuth's reigning Brunnhilde (whom Covent Garden, curiously, treated with little interest), giving the lie to the old cliché that ENO never has great voices. Bayreuth's Wotan, the great John Tomlinson, is another ENO regular, even at the height of his international fame. ENO mounted a new *Figaro* for the then unknown Bryn Terfel before Covent Garden spotted him. And never let it be forgotten that before her

populist TV career, Leslie Garrett gave a star turn as Janáček's *Cunning Little Vixen*, as well as providing exceptional Handelian singing in *Xerxes*, in a landmark production by Nicholas Hytner (now running the National Theatre) that set the standard for operas by Handel, something of a favourite at the Coliseum.

At its best, ENO has always managed to give a sense of a tightly-knit company pursuing a coherent artistic vision (a season of 20th-century work was brave, as not even Puccini and Strauss can make up for the absence of Verdi, Mozart and Wagner). However, financial cuts have since threatened that ensemble ideal, and productions are now cast individually, rather than from a standing pool of available talent. Though singers still respond gratefully to the supportive ENO ethos, there have been some desperate clangers in choice of repertoire: *Kismet* with Michael Ball, anyone?.

The apparent vacuity at the artistic planning level is a cruel irony, given that for years it was Covent Garden, rather than ENO, that swiped and lurched its way through operas seemingly chosen for their obscurity. The shag-pile of discarded clichés that made up Giordano's monumentally trite *Fedora*, the inflated nullity of Massenet's *Cherubin* or the autopilot mediocrity of *La Donna del Lago* were expensive toys that a subsidised house cannot and should not afford.

With Pappano in Bow Street and a misplaced faith in movie directors reigning in St Martin's Lane, things aren't looking good for ENO. The metropolitan critics, who hunt as a pack, are busy kicking at its slightest hiccup, while swooning at Covent Garden's merest fart. But they can't change the atmosphere of the two theatres, one welcoming, the other not giving a toss. And ENO's new and not so secret weapon has got off to a good start: young Edward Gardner looks set fair to be the most successful music director since Mark Elder.

In 1968, there wasn't really any competition between the two houses. And opera audiences in the capital behaved very differently. Drag queens didn't enliven first nights by standing up and shrieking (Coliseum, *Princess Ida*). Dowagers in tiaras didn't scream 'rubbish!' (Covent Garden, *Flying Dutchman*). Opera buffs didn't engage in fisticuffs (Coliseum, the film noir production of *A Masked Ball*). Since then, Nigel Kennedy's Four Seasons entered the Guinness Book of Records, and the Three Tenors made people think they liked opera on the strength of 'Nessun dorma'. Both phenomena have faded away. But London's two opera houses have kept changing over the past 40 years, as has their public. Long may high notes hit the rafters and fists fly in the foyer.

Martin Hoyle was Classical Music Editor of *Time Out* between 1989 and 2007. He now writes about the arts for the *Financial Times*.

PERFORMANCE

London's all ha ha hee hee

Largely an '80s invention, the capital's once unruly comedy clubs have become a slick component of its rich nightlife.
By Malcolm Hay

Legend has it that alternative comedy was born in Soho in summer 1979, with a strip club entrepreneur and an insurance salesman as an unlikely pair of midwives. Around 30 acts, led by formidable newcomer Alexei Sayle, struggled to hold the attention of an audience drunk on free champagne at the opening night of what became the Comedy Store. I wasn't there. My first glimpse of the bright new dawn in entertainment came one winter night, 18 months later, in a windswept street outside the Tramshed in Woolwich.

Marcel Steiner's Smallest Theatre In The World, conceived in the grand style with a proscenium stage, plush velvet curtains and a ceiling painted to resemble the Sistine Chapel, blew my mind. It was mounted on the sidecar of a motorcycle. The audience capacity was two, although ticket-less fans could peek at performances through a small back window. Steiner, along with his supporting cast (often no more than one), would take a repertory of classics to clubs, pubs and public spaces. That night in Woolwich, settling back into a comfortably padded seat under a glittering chandelier supplied by Woolworths, I watched a four-act, 15-minute version of *A Christmas Carol*, complete with the Great Blizzard of 1843.

On subsequent pilgrimages to this diminutive palace of culture, I sampled *War and Peace* and the *Raising of the Titanic*. Sadly, I never caught the *Guns of Navarone*. I was told the scaling of the cliffs presented problems. Steiner – a lanky, bearded loon – claimed he was the only actor who could play Quasimodo without make-up. He'd wow audiences by setting fire to himself and hammering six-inch nails up his nose. A gloriously eccentric showman, he provided an essential counterblast to the more serious ethos of early stand-up.

Throughout the 1980s, a sprinkling, then a minor flood of clubs followed the Comedy Store's lead. Outlandish acts roamed the still virgin territory of alternative comedy, like vast herds of antelope on an African plain. Clown, acrobat, juggler, fire-eater, sword-swallower and inventor of surreal images Chris Lynam made his mark with a firework-up-the-bum routine: he stripped naked, inserted a large

Gerry Sadowitz begins the Ben Elton backlash in *Time Out*.

Roman candle in his orifice, lit the blue touch-paper and blazed a path to fame. Les Bubb combined frenetic visual comedy with gravity-defying callisthenics until, for his grand finale, he would fasten seven or eight rubber bands at different angles across his face, transforming his features into a grotesque mask until his brain exploded.

At Comedy in Tatters, situated on an old paddle-steamer at the Thames Embankment, I watched with incredulity as the Iceman tried to melt a block of ice roughly the size of a washing-up bowl. His tools included hammer, chisel, blow-torch, strategically placed candles and heavy breathing. My own favourite, though, was Graham Walters, aka Arlo Barlo, a silent grotesque he'd created and christened 'the rubber executive'. This pot-bellied, bank manager-like figure stood rooted to the spot while, through a series of revolting contortions accompanied by the soundtrack to the movie *2001*, his head disappeared into his trunk and the arms and legs grew longer, then shorter, before your eyes.

They were riotous times. I say this without nostalgia, because club promoters often seemed amateurish and shambolic. The behaviour of audiences, and acts, veered from the brutish to the silly. An unruly double act called the Port Stanley Amateur Dramatic Society got banned from Earth Exchange, a tiny comedy venue in a veggie restaurant in Highgate, for pelting punters with corned beef sandwiches. Less playfully, comics would harangue and abuse audiences if their response was less than rapturous. Audiences could turn ugly. I lost count of the times I saw drunks splash beer or throw up over a stand-up's shoes from a vantage point in the front row.

South-east London, in particular, resembled the Wild West. The infamous Tunnel Palladium, run in a scruffy pub at the southern end of the Blackwall Tunnel by roguish comic and entrepreneur Malcolm Hardee, was the Last Chance Saloon. Hardee, subsequently in charge of the equally rowdy Up the Creek club in Greenwich, specialised in gross humour. He won admiration for his versatility, once putting his bollocks into a star-struck punter's glass of beer, playing a mouth-organ, singing a blues song, and then, with a flourish, picking up the pint to drink it down.

Alternative comedy veteran Arthur Smith attributed Hardee's crowd-pulling success to his being the antithesis of charm. But this rough, rabble-rousing attitude towards the acts he introduced sometimes backfired. At the Tunnel, back in 1988, the female half of the double act Clarence & Joy Pickles suffered serious concussion and scarring when she was struck on the forehead by a flying glass. In the inquiry that followed, a member of staff identified the culprit. He wasn't, as they'd initially suspected, a yobbish Millwall supporter. He was a social worker.

Back at the Woolwich Tramshed, in 1987, a Glaswegian stand-up in his twenties set the crowd roaring with his bleakly nihilistic, venomous and obscene tirades. With his cascading curly locks, Jerry 'Gobshite' Sadowitz looked like a malevolent fallen angel. He raged indiscriminately against Paul Daniels, politicians, pensioners, second-generation (oh, the liberal horror!) Pakistanis and much else, mixing throwaway magic tricks (he'd pluck a dove from his flies) with snatches of savage mime (slashing with a razor blade at a Jehovah's Witness who'd invaded his doorstep, kneeing a senior citizen in the groin, venting his spleen about Lady Diana in terms that involved a very private part of her anatomy and an electric toaster). No taboo was respected. Bad-taste humour, Sadowitz would argue, simply reflected the horror of real life.

Before long, many nervous promoters had excluded this dangerous talent from their clubs. When Sadowitz made the front cover of *Time Out* in 1988, he was shown strangling a Ben Elton puppet in what amounted to a symbolic act of patricide. To the general public, Elton typified the new comedy, born just nine years earlier, still in its infancy and yet already feeding on itself. Was this

Above, captain of south London's comedy clubs, the outrageous Malcolm Hardee; below, bad boy Russell Brand.

'Steiner would wow audiences by setting fire to himself and hammering six-inch nails up his nose.'

an ominous sign? Almost from the beginning there were prophets of doom within the business: 'How many clubs do we have in London now? A dozen or more? That's far too many. It won't last. The bubble's about to burst.'

How wrong they were. The past 20 years are crammed with memories of fledgling comics starting out in atmospheric performance spaces, then going on to become household names. Jo Brand, at the very early stage of her stand-up career as the Sea Monster, coping with the Tunnel Palladium by standing, silent and contemptuous, for minutes on end, until the baying crowd wore itself out and listened with respect. Lee Evans, in the basement room that housed Peter Grahame's admirable Downstairs at the King's Head, spraying sweat as he tried out an early prototype of the routine where he's pumped full of air and his body collapses when he's deflated. Linda Smith, amazingly bright and witty, full of scorn for hypocrisy, and an emblem of hope for anyone with faith in the power of reason, turning the dingy hall at the Wood Green trades union centre into a wonderland through the radiance of her humour.

And many others. Most recently, Russell Brand, as a contestant in the final of the Hackney Empire New Act of the Year competition in 2000, hurling out thoughts and conjuring black visions at great speed. He didn't win. TV and the tabloids, as well as his own hyperactive courting of celebrity status, have since turned him into an infamous bad boy, but he remains a phenomenally skilful stand-up who started out in small London clubs.

Inevitably, over 30 years, there were casualties. Most tragically Linda Smith, who died of ovarian cancer at the age of 48. Most dramatically Malcolm Hardee, who drowned in the Thames, close to his Wibbly Wobbly Boat at Surrey Quays in, of course, south-east London.

Hardee's departure from the scene in January 2005 signalled that alternative comedy had run its course. The live comedy business has grown into a major industry. It's now highly professional and hugely influential. Like an immaculately manicured suburban lawn, it's an inhospitable environment for wildlife. Jerry Sadowitz still gets occasional work. In 2007 he managed to secure one London gig.

Malcolm Hay was *Time Out's* Comedy Editor from the mid 1980s to 2007.

Alternative comedy

Ben Elton, sharp in a lurid red jacket that has already seen service at two gigs earlier in the evening, opens the new Comedy Store as first night compère. He's a confident, fast-talking, scintillating comic who burns up a prodigious amount of material in the course of an evening: over the past two years he has seasoned his craft and now gives the impression that little could seriously interrupt the flow. 'I hope you can hear me, sir, because I can certainly hear you.' And on he goes, without a pause.

Soho entrepreneur Don Ward, who added comedy to his portfolio when the spangled bottom began to fall out of the striptease market, had seen the San Francisco Comedy Store in action, and found there was no legal bar to introducing the concept and the name over here. At the time, 1979, there was no such thing as 'alternative comedy' – the routes into this traditional profession had merely evolved from bottom-of-the-bill music hall, through to the equivalent of the working men's clubs and 'chicken-in-a-basket' circuit, with a chance appearance on *New Faces* or *The Comedians* as a vital leg-up. The other path of the past 20 years, in the wake of *Beyond the Fringe*, was into radio and TV via Oxbridge, and was thus closed to most.

'When we started the Store, there was no pool of tried-and-tested talent to draw on,' says Ward. 'I put ads in *the Stage* and so on: "If you've ever wanted to be a comic, here's the chance to get the frustration out of your system", that sort of thing. But the response was so huge it became unmanageable to hold private auditions. We decided we had to audition "live", so we needed a way of getting an act offstage if it wasn't going anywhere.' So, everyone who worked at the Comedy Store in the early days had to accept a simple rule: when the gong sounded, they were required to vacate the stage immediately, with as much dignity as possible.

In 1981, Ward, under pressure from the now-established Elton, dispensed with the gong. 'It wasn't used with discrimination,' remembers Elton. 'It was usually a load of drunken prats sitting around the front tables, ordering more beer at three in the morning and shouting "gong" because they thought it was funny.'

Starting off in an entertainment vacuum, the Store nevertheless gave rise to a whole new generation of comics, and established an 'alternative' route into the comedy game. Alexei Sayle was the first to emerge as a star, but he was quickly joined by Rik Mayall and others, and this group eventually found the Store concept inhibiting to what they wanted to do. They broke away to start a 'rival' club, the Comic Strip. Ward says that the parting was amicable.

'They'd worked out what they wanted to do, they were writing their own material, and they needed a format that let them present it in their own way. But the Comedy Store is essentially a factory, a conveyor belt. They'd developed to a stage where they couldn't fit in with that, and also television was beginning to show an interest in them by then.'

The Store itself survived, gong-free, until just before last Christmas, when spiralling rents in Soho made it uneconomic. It has now been revived from midnight on Saturdays, at Club 28 in Leicester Square: no gong, just a set bill of 'reliable' acts linked by the compère, with an 'audience spot' at the end.

Between the opening of the pioneer Store in '79 and its phoenix a month ago, the centre of gravity of cheap pub-and-club entertainment in London had shifted from its rock band domination: it would be hard to deny that the Store was an important catalyst, along with the biting recession.

A general lack of direction and energy in grassroots rock encouraged this change; when a new band is formed these days, it no longer thinks in the first instance of trying to blag a gig at the Hope & Anchor; it thinks of making its video. Something else had to come along.

An informal circuit of pub and restaurant rooms, nightclubs and trade union halls provides the outlets. Cartoon Archetypal Slogan Theatre (CAST) operate their New Variety nights four times a week, with four varied acts to each bill. There's the pioneering Crown & Castle, now temporarily housed in Stoke Newington's White Hart; the Finborough Theatre, who have just expanded to include a second venue in Charlotte Street; the venerable music-hall room in the Pindar of Wakefield; and the Earth Exchange, a vegetarian restaurant in Archway.

The comics who form the basic grist to this mill arrived from any number of directions. John Hegley and the Popticians are buskers looking for a record deal, who prefer to work in the warm in the evenings. Hegley's sharp little songs are usually concerned with turning the wimp into the superhero. The Oblivion Boys' route was though drama school into rep and subsidised theatre. The formal training shows through the nervous surface of their double act; they can wander off in pursuit of a promising ad lib, but know just when to guide the routine back on course.

The other outstanding double act on this circuit, French and Saunders, are writers and performers with the Comic Strip team, moonlighting as a duo. If they are the best female comics in town, it is partly because their feminism is not driven home with a sledgehammer. Their act consists of a number of set pieces – mother and daughter, TV children's show presenters, a pair of Dolly Partons – linked by tightrope-walking explorations of their assumed relationship as performers. There is barely a 'joke' in their routine, but a constant comic alchemy.

So, if there is no alternative to professionalism in comedy, to the traditional skill of using your craft to keep an audience laughing, is there anything that can usefully be defined as 'alternative comedy'? Ben Elton, though proud of taking his place in a skilled trade that goes back centuries, and ambitious to be a successful television writer and performer, insists that there is.

'An "alternative" principle did evolve in the early days. It was to find new subjects to amuse people while being non-racist and non-sexist. Some people took a wholly political line in doing this, others – like Rik Mayall, say – simply didn't do anything politically objectionable. I'm somewhere in the middle myself – sometimes political, sometimes simply non-objectionable.'

Isn't there a risk that this can become self-congratulatory and unchallenging?

'Oh yes, you must have a sense of danger. Otherwise it's just "Thatcher out!" "Right on!", which becomes very sickly and empty.'

But, if a revolution has been going on, Don Ward has another warning against complacency.

'I worry about the amount of new comic talent coming up. The original Store shook the tree and a lot of good apples came down. But once the Comic Strip went off to do their own thing, they left behind only a handful of really good acts. Do you only think that this "alternative comedy" is just another fad? I sometimes wonder if the bubble will burst, and what will we all move on to next?' *Malcom Hay*

The Comedy Store is currently at 1A Oxenden Street, SW1, and has shows seven nights a week. Ben Elton has written several successful novels, TV comedies and West End musicals, including *We Will Rock You*.

PERFORMANCE

Harold Pinter

PERFORMANCE

Perusing the Pinter cuttings file in preparation for an interview is rather like being marked down for a kamikaze run or a raid on the Emperor's bunker. The tantrums are well documented: violent rows at the drop of a dictator's name; an assault on an American ambassador's ear; reducing friends and strangers to tears; denouncing the jackals of the press; celebrated fallings-out with loyal friends like Simon Gray and Peter Hall. And yet the chance of a rare audience with a man who made us redefine our attitude to communication, gave an adjective to the dictionary, and jolted our belief in a playwright's control over his creations, is worth the risk.

As it turns out, Pinter is ever the courteous host, even if the initial seating arrangements seem to resemble stage directions from *The Caretaker*. Pinter has never really forgiven the intrusions into his private life when his marriage to actress Vivien Merchant broke up spectacularly in 1975 after his affair with Lady Antonia Fraser. The latterday brickbats of 'Champagne Socialist' and 'Angry Old Man' haven't helped either, though some of the maturer critics have been perceptively tolerant of Pinter's increasing political activity, an interest that dates from the overthrow of Chile's Allende government in 1973.

Pinter: 'The attacks represent a well-established tradition of mockery of the artist in this country. I was going to say "intellectual", but I'm not that, I'm just a working writer; but any writer who pops his head over the trenches and dares to speak in this country is really placed outside the pale. I suppose it stems from the fact that a writer is supposed to be some kind of entertainer; it's true in the United States too. But this has never been the case in Europe or Latin America.

'There was a time when I was attacked by everyone in sight and I've survived that. So there's no way I can go under. I did a programme on Channel 4, *Opinions*, on American foreign policy and I was accused of ranting, of being a 'ranting emotional playwright', the usual accusation the press deliver to someone they wish to discredit. But I got a record number of letters from people who said, "We feel the same way as you do, but we can't say it as a bus conductor or a factory worker because if we do we'll be ostracised or even sacked." But I can't be sacked, you see, because I haven't got a job. Therefore I'll continue to say whatever I like.'

I want to put something on the record,' Pinter declares, in that famously rich voice that once belonged to a jobbing actor called 'David Barron' 44 years ago. The record seems to imply that I haven't written anything since 1978. I looked it up the other day; I read that I'd been blocked for 15 years. I've actually written six short plays, but *plays*, including *A Kind of Alaska*, which won an award somewhere. I've also written seven film scripts that were important to me, including *The French Lieutenant's Woman*, so that's seven and six, I make 13. It's about time that was recorded. To say that I've been doing fuck all for 15 years is a slight exaggeration.'

Harold Pinter photographed for *Time Out* in 2008.

Original interview by Steve Grant. Harold Pinter was awarded the Nobel Prize for literature in 2005.

The People Show

New Arts Lab
11 July 1970

The theatre has been transformed into a working men's club. The acts are Heinz, the boy singer (imagine Danny La Rue as Marilyn Monroe as a 14-year-old school kid); Mr Wild Wisdom, who does bird call imitations; Lazlo, the magician; Mr One Hundred Percent, the memory man, whose mystical insight correctly divines an article taken from an audience member's left foot as a wrist strap; and, finally, a complete transcript of an Enoch speech seen on TV the previous night.

The People Show are not actors in the traditional sense – they are actors who have explored improvisation. Their characterisations are imaginative projections of their own obsessions and what they present is not a play, it's a show, a display, an exhibition, and entertainment. The People Show is unique, and uniquely English. It is the only English experimental theatre group. *John Ford*

Oh! Calcutta!

Roundhouse
8 August 1970

First, what *Oh! Calcutta!* is. It's a review, a dozen sketches, slick, fast, super-sophisticated, plus some dancing. Some of the sketches and all the dances are performed naked. Sex acts are, contrary to rumour, mimed but not

performed – any of them; the cast remain totally uninvolved. The title is that of a Surrealist painting by Clovis Trouille and is a pun on *O quelle cul t'as*. The authors are as good as anonymous: prestige names are listed – Joe Orton, John Lennon, Edna O'Brien – but none of the sketches is attributed. Music is by the Open Window.

Now what it's not. It's not art untongue-tied by authority's retreat from theatre censorship. It's not a hymn to free, liberated love. It's not the arrival in the world of *What's On* and the *Daily Telegraph* of experimental, underground theatre, with the aid of Ken Tynan, who, in the 1950s, was midwife to a new intelligence, originality and seriousness in the theatre.

The truth is, it's lousy, and the midwife has turned bawd, with the Roundhouse taking £3,000 a night and sold out till the end of August. *Bradley Winterton*

Jesus Christ Superstar

Palace Theatre
15 September 1972

Full marks for King Herod, played by Paul Jabara as a catty, flouncy queen who shimmers forward on a silver-lamé waterbed swathed in dolly birds: his show-stopping number 'King of the Jews' is the one moment in the evening when *Superstar* looks what it is – a brash, vulgar,

fun-loving, camped-up romp produced by the middle-aged for the middle-aged with youth trapped in between like the nearest thing we'll ever get to sacred prostitutes in this godless age.

Abigail's Party

Hampstead Theatre
29 April 1977

Mike Leigh's latest improvisational excursion is a behavioural masterpiece despite one's occasional feeling that such theatre is little more than an A-level for actors. The titular event provides an intriguing backcloth; a

Abigail's Party

punk rock adolescent's party, which forces her recently divorced, humanitarian mum into the arms of a revoltingly kitsch foursome: overworked estate agent; coarse, sexually aggressive wife; sullen computer operator; and cretinously materialistic nurse.

The evening moves with carefully etched clarity from aching hilarity to juddering horror, despite the occasional lapse into silly names ('Wibbley Webb'). The women are superb and my only

unpleasant reminder comes from an extremely sophisticated audience laughing at those unfortunates from 'Affluent Yobbonia' who keep Beaujolais in the fridge. *Steve Grant*

Cats

New London Theatre
9 October 1981

What a glorious glossy treat this bit of frivolity is, from the start, when the huge rubbish dump revolves to reveal the stage, to the final, feline, furry jump up. TS Eliot's whimsical verses are interpreted with much zip by director Trevor Nunn, choreographer Gillian Lynne and 31 dancers out of whom (not surprisingly) Wayne Sleep wins *Time Out's* Kit-e-Kat award. This is bouillabaisse of theatre – you can get by without it, but doesn't it make life nicer. *Naseem Khan*

Top Girls

Royal Court
10 September 1982

A Japanese geisha, concubine to a medieval emperor; the brilliant Pope Joan whose unforgivable gender was discovered when she gave birth during a papal procession; the

adventurous Victorian traveller, Lady Isabella Bird; Patient Griselda, immortalised by Chaucer for a life of high, if brutal romance; Brueghel's primitive Dull Gret; these exotic, eccentric *Top Girls* from different centuries and cultures assemble for dinner to tell tales of horrendous male cruelty and callous custom – most have been deprived of their children – as they celebrate the success of 20th-century boss girl Marlene.

This exquisite and stylish first scene of Caryl Churchill's brilliant new play opens into scenes of crisp social realism, Bondian in their resonance and clarity. We see Marlene at work, resplendent in her Queen Bee status; yet this 1982 superwoman has also had to abandon her child, and her private life is revealed to be as careless and selfish as her Thatcherite politics.

Ms Churchill's rich, ambitious play is a powerful exposition of the way in which top girls, like top men, often achieve success at the expense of their less able sisters. Max Stafford-Clark's immaculate production gives us some of the most inspired ensemble playing in London. *Ann McFerran*

West

Donmar Warehouse
13 May 1983

Like the earlier *East*, Steven Berkoff's *West* is a paranoid exploration of the sexuality,

PERFORMANCE

language and violence of East End life. Can things really be like this?

Berkoff's characters are a group of likely lads from Dalston Junction, all twitching shoulders, casual sexism and sparkling tie pins. Their leader is Mike, a tough nut with a sleek suit on his back and a flash bird in the wings. A contender then, and he's preparing for a confrontation with the leader of an oppo mob, a character billed as a cross between Superman and Ronnie Kray.

In part an exploration of the macho ethic, in part a deliberately non-realistic look at London low life, *West* is at its best when joyously celebrating the possibilities of language. Once again, Berkoff plunders the entire Shakespearean canon to create a dialect that is fast, witty, obscene and spoken in iambics. *Richard Rayner*

As You Like It

Lyric Hammersmith
11 December 1991
All the world may be a stage, but in Declan Donnellan's production it is only the men that are players. Instead of the usual, complicated enough, woman playing a man playing a woman, in Adrian Lester's delicate hands it is as it was in Shakespeare's time, a man playing a woman playing a man playing a woman.

For me, this is by far the most fascinating of all Cheek by Jowl's

Shakespearean productions. *Jane Edwardes*

Swan Lake

Piccadilly Theatre
18 September 1996
Already a hit on the dance circuit, Matthew Bourne's production with Adventures in Motion Pictures takes on the West End and remains virtually intact. Much has been made of the fact that the Swans are danced by a group of bare-chested men led by Adam Cooper, the handsome young star from the Royal Ballet. But if you're in the mood for camp, then you're in the wrong theatre. These Swans are feral. Strong, menacingly wild and fiercely dangerous, they embody the repressed, ultimately loony Prince. *Allen Robertson*

Shopping and Fucking

Royal Court Theatre Upstairs at the Ambassadors
9 October 1996
After the furore over the title, Mark Ravenhill's new play had something to live up to, and with one person leaving before he fainted and everybody, surely, feeling queasy, the playwright more than delivers. But this remarkable play is a lot more than mere schlock. Once again, like Sarah Kane's *Blasted*, sex and violence are inextricably entwined. The general concern is for a society of lowlifers, consumed by cheap

culture, junk food, easy drugs and sexual transactions rather than relationships. *Jane Edwardes*

The Weir

Royal Court Theatre Upstairs
2 July 1997
Over the past 12 months, the 25-year-old Dubliner [Conor McPherson] has taken a prominent place in the line-up of young Irish scribes making their mark in London – he can hardly take a breath, it seems, without winning a prize for it. His latest play is a departure from the monologue format. The cast list boasts five characters who make themselves cosy in a rural Sligo pub and swap ghost stories.

'Ghost stories fulfil our need for answers,' says McPherson. 'They are a playful way of addressing our fears and hopes. My play is also about the need for community and loneliness – the way storytelling fills a fundamental human need.' *Kate Stratton*

The Blue Room

Donmar Warehouse
30 September 1998
Although you wouldn't know it from reading the review in the *Daily Telegraph*, the *Blue Room* is rather more than an opportunity for a Hollywood star to take her clothes off and display her flawless body. And yet that perfect body, so unlike

the usual run of flabby, ungainly flesh that is seen onstage, is typical of a production that is chic, cool, beautiful to look at, and quite detached from a reality that most of us recognise. Mendes's crucial decision was to use just two actors – Nicole Kidman and Iain Glen – providing plenty of opportunities for Kidman to prove that she can act. *Jane Edwardes*

Jerry Springer – The Opera

National Theatre, Lyttelton
7 May 2003
Many Londoners have had the chance to play their part in this musical – sorry, opera's – development, a great vindication of Tom Morris's experimental Scratch Nights at BAC. The combination of relentlessly foul-mouthed trailer trash and posh music – exploring TV's eagerness to exploit our strange compusion to confess all on the box – is exhilarating, unexpected and sometimes even moving. It may not look like it now, but it took

some courage for new artistic director Nicholas Hytner to bring *JS* to the National. With this blast of new energy, he makes his mark immediately on the building. The cult of the *Rocky Horror Show* has finally been usurped. *Jane Edwardes*

War Horse

National Theatre, Olivier
24 October 2007
The Olivier may have been built to stage Shakespeare and Brecht, but it has really come into its own with a new generation of theatremakers who imaginatively enhance the text with powerful imagery that fills the space without resorting to the high-tech wizardry of a West End musical.

Nowhere is this more true than in Marianne Elliott and Tom Morris's production of Michael Morpurgo's popular and moving book. The horses don't speak, but they are so imaginatively created by South African company Handspring and so eloquently manipulated by the puppeteers that they effortlessly hold the stage. *Jane Edwardes*

Jerry Springer – The Opera

On the edge

Bras full of baked beans, performances on a tube platform, a giant mechanical pachyderm, or a burning Sellotape phallus… life's better with a little eccentricity.

By Brian Logan

In 1968, to experiment wasn't a luxury, it was a moral responsibility. According to Charles Marowitz, director of London's first fringe theatre, the Open Space, 'You were either with the revolution or against it – ie indiscriminately supporting the Extreme, the Extravagant and the Experimental, or helping the fuzz bust pot-heads and send [bookseller] John Calder to jail for publishing *Last Exit to Brooklyn*.' This was an age in which the outré was encouraged, and in which London became habituated to spectacles of surprise and subversion. There's been a corner of its theatre reserved for the extreme, the extravagant and the experimental ever since.

In the late 1960s, experimental could mean anything from the off-the-cuff antics of director Keith Johnstone's Theatre Machine, which launched improvisation on an unsuspecting world, to Joan Littlewood's proposed Fun Palace, a radical 'university of the streets' to engage factory workers in role-play, theatregoers in metalwork and everyone in shamanistic poetry readings till dawn. The LSD-tinged spirit of the age was distilled in the work of the People Show (who carried on until 2008), who, in 1969, lured Sloane Square passers-by into a phone box before offering them two sugar lumps coloured with red ink, or a bra stuffed with baked beans. The ginger-bearded gadfly Roland Muldoon, meanwhile, ran the Cartoon Archetypal Slogan Theatre, or CAST, which took on capitalism using mainly

white face-paint, a wardrobe full of leotards and an impish spirit. (Capitalism won.)

By the 1970s, theatre was spilling off the stage and onto the streets. The Natural Theatre Company became the so-called 'royal family of British street theatre', renowned for their 'egg-headed aliens' walkabout show that looked at the world through extra-terrestrial eyes, and for topsy-turvy depictions of authority, such as their snogging, dope-toking policemen. Forkbeard Fantasy sent up the Queen's Silver Jubilee in 1977 with the *Great British Square Dance*, in which four bowler-hatted businessmen, attached at the feet by planks of wood, danced around a giant Union Jack. Meanwhile, on stage and off (with his legendary Roadshow), Ken Campbell was establishing himself as Ilford's most eccentric son. Campbell helmed two of the decade's oddest offerings: *Illuminatus!*, a sci-fi trilogy that opened the National Theatre's Cottesloe stage; and the *Warp*, a time-travelling hippie quest lasting a bum-numbing 22 hours.

But London theatre was about to turn away from British eccentricity towards a more international sensibility. In 1981, LIFT – the London International Festival of Theatre – was founded by two enterprising twentysomethings, Rose Fenton and Lucy Neal. By bringing to the city work from every cranny of the planet, LIFT transformed London's notion of what theatre could be – and sometimes of what London could be too. At LIFT,

Freezies, one of numerous 'scenarios' offered by the Natural Theatre Company.

theatre could take place anywhere – in a park, a zoo cage or (in 1999's two-week-long performance *Urban Dream Capsule*) a shop window in Clapham Junction. And it could be as unlike 'normal' theatre as the imagination would allow.

Thanks to LIFT, and to producers such as Artsadmin and Artangel, Londoners were exposed to never-before-seen spectacles from groups such as North American visionary Robert Wilson, who filled the former Clink prison on Bankside with eerie tableaux of the building's history in 1995's *HG*; the Argentinians De La Guarda, who staged the sexy aerial-aquatic spectacular *Periodo Villa Villa!* at the Roundhouse in 1997; and the alarmingly indecipherable Italian Romeo Castellucci, whose not-very-Biblical *Genesis* at the Festival Hall starred a cast of robots and dogs.

Londoners were now regularly regaled with theatre by turns more intimate than before (director Deborah Warner's 'fantastical walk' for an audience-of-one through St Pancras Tower) and more public: the carnivalesque street artists Welfare State burnt down the (fake, alas) Houses of Parliament for an audience of 15,000 people in Catford in 1981, then raised the *Titanic* from the Regent's Canal in Limehouse in 1983.

The globalisation of London's theatre filtered down to local companies, with electrifying results. Theatre de Complicite, which imported the body-based theatre of French sage Jacques Lecoq, won the Perrier Award for comedy, then became the pre-eminent theatre ensemble of the '90s. In their wake followed vivacious, always-unexpected work from Told By An Idiot, Peepolykus and the demented duo Ridiculusmus, who chucked themselves into the Thames in 2000 for a Hammersmith audience, and who reduced their performance philosophy to the natty acronym ARSEFLOP.

Meanwhile, Forced Entertainment (founded in Sheffield in the 1980s) rocketed to international prominence with their bloody-minded brand of mixed-media, Dadaist 'durational performance'.

Director Tim Etchells called for 20-hour performances, hankering after that moment at which 'your tongue is loose, the connections in your brain are scrambled. Fatigue has set in and been followed by hysteria.' But if Forced Ents craved fatigue, the experimentalism of the '80s had a revitalising effect. A new generation of inquisitive entertainment soon dawned: Improbable Theatre, whose giant burning Sellotape phallus, *Sticky*, lit up the South Bank in 2000; Blast Theory, whose 1998 project *Kidnap* involved abducting members of the public and webcasting their incarceration; and Shunt, staging hip, abstract cabarets under a railway arch in the guts of the East End.

Today, offbeat performance thrives on the margins – and infiltrates the mainstream. At the Shunt Vaults, at BAC and, increasingly often, in non-theatre sites around the city (Simon McBurney's the *Vertical Line* on a derelict tube platform, Mem Morrison's *Leftovers* in a greasy-spoon cafe, the Australian company Back to Back's *Small Metal Objects* amid Stratford's teeming station concourse), artists are reinventing theatre and storming Londoners' imaginations.

When the *Sultan's Elephant* arrived from France in 2005 to take a two-day parade around our city, Londoners spilled out in their thousands to follow this giant puppet pachyderm and, in doing so, to celebrate their own togetherness. In 2008, they crowded round the end of a giant mechanical eyepiece outside City Hall, the Telectroscope, to peer at New Yorkers peering back at them, making bizarre momentary connections through a hypothetical undersea tunnel. In London, the Extreme is often to be found meeting the Extravagant and the Experimental. And the memories can last a lifetime.

Clockwise from top left: *The Sultan's Elephant*, 2006; Mem Morrison's *Leftovers*, 2006; Anne Bean's *Remember Me*, 2004.

HEDONISM INTRODUCTION
SEX CITYSCAPE FASHION
SOCIETY SHOPPING COMEDY
DRAMA PROTEST & POLITICS
VISUAL ARTS PERFORMANCE

LITERATURE GANGS OPINION

COCKNEYS BARS ON SCREEN
DANCE MUSIC TELEVISION
BUILDINGS CLUBS NIGHTLIFE
SPORT & FITNESS MEMORIES
STYLE FOOD & DRINK GIGS
CONSUME RIOTS REFERENCE

Metropolitan lines

Is there any such thing as the London novel?

By DJ Taylor

'Millwall,' said Muncie, tapping the glass. 'It looks like an island,' said Hood. 'It is an island,' said Murf. 'Isle of Dogs. I wouldn't live there for anything.' Paul Theroux, *The Family Arsenal* (1976)

Back in the early 1950s, newly divorced, strapped for cash and looking to fund an agreeable-sounding lifestyle of genteel globe-trotting, Evelyn Waugh's elder brother Alec sat down with the aim of writing a work that would rejuvenate his career. But what should he write about? An England only just emerging from the tundra of rationing and Attlee-era state socialism? The chill, egalitarian air sweeping in from beyond the Iron Curtain? No, Waugh, as recounted in his autobiography *The Best Wine Last* (1978), settled for 'an ambitious novel about London life'. The book, *Guy Renton* (1953), was not a great success. Perhaps it was just that, even in the age of Churchill, Truman and John Foster Dulles, 'London life' was moving rather beyond the novelist's radar.

Half a century later, the task of arranging the countless discrete societies of which London consists into some kind of plausible whole has turned more problematic still. 'From where I live, it is difficult to have a complete picture of London,' Tim Curtiz, the Belgravia mews-residing US journalist of Justin Cartwright's *Look at it this Way* (1990) ruefully concedes. Curtiz's inventory of the capital's contending tribes ('the barristers with their anally-retentive tailoring and Lionel Barrymore haircuts; the vicious little bastards in white vans with ladders on the roof; the crazed minicabbers... the febrile gay boys filing into the public conveniences in Clerkenwell... the cub mistresses eating fairy cakes in church halls... the gypsies selling candy floss beside the dodgems

on Hampstead Heath, the schoolgirls in their little green uniforms and white socks') runs on to the end of the page. Where do you stop, Curtiz wonders. 'You can't even begin. Like the notion of infinite space, London is not susceptible to human reason.'

As all this may suggest, the idea of a 'London novel' is what scientists call a false isolate: no such thing exists, merely a bumper selection of novels set in that cramped and pullulating space within the M25, whose coign of geographical vantage can often turn out to be uncomfortably narrow. One sees this in the titles of books that use their metropolitan tethering as part of the sales pitch. There is an ominous particularity about a novel that calls itself *A Kilburn Tale*, *Notting Hell*, *A Far Cry from Kensington* or *The Sweets of Pimlico*, the thought of enclaves, compartments and demarcation lines; even the works that advertise themselves as panoramas – Patrick Hamilton's '30s trilogy, *Twenty Thousand Streets Under the Sky*, say – usually end up settling for a very small patch of territory.

This titular shakiness is compounded by the signposts of tradition and influence to which practically all 'London novels' defer, almost from the moment of their conception. The London crime novel is as old as Defoe and Fielding. The young man from the provinces making his timorous way to the thronged and clamorous city has been stalking the area around Oxford Circus for over a quarter-millennium. The London bohemia novel, gestured at in Thackeray's *Pendennis* (1850), with its accounts of roister-doistering at the Cave of Harmony and the Cyder Cellar, derives from Pierce Egan's *Life in London, or The Adventures of Corinthian Tom, Jeremiah Hawthorne and their Friend Bob Logic* (1821), with illustrations by Cruickshank, which itself goes back to the

'The idea of a "London novel" is what scientists call a false isolate: no such thing exists.'

night-life of Augustan young men about town. The terrorist-revolutionary-espionage novel, brought into being by the mid-Victorian panic about 'spies' and Fenian plotters, moves on through Henry James's *The Princess Casamassima* (1886), Joseph Conrad's *The Secret Agent* (1902), Graham Greene's *It's a Battlefield* (1932) and Paul Theroux's *The Family Arsenal* (1976) – IRA terror cells operating out of a Catford terrace – to contemporary despatches from the jihad frontline. Even so necessarily restricted a sub-genre as the novel of London literary life has a recognised chain of descent, taking in *Pendennis*, George Gissing's mordant *New Grub Street* (1891), Orwell's *Keep the Aspidistra Flying* (1936) and Anthony Powell's *Books Do Furnish a Room* (1971), before ending up with a work like Nigel Williams' *My Life Closed Twice* (1977). And this is to ignore such obvious fictional categories as the London gay novel, the 'Hampstead novel' (still going strong, if in increasingly stylised form), the migrant novel, the East End novel, the Kensington novel – each of them sanctified and mythologised by a century or so of hard, professional use, and nearly all of them capable of being re-imagined and re-invented in startlingly unexpected ways.

But perhaps one ought to start with the idea of London as a place of refuge and enticement, the magnet to which no self-respecting provincial hick or chancer can fail to allow himself to be drawn. If novels of 1950s British regional life have an authenticating mark, it is the scene in which our hero, terminally ground-down by his footling job and non-existent love-life, plots a decisive relocation. Kingsley Amis's *Lucky Jim* (1954) ends with the absconding Jim Dixon on the railway platform waiting for the train that will bear him away, his mind buzzing with London place-names ('Bayswater. Knightsbridge. Notting Hill Gate. Pimlico. Belgrave Square. Chelsea. No, not Chelsea.' Early versions have 'No, not Bloomsbury.') Sometimes the motive is straightforward escape: Margaret in David Storey's *Flight into Camden* (1960) heads south from her staid South Yorkshire home to cohabit with her married, schoolteacher lover. More often the lure is a job or, in the brave new world of the post-war welfare state, an education.

Some of the most interesting 'London novels' of the post-war period are those in which different strands of literary ancestry are mixed together. Alan Sillitoe's *A Start in Life* (1970), for example, is a very different proposition from the backstreet

Nottingham reportage with which he made his name. For one thing, there is its form, which is picaresque, taking its hero Michael Cullen from the Midlands to a wide-boy career among the Soho fleshpots.

Then there is the self-conscious awareness of literary models, which exchanges the wary reticence of the early books for a succession of characters whose first act, on arriving in the text, is to recapitulate their lives to date. The thought that a more or less realistic premise – the young man making his way in the world – has been high-jacked by a series of fantasy projections is reinforced by the almost surreal tone of the final chapters, full of gangsters zealously double-crossing each other amid a hail of bullets and the reek of cordite.

Among other accomplishments, Cullen is a kind of skit on the idea of the existential hero, playing off one girl against another and lying his way out of trouble at a moment's notice. Deviously at large in 'Swinging London', he works as a strip-club bouncer and chauffeur-factotum to a racketeering bullion smuggler before falling calamitously in love with his employer's daughter. In fact, most of these accounts of provincials on the make in the '60s and '70s metropolis were painfully realistic. They also – a tribute to the profound demographic changes brought about by an expanding jobs market and the new educational opportunities – tended to be about women.

It's a woman's world

While some of the usual continuities of form and ancestry apply – Hilary Mantel's account of a London university student residence

Capital writers, clockwise from left: Justin Cartwright, Monica Ali, Paul Theroux and Zadie Smith.

An Experiment in Love (1995) self-consciously borrows from Muriel Spark's *The Girls of Slender Means* (1963), which itself owes something to the spiritless zenana of the Burpenfield Club in JB Priestley's *Angel Pavement* (1930) – the tone of this new wave of women's fiction is often sharply opposed to the compromising spirit of some of its forebears. The '60s-to-'70s London girl was hot in pursuit of a freedom – sexual, economic, intellectual – mostly denied her predecessors. Clara Maugham, the heroine of Margaret Drabble's wonderfully acerbic *Jerusalem the Golden* (1967), is a pattern example of this new breed of colonists, raised in the philistine fortress of 'Northam' (Sheffield), desperate to prise herself free from the stifling embrace of her puritanical mother. Gaining a place at the University of London, and later feeling that 'her years in London had merely strengthened her desire to live there for the rest of her life', Clara takes the *Brideshead Revisited* route of falling in love with an entire family.

The stylish, well-connected Denhams, who live chaotically in bohemian Highgate, include Clara's college chum Clelia, with whom she is infatuated, and an unhappily married brother, Gabriel, with whom she begins an affair. Called back to Northam to attend her mother's terminal illness, and temporarily quartered in the family house, Clara finds herself balanced on a pontoon bridge between two worlds. Eventually she summons Gabriel to take her away: she will not make the mistakes that a trawl through some ancient photographs reveals her mother to have made.

Novels about '60s and '70s London are full of girls trying not to make the mistakes their mothers made, fearful of being trapped in sterile relationships, moving on from adolescent inertia

The same could be said of most post-war British novelists. The 'City novel', an ancient genre inaugurated by *Dombey and Son* (1848), if not before, generally falls into two categories: novels by writers with a great deal of relevant expertise which are not terribly good as novels; and works with a Square Mile background that are somewhat short on forensic detail. Desmond Briggs' *Standing into Danger* (1985), an account of the Lloyd's insurance market, falls into the former category, and Ferdinand Mount's *The Liquidator* (1996), one of whose characters is a celebrated insolvency specialist, into the latter. But the tradition of not knowing, or, in some cases, not caring, about the intricate patterns of City life is as old as the genre. Nowhere in all of *Dombey and Son*'s 900 pages, for example, do we actually discover how Mr Dombey – presented as a figure of quite deathless power and influence – makes his money. *Angel Pavement* is quite as indifferent to the veneers and inlays in which the moribund firm of Twigg & Dersingham melancholically trades.

A genuine City novel, in which the novelist has the material at his finger-tips, can consequently be a bracing experience: Piers Paul Read's *A Season in the West* (1988), for instance, which contains a detailed account of the financial collapse of autumn 1987, or Justin Cartwright's

into a world where anything seems possible. Distance tends to give these individual lives an occasionally exaggerated sociological importance.

AS Byatt's *Babel Tower* (1996), written nearly 30 years after its author's own arrival in London, finds twentysomething Frederica Potter fleeing a vicious husband and backwater Herefordshire for a career as a publisher's reader and art school lectrice. The call of zeitgeist is everywhere apparent: the Who are playing 'My Generation'; the first Wilson government is in Downing Street; the High Court resounds to the fury of obscenity cases. Clara Maugham is, of course, quite as much a symbol of the wider social landscape as her distant cousin, but history, hindsight and literary politics can sometimes make Frederica seem much more narrowly representative of her time. One of *Babel Tower*'s most marked characteristics, for example, is the loathing that its author clearly feels for the whole idea of the swinging '60s metropolis.

None of this, though, wholly disguises the pull of memory. Frederica, as keen on undiscovered country as any other '60s heroine, is 'excited' and at the same time slightly confused by London. 'She knew little of it, and could not connect the parts she knew in a coherent map in her head. What she liked was the anonymity and variety of her possible journeys from territory to territory.' There is a significant moment in Byatt's earlier novel, *Still Life* (1985), when Frederica approaches St Paul's and is horribly baffled by the tide of office workers making their way east to the City. 'She had no idea where they were going, or how they lived, or what they did, and stared at every advancing young man as if to extract some sense of his habits, his slant of mind.'

BRICK LANE E.1.
इंटলেন

'Tribalism has its dangers: insufficient expertise, the supposed gap between writer and territory.'

despatch from the death throes of Thatcherism, *In Every Face I Meet* (1995). Northleach, Cartwright's fortysomething hero, is a particularly symbolic figure: a management consultant whose promotion to the directorship of an ailing firm is simply a way of extending liability for the business's debts. Just as symbolic is the novel's finale, in which he is near-fatally waylaid by a scheming drug-dealer who uses his prostitute girlfriend as bait.

Cartwright's interest, as in *Look at it this Way*, lies in the myriad compartments into which London endlessly sub-divides, and the factors that sometimes work to bring them together: as Northleach discovers to his cost, the walls between one London community and another can be paper-thin. The London bohemia novel, into which several of Cartwright's books intermittently threaten to mutate, reflects these edgy translations. Like many another branch of London fiction, it is hard to define: not quite low-life (Martin Amis's *London Fields*, 1989, and its many successors), overly self-conscious, occasionally, in its staking out of too-familiar territory (Colin Wilson's *Adrift in Soho*, 1961). Unsurprisingly, *The Family Arsenal* strays into its upper level: Lady Arrow, its dotty libertarian aristocrat, and Araba Nightwing, its politically engaged actress, would not look out of place in *The Princess Casamissima*, to which Theroux obliquely refers.

All the same, the real novels of London bohemia inhabit a landscape well beyond the world of the Chelsea lofts and the Soho drinking clubs. At first glance, Carol Birch's *Life in the Palace* (1988), set on a run-down Kennington estate in the 1970s, seems to be a straightforward depiction of London working-class life. Close inspection of its main characters – the former schoolteacher Judy Grey, brittle, demon-haunted Raff – reveals a community of fiercely intelligent individualists who have taken a deliberate decision to opt out of the processes of conventional society. When the public world impinges on Kinnaird Buildings, it does so almost parenthetically. One of Birch's characters works at what sounds like Selfridges in Oxford Street at a time when there are 'bombs in the West End'. At one point, the noise from some royal celebration floats over the rooftops. The 1977 Jubilee? Birch doesn't say. Her characters are resolutely detached from the formal world going on a couple of miles from their doorsteps.

Tribes and tribulations

Another sign of *Life in the Palace*'s bohemian underpinning is its unshowy use of 'ethnic' characters: girls have West Indian boyfriends from Stockwell; one of the Kinnaird Buildings habitués is black. What sometimes gets called the 'multicultural' novel is over half a century old – Samuel Selvon's report on the Windrush diaspora, the *Lonely Londoners* (1956), and the Nigerian Buchi Emecheta's *In the Ditch* (1972),

From page to screen: Tannishtha Chatterjee as Nazneen in the film version of Monica Ali's *Brick Lane*.

were two notable pioneers – but in some ways the multicultural tag is misleading. Such novels – Hanif Kureishi's *The Buddha of Suburbia* (1990), Zadie Smith's *White Teeth* (2000), Monica Ali's *Brick Lane* (2003) – tend, like almost every other kind of London novel, to be confined to particular locales and concentrate on particular ethnic groups. This kind of tribalism has its dangers – insufficient expertise, the supposed gap between writer and territory – exemplified by the long-running row that followed publication of the immensely successful *Brick Lane*, the discovery that the author was Oxbridge-educated posh whereas her subjects were Sylheti migrants, and the assumption that Ali was merely peddling 'negative stereotypes' about the area. The nadir in these exchanges was reached in a *Guardian* leader effectively rebuking Ali for having the cheek to write a novel about the Bengali East End in the first place. The novelist Hari Kunzru offered a brisk rejoinder in which, assessing the qualifications which the *Guardian* seemed to find necessary for writers of novels on these subjects, he demanded, 'How black do I have to be?'

Naturally enough, there are points to be made on both sides. In a free society, novelists can presumably write the kind of books they want to write in the ways they want to write them; most of the community leaders who complained about *Brick Lane* would probably not know what a novel was if they fell over one in the street. On the other hand, no one should doubt the power of fiction – see the Rushdie affair of the late 1980s – to alarm the sensibilities of disadvantaged people who feel, or have been told to feel, that they are being got at. Perhaps the strongest argument in *Brick Lane*'s favour was the brisk sale of copies in the area's bookshops: whether or not they agreed with her, locals seemed to be interested in what Ali had to say.

However different the geographical or procedural circumstances, we are back with the cast of *Look at it this Way*: advertising executive Victoria; venal City dealer Miles unwillingly caught up in organised crime; Mike the yobbish art director; Curtiz the émigré journalist; Bernie the ageing Jewish actor with his dream of starring in a musical about the Blitz. Each, in some sense, is the representative of a tribe, hardly any of whose members understand their opposite numbers, and whose engagement with the city of which they are a part is founded on a series of jealously guarded myths. This, together with the sheer pace of metropolitan history's forward march, can sometimes give even the best 'London novels' an air of immensely sophisticated reportage. 'London life', if there is such a thing, hangs some way above their heads – dense, vagrant, ineluctable, and as unyielding to the chroniclers of the 21st century as it was to Alec Waugh.

DJ Taylor is a novelist and critic.

TIMELINE

1969
The first Booker Prize event is held at Stationers' Hall in the City. PH Newby wins for his novel *Something to Answer For*.

1973
The Rachel Papers by Martin Amis is published. Amis goes ton to earn a reputation as one of the foremost literary chroniclers of contemporary London.

1979
The fortnightly literary and political magazine the *London Review of Books* is founded. Its rival, the *Times Literary Supplement*, is kept off the newsstands for a year by a printers' strike.

1983
Granta chooses its first Best of Young British Novelists list. Many of those nominated go on to enjoy stellar careers. They include Martin Amis, Pat Barker, Julian Barnes, William Boyd, Ian McEwan and Salman Rushdie.

1984
Ted Hughes succeeds Sir John Betjeman as Poet Laureate.

1989
Salman Rushdie goes into hiding after the Ayatollah Khomeini issues a fatwa against him following the publication of *The Satanic Verses*.

1993
Salman Rushdie's *Midnight's Children* wins the Booker of Bookers. The award is for the best novel to have won the Booker Prize in its 25-year history.

1997
Harry Potter and the Philosopher's Stone is published. The success of the following six books in the series, together with the films, video games and assorted wizard-themed merchandise, makes J.K Rowling the highest-earning novelist in history.

Iain Sinclair publishes *Lights Out for the Territory*, the first of several books about London that will obsessively mine the urban unconscious.

2003
Monica Ali is named as one of *Granta*'s Best of Young British Novelists on the basis of the unpublished manuscript of *Brick Lane*. The novel, about the Bangladeshi community in East End, is published later in the year and is subsequently made into a film.

2006
Will Self publishes *The Book of Dave*, a novel about a London cabbie whose scribblings are disinterred 500 years after his death to become the blueprint of a post-apocalyptic civilisation.

2007
Southbank Centre launches the first London Literature Festival. This coincides with the 25th anniversary of the daily Southbank Centre Book Market, held underneath Waterloo Bridge.

LITERATURE

Jamar Allen in full flow.

Poetry slams

Live poetry has captured the imagination of London's youth. Andrew Motion, the poet laureate, visits one of the competitive heats in the Rise Londonwide Youth Slam Championship to see the dynamic art form for himself.

For the uninitiated, first things first. A poetry slam is a competitive poetry performance in which participants present an original piece of work and are judged by members of the audience. Slams first took off in the States during the late 1970s, often (but not exclusively) giving a voice to young black people who felt drowned out or ignored by more establishment forms of writing. Typically, they addressed tough urban themes (domestic violence, gun crime, racial tension) in high-voltage raps and plain-speaking free-forms.

Previously, poetry readings had been just that – readings – and were usually pretty sedate affairs. Suddenly they were fun, noisy and packed. It was only a matter of time before slams crossed the Atlantic and bred a British counterpart.

The Poetry Society was quick to see their potential – not just as things in themselves, but as a way of proving that poetry could take centre stage in lives that might otherwise consider it irrelevant or (more likely) merely something that had to be endured in school.

This year's slam is now well under way, and the qualifying round, held at the Jackson's Lane

'Slamming is visceral,
driven by strong rhythms
and rhymes, and direct.'

Theatre in Archway on 26 April, suggests that it's
going to be the most successful yet. As with the
three other rounds being held elsewhere in London,
the theme was 'respect', the participants were aged
12 to 18, the poems took three minutes (maximum)
to deliver, and the poets were allowed to perform
alone or in a group of which each member had
contributed to the writing of the poem. Nineteen
people took part, and by the time DJ Concept and
DJ Trinz had played people into their seats, and
the MC Joelle Taylor had shaken the rafters in her
introduction, the theatre felt more like Wembley
than the slopes of Parnassus.

Without exception, the performers captured the
authentic and unignorable sounds of modern
London in their work, rhyming and chiming and
chanting and ranting in a mood of quickly rising
excitement. Familiar phrases were broken open by
contact with new structures, slow thoughts were
wound around quick beats, hilarity jostled with
anger, and pathos with passion. Slam competitions
may rely on the energy of individual speakers, but
they create a terrific feeling of community.

These days, we happily accept that poetry is a
broad church, reflecting the variety of our culture
in the diversity of its voices. Which means it's
proper to celebrate everything distinct and
individual about slamming. It's visceral, driven
by strong rhythms and rhymes, and direct.

Although the form and the presentation of the
slam felt absolutely contemporary, its emphases
were often orthodox. Not just because performer
after performer insisted that respect needs to be
earned, but because they generally associated it
with ways of behaving that even the most old-
fashioned poetry-reader would recognise.

Slamming is, in the best sense, a self-centred
form, and among young performers is especially
likely to establish a sense of threatened innocence
in the speaker before turning to the wider world.
If the poems were delivered with less energy, this
might become sentimental; generally, though, it
creates a sense of integrity that in turn licenses
outrage, disappointment, offence – and celebration.

From Derrida
to Dr Martens

One of the first outposts of London's late '60s
counterculture to sprout in the grimy bohemia of
Camden Town was Compendium Bookshop.
Opened in 1968, Compendium rapidly established
itself as a conduit for the radical and avant garde
literature that was beginning to arrive in Britain
from Europe and the United States. Upstairs, it
stocked the kind of experimental poetry and
fiction unobtainable anywhere else in the capital.
Downstairs, the basement was a gloomy mecca
for adepts of the chicest, most obscure strains of
continental theory and philosophy. Compendium
survived the political disappointments of the
1970s and '80s, only to succumb, in 2000, to more
prosaic, economic forces. The demise of the Net
Book Agreement and the growth of internet
retailing meant it could no longer survive on the
patronage of London's radical intelligentsia.
Today Camden High Street today is more Dr
Martens than Derrida and Debord.

Martin Amis

The thing that strikes you first about Martin Amis is a near-neurotic concern to safeguard his own image. At four o'clock on a Friday afternoon, the TV set in his flat was on, scenes from a B-feature flickering above a gleaming IBM typewriter on the floor. Amis quickly turned the set off. 'It was for the cleaning lady's kids,' he explained. 'I wouldn't like you to think I spend all day watching crappy Westerners.'

Eight years after the publication of *The Rachel Papers*, Amis is, at 31, London's most publicised and most notorious literary figure. After leaving Oxford with a first in English, he started work on the editorial staff of the *Times Literary Supplement*, where it is unlikely that the name of his father actively hindered his chances. Four novels, three screenplays, innumerable articles, and the prestigious literary editorship of the *New Statesman* have followed, in less than a decade. During this time, Amis has learned a lot about marketing his product: people expect him to be mordant, flashy, controversial, and it is precisely this gossip column persona that he cultivates.

Along with his friends Clive James of the *Observer*, Julian Barnes of the *New Statesman* and *Sunday Times*, Craig Raine of *Quarto*, and Tina Brown of *Tatler*, Amis represents a powerful lobby of youngish Oxbridge critics who signalled the emergence of a new style of narcissistic journalism in the mid '70s. He has established himself as a prominent figure in a literary scene which, he admits, has its Mafia-like aspects.

'Yes, I suppose it's like a Mafia in some ways. Books may get given to a writer's friend for review. Certain writers are in bad with certain magazines and get dumped on. What it isn't is the Leavisite fantasy of a Zanzibar where writers and editors exchange wads of notes. The corruption is much more haphazard and subtle than that.'

Amis is not among that small group of writers who can earn a living from novels alone, and relies on journalism for much of his income. Currently he works from home – a small rented flat off Queensway, an area which animates much of his fiction – as a staff writer/reviewer for the *Observer*. His features consist largely of going to America and being neurotic there, detailing intensely subjective responses to bizarre phenomena: born-again Christianity, child murders in Atlanta,

Norman Mailer. The process, which he says involves a great deal of cowering in hotel rooms, results in journalism that, although lacquered with his customary stylistic brilliance, is intellectually fragile and swiftly forgotten. The fact is that, whatever the ostensible topic, the author's mind turns inexorably to a subject it finds much more interesting: Martin Amis.

His conscious presentation of himself as the most cynical penman in town has made Amis familiar to a wide audience, while alienating many potential readers, with the result that his fiction is more talked about than read, more often the subject of unthinking approval or dismissal than analysis.

Amis's attitude to the dubious celebrity he has created is ambiguous: he is delighted about being controversial and sought-after, yet anxious to promote his more serious literary credentials: 'I've been accused of not taking my work seriously enough,' he says. 'Of course my writing is serious. It's much too serious to talk seriously about it.'

In fact, his four novels – *The Rachel Papers, Dead Babies, Success* and *Other People: A Mystery Story* – have established him as one of the most provocative and consistently daring writers of fiction around. His expressed intention is to sweeten the pill of modernism, annexing complex narrative structures to a certain commitment to the populist techniques of realism. At best, his books are both penetrating and funny, meticulously contrived comedy counterpointing the almost surreal quality of the environments he describes, particularly that of contemporary London. Amis has developed his writing to show an increased concern with London street scenes, where a general sense of unease is translated into the specific experiences of a single character.

'Psychosis is the normal answer to urban life. Perhaps the inevitable result of the city idea is to push people to extremes – concentrated lifestyles, emphasis on speed, complete subservience to money. In Queensway you can walk around at any time and hear ten people screaming a mad commentary on life. The streets sing.'

Other People is easily his most controlled and assured novel to date, less extravagant and self-indulgent than its predecessors. It opens with an eerie, memorable description of a woman waking up in a mental hospital. She is an almost total amnesiac, having forgotten not only who she is but also the nature of 'everyday' reality. She escapes from the institution and dubs herself Mary Lamb after hearing tramps chanting a nursery rhyme. For Mary, other people are the mystery story.

A malign and omnipotent narrator traces Mary's attempts to transcend this state of solipsism and reconstruct her own identity. There is some familiar Amis stuff about the-horribleness-of-sex-and-life-in-general before the novel closes enigmatically with a scene reminiscent of the closing shots of Hitchcock's *Psycho*.

> 'If you want to talk in feminist terms, my fiction isn't anti-women, it's anti-people. Everyone has a bad time.'

Of course, there is a problem, as it seems there must always be with Amis. For all its qualities, *Other People* still remains open to the charge that Amis's fiction parades violence, despair and sexism in a wilfully gloating, even sadistic fashion. In all of his novels, there are characters who are dismissive and contemptuous of women. Amis admits that the most consistent criticism of his work is sexism, but doesn't regard it as anything worth losing his cool about.

'I really think that it's just fashion criticising me. My stuff will still be the same when feminist criticism moves away from it and on to something different. If you want to talk in those terms, then my fiction isn't anti-women, it's anti-people. Everyone has a bad time in it. And people assume that these characters express my attitudes. That just isn't so – my books are satires.'

The relationship between Amis and his narrators suggests that their presence operates only as an element in an artistic game, rather than to make any moral or intellectual point. 'The idea that the novelist punishes bad characters and rewards good ones doesn't bear up any more. Of course the nastiness is an element in my stuff. I write about that because it's more interesting. Everyone's more interested in the bad news. Only one writer has ever written convincingly about happiness, and that's Tolstoy. Nobody else seems to be able to make it swing on the page.'

Amis has written that idea's are 'the novelist's fatal disease', and perhaps he regards all politics as irrelevant to literature. It seems difficult not to conclude that his novels are merely experiments with different patterns of expression, all surface and no depth, and that he believes style to be the crucial factor in fiction, not ideas and content.

'I think that expresses half the truth. The structures of my books come on a bit like that. But I see things as being more chaotic. It's true that I'm not particularly interested in politics. I'm more interested in rival versions of sanity – one person saying to another, "My sanity is saner than yours". Nonetheless, I'd calculate my imagination to be of the Left. I'm more obsessed by down-and-outs and the griefs of ordinary people than in life at the top end of the scale. It's not the novelist's business to worry about social causations. All he must be alive to is the effects they have.'

Original interview by Richard Rayner.

LITERATURE

Bookslam

This 'literary nightclub' was founded by writer Patrick Neate and musician-cum-DJ Ben Watt. It takes place once a month at Neighbourhood, in the shadow of the Westway in Ladbroke Grove. Bookish luminaries to have tried their hand at stand-up literature here include Dave Eggers, Nick Hornby, Hari Kunzru, Toby Litt, Will Self and Zadie Smith. A typical evening involves DJ sets and live music, as well as writers promoting new work. Neate calls its 'clubbing for grown-ups'. His empire is growing: the monthly Bookslam podcast, which features interviews with authors as well as readings, won a Sony Radio Academy Gold Award in 2008.

Literary London

By Jonathan Derbyshire. Illustrations by Quinton Winter

LITERATURE

Coach & Horses

The Coach & Horses in Soho's Greek Street was immortalised in Keith Waterhouse's play *Jeffrey Bernard is Unwell*. The play's title referred to the notice often posted in the *Spectator* whenever Bernard, who was frequently incapacitated by the prodigious quantities of alchohol he consumed at the Coach, was unable to file his column for the magazine. Shortly before he died in 1997, Bernard mourned the disappearance of 'decent pubs', places that didn't sell cigarettes or 'chemical beer' and 'didn't have fucking music'.

Shepperton

Most of JG Ballard's fiction, including the dystopian *Crash* and the partially autobiographical *Empire of the Sun*, was composed in a semi-detached house in Shepperton, in the distant suburbs west of London. 'I came to live in Shepperton in 1960,' Ballard has written. 'I thought: the future isn't in the metropolitan areas of London. I want to go out to the new suburbs, near the film studios. This was the England I wanted to write about, because this was the new world.'

London Library

AS Byatt's Booker prize-winning intellectual mystery *Possession* is partly set among the heaving stacks and distinctive cast-iron latticed floors of the London Library. This St James's Square institution, presided over by Sir Tom Stoppard, has a stellar membership, many of whom are attracted by the highly idiosyncratic system for classifying the books.

London Review of Books

The *London Review* was founded in 1979, during a strike that kept the *Times Literary Supplement* off the newsstands for more than a year. The paper's first 'office' was a desk in the packing department of Waterstone's (formerly Dillon's) on Gower Street. So cramped were the conditions that an assistant to editor Karl Miller once elbowed an entire month's invoices into the bin by mistake.

Hampstead

The only area of London to have a literary sub-genre named after it, Hampstead is historically a bookish enclave. But like other regions of the capital's former bohemia, these days one's neighbours here are more likely to be hedge fund managers or footballers than struggling writers. Some literary grandees are holding out, however: novelist and broadcaster Melvyn Bragg lives in Hampstead, as do the Nobel laureate Doris Lessing and the novelist Fay Weldon.

Bertorelli's

Throughout the 1970s, the poet and historian Robert Conquest hosted 'Fascist lunches' for right-leaning writers and intellectuals at Bertorelli's in Charlotte Street. Regular fascist lunchers included the novelists Anthony Powell and John Braine, the historian and polemicist Tibor Szamuely, newspaper columnist Bernard Levin and Conquest's close friend Kingsley Amis. The F-word was intended as a provocation to metropolitan lefties like Amis's son Martin, against whose 'fucking fool' politics the ex-Communist Kingsley would rail entertainingly.

Spitalfields

Jeanette Winterson, whose first novel *Oranges Are Not the Only Fruit* won the Whitbread Prize in 1985, has diversified her operations in recent years. She is now the proprietor of Verde's, a bespoke delicatessen in Spitalfields. The shop is a temple to 'real food', which Winterson describes as 'one of life's true pleasures'.

Pillars of Hercules

This gloomy Soho pub was frequented in the mid 1970s by literary young turks such as Martin Amis, Clive James, James Fenton, Christopher Hitchens, Ian McEwan and Julian Barnes. The offices of the *New Review* were next door, and that magazine's editor, Ian Hamilton, preferred to do his editing in what one of its habitués described as a 'sticky-carpeted dive'. Proofs were corrected and judgements handed down over the house red.

East End

Iain Sinclair is a laureate of the East End, a tireless psychogeographer of the territory between Whitechapel and West Ham. His novel *White Chappell, Scarlet Tracings* features an bookseller obsessed with Jack the Ripper. And in *Rodinsky's Room*, co-written with Rachel Lichtenstein, Sinclair probes the mystery of the eponymous inhabitant of 19 Princelet Street in Spitalfields.

LITERATURE

John Betjeman

LITERATURE

The following conversation took place at Sir John Betjeman's house in Chelsea in the middle of a sunny day: blue sky, daffodils and daisies.

'You've done your hair up in a new colour!' was the first thing he said, with his toothy, crooked grin which is so open and fresh and artless and hasn't changed since he charmed his mother's tea guests with it as a little boy carrying a teddy bear by one arm.

'No, no, I went to the tropics.'

'Would you like to have a little bubbly? Mr Glover, where are you? Oh, there you are, let's have another glass. And let's have another bottle.'

Fallowell: Sorry, I'm a bit late actually. The King's Road is blocked off.

Betjeman: It's not the punks, is it?

Fallowell: No, steamrollers. They're making a new road.

Betjeman: Mechanical punk… Can't offer you a cigarette. Haven't you got any?

Fallowell: I've got some Camels.

Betjeman: I love the smell of it.

Fallowell: Have you an ashtray?

Betjeman: Use that Chelsea Arts bowl. They kindly presented it to me, the Chelsea Potters, a lovely firm.

Fallowell: Why did you move here from the City?

Betjeman: Driven out by the noise. I really liked the City better. But you know that great Barbican thing glaring down at one. Horrible great thing. It's only in the morning that you need this champagne to drink, you know.

Fallowell: What do you have in the afternoon?

Betjeman: Sometimes I have a rest.

Betjeman: I like your things in the *Spectator*.

Fallowell: Did you ever know any of those *Spectator* people?

Betjeman: I knew Peter Fleming. He said that each number of the *Spectator* was *semper idem sed numquam verbatim*. Which do you think is the dullest periodical? *Punch*, I suppose. I dare say the *Investor's Chronicle* is quite dull.

Fallowell: *The Farmer and Stockbreeder*. Did you get any of my postcards from India?

Betjeman: Yes, I did! Lovely. Those wonderful Raj churches that should have been in Surrey or Edinburgh.

Fallowell: Yes, I sent one of St Paul's Cathedral in Calcutta.

Betjeman: That's obviously wonderful.

Fallowell: It's the Regency version of Canterbury Cathedral.

Betjeman: Is it well attended, St Paul's Calcutta?

Fallowell: Mm, well, the outpatients department is. They have a crack Samaritan service in jeeps.

Betjeman: I've never been there, but my wife has.

Fallowell: I saw her in Hay-on-Wye, incidentally.

Betjeman: I used to go and stay there, but she has no water or electricity or heating, and all the windows are open with the wind whistling through the place – well, I'm rather frightened to go now, in case it kills me. Look what I had in today, from Southend-on-Sea, a lovely place. This letter, read it, it seems they've saved the Royal Hotel there from demolition. It cost £350,000. The little picture at the top shows you what Southend's like – a lovely Georgian terrace.

Fallowell: Ah, for a moment I was thinking of another hotel. Like a château on a bluff, one of the first purpose-built Victorian hotels – near Skegness, was it?

Betjeman: Scarborough! Now, that's strange, I also had a letter about that one today. I wish they would hold on to these things. These buildings are worth anything to the country. Anything with a gable or a tower is worth saving.

Fallowell: I like the new aerial roadways in Birmingham.

Betjeman: Newcastle was lovely until Poulson was let in. Now there are just a few streets left in order to show you what it was once like. Newcastle Central Railway Station is still there. Forgive my brushing my hair, but I suddenly found this hairbrush, and it's the most delightful sensation, what little hair I've got left, like a scalp massage. It's an ivory-back brush. The bristles are so delicate. Whenever you go bald, should that ever happen to you, and I don't think it will –

Fallowell: I think it might.

Betjeman: No, it seems to be bursting out boldly.

Fallowell: Are you working hard for the Queen?

Betjeman: I tell you one nice thing I discovered – the Poet Laureateship is not what the newspapers presume it to be, it isn't a command to work when something important happens. It is meant to be a kind of reward for having worked for a long time – much better. Still, official people do sometimes phone up – one must avoid promising too many things on the telephone.

Fallowell: Are you invited very often to Buckingham Palace?

Betjeman: Not much, but I have had invitations.

Fallowell: Do you enjoy going there?

Betjeman: Yes. The Queen is very bright in the head, very well informed. She's an awfully good

Sir John Betjeman
in the courtyard of
St Bartholomew the
Great, Smithfield.

Fallowell: I received a poisonous letter from a writer called Michael Moorcock.
Betjeman: Who is he?
Fallowell: He writes fantasies for children and old hippies, churns out about five a year. Pretty feeble stuff, I'm afraid, and I said so. He said if I said so again he'd break both my legs with an iron bar.
Betjeman: Where did you run him down?
Fallowell: In print.
Betjeman: Oh, they never forgive print. They think it's going to be there forever. I always believe anything that's said against me. And if anything is said in my favour I think they're only trying to be nice. To this day I think that. And I can only remember things said against me.

The Reverend Gerard Irvine arrives with his sister Rosemary Irvine. He is wearing a soutane, is very jolly and flushed and 18th-century looking. His sister is more contained, wears intelligent shoes, and has a dry sense of humour.
Fallowell: Do you smoke?
Gerry: No, thank you.
Rosemary: We're all too scared of lung cancer.
Betjeman: Have you got anything in your glass, Rosemary? Have some more – isn't it lovely stuff in the morning?
Rosemary: Mmm, it is good stuff.
Gerry: Gorgeous stuff.
Betjeman: We're going to Au Fin Bec in Draycott Avenue. We'll start with oeufs Benedict, which I think are better there than anywhere else I know. Oh, I was with somebody holy – I went to Mass at the Traveller's Club.
Gerry: Upstairs with the old Father?
Betjeman: That's it. There were some extremely right-wing people there.
Gerry: I'm sure there were. Everybody. I'm not a member any more. I've gone off it. It is now £150 a year – it used to be £45.
Betjeman: The food's better there than at the RAC. I joined the RAC because it was so empty and nobody spoke to one. And because it had a country club at Epsom, which I've never been to, but I always like to think that it's there if ever I want to. Perhaps we should have gone there for lunch, since we've got a motor car. Shall we go and eat?

Rosemary drove and there was a moment of frisson while crossing the King's Road, followed by some disorientation in a cul-de-sac. There were several ribald remarks about a certain block of flats used for prostitution, by which time the car had been brought back to dirigibility. They eventually found themselves at their destination. There, as the oeufs Benedict broke and dribbled, the conversation became libellous.

conversationalist. The family really are better company than almost anyone you could meet, certainly better than the local council would be. Is it right to put all this down, do you think? On the whole, I think it's better that people should say what they like. Whether it should all be printed and read – I'm not so sure. Have some more champagne. Mr Glover, can we have another bottle? Where's he got to, do you think?
Fallowell: It's a fine name for a butler.
Betjeman: No, he's not a butler or anything. He does odd jobs around. At the moment he's doing some electrical re-wiring.

Original interview by Duncan Fallowell. John Betjeman died a month later, in May 1984.

Urban invention

Hundreds of independent literary magazines are published in London each year.
And many of them take the capital itself as their theme.

By Nicholas Royle

LITERATURE

It's easy to be nostalgic for the Golden Age of 'little magazines', a time (at some unspecified point in the distant past) when a Grub Street hack could make a passable living writing stories and reviews in any number of metropolitan periodicals. The economic realities of such literary piecework may have changed, but London today is home to as a varied and lively a range of small magazines as it was in Hazlitt's day, or Matthew Arnold's, or George Orwell's.

Iain Sinclair, Chris Petit, Michael Moorcock, Peter Ackroyd, Christopher Fowler, Will Self, JG Ballard. Why do London's psychogeography nuts seem to be mainly men? Where are all the women writers with a thing about place? One of them – Laura Oldfield Ford – is writing and producing a fanzine-style publication called *Savage Messiah*.

One issue of the A5-size magazine might read like a series of cut-ups: disjointed descriptions of Dalston, Hackney and the River Lea, local colour in black and white, establishing shots in pre-production. Another, focusing on Heathrow and around, will edge a little closer to coherent narrative, while still keeping its distance. There's a suggestion of almost limitless potential, as if the writer could break out in any number of directions: fiction, film, graphic novels, illustration, fine art. The material touches on direct action, drugs, lawlessness, surveillance. We negotiate canals, gated communities, perimeter fences; the mood is one of paranoia, desperation, hunger, intellectual inquiry.

The *Other Side* is that rare thing, a freebie that's worth reading. Given away on the Northern line (they handed out 5,000 copies of a recent issue), it features humorous articles, interviews with creative folk and general arts coverage. It's written in a lively popular style, and offers ample diversion on the slog from Mill Hill East to Clapham North.

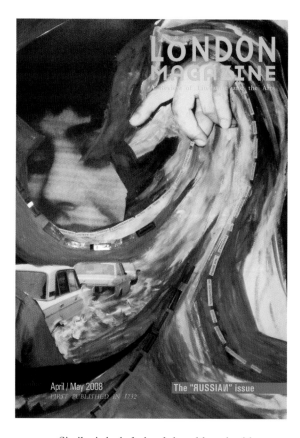

April / May 2008
FIRST PUBLISHED IN 1732

The "RUSSIAN" issue

Similar in look, feel and size, although with more content, the *Eel* draws its inspiration from Hackney's Broadway Market. The articles are about market traders, encounters on the Silverlink train service, and the Olympics. 'Stuff the Olympics' is a rallying cry. Its writers and editors give it a campaigning edge; local knowledge is their currency, and they are rich. You can read folk tales, personal anecdotes and blistering polemic alongside pieces about allotments, city farms and smoked eel.

A guide to the Greenway takes you as far as Maryon Park in Charlton 'where a famous film was made'. A footnote mischievously names the film as Polanski's 1965 movie *Get Swinging*, starring Terence Stamp, Una Stubbs and Jim Davidson, which you won't find in the *Time Out Film Guide*, or any other guide for that matter. 'Ask in the Film Shop for more details,' it advises. The Film Shop, at 33 Broadway Market, would probably enjoy a chuckle at your expense, but they might well have a copy of Antonioni's 1966 movie *Blowup*, starring David Hemmings, Vanessa Redgrave and Sarah Miles, which does include key scenes shot in Maryon Park.

Folk tales are at the heart of the more classically designed pamphlet *One Eye Grey*, styling itself as a 21st-century penny dreadful and featuring modern short stories based on traditional London tales of

'We negotiate canals, gated communities, perimeter fences; the mood is one of paranoia, desperation, intellectual inquiry.'

with publications that can showcase their students' work. Birkbeck writing school publishes an annual anthology in book form, *The Mechanics' Institute Review*, whereas the University of Greenwich has opted for a magazine format: *Brand*, enthusiastically edited by Nina Rapi, publishes stories, poems, plays, poems and non-fiction.

Another growth area is art and artists' magazines. The trouble with artists' magazines, if written by artists, is that, by and large, artists can't write. One of the best, however, is *Garageland*. Editor Cathy Lomax has attracted writers of the calibre of Stewart Home and Marina Warner to appear alongside her regular contributors.

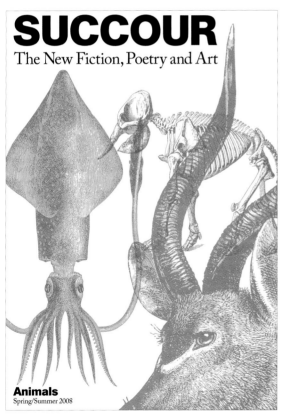

SUCCOUR
The New Fiction, Poetry and Art

Animals
Spring/Summer 2008

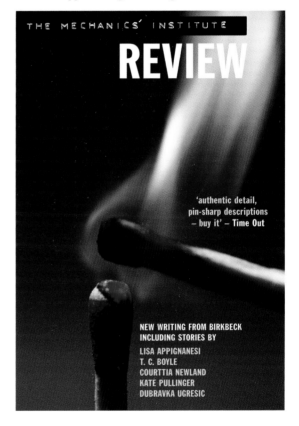

THE MECHANICS' INSTITUTE
REVIEW

'authentic detail, pin-sharp descriptions – buy it' – Time Out

NEW WRITING FROM BIRKBECK INCLUDING STORIES BY
LISA APPIGNANESI
T. C. BOYLE
COURTTIA NEWLAND
KATE PULLINGER
DUBRAVKA UGRESIC

the supernatural and uncanny. Early issues were written entirely by Carl Gee and Chris Roberts, but contributions were later sought from other writers, of which there is no shortage these days, with the massive expansion in university creative writing programmes. Indeed, many of these institutions have experimented in different ways

Read all about it, in three of the numerous literary magazines based in London.

Steve Lomax has an effectively creepy short story about paranoia and alienation on the Underground in a recent issue on the supernatural. Other themes have included machismo, the baroque, nature, and beauty. The magazine looks fantastic, with lots of colour, excellent reproduction and a simple, attractive design, making it easy to read.

Altogether more venerable than any of the periodicals mentioned so far, the *London Magazine* (founded in 1737) and *Ambit* (1959) are two of the best literary magazines in the country. Both are based in London, but neither is exclusively metropolitan in outlook. Both were hit hard by recent Arts Council cuts, but continue to publish regularly and to an excellent standard, filling their pages with poetry, short stories, essays, reviews and art. A list of names of the fine writers – and artists – who have contributed to both magazines over the years could have filled the space allowed for this piece.

Newer and with only a slightly narrower focus (it doesn't publish reviews), *Succour* is a twice-yearly magazine published in London. Regional editors based in Manchester, Exeter, Brighton and Dublin attract contributors from outside the M25. The magazine features a mixture of new writers and more established authors contributing short stories, poetry and art. Themed issues, clean design and overall quality suggest a *Granta* for

Literary giant *Ambit*, established in 1959.

the Facebook generation. The 'Animals' issue, for instance, provides a home for everything from humble mutts to 'the Kraken', via hares, moths, pigs, a black tiger and flocks of birds.

Nicholas Royle is a novelist, short-story writer and journalist.

Notes from the underground

Among the hundred flowers to bloom in the hothouse of London's late '60s counterculture were a number of newspapers and magazines. Smudged, mimeographed freesheets came and went all the time, but three products of this cultural ferment proved more durable than most: *Black Dwarf*, *International Times* (*IT*) and, perhaps most notorious of all, *Oz*.

Whereas *Black Dwarf* (initially edited by Tariq Ali) and, to a lesser extent, *IT* were identified with the neo-Leninist politics of the New Left, *Oz* was the mouthpiece of what its co-founder Richard Neville called the 'psychedelic left'. Its concerns were broadly cultural as well as political. Regular contributors included Germaine Greer, the cartoonist Robert Crumb, and David Widgery, who tried to keep open channels of communication between the hippy idealists of *Oz* and more austere, *marxisant* tendencies in the underground.

Oz had been monitored by the Obscene Publications Squad at Scotland Yard ever since its launch issue in January 1967, which included an essay by Greer on the 'English man' and an 'LBJ playmate' foldout. But the magazine would collide with the law most spectacularly in 1971. The previous year, the editors had invited 20 teenagers to edit a special School Kids issue. One item in particular caught the eye of the 'Dirty Squad': Vivian Berger's 'Rupert/Crumb' montage, in which the head of Rupert Bear was superimposed on a sexually explicit cartoon by Robert Crumb.

In 1971, the *Oz* offices were raided, the School Kids issue seized, and Neville and his fellow editors Felix Dennis and Jim Anderson were put on trial for conspiring to 'corrupt the morals of children and other young persons'. Lawyer and playwright John Mortimer (creator of *Rumpole of the Bailey*), worked for the defence team, and George Melly and John Peel were called as defence witnesses. *Oz* lost the case, though the verdict was overturned on appeal. The magazine folded in 1973.
Jonathan Derbyshire

HEDONISM INTRODUCTION
SEX CITYSCAPE FASHION
SOCIETY SHOPPING COMEDY
DRAMA PROTEST & POLITICS
VISUAL ARTS PERFORMANCE
LITERATURE GANGS OPINION
COCKNEYS BARS **ON SCREEN**
DANCE MUSIC TELEVISION
BUILDINGS CLUBS NIGHTLIFE
SPORT & FITNESS MEMORIES
STYLE FOOD & DRINK GIGS
CONSUME RIOTS REFERENCE

London
invisible city

Cinema has recorded the capital's changing landscape, its shifting values, its disaffected youth, its criminal underworld, its paranoias, its history, its gritty council estates and its bourgeois villages and even its bourgeoisie, but has it ever really captured its soul?

By Sukhdev Sandhu

London was invisible to me as a child. Oh, I could hear its bass materialism and frontline dramas in the records of the Clash and Linton Kwesi Johnson; its raggedy, romantic tumults in the Band of Holy Joy; its sampledelic, messthetic hybridity in the electro cuts on Street Sounds compilations. But on television, which is where I schooled myself in the history of film, the city seemed as remote and mythical as the oriental kingdom in *The Lost Horizon* (1937).

By contrast, it was the American metropolis – be it in the gangster thrillers of Jimmy Cagney, in the teeming sidewalks on to which Harold Lloyd, desperately clinging to a clockface in *Safety First* (1928), seemed forever on the brink of falling, or in the menacing Chinatowns of Fu Manchu shilling shockers and *Blade Runner* (1982) fantasias – that represented, in all its thrilling variations, the key cartographies of 20th-century cinema.

Whether seen dimly through the fogscapes of Dickens adaptations or Hammer horror films, or as backdrops for the ballroom waltzes and crinolined melodramas of Gainsborough pictures, London was a place defined by its past more than its present. Big Ben, Nelson's Column, Buckingham Palace; this landmark city, a mausoleum of aristocratic and imperial monumentality – as stiff as a waxwork at Madame Tussauds, as cornily prestigious as a Harrods plastic bag – had been reduced to the status of a series of generic establishing shots. It seemed rarely to be the object of directors' fascinations, a landscape to be explored, a torque to trad filmic narratives.

London in the 1960s certainly had its dark archive – Michael Powell's *Peeping Tom* (1960), Roman Polanski's *Repulsion* (1965), Yoko Ono's Rape (1969), Donald Cammell and Nicholas Roeg's festering *Performance* (1968), an archive that, in retrospect, comprises many of the most challenging and quietly influential films of the era – but its dominant visual iconography, both at the time and endlessly recycled over the next few decades, was a cheery rush of Formica'd coffee bars, paparazzi-pursued Beatles and mini-skirted babes sashaying down King's Road.

In the 1980s, when I was growing up in a small town near the Welsh border, the idea that London could be one of the centres of the creative universe seemed a joke. Compared to the lush gardens of *Brideshead Revisited* or *The Raj Quartet*, it seemed sickly, cancerous. It was difficult to watch news coverage of race riots or to hear politicians on *Question Time* lamenting its sink estates and inner-city ghettoes without assuming that the capital was doomed.

Viewed today, the films of the period, even and especially the ones that in recent years have been revived and held up as evocative snapshots of subcultural communities and teen aesthetics – *Bronco Bullfrog* (1969), *Pressure* (1974), *Rude Boy* (1980), *Babylon* (1980) – are, no matter how funky their soundtracks, strikingly dour in tone and mood. Their sound mixes are patchy. Their actors, often non-professionals, are wooden, as if they can barely muster the energy to communicate the anomie of their prematurely defeated characters.

Anne Gooding and Del Walker in cult movie *Bronco Bullfrog* (1969), set on a Stratford council estate.

The alleys and side streets through which bad boys and posse members chase each other are ramshackle and puddled. Everywhere there are brick walls, not repurposed as canvasses for elaborate and colourful graffiti, or even as bulletin boards to advertise and hype up club nights and basement parties, but at best sporting semi-faded slogans about the IRA or George Davis.

An exception was Derek Jarman, whose *Jubilee* (1977) channeled a mad, gladsome spirit of heterotopian anarchism and outlaw resistance among the ruins of a borderline-apocalyptic capital. *Jubilee*, while it sought to exalt designs for living and dissent that echoed those being captured in New York by No Wave film-makers such as Nick Zed and Amos Poe, and while its frame of reference – linking Queen Elizabeth I's astrologer-magician John Dee to the subversions and *détournements* of punk philosophy – prefigures some of the intellectual scope and tactical nous of today's psychogeographic fraternity, was simply too far ahead of its time to be understood as offering an escape route from London's sterility and discontent rather than being an embodiment of it.

Screen prescience

Equally in and out of its time was John Mackenzie's *The Long Good Friday* (1980), that, in retrospect, anticipates many of the shifts in metropolitan politics and culture that would help to transform, and very possibly deform, London over the course of the 1980s. In it, Bob Hoskins plays Harold Shand, an old-school London villain on the brink of rubber-stamping a deal with Yank financiers

after which, helped by bent local councillors to whom he's siphoned kickbacks, he'll have carte blanche to develop huge swathes of the Thames in east London.

The film, based on a screenplay by Barrie Keefe, is astute in its depiction of the extent to which the shift from London as a residually industrial city to post-industrial, financial services hub was ushered in by wide-boy crooks vying for land-grab mastery with IRA mobsters. It's also on the money in terms of location: in 1981, a year after the closure of the West India Docks sounded the death knell for the capital's status as a historic maritime city, Margaret Thatcher established the London Docklands Development Corporation that helped create Canary Wharf, symbol of priapic globalisation, as well as turn an area long seen as a working-class enclave into a private playpool for money merchants and media folk.

What's most prescient about Shand is his unscrupulous exploitation of London's past – he styles himself 'a businessman with a sense of history' – in order to justify and sell his riverine imperialism. As he and his compadres sail past Tower Bridge, orating forth before an invited coterie of champagne-grasping speculators, he gestures towards the derelict plains around them and, deploying a rhetoric of ownership rather than community, one that invokes the future rather than an Ackroydian genuflection to the Thames as an ancient capillary of eternal recurrences, announces: 'I believe this is the decade London will become Europe's capital, having cleaned away the outdated. We've got mile after mile, acre after acre of land for our future prosperity. No other

Left, Eddie Constantine, Helen Mirren and Bob Hoskins in *The Long Good Friday* (1980) and, above, Cillian Murphy walks eerily deserted streets in *28 Days Later* (2002).

'The London that we inhabit today, far less the London of tomorrow, is still missing in cinematic action.'

city in the world has got right in its centre such an opportunity for profitable progress. So it's important that the right people mastermind the new London.'

A companion piece to *The Long Good Friday*, though it's rarely seen as such, is *My Beautiful Laundrette* (1985), directed by Stephen Frears from a script by Hanif Kureishi. Here it's second-generation Asians, some of them also crooks, who exude a spirit of can-do entrepreneurialism that gibes against notional class solidarity. Karim is a mixed-race low-achiever born to Pakistani and white English parents, who, when he's not fending off his family's efforts to push him into an arranged marriage, is getting it on with a skinhead played by Daniel Day-Lewis and setting up a state-of-the-art launderette part-financed by embezzled drug money.

For all the racist violence it acknowledges as an ongoing part of daily reality for minority groups in the capital, *My Beautiful Laundrette*, like many of Kureishi's later films and novels, is both a document and a celebration of an emergent metropolis. This London, like that of *Absolute Beginners* (Colin MacInnes's 1959 novel rather than the 1986 Julien Temple film) or *Catch Us If You Can* (1965) before it, is a magnet for young people keen to throw off the shackles of dull, family-focused conformity. It's a place for bastards, misfits, in-betweeners – those young men and women who, like Karim, are dazed and a little repelled by the hypocrisy and desire-quashing values that govern suburbia, and who are hungry for new liaisons, opportunities, structures of feeling and living.

Kureishi's film ironises Thatcherite ideology, decoupling laisser-faire economics from Victorian values, and presenting a vision of urban regeneration propelled not by tightly neck-tied scions of the Establishment, but by Pakis and sexual deviants. It maps a capital in which people from ethnic backgrounds are increasingly ascendant drivers of the economy. White Londoners are portrayed as marginal, relics of a fading metropolitan order (one signalled by the change in the launderette's name from Churchill's to Powders), required to get to grips with the shifting cartographies of power or face being consigned to impotency.

In search of the city's psyche

The Long Good Friday and *My Beautiful Laundrette* are important London films primarily because of the themes they address; Patrick Keiller's *London* (1994), like the Black Audio Film Collective's *Twilight City* (1989), is important because of its form. It's a cine-essay, a mesh of documentary and fiction, influenced by the writings of Daniel Defoe, that chronicles the capital through the course of 1992. The narrator (Paul Scofield) describes a series of perambulations he and his (unseen) one-time lover Robinson undertake to explore the 'problem of London'.

Journeying through and to such places as Ealing, Neasden and Stoke Newington, in what the narrator calls an 'exercise in psychic landscaping, drifting and free association', that problem proves to be complex and multiple. In a year of economic crisis, IRA attacks and a fourth successive Tory election victory, what are the historical factors that might explain the lack of any revolutionary impulse within the capital? How might one talk coherently about London when it is a hodge-podge of distinct wards and communities, a 'city of fragments'? Where is the heart of modern London?

The breadth of Keiller's urban tableaux, the proximity between his 'psychic landscaping' strategies and those of contemporary psychogeography, and the extent to which his choice of still photography resonates with legions of modern-day snappers racking up hundreds of images on their digital cameras, means that London has had a big impact on film makers.

Not least in *Finisterre* (2003), a collaboration between Kieron Evans, Paul Kelly and the band Saint Etienne, in which a pantheon of pop cultural schemers and dreamers, among them Vic Godard, Vashti Bunyan and Julian Opie, are heard reflecting about the capital over a series of images – of Banksy graffiti, Primrose Hill panoramas, Hackney vinyl-pressing plants – and segued between specially-composed incidental musical pieces to build up what amounts to the nearest to a city-symphony treatment London has so far received.

Finisterre is a much more optimistic film than *London*, partly because Saint Etienne have always been motivated by love rather than rage or disappointment, but also because of the time when the film was made. As the city's economy, as well as its population, swelled and boomed, London, for so long a pimply teenager almost embarrassed to look at itself in the mirror, seemed unable now to stop pointing a camera lens at itself. Grime-lovers chronicling the scene in Bow and sticking up footage on YouTube or via Channel U;

'London is shown as manicured and picturesque, a theme park unspoiled by too many encounters with poor or non-white people.'

the growing recognition for experimental artists such as William Raban (whose 2000 film *MM* is a radical reframing of the Millennium Dome) or Anja Kirschner (whose 2006 *Polly II: Plan for a Revolution in Docklands* updates *The Beggar's Opera* to contemporary, waterlogged east London); the rediscovery of eccentricities such as Norman Cohen's *The London Nobody Knows* (1967) or Douglas Hickox's *Les Bicyclettes de Belsize* (1967): this is, at least in the margins and in terms of accessing marginal work, a golden age for London film.

Some would add *Notting Hill* (1998), *Sliding Doors* (1998) and *Bridget Jones's Diary* (2001) to that list. All are films that offer an enchanted London closer in spirit to *Friends* and *Sex and the City* than, say, to Mike Leigh's *Naked* (1993) or Gary Oldman's *Nil By Mouth* (1997). Indeed, their presentation of the capital as a quirky, bucolic wonderland seems tailored for transatlantic audiences. London is shown as manicured and picturesque, a theme park of private gardens, quaint bookshops and riverside boulevards unspoiled by too many encounters with poor or non-white people. Then again, in a city where there is increasingly little correlation between the amount one works and what one earns, and across which a dismayingly large proportion of new developments are 'boutique', 'luxury' and 'gated', this pasteurised version of urbanism is a lived reality for the lucky few.

London as tourist cliché: Hugh Grant on location for *Notting Hill* (1998).

What lies beneath?

In the past, the crime genre, in pictures such as Alfred Hitchcock's *The Lodger* (1926) or Ken Hughes's *The Small World of Sammy Lee* (1963), was the place to turn to for less varnished snapshots of London. The success of Guy Ritchie's *Lock, Stock and Two Smoking Barrels* (1998) has spawned a rash of dismal knock-offs that, owing to the enfeebled political imaginations of their directors, has been unable to convey with any plausibility the corporate, deterritorialised and digital landscapes of much contemporary crime.

It seems that film, compared to pop music, visual art or even literature, has served London poorly. Where is its JG Ballard? Its Burial or Kode9? Who are the directors penetrating its surface to show the grind and inequalities that underpin its bling façades? Stephen Frears' *Dirty Pretty Things* (2002) had a good if somewhat melodramatic stab at charting a subaltern network of prostitutes, fixers, minicab drivers and security staff united by marginal legal status, cultural invisibility and personal desperation. More typical, though, is Mirjam von Arx's *Building the Gherkin* (2005), an insightful documentary about the construction of 30 St Mary Axe that includes testimony from planners, architects, office workers – everybody but the men who actually built the structure itself.

Horror and sci-fi films such as Danny Boyle's *28 Days Later* (2002) and Alfonso Cuaron's *Children of Men* have, in the tradition of Gary Sherman's *Death Line* (1972) and even David Lynch's *The Elephant Man* (1980), offered visceral and jarring visions of the capital that tap into contemporary fears and neuroses. And yet the London that we inhabit today, far less the London of tomorrow, is still missing in cinematic action. Chris Petit, in *London Orbital* (2002) and *Unrequited Love* (2006), is one of the few directors to analyse its suburbanising, pixellated, Ring of Steel'd, military-zone-cum-Bluewater'd non-space into which the capital threatens to morph.

London – on digital billboards, on the sponsored news programmes in the backs of taxi cabs, via the visual armoury of webcams, cellphones and cheap digital cameras, to say nothing of the CCTV panopticon everywhere from malls to office lifts – is becoming an enormous movie screen. And to be a Londoner is, increasingly, to be framed, remotely tracked, pixellated, downloadable. Perhaps this is a notion we don't wish to entertain. A notion that many people would view as the very opposite of entertainment. If that's so, it explains why, nearly 30 years after I was making do with Dick van Dyke and Julie Andrews mockneying it up on the rooftops of Victorian tenements, the London I see around me and the London I see in the movies have so little in common.

Sukhdev Sandhu is a writer and chief film critic of the Daily Telegraph.

TIMELINE

1968
Thames TV and LWT launched.

1971
A Clockwork Orange filmed. Director Stanley Kubrick chooses almost exclusively London locations, in particular the new Thamesmead estate, to represent Anthony Burgess's nihilistic world.

1979
Quadrophenia shows the clash between Mods and Rockers. It is based on the Who's 1973 rock opera album of the same name.

1981
Only Fools and Horses hits the screens to lukewarm critical and viewer response. A second series is commissioned anyway, and the Trotters go on to grace seven series, and many Christmas specials.

1982
Channel 4 launched with a remit of 'provision of a broad range of high-quality and diverse programming, which, in particular: demonstrates innovation, experiment and creativity in the form and content of programmes; and appeals to the tastes and interests of a culturally diverse society.'

1985
The BBC launches the first London-based soap set in the fictional borough of Walford. *EastEnders* is given two years to become a hit.

1986
The London Lesbian & Gay Film Festival is founded.

1988
NFT opens the Museum of the Moving Image. It lasts until 1999.

1994
Patrick Keiller takes a psychogeographical tour of the city in the simply named *London*. It now stands as a poignant document of cultural decline in the early 1990s.

1997
The Lumière cinema on St Martin's Lane closes after 30 years, to much sadness from indie film fans. It is now a Gymbox, underneath a boutique hotel.

The Lux Cinema opens on fashionable Hoxton Square, showing a mix of mainsteam and arthouse fare. It closed suddenly in 2001 and, after laying unused for a while, is now a restaurant.

Garry Oldman returns to the south-east London estates of his youth in *Nil by Mouth*.

1999
London's IMAX cinema opens in the middle of Waterloo roundabout. Designed by Avery Associates, the glass drum features an ever-changing display that has brought colour to the drab environs.

2000
Channel 4 locks up five men and five women in a purpose-built house in north London, and subjects them to round-the-clock live TV surveillance. Who knew the deformed monster *Big Brother* would eventually become?

2002
Chris Petit and Iain Sinclair pay homage to the M25 in *London Orbital*.

2005
Chris Morris and Charlie Brooker's *Nathan Barley* (Channel 4) lampoons the whole Shoreditch Twat scene.

2006
The London Film Festival celebrates its 50th anniversary.

2007
The NFT rebrands itself BFI Southbank and, after a £6m redevelopment, opens a flash new bar, film store, gallery and mediathèque.

Mick Jagger
on *Performance*

Donald Cammell's and Nicholas Roeg's
Performance cast Mick Jagger as
reclusive rock star Turner, living a
bohemian fantasy in a grand house
in pre-gentrification Notting Hill.
Here Jagger talks about the film.

ON SCREEN

I think Turner is a projection of Donald's fantasy
or idea of what I imagine I am. The thing is that
it's very easy for people to believe that's what I'm
like. It was easy to do in a way, because it's just
another facet of me, if I felt inclined to go that way.
But now, when I look at it, there's so many things
I could have done to make it stranger or more real,
to my mind, of how Turner would be and how he
would live. I think it was a bit too much like me
in a few ways. But he's not quite hopeless enough.

I don't think there's many people like that
individual. I found his intellectual posturing very
ridiculous – that's what sort of fucked him up.
Too much intellectual posturing in the bath when
you're with two women is not a good thing – that's
not to be taken too seriously! It made me skin go
all funny! I know people like that.

It isn't me really. You just get into the part – that's
acting, isn't it? You just get into the feeling of that
person and I got into feeling like that. You know
you don't want to make any decisions, and there's
certain things you know you've got to do and there's
certain things in your fate that you know. Some
people like to sit down and get really involved in the
things that they know and some people just want
to take what they are and just carry on. Turner was
just a person who'd stopped all that and become
very tuned in to it. After a while you really get into
thinking like that and driving everyone crazy. I
drove everyone a bit crazy, I think, during that time.
It was taken for granted that I would do anything!

I've known Donald on and off for several years.
But I didn't know him that well. But when you work
with someone, you really get to know them, and we
had terrible rows because I didn't think he knew
what he was doing. He'll probably say that I didn't
really, either. Roeg was the professional doing his
thing. He was always reliable and he had his little
lighting cameraman job to do as well. But he was

doing more than that, and I don't know how much of the composition etc was due to him. Donald wrote the story and he was the driving force as far as the actors were concerned. Between the two they were working out the delineation of their authority.

At the time I couldn't see the film because I was very hung up about it. I'd rather it had come out. It should have been out years ago. I still think it's good, but I think it was a better film two years ago.

I feel I did create something. It was enjoyable as far as that's concerned. That's what made it such hard work. Although you can say it was

contributing something creative, it wasn't shot with one camera, taking Anita and I out into the middle of nowhere for three days and saying this is the sort of feeling we want you to have. It was shot just like a regular movie. It wasn't just a question of improvising for hours and hours. We had to work it all out before, otherwise you just got in a mess. We'd suddenly stop shooting one day because I'd say I wasn't going to say those lines. The regular technicians would go, 'Blimey I've never seen anything like it!' Donald's whole thing is casting people for what they are and how they fit into the part, to make them work out and create the part, rather to work on things that were already in their own minds.

There's two important things about the film to Donald. There's the sexual thing – not only physically sexual, but the interrelating of the sexes and the interchanging of roles. And the role of violence and the role of women, vis-à-vis the role of violence of a man. How the two things can balance each other out. And the ritualistic significance of violence. That's one of the main themes if you can gain any conclusion out of it.

I don't understand the connection between music and violence. Donald's always trying to explain it to me and I just blindly carry on. I just know that I get very aroused by music, but it doesn't arouse me violently. I never went to a rock and roll show and wanted to smash the windows or beat anybody up. I feel more sexual than physically violent. I get a sexual feeling and I want to fuck as soon as I've been playing. I cool down very quickly. I can come off stage and be back to normal in five minutes.

The only time I've felt violent was in some street demonstration, and you really get the feeling of being in with a crowd that wants to do something, and you get really carried along whether they're right or wrong. Whether the policeman is doing his job or whether the cause that you're hitting the policeman for is really right, what's it fucking matter? The point is that the act of violence is more powerful than the intellectual political act. I never felt that feeling in a crowd with music, although I've felt very turned on – but not like that.

Mick Jagger was interviewed by Tony Elliott.

Time Out's special fold-out supplement on *Performance*, which included a poster of Jagger on the back.

Mike Leigh's London locations

Mike Leigh might be Manchester-born, but his films, most of which are set in London, are testament to his love of the capital. The director, who always makes intensive use of location, took *Time Out* on a two-day, whistle-stop tour of the streets, shops, flats, office blocks and markets that, over the past four decades, his characters have made their own.

ON SCREEN

Life Is Sweet (1990) Tuesday, 8am, Enfield

We're in a cab on the way to Enfield, site of the fictional 'Regret Rien' restaurant, run by the ridiculous Aubrey (Timothy Spall). We drive through Wood Green and past a street where Leigh lived for 30 years.

'I moved out three years ago and haven't been back,' he says, remembering how convenient it was to film up the road, not least as his then wife Alison Steadman was one of the cast. We reach the 'Regret Rien'; it's now an Indian restaurant.

Why always shoot in London? 'Frankly, we can't afford to go anywhere else,' he says. 'And the city is a great canvas. You can make anything you want here, short of a film about farming.'

Secrets & Lies (1996) 8.45am, Winchmore Hill

We stop outside the photo studio run by Maurice (Spall) in Leigh's *Secrets and Lies*. It's now a brasserie. He tells how, during rehearsals, an agitated Greek-Cypriot woman screeched up demanding to book her wedding photos. 'I said something that she had no way of decoding: "This is not real." She was very angry.'

High Hopes (1988) 10am, King's Cross

Opposite the new entrance to St Pancras are the remnants of Stanley Buildings, a 19th-century block of railway-workers' flats that housed Cyril (Phil Davis) and Shirley (Ruth Sheen) in Leigh's touching film *High Hopes*, a story of a disenchanted bike courier (Davis), his girlfriend (Sheen) and his elderly mum (Edna Doré), all facing up to a changing city. 'Weird, weird,' mutters Leigh, looking up at the building, which is spliced in half and derelict. Net curtains still hang in the windows. 'One of the first things we invented with the backstory was that Cyril's father worked on the railways. It was synchronicity that we shot here, and at the end they're able to look down at St Pancras and talk about Cyril's father.'

Meantime, Regent's Canal.

Happy Go Lucky, Camden Market.

High Hopes, St Pancras.

Career Girls (1997)

10.45am, Agar Grove, Camden

We stop outside the flat where Leigh filmed *Career Girls* in 1996. Katrin Cartlidge (who died suddenly in 2002, aged 41) and Lynda Steadman play Hannah and Annie, two women we meet first as 20-year-old students, then a decade later as disappointed professionals. Leigh and his team invented a Chinese takeaway on this spot: it was only when Leigh arrived to check the set that he found that his production designer, Eve Stewart, had named the fake takeaway the 'Lo Hung Lee'.

Naked, Dalston.

Life is Sweet, Enfield.

Secrets & Lies, Quilter Street.

'I was very amused, which was fortunate. It's entirely true, of course.' For Leigh, the memory of Cartlidge, who also worked with him on *Naked* and *Topsy-Turvy*, hangs over the place. 'It's emotional. I can only think of Katrin Cartlidge, standing there and being very emotional about memories and lost things.'

Happy-Go-Lucky (2008)
11.20am, Camden Market
We drive through Camden Town and past an osteopath's surgery, a burger stall near the tube, the Lock Tavern pub – all locations in Leigh's new film, *Happy-Go-Lucky*. We get out and retrace an early scene, in which the lead character, Poppy (Hawkins), her sister and three of their mates stagger over Camden Lock at dawn on their way back from a night out at Koko.

'We shot in Koko for real. We went in at 9pm but from 11pm onwards it was so full we had to get out.' Leigh remembers what the area was like when he moved to London in the early 1960s. 'All along there,' he says, pointing up Chalk Farm Road, 'there were shops that sold only second-hand cookers and fridges. It was totally different back then, quite laid-back.'

Naked (1993)
2.30pm, Lina Stores, Brewer Street, Soho
'We shot some of *Naked* around Soho at night. There's a famous scene between David Thewlis and Ewen Bremner. We had first improvised it on the steps of a church in Marylebone. To film it, we went to Brewer Street, picked Lina Stores and made it happen there. We made no attempt to control traffic or crowds.

3.30pm, Charlotte Street, Soho
We find the office block where Thewlis' Johnny rants and philosophises to Brian (Peter Wight), a night guard. Fittingly, Leigh, who briefly worked for Securicor in the 1960s ('when you didn't have to be brawny') starts chatting with the current guard, who hasn't seen *Naked*. When he hears the film's name, he looks worried.

Meantime (1984) Wednesday, 8am, Haggerston
To Haggerston, off Kingsland Road in Hackney, to find the council estate where Leigh shot *Meantime* with young bucks Gary Oldman, who plays skinhead Coxy, and Tim Roth, who plays his taciturn pal, Colin. The estate is pretty much as it was then, although Leigh is impressed that there's now a civic garden where before there was just concrete. 'Gary and Tim were doing an improvisation in the

rehearsal space round the corner, a big room with striplights. Gary threw a milk bottle that hit a fluorescent light and suddenly I saw his head erupt in red. We jumped in my car and rushed to the hospital. Gary was dressed in braces and boots and was worried they'd think he was a real skinhead.'

We walk to the bank of the Regent's Canal, site of Oldman and Roth playfighting. 'That's where they squeezed through,' says Leigh, pointing to a hole in the railings and clambering through.

Secrets & Lies (1996)
10am, Quilter Street, Bethnal Green
We go looking for the two-up, two-down that houses Brenda Blethyn's Cynthia. 'Hello Mr Leigh, I think that's the door you're looking for,' says a neighbour. 'The house had been bought by a lawyer as a pied-à-terre. A well-known sculptress next door got a bit fed up with us.'

Naked (1993)
11.10am, St Marks Rise, Dalston
We drive to the house in Dalston used in *Naked*, where Johnny (Thewlis) shows up and plays havoc with two flatmates (Katrin Cartlidge and Lesley Sharp). Leigh hobbles down the street exactly as Johnny does for the film's final shot. With *Naked*, Leigh was looking for a location to match a film that took his filmmaking somewhere more unusual, more poetic. 'You didn't want it to be just another domestic space.'

All or Nothing (2002) 12.20pm, Greenwich
We're on the site of the council estate where Leigh shot *All or Nothing*; at the time it was derelict. 'There was one couple left, who had refused flatly to move out.' Most of the estate has gone, replaced by flats. Leigh made the film after *Topsy-Turvy*: 'I wanted to do a contemporary piece about working-class people, a film about the emotional struggle to hold onto relationships.'

Bleak Moments (1971) 1.30pm, Tulse Hill
We end where Leigh began: outside the semi-detached house where, in 1971, he shot *Bleak Moments*, his first film, which was backed by Albert Finney and told of Sylvia (Anne Raitt), a repressed young woman with a hippy lodger in her garage. Leigh hasn't been here for 37 years. 'It's got the same front door and the garage is the same.'

How does it feel to be back? 'Some people say you should never go back. I think that's bollocks. It's fantastic to come back to the location where I shot the first of 18 full-length films.

'On this spot, I was a crazy, ambitious 28-year-old, and I couldn't have imagined all the things that would come later. What's particularly fantastic is that I can stand here and think I've made 17 more films with just the same freedom.

'What do I feel? Actually I'm overwhelmed. It's very exciting, without being smug about it.'

ON SCREEN

Electric dreams

Geoff Andrew remembers London's greatest independent cinemas.

'Cinema is there for eternity, and that's incredible.'
Gérard Depardieu

Like many people, the older I get, the greater my concern with the passing of time; it must have something to do with the awareness of it running out. Film was the first medium or art form properly able to depict, reflect and record time's passing. To get philosophical for a moment, didn't some bright spark – Cocteau, maybe – argue that to film someone was to record death's inexorable approach? Certainly, Godard's typically pithy and problematic claim that cinema is 'truth 24 times a second' is often quoted, and years earlier, HG Wells likened cinema to a time machine. And film itself, in material terms, is notoriously fragile, volatile and vulnerable to the ravages of the advancing years. Film is inextricably linked to the passage of time, which is in turn inextricably linked to change. In short, film is about change – and how!

'At 21 or 22, so many things appear solid, permanent… which at 40 seem nothing but disappearing mire. Forty can't tell 20 about this; 20 can find that out only by getting to be 40.'
Joseph Cotten in *The Magnificent Ambersons*

Whenever we watch a movie, we see constant change – of expression, place, light, whatever — and when we watch any old film, we see how the world has changed. But there have also been huge changes in the way we watch movies, from the Lumière brothers' first public screenings, through the movie palaces of the golden age, to the more isolated experiences of recent years.

Even in my own limited experience of working in London's indie and arthouse circuit over the last 30 years, those changes have been remarkable. Currently I am Head of Film Programme at BFI Southbank, an enlarged and enhanced version of what was known, for over half a century, as the National Film Theatre. When I leave work, I see crowds milling around a buzzy venue that includes four auditoria, two restaurant-bars, a shop, a gallery that presents moving-image work by artists, and a mediatheque in which visitors can watch, for free, on monitor screens, hundreds of hours of digitised

footage from the BFI's National Archive. Even at the NFT, this would have been wholly unthinkable in 1977 when, still fresh from university, I took a job, first as manager, then as co-programmer, at Portobello Road's Electric Cinema Club.

These days, the Electric is a ritzy joint serving gentrified Notting Hill; back then, it was an impoverished if characterful fleapit that attracted cinephiles from all over London, while trying to keep out the drunks, dealers, whores and various crazies populating Portobello by night. The programming has changed too. Where we used to screen around 25 different movies a week, ranging from silent classics to *The Harder They Come*, Hollywood film noir to *Ai No Corrida*, the New German cinema to the American underground – and all points between – today's Electric offers a safe-as-houses handful of new commercial or 'crossover' titles each week.

One of the first purpose-built cinemas in the UK, the Electric, above and right, opened for business in 1910.

ON SCREEN

'I am big. It's the pictures that got small.'
Gloria Swanson in *Sunset Blvd.*

The Electric is far from alone in its unadventurous programming, but nor was it alone in its audacity during the five years I spent there. Though the late '70s the Electric was described by the *Observer*'s Philip French as 'possibly the best repertory cinema in Europe' – and by *Time Out* as 'a galvanising alternative to the NFT'. It was complemented not only by the BFI's flagship (which then had two auditoria), but by a host of healthily independent repertory houses, like the Scala, the Essential, the Ritzy, the Rio, the Riverside and, in the Mayfair Hotel, the Starlight. Then too there were the older arthouses: although, for a newcomer like me, some '60s cinephile havens were just names (I missed out on the Tolmer, the Berkeley, the Continental and others), London in the late '70s and early '80s could still boast Oxford Street's three-screen Academy, the Paris Pullman, the ICA, the Everyman, the various Gate cinemas, the Camden Plaza, the Lumière, the Chelsea, the Screens, the Curzon Mayfair, the Phoenix, the London Film-makers' Co-op and the Minema.

A few – very few – of these survive to this multiplex-dominated day, some with names changed; and they were supplemented, at one point or another, by the Barbican, the Prince Charles, the Curzon Soho, the Ciné Lumière and the Lux. But too many of our rep cinemas and arthouses have gone, and so too has the diversity of programming. True, there are more films than ever opening each Friday, but many vanish after a week; the exhibitors are reluctant to retain anything after a remotely disappointing opening weekend. Meanwhile, the repertory on offer is probably weaker now than at any time I can recall during my 30-odd years in the capital. To make matters more worrying, the programming of London's – indeed, the UK's – screens, arthouse or otherwise, is increasingly the

province of fewer and fewer individuals. Though many of the small, one-off venues are making sterling attempts to offer an alternative to what's provided by their circuit counterparts, they're often limited to one or two screenings a week, on DVD or video – not exactly the full cinematic experience.

'Mother of mercy, is this the end of Rico?'
Edward G Robinson in *Little Caesar*

Is there hope for London's indie cinemas? More importantly, is there hope for anyone who wants something more varied than what's on the menu at the vast majority of cinemas? In this increasingly homogenised conglomerate world, the clear answer would appear to be 'no'… except that although most suppliers always aim to steer a market to their own financial advantage, they also tend, however slowly and unimaginatively, to respond to demand. And judging by audiences at some of the venues providing an alternative to the mainstream, there is a significant demand for something else; think of the box-office success of films as different as *Hidden*, *Volver* and *The Lives of Others,* or revivals like *The Passenger*, *The Conformist* and *The Lady Vanishes.* True, many other equally fine, lower-profile films – think *Climates* or *The Child* – fall by the wayside; but at least it's clear that not all cinemagoers are as cautious or narrow-minded as some choose to think they are.

People do, however, need to be properly informed about what's on offer; they do need to see a film in comfort, with good projection and sound provided at a reasonable price; and that film does need to be kept on at a cinema for long enough for them to catch up with it. There we go again. As ever with the movies, it's all a matter of time.

Geoff Andrew was Film Editor of *Time Out* from 1989 to 2006.

Memory bank
Adam Buxton on late nights at the Scala

Joe Cornish and I spent most of our childhood in the cinema. We used to go to the Scala in King's Cross, which is now a music venue. It used to be a cinema where they'd do these all-nighters, like a triple bill or sometimes even four or five in a row. It was a really strange place, and, as you can probably imagine, it

used to draw this really weird crowd. It was very different from your average West End cinema, as it was a little bit grotty, and it felt a little bit illicit and seedy.

They showed a really wide range of films, from horror films, art films and even most of the mainstream movies. One night they might show the *Back to the*

Future trilogy back to back; on another, a series of zombie movies.

The night that really sticks in my mind is an early preview screening of *Nightmare on Elm Street*. It hadn't been rated, and they hadn't finished editing it. It was like a test screening. I remember being really excited about it. When we arrived, they showed a load of Roger Corman-style B-movies, then *Blade Runner*.

The night climaxed with *Nightmare on Elm Street*. It just totally blew our minds. We were too young at the time, so we got in with forged IDs. That's the best way to do it, really.

I actually remember going to see my first 18-rated film there – Neil Jordan's *The Company of Wolves*.

The Scala was definitely the place to go to if you just wanted to see a lot of interesting cinema. It was

friendly… They had a cat that would run along the seats and would freak you out… The trains going in to King's Cross over the road would make the whole room vibrate… There was water dripping from the ceiling… It was just amazing.

Adam Buxton is a broadcaster and comedian. He has been working with his comedy partner Joe Cornish since they were 14.

ON SCREEN

Withnail & I

L ast year, Handmade Films and its executive producers Dennis O'Brien and George Harrison had a surprising critical and box-office success in Australia and the USA with a movie called *Withnail and I*. It was written and directed by Bruce Robinson, who also wrote the screenplay for *The Killing Fields*, and made in 30 days for a mere £1.5m. It is very English, nostalgic and low on plot (if not incident), and it ran successfully for six months in New York, and was playing to full houses when it was pulled.

Paul McGann, left, as 'I' and Richard E Grant as Withnail.

It's set in the autumn of 1969, in the death agonies of that now often despised and misunderstood decade; its humour is trickily alien on grounds both historical and geographical. But Yanks and Aussies young and old seemed to love it, and its weirdly wonderful array of English-speaking eccentrics: from Withnail (pronounced Withnell), a Byronic but emaciated actor with a taste for lighter fuel and a use for Deep Heat medicinal rub not approved by Boots; the eponymous 'I', played by Paul 'Toplis' McGann, a pretty and desperate

thespian pursued by amorous, aristocratic queens and sullen Cumbrian poachers; and Danny, the drug dealer who haunts the miasmically awful Camden flat where most of the action takes place.

Though the film was shown at the last London Film Festival and has been looking for a suitable spot since October, its London release this month comes at a fortuitous time: just on the cusp of the late '60s celebration that may well make 1988 even more tedious than 1984, which did for George Orwell what the A6 murder did for hitch-hikers. Already Tariq Ali seems as ubiquitous as Anne Diamond (and just as convincing): books on the red revolution are pouring off the presses and County Joe and the Fish are no doubt poised for a world tour. And will Daniel Cohn-Bendit open a wine bar in the Mile End Road? To all of us who lived through the '60's, *Withnail & I* is a welcome recapturing of the period: no vague burst of political rhetoric, but a cameo of a time when squalor, indolence and failure could still be fun, when innocence was still possible and when, to paraphrase De Niro in *Angel Heart*, the future really was like it used to be.

Withnail & I is 25 per cent autobiographical, says Robinson, in so far as most of the incidents in the film happened to him. 'I was a perpetually skint, hairy, scruffy London drama student who used to do all the drink, drugs, sex and rock 'n' roll stuff in that period. I did meet some extraordinary people and yes, when I was in my early twenties and I was a struggling actor, I did have trouble with artistic gents who were after my bum. To put it mildly.'

Withnail and 'I' share the same diseased flat and the same unsanitary, sleepless, poverty-stricken existence. But only one of them seems destined to make it out of the toytown decade of silly, selfish indulgence. While 'I' goes off to star in a stage play, the crazy but hungry Withnail is left quoting *Hamlet* in the rain… 'Yes, I am 'I'. But I'm also Withnail. I didn't wander around with a tape recorder in 1969 thinking, "I'm going to write this down." But half of Withnail is definitely me; that tendency to the verbose, the self-dramatising. Then it would be ranting about not having the price of a packet of fags; today it would be ranting about politics to my wife, driving her fucking barmy.'

We met in his splendid house in Wimbledon, bought only two years ago for a mere £100,000 and already worth three times that amount, where he lives in some comfort with his painter wife Sophie, their baby girl Lily India ('conceived on a swarthy night in Kerala, good job it wasn't Bournemouth') and a collection of paintings and Dickens memorabilia. There's also the other love of his life: the DB4 Aston Martin (as featured in the Bond films) of which there are, he proudly murmurs, only 34 left in the world. There's no alcohol on the premises, though, neither shaken not stirred. The problem being not alcoholism 'exactly', but Robinson's need for at least three bottles of good

red wine before he can start to write: 'As necessary to me as a typewriter or a sheet of paper, so when I'm not working I tend to knock it on the head.'

Withnail & I is set to no small extent in a rugged Lake District landscape near Penrith. 'That was all true. Around '68, '69, all my friends used to call me the Bard, 'cos I was always writing. My friend Micky Feast, the actor, and me, went on holiday to the Lake District 'cos we wanted to write this screenplay. He saw this ad in the paper for this idyllic cottage in the Lake District, ten quid a week. So we got in this battered old Jag of mine, just like in the film, no money, drove up here, and arrived in this pigsty in a fucking gale on a hillside, drove the car into the ditch. We got the farmer next morning to pull the car out of the ditch with his tractor, but the car was so fucked that the front flew off. We stayed there a week, lived on a fiver, put polythene bags round our feet 'cos we had no wellies, got worried by sheep, the locals were rude to us. It wasn't remotely funny at the time. But out of that disastrous adventure came that bit of the film.

> 'We stayed there a week, lived on a fiver, put polythene bags on our feet 'cos we had no wellies.'

'I'm primarily concerned with dialogue and the acting. I'm not one of those people who comes out of a film saying, "Wow, what a great shot, that crane shot moving into a dissolve, into a 50-mil close-up of Sarah's face." I didn't even know what dimensions the lenses were, but I did concentrate on the actors. Richard E Grant, who plays Withnail, is astonishingly good; if he'd gone two degrees to the left or right he'd have blown that part. Mike Elphick did Jake as a favour, 'cos we were at drama school together. We couldn't afford his rates, but he did it for a few quid and a bottle of scotch. Uncle Monty came from this book that I picked up in a junk shop in Putney, a privately published book by some old queer, who lived in Hampstead in 1926, called A Newman, full of poems like "In trousers now by boys arrayed", and all that old shit.'

'George Harrison was great, just like he was in the old Beatles days. The worst scene we did in *Withnail* was this mad chase on the motorway with cheap '60s cars and a guy with a walkie-talkie who got the cars to surround any car that got into the shot and looked too modern! It was a nightmare! And all George said at the end of the production, his only comment on the movie, was: "Here, Bruce, they didn't build that stretch of the M25 till after 1969." He was right of course – but only just.'

Bruce Robinson was interviewed by Steve Grant.

Here's looking at you

The city under surveillance.

Gaining access to Westminster's CCTV control centre is a bit like stepping into a John le Carré novel. I turn up (under strict orders not to divulge the address) at a Starbucks in a West End location. At 11am precisely, I'm met by Westminster's CCTV operations co-ordinator, Dan Brown, who, in his striped shirt, grey suit and goatee, looks more like a car salesman than the eyes of London. He leads us through some double doors, down some stairs and into a dark, dank subterranean world. We stop at a blond wood door. Dan taps in a code, and we walk through. There's another door. The first one locks behind us before the second opens.

A bank of TV screens looms into view. And there, spread out before me, are the streets of central London – viewed from every conceivable angle. Above us, couples stroll through the spring sunshine, tourists pore over maps and bored teens amble in and out of shops, unaware that below them is a state-of-the-art CCTV facility where a team of suits watches their every movement.

Brown oversees a crew of three, who operate 160 cameras across Westminster: the West End, Belgravia, Jubilee Bridge, Trafalgar Square, Knightsbridge and Oxford Street. The team works 12-hour shifts and the centre operates 24 hours a day, seven days a week, 365 days a year –

Westminster's secret CCTV operations centre, watching London's West End round the clock.

including Christmas Day. Since its launch in 2002, the control room has recorded 24,000 'incidents', ranging from graffiti, fly-tipping and public urinating to robbery, drug dealing and prostitution.

I join one of the operators as he peers into his screen. On an adjacent screen, he has a map of the area. He hits a blue button and suddenly I have a bird's-eye view of Trafalgar Square. He can rotate the camera 360 degrees sideways and 180 degrees up and down and zoom in and out. I get a high-resolution close-up as a man grabs his girlfriend from behind. They look like young tourists larking around. Isn't it a bit embarrassing to watch such intimacies? 'We don't linger on things that aren't suspicious,' says the operator matter-of-factly. How do they recognise suspicious behaviour? 'We look for body language, loitering, anything out of the ordinary,' says Brown.

It's estimated that the average Londoner is monitored by 300 CCTV cameras a day. Roughly 1,800 cameras watch over London's railway stations, another 6,000 peer permanently at commuters on the Underground or London buses, and if you include banks, schools, shops and other private companies there are probably 4.2 million closed-circuit cameras watching us every day. Yet, although civil-rights groups regularly emphasise the intrusive nature of such cameras, they have become an integral, and sometimes useful, part of our lives. *Rebecca Taylor*

World view

It beams a constant stream of London's tourist hotspots into homes around the globe, but television has also made unlikely stars of Peckham, Tooting Broadway and Wood Green bus depot. **By Alkarim Jivani**

Television is all about pictures, and no location in Britain provides more emblematic images than London. The capital can be used to illustrate fabulous wealth as well as wretched poverty, entrenched conservatism as represented by pin-striped financiers, or extreme rebellion as depicted by youth tribes. Then there are the iconic sights, instantly recognisable to the world: Big Ben, Buckingham Palace or a piece of Banksy graffiti. Even the most casual viewer of British television is bombarded by images of London. Sometimes they are almost subliminal – a quick shot of the

John Thaw (left) and Dennis Waterman as the Met's finest in *The Sweeney* (1975-78), still one of television's most influential police dramas.

Millennium Wheel here, a black cab flashing by in the background there – and at other times they are right up front, having every last drop of symbolic value squeezed out of them, as with *News at Ten,* which has been milking Big Ben and its bongs since 1967.

Whereas ITV used the Palace of Westminster to signify a sense of authority and probity, others have used it to imply the opposite: dishonesty, cynicism and greed. There was Margaret Thatcher's favourite TV programme, *Yes, Minster,* and its sequel *Yes, Prime Minister*; Rik Mayall's monstrous invention Alan B'stard MP, in *The New Statesman,* who lied, cheated and slept his way to the top; and Michael Dobbs's *House of Cards*, a Shakespearean tale of corruption and avarice that culminated in a putative prime minister pushing a journalist off the roof of the Houses of Parliament.

The golden age for London's representation on television began in 1968, when two newly formed companies with big ideas and lots of bright people – Thames Television and London Weekend Television – won the franchise to broadcast to Londoners. They were legally obliged to reflect their region, so out poured a succession of programmes that could only have been set in London. Representing London's great institutions was *Rumpole of the Bailey*, about a barrister who only came to life when he rose to his feet at the Royal Courts of Justice or sank down with a drink at the Fleet Street boozer Pommeroys, a thinly disguised version of the celebrated journalists' drinking hole El Vino's, drinking wine he referred to as 'Chateau Thames Embankment'.

At the other end of the criminal justice system was a parade of loveable rogues: one of the many stereotypes of the native Londoner that television has enthusiastically exploited. Leading the procession of camel coat-clad wheeler-dealers is Arthur Daley, as played by George Cole in *Minder*. The series used cockney rhyming slang, and took a bit of jargon from the criminal underworld as its title and put it into the general lexicon. It was one of the first series to exploit new camera equipment, which had become lightweight and flexible enough to allow directors to shoot on location without huge inconvenience. And it made the most of it. Londoners recognised their city in the backdrops – not just the big landmarks, but also ordinary west London streets and quirky features, most notably the crooked lamp-post at the bottom of Newman Passage, W1 (now sadly replaced by a straight one) that featured in the credit sequences.

Dennis Waterman, who played Arthur Daley's personal heavy, was fresh from *The Sweeney*, the most influential of the many cop shows that dissected the Metropolitan Police Force. A visceral policier, it took its title from cockney rhyming slang (Sweeney Todd = Flying Squad), and in its three-year run from 1975, set up a template for the hard-bitten Metropolitan police officer who thinks nothing of cutting corners or twisting a suspect's arm. Each episode was filmed in just ten days, so there was no time to hire studios or build sets; in any case, the show's gritty aesthetic would have been stifled by a sterile studio interior. Much of it was filmed out on the street – usually in west London, so the cast and crew didn't have to go too far from the production office in Hammersmith. The ideal places were waste grounds and disused factories, still plentiful in London before the '80s property boom – although one episode had a number of scenes in Julie's wine bar in Notting Hill, then a posh but relatively unassuming watering hole for locals, and now a celebrity hangout for Stella McCartney and co.

'There was a parade of loveable rogues: one of the many stereotypes of the native Londoner that television has enthusiastically exploited.'

Cheeky transport caper
On the Buses (1969-73).

The emergency services provide TV drama with two key ingredients: life-and-death situations and a constant stream of new characters in states of high emotion. There's the soapy police procedural, *The Bill,* which has been plodding along since 1984, and *London's Burning,* which ran for 16 years from 1986 and differed in one key respect from the policiers: firefighters rose in the public estimation as a result of the show.

London's transport infrastructure has also made excellent television fodder, to whit *On the Buses,* which, despite much critical drubbing, was a huge hit with viewers and spawned several movie spin-offs, as well as being sold to NBC in the United States. Even though the writers could have chosen to send the distinctive red double-deckers around Piccadilly Circus or down Park Lane, they chose to locate the show in suburbia – Wood Green bus depot in north London. Perhaps they calculated that viewers were more likely to identify with a setting that was down to earth and familiar, rather than a more famous sight that was psychologically more remote.

Other unassuming corners of the London boroughs have taken on new significance through television. The south London commuter suburb, Surbiton, became a byword for middle-class snobbery after *The Good Life* (though the series was actually shot in Northwood). Peckham has become forever associated with wide boys and smooth-talking market traders since *Only Fools and Horses* was set there. *Citizen Smith* played on the ridiculous notion of ineffectual revolutionary Woolfie Smith's (Robert Lindsay) 'Tooting Popular Front' with its slogan 'Freedom for Tooting', and ensured an obscure south London tube stop gained nationwide fame.

But the best known of the inner London suburbs is one that doesn't exist: Walford, the fictional setting for *EastEnders. EastEnders* was the first soap to be set in London, and established the tone from its opening scene – the death of an old man in his bedsit. The BBC wanted to give it a sharp edge, not just to differentiate it from its key rival, *Coronation Street,* which relied on cosy northern whimsy for its appeal, but because a soap set in London that didn't have tough storylines would be ducking the issue. The show was the first soap to have a gay character, the first to have an AIDS storyline, and the first to feature prostitution and drug abuse; but perhaps the most distinctive

Thames & London Weekend Television

On 30 July 1968, two new television companies came into being with a mission to broadcast to Londoners: Thames would fill the airwaves during the week, and on Friday the baton would be passed to London Weekend Television.

Delighted to have the franchise for the capital, Thames made the most of its distinctive geographical situation with a station ident consisting of as many big London landmarks as could be crammed into it. For the next 25 years, a composite but geographically warped cityscape consisting of Tower Bridge, Big Ben, Telecom Tower and St Paul's was beamed into homes up and down the country several times a day, announcing some of TV's best dramas and documentaries.

The opening night, however, was something of a disaster. The technicians' union had timed industrial action to have the maximum impact. Although the first programme – luncheon at London's Mansion House – was broadcast unscathed, subsequent programmes took a hit, notably the highlight of the evening schedule: a new series from comedian Tommy Cooper. Screens went blank across the country and remained so until 10.30pm.

LWT was just as unlucky when it took over on the Friday evening, three days later, with more industrial action. Even after the dispute was settled, LWT's highbrow schedule of opera and *Hamlet* was no more appealing to viewers than a blank screen, and ratings, and therefore revenues, were rock- bottom. There were serious concerns that the company would go bankrupt, until an unlikely saviour rode to the rescue: Rupert Murdoch.

The Australian media tycoon , newly arrived in London, did what he does best: knocking heads together until he got what he wanted, a populist, crowd-pleasing schedule that pandered to audiences rather than challenging them. Out went the arts discussion shows, in came *Please Sir!*, an anodyne sitcom starring John Alderton and set in a school. The regulatory body, the Independent Television Authority, took the view

that Murdoch's newspaper interests not only represented a conflict of interest, but gave him too large a share of the British media. In 1971 he was issued with a discreet ultimatum and, uncharacteristically, he withdrew.

However, he didn't give up. Having been pushed out of the charmed circle of TV franchise holders, he has tried every other alternative route, launching Sky Television in 1989 and buying a large chunk of ITV in 2006 – the maximum he was permitted to own under British financial regulations.

Ironically, Thames, which has always been the dominant partner in the relationship between the two London franchise holders, was outlived by LWT, which still broadcasts today. The corporate structure remains, even though the name has been buried under a unified ITV brand. Thames lost its franchise after 24 years and put out its last programme on 31 December 1992, when its chief executive broadcast a farewell speech followed by a montage of the channel's greatest hits, set to Dusty Springfield singing 'I Only Want To Be With You'.
Alkarim Jivani

thing about *EastEnders* was that it was the first mainstream soap to have regular black characters – crucial if any depiction of a city as diverse as London wants to be taken seriously.

London is one of the most cosmopolitan cities of the 21st century, with 300 different languages regularly spoken by its inhabitants, and television allows us glimpses of these multifarious ethnic cultures. *The Chinese Detective*, in 1981, was the first – and remains the only – dramatic attempt to look at British Chinese culture. David Yip was cast as the titular cop, which was a breakthrough in itself: previously Chinese characters had often been played by white actors who had 'yellowed up'. Moreover, his speech was free from any cod accent – in fact it had a faint tinge of cockney, thus affirming that he was as much a Londoner as he was Chinese. *King of the Ghetto* (from 1986) was a prescient and clear-eyed view of race politics in Brick Lane between the old white working class and the Bangladeshi community. Jack Rosenthal created a series of dramas set among London's

Jewish community, such as *Bar Mitzvah Boy,* and also turned his attention to London's cab drivers in the Thames Television play *The Knowledge*.

London's role as a destination for people from all over the place has also lent itself to storylines about disparate groups brought together under one roof. Every generation has had its own iconic flat share drama, going back to *Take Three Girls* in the late '60s, which sought to exploit the swinging '60s image of London with its story line about a debutante, an actress and an art student living together in Chelsea. In the '70s, that daring new phenomenon, the mixed-sex flat share, became the subject of *Man about the House,* where the 'dolly birds' were joined by Richard O' Sullivan, who had to pretend to be gay to the landlord to avoid a scandal. The '80s brought parodies of the form with the *The Young Ones*: a surreal, slapstick show about four students sharing a house in north London, who are constantly bored, even though their home is the scene of a terrorist siege and a hidden world that reveals itself when they are asleep. The show featured almost every big name from London's burgeoning alternative comedy scene, including Rik Mayall, Ade Edmondson, Alexei Sayle, Ben Elton, Dawn French and Stephen Fry.

More recently, *This Life*, which ran for two series in 1996 and 1997, with a reunion in 2006, was very different from other flat share series in tone and content. It gave us a group of young lawyers starting their careers, and was unflinchingly honest about their sex lives and drug consumption, using handheld cameras and lots of jump cuts to create a rough-and-ready texture. The characters were seen commuting on the capital's erratic transport system, and the action sprawled from the legal ghetto of Chancery Lane and Lincoln's Inn to the shabbier environs of Southwark Bridge Road where the central quintet lived.

Unlike film, television has never taken an unabashedly rosy look at the city. In the '60s and '70s, when British cinema was putting out images of swinging London and 'red bus' movies, TV was doing the exact opposite, and depicting the grittier, quirkier side of life with dramas such as *Cathy Come Home* and *Edna the Inebriate Woman*. Ironic, given that television is seen as the cosier medium. There is still no TV equivalent of *A Touch of Class* or *Notting Hill*, films that show the city as enticing and romantic without qualification.

That is not to say that there aren't TV depictions of London as a place of wealth, luxury and power, but they are few and far between, and

EastEnders

Albert Square in the London Borough of Walford, E20, will soon become as familiar as Coronation Street. Or so the BBC hopes.

'We chose the East End because it's a close-knit community of garrulous, noisy, vulgar, buoyant people, and has a history of shifting immigration populations,' says producer and co-creator Julia Smith.

'It'll be a multiracial community with all the problems you'd expect to find in an inner city, including racial tension, because it's a fact of life.' In other words, expect lots of stereotyped images: a young Bengali couple trying to cope with an arranged marriage, racial harassment and a supermarket; Ali, the Turkish Cypriot who runs the local café; a Caribbean builder; a cockney publican; a young single parent; a closet gay; and a loud, rather vulgar 75-year-old cockney mother. But fear not, there will be 'plenty of laughs'. And those who want a bit of glamour will find it in the shapely form of Debbie (Shirley Cheriton from *Angels*). She has all the right statistics to become a Fleet Street pin-up. *Belkis Bhegani Review from Time Out, 21 February 1985.*

From left: Paul Eddington, Nigel Hawthorne and Derek Fowlds win promotion from *Yes, Minister* (1980-84) to *Yes, Prime Minister* (1986-88). Mrs Thatcher named it as one of her favourite programmes.

often set in the past – such as *Upstairs Downstairs* and *The Duchess of Duke Street*.

The sunniest television depiction of London came not from a British production but an American one, and, ironically, it has probably been watched by more people around the world than any other TV show set in London. It is, of course, the final episode of the fourth series of *Friends*, when the Manhattanite mates cross the Atlantic for Ross's wedding. It showed a cleaned-up, toned-down London, complete with chirpy cockneys and guest appearances from Richard Branson and the Duchess of York. How Londoners chortled.

In consolation, Britain's biggest worldwide hit is a science fiction programme whose depictions of London seem more realistic than anything we saw in *Friends*. *Doctor Who* episodes that show London with Daleks invading across Westminster Bridge, UFOs crashing into Big Ben and evil Santas terrorising a south London council estate show the city as a place where anything and everything can happen. And that's the way Londoners like it.

Alkarim Jivani was TV Editor of *Time Out* from 1987 to 2007.

ON SCREEN

MUSIC

Art school
rock

London's rock history over the past 40 years can be traced through its art schools.

By John Lewis

A year before he launched *Time Out* in 1968, Tony Elliott was writing and editing a magazine at Keele University called *Unit*. A round-up of art and music articles, linked to the burgeoning alternative rock scene, one 1967 edition featured two features that might have looked a little incongruous, even in that fertile environment. One was a profile of an obscure conceptual artist from Japan, the other was an interview with an even more obscure lecturer at Walthamstow Art College.

The obscure Japanese conceptual artist turned out to be Yoko Ono; the art lecturer turned out to be Keith Albarn, who, a year later, would father a boy named Damon. Somewhere between the two of them, we can trace an entire history of British pop music. From the moment that Yoko's husband entered Liverpool School of Art in 1957 to the increasingly arthouse obsessions of Damon Albarn 50 years later, the art school has a unique place in the history of British pop. It has been the mechanism through which British mavericks processed African-American music, adding theatricality, politics, militancy, feminism, surrealism, high camp and androgyny.

Key members of pretty much every major British band who emerged in the 1960s – the Beatles, the Rolling Stones, the Who, the Kinks, the Animals, the Yardbirds, Herman's Hermits, the Small Faces, the Pretty Things, Manfred Mann, Pink Floyd, Fleetwood Mac, Led Zeppelin, Deep Purple – had at least one art school graduate in their ranks, and even some of the most innocuous pop stars of the 1960s and early '70s (Donovan, Cat Stevens, Gilbert O'Sullivan, Leo Sayer, 10cc) were art college graduates. It's a link that continued throughout glam rock, punk, New Romantics, shoegazers,

Britpop and beyond. Take away the art school from the history of British pop and you'd be left with a pretty threadbare record collection, or a near empty iPod.

The link between pop and art is a very British thing. There have been a handful of art school graduates in American pop (tellingly, most of them tended to be anglophiles, such as Devo, Chrissie Hynde, Talking Heads, Chris Stein from Blondie, Pere Ubu, Grace Jones, the Scissor Sisters, or Kurt Cobain and Krist Novoselic from Nirvana), but art schools in the US never had the cross-cultural, state-funded democratic appeal of their British counterparts. Before World War II, Britain's art schools had been the preserve of upper middle-class bohemians and well-bred girls from finishing schools. Fuelled by a socialist progressivism – coupled with the necessity to keep the labour pool clear for freshly demobbed servicemen – Britain's postwar art schools started to embrace a new demographic: lower middle-class and upper working class kids who were bright, lacked academic aptitude or discipline but hadn't the patience to learn a trade. It happened to be exactly the same upwardly mobile demographic (described by the music critic Simon Reynolds as the 'liminal class') that has been the bedrock of pop music for the past half century.

Part of the attraction of the art school to this liminal class was the promise of sex, drugs, creative freedom and flexible working hours. According to the Clash's Joe Strummer, art school was 'the last resort of malingerers, bluffers and people who didn't want to work'. According to Keith Richards, 'In England, if you're lucky, you get into art school. It's somewhere they put you if they can't put you anywhere else… Most of

Art school antics: Adam Ant at the height of his chart success in 1981.

the teachers were drunks, freaks, potheads who didn't care what the kids did.' Pete Townshend concurs. 'All those rules – that you had to be good-looking and smartly dressed, that you had to be intelligent and not pick your nose, that you had to always have something to say and you had to be big and you had to be strong – none of those rules applied at art college… Incredibly beautiful women would talk to you without needing to see your credentials. It took me about a year to get over that.'

It was London and its suburbs that were central to the postwar art school boom, and that continued to produce scores of pop stars well into the 21st century. From the 1950s onwards, London developed a network of suburban art colleges that fed 30 years of pop. Invariably, these colleges were in the same suburbs (Richmond, Croydon, Hornsey) that hosted 'rhythm clubs' in the 1940s and '50s, and which ended up, by the 1960s, hosting key venues in the blues, trad jazz and burgeoning rock 'n' roll circuit. They include institutions in Sidcup (whose alumni include Keith Richards, along with Phil May and Dick Taylor of the Pretty Things), Ealing (Pete Townshend, Ronnie Wood, Freddie Mercury, Thunderclap Newman), Kingston (Eric Clapton, Sandy Denny, John Renbourne, Keith Relf from the Yardbirds, Tom McGuiness from Manfred Mann), Camberwell (Syd Barrett, Humphrey Lyttelton), Wimbledon (Jeff Beck), Hornsey (Ray Davies, Roger Glover from Deep Purple), Croydon (record producer Mike Vernon), Sutton (Jimmy Page), Harrow (Charlie Watts), Walthamstow (Ian Dury) and Hammersmith (Cat Stevens). David Bowie, though not an art school student, was heavily involved with the Beckenham Arts Lab, and had worked briefly in graphic design.

Albert Goldman, in his biography of Lennon, observes that British pop music developed and distinguished itself from its American counterpart 'by taking the raw material of American rock 'n' roll and subjecting it to the techniques that the British art schools had inherited from the prewar European avant garde.' What, exactly, were these avant-garde techniques and sensibilities that proved so influential on rock music? One was certainly a Romantic pursuit of 'authenticity'.

In art terms it was the notion of the 'noble savage', the celebration of primitivism pursued by artists such as Picasso. In musical terms, this often meant a studied reversion to early forms of African-American music: in the case of London art school graduates like Humphrey Lyttelton, Wally Fawkes and Monty Sunshine (all key figures in the trad jazz revival of the mid to late 1950s), it meant New Orleans traditional jazz that predated Louis Armstrong's relocation to Chicago in 1922. This search for primal black music was continued by suburban London blues fans like Ronnie Wood, Jeff Beck and Eric Clapton, who viewed African-American blues as the gateway to a creative bohemia (legend has it that Mick Jagger bonded with art school student Keith Richards when he saw him at Dartford rail station carrying a pile of blues albums).

More directly influential on pop would have been the formal techniques of the avant garde (collage, montage, ready-mades), and the exposure to forms like abstraction, surrealism and automatic writing (one can certainly see the influence of these on John Lennon, Syd Barrett, Bryan Ferry and Donovan). More generally, if the postwar British art schools had a guiding ideology, it was the doctrine that art has something to say that produces unrest and movement. 'According to this definition,' say Simon Frith and Howard Horne in their detailed analysis of the scene in *Art into Pop* (1987), 'Art could not be a passive instrument of capitalism's social and economic interests: it had to win back its central, influential position at the heart of cultural production – the mode of expression of students (and of rock) in the '60s borrowed heavily from Romantic philosophy, with its emphasis on autonomy and creativity, and from avant-garde manifestos of the early 20th century… art school ideology casts the self love of the aesthete and the avant-gardist's sensitivity to the power of form into one style.'

Pete Townshend was the first art school graduate to knowingly apply these theories to pop music. His lecturer at Ealing Art College, Roy Ascott (who later taught Brian Eno at Ipswich Art College), pioneered a radical programme called the Groundcourse, which would introduce his art students to various leftfield linguists, sociologists, cyberneticians and biologists, and also invited various radical artists as guest lecturers. One of these was the Austrian Gustav Metzke, the mind behind 'auto-destruction'. Metzke talked about sculpting statues that would intentionally fall from their plinths; at one lecture, he methodically destroyed a double bass. When Townshend started to rigorously trash his guitar at the end of Who gigs, it was an explicit reference to Metzke. 'The rest of the band would say that this was pompous drivel,' says Townshend. 'I'd say, "No, no, no, it's auto-destructive art!"'

Townshend always used the conceptual vocabulary of the art school to describe his work, gleefully embracing notions like 'Pop Art Music' (the sardonic celebration of consumerism in *The Who Sell Out*), 'social realism' (the invocation of grim London landscapes in his lyrics, a trait influenced by Hornsey Art School graduate Ray Davies) and 'Rock Opera' (his later unified, conceptual works like *Tommy* and *Quadrophenia*).

Sound of the suburbs

By the late 1960s, a whole generation schooled in London's suburban art schools had started to permeate British pop music. The Bonzo Dog Doo-Dah Band – featuring graduates of Saint Martins College, Goldsmiths and the Royal College of Art – were fusing prewar trad jazz with psychedelia, mixing a love of fin-de-siècle aestheticism with a rigorous application of absurdist surrealism. Freddie Mercury, only a few years behind Pete Townsend at Ealing Art College, used his design training to create a flamboyant onstage persona for himself. Ian Dury, a former student of Peter Blake at Walthamstow Art School, and later a student at the Royal Academy of Art, cut an oddly theatrical figure on the drearily blokeish pub rock scene of the early 1970s.

Dury – born in 1942 and a full 36 years old when he finally had a hit single in 1978 – proved the link between the postwar art school boom and the punk revolution. He used his disability (he had a calliper on his left leg after contracting polio as a child) to create a confrontational persona that mimicked Laurence Olivier's Richard III. His stage costume in the early 1970s – bondage trousers, shaved head, safety pins and razor blades hanging from his pierced ears – was a source of fascination for a teenager from Finsbury Park called John Lydon and a young fashion student from Stoke Newington called Malcolm McLaren.

McLaren had studied fine art, design and fashion at a variety of London institutions (Saint Martins, Croydon College of Art, Harrow

The ultimate art school pop star? Blur's Damon Albarn, at Reading Festival in 1991.

'In many ways, Blur mined every historic manifestation of the art school in rock 'n' roll.'

Art College and Goldsmiths, and invited Dury to Let It Rock, the haute couture boutique that he ran with Vivienne Westwood, to be styled. Soon he was using Dury's stage persona as the basis for the Sex Pistols.

Although John Lydon and the other Pistols would violently dispute this, McLaren has always insisted that punk was fostered at London's art schools under his auspices (heavily influenced by the situationist ideas of the 1968 French student movement, and the mischievous pranks of the late '60s art school 'groupuscule' King Mob). It's certainly true that the Sex Pistols' chief songsmith, Glen Matlock, spent 18 months at Saint Martins, and three-quarters of the Clash emerged from London art colleges. Paul Simonon went to Byam Shaw Art School in Notting Hill, Mick Jones spent two years at Hammersmith School of Art, and Joe Strummer had dropped out of Newport Art College in south Wales and Central School of Art in London. All of them dressed like they'd just come out of their art studio, seeming to wear the influence of Rauschenberg and Pollock down their trousers.

In many ways, punk was the most distilled reading of the avant-garde art school aesthetic – the shock tactics of the Italian futurists, the rupture with the postwar consensus, the expressionistic howls of rage, the reversion to primal forms of American music (in this case, garage rock), the DIY aesthetics, the prioritisation of error, discordancy and indeterminacy. Dozens of

> 'All of them dressed like they'd just come out of their art studio, seeming to wear the influence of Rauschenberg and Pollock down their trousers.'

other punk and post-punk artists emerged from London's art colleges in the '70s. Adam Ant, Mike Barson from Madness, two members of Wire, Lester Square from the Monochrome Set and most of the Raincoats attended Hornsey Art College; while other art students include Billy Childish (Central), John Foxx (Royal College Of Art), Richard Butler from the Psychedelic Furs (Epsom) and two members of Wire (Watford Art College). Together with a handful of regional art colleges like Manchester (Howard Devoto, Mick Hucknall, John McGeoch from The Banshees), Leeds (Soft Cell, Jon King and Andy Gill from Gang of Four, Green Gartside from Scritti Politti), Liverpool (Budgie from the Banshees, Paul Rutherford from Frankie Goes to Hollywood) and Lanchester College in Coventry (Jerry Dammers from the Specials, Hazel O'Connor and Selecter), punk and post-punk started to develop a distinct art school sensibility.

These tropes dominated pop music – even mainstream British chart pop – for the best part of the next decade, as art school graduates with punk roots started to creep into the charts. Some, like John Taylor and Nick Rhodes from Duran Duran (Birmingham School of Art) or Dave Gahan and Alan Wilder from Depeche Mode (Southend Art College), harnessed their visual nous to exploit the possibilities of the promo video; others, like Green Gartside or Mick Hucknall, used the manifesto-laden discourse of contemporary art to justify a process of 'entryism' into the corporate pop world. The influence of art school – particularly fashion courses – also assisted the entry of many more women into the traditionally male bastions of pop, including Bananarama, the Slits, the Raincoats, the Belle Stars, the Bodysnatchers and Sade.

Even before art school ideas started to permeate the mainstream, however, a certain style of post-punk became synonymous with 'art school rock'. It tended to feature abstract, literary lyrics; choppy, angular, discordant guitar riffs; hypnotic basslines; and brittle, funk-influenced drum beats. Fittingly, whenever music in that style was revived over the next three decades – by Ride, Spacemen 3, Spiritualized, Radiohead, Elastica, Blur, Pulp and PJ Harvey in the mid '90s, or by Franz Ferdinand, Tom Vek and the Kaiser Chiefs in the noughties – the bands were invariably dominated by art school graduates.

Ex-fine art student Alison Goldfrapp at the V Festival, 2005.

Rock goes to college

During the '80s and '90s, as a higher proportion of the country was pushed into further education, academic university courses often seemed to usurp the art school as a breeding ground for pop stars. For instance, the members of Coldplay studied, variously, Greek and Latin (Chris Martin), anthropology (Will Champion), engineering (Guy Berryman) and mathematics (Jonny Buckland) at University College London; Tim Rice-Oxley from Coldplay's pals Keane graduated in classics at the same university; and UCL's Bartlett School of Architecture was the alma mater of both Justine Frischmann from Elastica and Brett Anderson from Suede. Other musicians ended up taking curiously apposite higher education options: Richard D James, aka Aphex Twin, studied electrical engineering at Kingston University; the oddball house producer and sonic prankster Matthew Herbert studied drama at Exeter University; and two members of the Manic Street Preachers graduated in political history.

Yet the vestigial links between the art school and the pop world continue well into the 21st century. Alison Goldfrapp – a fine art graduate from Middlesex University (formerly Hornsey Art College) – fronts the synth pop duo Goldfrapp, who seem to embody an art school lineage that takes in the experimental glam rock of Roxy Music, the flamboyant stage costumes of Freddie Mercury and the electronic flirtations of Soft Cell and Depeche Mode. Indeed, some of the most exciting music to be made by London's art school graduates has from come outside the realm of rock. Mathangi 'Maya' Arulpragasam, the London-born musician of Sri Lankan ancestry who goes by the name of MIA, studied fine art, film and video at Central Saint Martins College, and her music – a Technicolor blur of low-budget electronica from the shanty towns of Bombay, Rio, Jamaica and Nigeria – sounds like a sonic reproduction of the junkyard bricolage of Brazilian artists like the Campana Brothers, or the graffiti art of Keith Haring. Or look at rapper Steven Henry, better known as Infinite Livez, a Chelsea Art College-educated comic book artist, who has taken hip hop into astonishingly vaudevillian areas, performing with inflatable dolls, papier mâché props, and dancers in horses heads, and making sexually ambiguous music of a conceptual nature.

Perhaps the best example of the union of pop and art has come from the son of that Walthamstow Art College lecturer featured in the early predecessor of *Time Out*. Damon Albarn absorbed an earlier generation of postwar art school ideology from his father and briefly studied fine art at Goldsmiths, alongside his Essex pal Graham Coxon, around the same time that they formed Blur. In many ways, Blur mined every historic manifestation of the art school in rock 'n' roll – the Pop Art/social realist trajectory explored by Pete Townshend and Ray Davies, the retro-futurist whimsy of the Bonzo Dog Doo-Dah Band, the avant garde/psychedelic aesthetic of Pink Floyd, the back-to-basics rupture of punk. And in his various solo guises, Albarn has moved pop further into the visual sphere than any other artist. Gorillaz – his 'virtual 3D band' developed with the cartoonist Jamie Hewlett, himself a former art student at Northbrook College in Sussex – is the ultimate postmodern art school prank, anonymous, conceptual and existing solely in the studio.

As if to consummate the pop/art marriage, Albarn and Hewlett teamed up to create *Monkey: Journey to the West*, a multimedia opera fusing Hewlett's outrageous designs with Albarn's music, a riot of Chinese pentatonic modes and spiky orchestrations featuring a mix of Chinese and European classical musicians. The art school aesthetic is alive and kicking in music – you just have to look a bit further than rock 'n' roll to find it.

John Lewis is a former *Time Out* music critic.

TIMELINE

1968
The London Sinfonietta, dedicated to playing contemporary classical music and new compositions, set up.

The Doors play at the Roundhouse, their first, and last, gig in Britain.

The Sadler's Wells Opera moves to the Coliseum in St Martin's Lane and renames itself English National Opera.

1969
David Bowie catches the eye, and ear, of the public with the release of his first single, 'Space Oddity'.

The Beatles perform their final live gig on the rooftop of the Apple building at 3 Savile Row, W1.

1971
The Rolling Stones launch their own record company, Rolling Stones Records, and release the album *Sticky Fingers*. Andy Warhol designs the album's now famous cover.

Virgin Megastore opens on Oxford Street.

1975
Queen's 'Bohemian Rhapsody' becomes the first pop music video to be shown on *Top of the Pops*.

1976
The Rough Trade record shop opens on Portobello Road. Two years later, the Rough Trade independent record label is founded.

1977
The Sex Pistols release *Never Mind the Bollocks, Here's the Sex Pistols*. They perform their single 'Anarchy in the UK' on a boat on the Thames outside the Houses of Parliament.

1978
Some 80,000 people gather in Victoria Park for a Rock Against Racism concert. RAR was reborn in 2002 as Love Music Hate Racism, with a concert at the Astoria in London.

1979
The Clash release *London Calling*.

1985
Live Aid raises more than £40m for famine relief in Ethiopia. Pop stars Bob Geldof (the Boomtown Rats) and Midge Ure (Ultravox) organise the event at Wembley Stadium. It is attended by 82,000 people.

The Red Wedge collective of British musicians, including Billy Bragg and Paul Weller, promote Labour in the build-up to the 1987 general election. The Tories win.

1993
The London Art Board (now Arts Council) supports the first London Jazz Festival.

1995
Blur and Oasis bring Britpop to the nation's attention by each releasing a single on the same day. Blur's 'Country House' reaches No.1; Oasis come in second with 'Roll With It'.

1996
Jazz impresario Ronnie Scott dies, but his legendary club lives on.

Spice Girls shoot the video for their first single, 'Wannabe', in gothic and derelict St Pancras Hotel.

1997
Noel Gallagher and Meg Matthews move into Primrose Hill. All-night rock parties follow.

Indie and alternative music radio station Xfm is launched in London.

2002
Visitors can plug in their headphones and listen to Ian Dury after a musical bench is placed in Richmond Park in memory of the singer.

We Will Rock You opens at the Dominion Theatre, Tottenham Court Road. Written by Ben Elton, the medley of Queen's greatest hits confirms the trend for 'jukebox musicals'.

2007
George Melly, the flamboyant jazz musician, womaniser and London icon, dies.

Hammersmith Palais closes.

The Royal Festival Hall reopens after a two-year restoration project costing £91m.

MUSIC

Ian Dury

MUSIC

Tables, pigeons, hedge, chained metal cup on the fountain. The outdoor cafeteria at Kenworth House, Hampstead has become Ian Dury's new manor. 'Lovely place. They've got a Rembrandt over there. I know the staff by now. They're great. All working class, all people who're into art or gardening.' We sit in the garden and discuss his cancer. One feared finding him diminished. He is not. 'Oy-oy! Take a photo of me. Be fair,' he hollers at a tourist. 'Don't be a cunt all you life. Take your top off.' That took care of the does-he-take-sugar factor. 'I was in LA doing a part in *The Crow: Part Two* because they wanted a bit of Essex in the film. I wasn't very well though. I had a Kennington round me Newington's, as they say. I was being very, very sick from a long way down where I've never come from before. It wasn't the bit of caulie, bits of tomato that never evaporated, it was something new, and it worried me.'

He came home and was referred to a cancer specialist, but cancer of the colon developed secondaries in the liver. Ian lifts his T-shirt to show the plugs in his stomach connected to his heart through which the chemotherapy is delivered. 'We can possibly keep it at bay on the liver, but getting rid of it's more difficult. I'm not going to Lourdes next week, not that I'm knocking that. I'm very lucky. I'm early stages, I'm in no pain and I still have me own barnet [Barnet Fair: hair]. At least half of cancer treatment is how you feel. Spirit, man. You fight it much better.' He grabs my tobacco pouch – 'So, fuck it!' – and rolls one up.

He's in reminiscent mood. 'Man overboard!' he roars, remembering the state I was in after some bastard at a Marin County radio station slipped PCP into my drink. 'We thought we'd lost you! That was 20 years ago!' It's hardly possible to be more London, and loved for it, than Ian Dury, which gave him a few problems on that first *New Boots & Panties* tour of the US in 1978. Dury had a clenched regionality born of bus queues, bomb sites, draughts, winkles and celery on Sunday off the barrow, and hardship. Childhood polio left him painfully emphatic of progress; he jerked through San Francisco in his hobnails and callipers on his stick. LA's Roxy didn't know what to make of him either, though the *LA Times* felt that he lacked the elegance and sophistication of Roxy Music. 'Arrogant like I am, cocky dick, the warmth is what you're dealing in, smothering people in jollification. We're trying to warm them up.'

Dury remained unchanged by lucrative chart hits such as 'Sex and Drugs and Rock 'n' Roll' and 'Hit Me with Your Rhythm Stick', and *New Boots &*

Panties going platinum. 'It's very important not to be impressed by what happens to you. The main thing is to work out how to get what I need without needing too much. If a yacht floats past my eyeballs and I get on it, I'm a cunt. I'd rather get on with the gig. My life has been good because I've been tooled up. I'm a half-breed geezer because I've got a natural inherited academic cleverness from my mother's side, and I've got my old man who'd be an artisan, bus-driver type.'

We share memories of Soho. 'It was a jubbly ol' mixture of people round the Duke of York and the Champion in the '50s. You was either a Modern Jazz or a Traddie at art school, right? I was both.

A more youthful Dury poses in 1970.

I was into Traddiness 'cos the dollies was nice. Cy's, Colyers, Studio 51. We used to use that Peter Cook "yerst" language, and it got mixed up with McVooteroonie language. Then I learned about cockney rhyming slang being a current thing, not all that apples-and-pears bollocks. Every ten years there'd be a new word for telephone – Al Capone, eau de cologne, rag 'n' bone.'

He then delivers a labyrinthine definition of the cockney word 'sort'. 'Sort is a right good-looking girl, half a sort is a doubly good-looking girl. Sort yourself out, you know. "Mort" is the other one. That's Fulham for your girl, for your Richard [Richard III: bird]. I know Fulham people who use it without even thinking about it. "I gotta bell me mort, in I?" I had this girl come in my dressing room sit down on my knee, she goes, "I love you". And this minder, he goes "Half a sort, your three o'clock." You know this 12 o'clock code? It's a prison thing. Spider taught me this. Here's your clock face, there's your imaginary hands. To me you're at exactly my 12 o'clock, to you I'm at my six o'clock. It tells you the position of somebody you're talking about without giving it away or looking at them. Bosh! Boom! Over there!'

He'd always been snowed under with requests to do charity gigs, but his attitude towards the affliction is complex. His single, 'Spasticus Autisticus', ran into a storm of protest. 'I'm the raspberry [raspberry ripple: cripple] that became glamorous. I didn't step out of the ring because I was a fuckin' cripple. I got out because I was magnificent. I tell that to all the cripples that I meet. Magnificent takes a little longer than being crippled, and the only way to sustain it is to know that you're crippled.'

Years ago, he'd formulated an interesting theory about drugs. 'You know, they only give Thai sticks to old people in Thailand, and opium's an old people's drug in the Orient. Coke is really a post-menopausal drug. I intend to be 55 before I get i nto it. I won't take heroin till I'm 75. I'm looking forward to it. I'll have acid when I'm an old boy in case I don't come back.' At 56, things have changed. 'Well, now I've been told I may not make it to be old. I'm not tempted because what I know now is already working well.' He has a boy of one and another of three. 'If you ain't got one you can't get one, if you get one you get hundreds. Two babies, I've got many reasons to be extremely cheerful, and you can't steal cheerful.'

Original interview by Brian Case. Ian Dury died of cancer on 27 March 2000.

Rock Against Racism

When I was 14, I was a fan of punk bands. I loved going to the gigs, but was terrified of the violence that surrounded them: the shows were frequented by gangs of National Front supporters and you ran the risk of getting your head kicked in. I lived in Sutton and remember travelling back on the Northern Line from a Generation X gig at the Roundhouse in Camden. A group of skinheads got on the train and started laying into people with their boots and fists. I narrowly escaped a beating. I didn't know many black people, but I was aware of the racial tensions of the time. But there was no organised resistance to it.

It was spring 1978, and I heard about a group called Rock Against Racism, which had been set up in 1976 to fight the NF and racism. When I found out they were organising a carnival in April at Victoria Park, I decided I was going to be there. The march left Trafalgar Square and went down Brick Lane, past some well-known skinhead pubs. People shouted abuse at us, but the column of marchers was so long, that they got fed up after a while. As we marched, the Members were playing on an open-back truck. The Clash played at Victoria Park, but we couldn't hear much because the organisers had only planned for around 20,000 people – there were nearer 100,000. It was my first political experience, and I saw things I had never come across before – openly gay couples and radical Trotskyists handing out leaflets.

Back at school, I set up a local group called Schoolkids Against the Nazis. We went to concerts, and listened to bands we would never have listened to otherwise, such as Steel Pulse, Misty in Roots and other reggae bands. We went to RAR events, such as the concert in Brockwell Park in September '78, where we distributed their stickers and leaflets.

The RAR gigs also introduced me to Two-Tone music. It was the first time that I'd seen black and white musicians perform together. The gigs were fantastic, but they were also heavily targeted by the NF. At one Specials gig, the band jumped into the stalls to stop some kids getting beaten up.

I got a job as a porter at the Royal Marsden Hospital, and eventually became a shop steward for the union there. I would never have done that without my involvement with RAR, which showed me that you have to stand up for what you believe in. These days, I organise the Leftfield at Glastonbury, which I hope retains the RAR spirit. But 30 years on, the far right has more political clout than ever, with BNP councillors in Barking and Dagenham and a BNP member on the London Assembly. We must keep on fighting racism – it certainly hasn't gone away.

**Geoff Martin,
Rock Against Racism activist**

Northern exposure

From the Dublin Castle to the Hawley Arms, Camden has always rocked.

MUSIC

It may have had some of its thunder stolen by Shoreditch at the start of the noughties and, more recently, by the feverishly creative hub that is New Cross, but Camden's status as the white-hot epicentre of London's live music scene has gone largely unchallenged for several decades.

Fired up in the '60s by the Roundhouse – which hosted gigs by Hendrix, Pink Floyd and the Doors, among countless groovy others – the dynamic neighbourhood has since embraced every musical genre, even spawning one of its very own, the 'Camden lurch' scene of the early '90s. Its main claim to fame, however, and one that still exerts a powerful pull for music-obsessive tourists and locals alike, more than a decade after the event, is as the beating heart of Britpop. Unarguably key to the mid '90s scene that produced Blur, Suede, Pulp, Elastica, Sleeper et al and came to define 'Cool Britannia', was the Good Mixer, a scruffy, singularly unprepossessing boozer in Inverness Street, where Britpop's movers and shakers – and plenty of second- and third-division players and hangers-on – held their business meetings, drank away their days and nights and generally ran off the behavioural rails. When they weren't in the Good Mixer, Damon, Justine, Brett and the rest were likely in the tiny Laurel Tree, home (between 1993-96) to Paul Tunkin's hugely hip, neo-Mod club Blow Up, which later moved to the West End.

Before Britpop there was Madness. In the early '80s, the original nutty boys established themselves at the Dublin Castle in Parkway, filming the video to 'My Girl' there and returning in 2004 to play a series of reformation gigs as the Dangermen. Lead singer Suggs even paid solo homage to his 'hood in 1999 with the song 'Camden Town'. Madness's punk peers (Sex Pistols, The Clash, Ian Dury and the Blockheads,

Joy Division…) all played at the Electric Ballroom, a venue still in rude health but now under threat from plans to extend the adjacent Camden Town Underground station.

It's hard to name a local pub that doesn't dance to the beat of music history's drum: Suede played their very first London gig in a dank sweatbox called the Falcon in Royal College Street, which was for several years a destination venue for the more committed, underground rock fan (anyone remember Fudgetunnel?); one of Pulp's earliest London showings was at the Underworld, which also hosted countless touring American bands in the glory days of grunge. Further up the road towards Chalk Farm, Dingwalls first opened its doors in 1973, embracing everything from punk to reggae, baggy and acid-jazz acts, while the tiny, upstairs room at the Barfly (previously the Monarch) quickly carved out its name as a place in which to see successful bands in their formative days (Stereophonics, Muse and Doves all played early gigs there).

A constant hunger for the new means sub-cultural shifts are inevitable but, as the popularity of some Camden venues wanes, that of others waxes. The Hawley Arms was once a rough Hell's Angels hangout; a makeover turned it into London's coolest boozer, simply because Pete Doherty, Razorlight, Kelly Osbourne, Sadie Frost, Noel Fielding and – most famously – Amy Winehouse (collectively dubbed the 'Camden Caners') drank there. A devastating fire tore through the canal area of the market in February 2008, all but destroying the Hawley Arms, though it vowed to reopen before the end of the year. The music-mad, historically hedonistic spirit of Camden, it's safe to say, will not stand still in the meantime. *Sharon O'Connell*

Teenage kicks

Unfortunately for history's sake, my first ever gig was not cool: David Essex at the Dominion on Tottenham Court Road. It would have been hip in 1973, but this was 1980. Still, my friend Jane and I liked his old stuff, and thought there was something strangely appealing about the tousle-haired thirtysomething on a motorbike. My dad stood in the queue with us 13-year-olds to make sure we got in OK. A woman collecting for charity walked along the line, and when my dad bought a couple of badges, she said, 'Yes sir, would you like one for your girlfriend?' I know that both my father and I were thinking, 'This is it, Lee's future is going to gigs where young girls go out with men twice their age.'

My second gig was an under-18s concert by Madness at Hammersmith Odeon. There were no older men, just younger boys in the row behind us trying to steal my poster without dropping their fags. It was the first of too many wonderful Madness gigs to count, each one thereafter like being Alice in Wonderland, trying to get my feet free of sticky rock venue carpets to a ska pop soundtrack.

Although you could usually bluff your way into gigs, a lot of bands had begun putting on under-18s gigs as matinees. Depeche Mode in the Afternoon sounds like a sequel to *Bonjour Tristesse,* but actually it was Essex's finest putting me in touch with my electronica side. It was also my first experience of the Venue in Victoria. There was always a 'spicy' aroma in the foyer of the Venue, and, because it was a compact old theatre, you always felt close to the band. So close you could smell the gladioli when the Smiths played there in September 1983, just before 'This Charming Man' was released. The support acts included the Go-Betweens. It was sublime. The Venue was eventually turned into a ribshack.

The early 1980s were a heyday for gigs: bands such as UB40 were introducing concessions for the unemployed, nurses and students; ICA Rock Weeks crammed all the hottest acts into a handful of shows for less than a tenner a night; and you could buy tickets for their face value rather than pay an extortionate booking fee.

Indeed, your ticket money often went a long way. If a band was playing the Lyceum on more than one night, you'd always pick the Sunday gig, because on Sundays you got four bands no matter what, so alongside the main and support acts would be some marvellous European curiosity.

After a major indie event like one of the Norwich nights (the Higsons, the Farmer's Boys, Popular Voice and Serious Drinking), sweating right through to our coats because we hadn't checked them in, we'd spill on to the Northern Line and make the late night trek back to Morden, where a parent in pyjamas would pick us up.

My girls' school wasn't ideal for making male friends, but I got together with one of my mate's boyfriends over almost anything available on vinyl. Having crossed over to the boys' music club, I didn't look back. For three or four years, Patrick and I went to countless gigs. He was already at poly, so my parents approved of his older presence – especially one that was romantically attached elsewhere.

Those crazy Madness boys strut their stuff in 1980.

In fact, I probably spent more time with Paddy than any of his girlfriends did. Hours on Waterloo station waiting for the one late-night train home, midweek evenings working on our fanzine *This Year's Model* (he was a big Costello fan) or trekking to new corners of London to interview Prefab Sprout or Microdisney. We even helped organise gigs at the Loughborough Hotel in Brixton. For some reason, punk nights sold the best.

In September 1984, I went away to college, keen to see what Manchester and Liverpool had to offer. I'd like to think I'd left a space in the mosh pit for another 18-year-old in a thrift-shop dress and knitted tights travelling in the opposite direction down the M6.

Laura Lee Davies was Music Editor of *Time Out* from 1994 to 1998, and its Editor until 2004.

MUSIC

Bands on the run

The Clash at the Rainbow? Bob Marley at the Lyceum? Led Zeppelin at the Marquee? These are some of the performances over the past 40 years that have helped make London the greatest gig city in the world.

Her Madgeness points the way forward for pop at Wembley, 1990.

THE DOORS + THE GRATEFUL DEAD
ROUNDHOUSE, 8 SEPTEMBER 1968

The venue was actually half empty for the Doors' London debut – but those in-the-know punters who did turn up were treated to an astonishing performance, one that was filmed, fortunately, for BBC television.

LED ZEPPELIN
MARQUEE, 18 OCTOBER 1968

Billed here as 'the New Yardbirds' – the four-piece only acquired the Led Zep moniker a week later. But heavy metal was born at this London debut, as ex-Yardbird Jimmy Page applied a violin bow to his bass and Robert Plant wailed his mournful banshee wail. The song? 'Dazed and Confused'. Said one *Melody Maker* reviewer: 'Generally there appears to be a need for Led Zeppelin to cut down on volume a bit.'

SUN RA AND HIS ARKESTRA
QUEEN ELIZABETH HALL, 9 NOVEMBER 1970

His first UK show was far from anyone's notion of a 'jazz concert'. There were fire-eaters, a golden-robed dancer carrying a sun symbol, musicians wandering around the crowd, back projections of images from Africa and outer space, and ferocious electronic blasts from Sun on Moog synth and Farfisa organ. 'One of the most spectacular concerts ever held in this country,' said critic David Toop. 'It presented a complete world view, so occult, so "other".'

CURTIS MAYFIELD
RAINBOW, 23 JANUARY 1972

It's difficult to imagine now, but US funk hadn't crossed over to a wider – read 'white' – audience, so memories of this bill are of the ex-Impressions man purveying funk-soul stew to a black crowd. As Mayfield ripped through 'Move on Up', 'We Got to Have Peace', a few old Impressions favourites and some previews of his *Superfly* soundtrack, the crowd seemed to throb as one.

BOB MARLEY
LYCEUM BALLROOM, 17 JULY 1975
The London leg of Marley's Natty Dread tour was immortalised on a best-selling album. It was described by Marley's biographer Timothy White as 'combining the ritualistic fervour of a Jamaican Grounation meeting with the abandon of a rock concert.' After a high incidence of theft and intimidation (from what the tabloids referred to as 'Rastafarian youths'), Marley returned only to play much larger venues. But, as he admitted himself, none of them ever matched this gig's hypnotic steamy appeal.

BRUCE SPRINGSTEEN
HAMMERSMITH ODEON, 18 NOVEMBER 1975
Even Springsteen was outraged by the pre-gig hyperbole for his European debut (he ripped down a flyposter that read 'At Last London is Ready for Bruce Springsteen'). So when *Born to Run* stiffed at number 36 in the UK album chart, the backlash kicked in just as the hype went into overdrive. Still, it didn't stop this show – all guts and glory – from being one of London's best.

SEX PISTOLS + THE CLASH + BUZZCOCKS
SCREEN ON THE GREEN, 29 AUGUST 1976
These days, the Screen on the Green is a rather dainty arthouse cinema in the middle of gentrified Islington. In 1976, it was a rundown fleapit that showed cowboy films. In Greek. Which, curiously, made it the ideal venue for this era-defining punk rave that started at midnight and ended at dawn. Pistols aide Nils Stevenson admits that 'it was very hippy in a way… a very 1967 type of event.' There were a few freakshow Vivienne Westwood punks fresh from the King's Road – notably a swastika-clad Suzi Dallion, later to rechristen herself Siouxsie Sioux – but most of the crowd were a hybrid of skinhead, glam rocker and lapsed hippy.

Many thought Buzzcocks stole the show. The Pistols played a 30-minute set, in which Johnny Rotten knocked out one of his teeth on the microphone and had the front two rows on their hands and knees looking for it.

THE CLASH + THE JAM + BUZZCOCKS + SUBWAY SECT + THE PREFECTS
RAINBOW, 9 MAY 1977
This gig was a shift in gear for the Clash, as the Rainbow was twice as large as many of the venues they'd played before. But, as Jon Savage reported in *Sounds*, it proved that they could 'communicate just as directly and devastatingly with 3,000 people as… 300.' The Clash also proved they could put on a show, something often thought to be anathema to the punk ethic. Picture it: a huge picture of the Notting Hill riots as a backdrop. Paul Simonon's father, curious to see what his son had been doing since quitting art college, stood at the back as the audience proceeded to rip up the seats around him.

A huge picture of the Notting Hill riots was the backdrop for the Clash's gig at the Rainbow in 1977.

BLACK SABBATH
ROYAL ALBERT HALL, 17 FEBRUARY 1972
A hilariously inappropriate venue for the kings of sludge rock. Prince Albert's gaff had not yet witnessed music at this volume as the definitive Sabs line-up – Osbourne, Iommi, Butler, Ward – continued their Masters of Reality tour. The bass and drums were not so much heard as felt, hard, in the stomach.

KILBURN AND THE HIGH ROADS
TALLY HO, KENTISH TOWN, 24 JANUARY 1973
Around this time, venues like the Tally Ho, Greyhound, Hope & Anchor, Kensington, Red Cow and Nashville all specialised in pub rock – a back-to-basics R&B that paved the way for punk. Ian Dury's seminal outfit (the Blockheads arrived a few years later) were the most bizarre and interesting of the lot.

STEVIE WONDER
RAINBOW, 24 FEBRUARY 1974
Eight months earlier, Stevie had spent four days in a coma after a near-fatal car accident in North Carolina, but this UK return was more than just a piece of rubbernecking – it was a chance to see the narrative funk of *Innervisions* and his backing band Wonderlove. This crack jazz-funk collective succeeded in translating the studio-bound creations that Stevie had forged with Malcolm Cecil and Bob Margouleff, turning each song into an extended, loose-limbed jam. The gig was recorded by Motown but never released; sections of it have since emerged on bootleg.

Above, good times all round for Chic's appearance at Hammersmith Odeon, 1979. Right, Wham!'s Andrew Ridgeley (on the left) and George Michael in all their sweaty glory at Wembley, 1986.

TELEVISION + BLONDIE
HAMMERSMITH ODEON, 26 MAY 1977

Is this the hippest double bill in history? New York's godfathers of prog-punk visited London in the wake of their lauded debut album, *Marquee Moon*, with a fresh-faced Debbie Harry as support. Stick-thin Tom Verlaine stole the show with his transparent plexiglass guitar, which reflected spotlights back at the audience like laser beams.

CHIC
HAMMERSMITH ODEON, 20 JANUARY 1979

'Le Freak' had just gone into the Top Ten, and Nile Rodgers and Bernard Edwards issued a triumphant 'up yours' to the homophobic and racist 'Disco Sucks' purists.

GANG OF FOUR + STIFF LITTLE FINGERS + THE FALL + HUMAN LEAGUE + THE MEKONS
LYCEUM, 25 MARCH 1979

The ultimate post-punk bill – most of the audience were there to see the sub-Clash posturing of Stiff Little Fingers. The Fall were bottled mercilessly throughout their set: Mark E Smith was met onstage by a skinhead who poured a pint of lager over his head and landed two punches on his jaw. Smith continued to perform. The bottling resumed when Human League launched their synths-and-slideshow shtick with 'Blind Youth', although they won the crowd over with 'You've Lost That Loving Feeling', Gary Glitter's 'Rock and Roll' and Iggy Pop's 'Nightclubbing'. Gang of Four were – then, at least – punky enough to keep the bottles at bay.

YOUSSOU N'DOUR
VENUE, 10 MAY 1984

Worldbeat guru Charlie Gillett admits that he found Youssou a little baffling on record, but it all made sense when he saw him live, accompanied by swirling backing band Super Etoile de Dakar. Youssou's voice soared through the intense percussion, the stuttering guitars, the wailing horn section and the wild dancers. 'It literally changed my life,' says Gillett.

THE SMITHS
JUBILEE GARDENS, 10 JUNE 1984

Hippies will gleefully wax lyrical about the fabled free gig in Hyde Park in the late '60s, but the truth is that the mid '80s were *the* high point of the free festival in London – courtesy of Red Ken's doomed Greater London Council. The Smiths were in their prime on this unforgettably sunny, flower-festooned, GLC-sponsored session, as gladioli flew and Moz writhed around in a big girl's blouse. The festival was marred earlier in the day by a feeble riot by some right-wing skinhead groups. And, during the Smiths' one-hour set, two events distracted the attention of the crowd: one was an idiot dangling from the gargoyles of County Hall, 100 feet in the air, before alighting on a window ledge (he got a round of applause); another was a gentleman on a balcony, who sported only a large beard to cover his modesty.

WHAM!
WEMBLEY STADIUM, 28 JUNE 1986

At a sweltering Wembley, 72,000 Wham! fans sat through sets from Gary Glitter and Nick Heyward while being squirted with water by security – patiently waiting for their pop heroes to play their last gig. They finally appeared and delivered over an hour of hits that had even the police officers dancing. Guests on stage included Elton John dressed as Ronald McDonald and jet set chum Simon Le Bon.

THE STONE ROSES
ALEXANDRA PALACE, 18 NOVEMBER 1989
'I'm hopeful there'll be a big police presence at Ally Pally,' said Ian Brown in *Time Out* before this gig. 'That'll make it more of an event.' This was a coming together for the acid house generation, in their flares, Reni hats and Kickers. All 7,000 tickets sold out in days. Those who went can't talk about it without getting decidedly misty-eyed.

MADONNA
WEMBLEY STADIUM, 20 JULY 1990
She'd played in London before, but the Blonde Ambition tour was Madonna at the height of her powers: a mix of McLarenesque hyperbole, hubristic flights of fancy and unalloyed pop genius.

NIRVANA
ASTORIA, 5 NOVEMBER 1991
This wasn't the first time Nirvana played the Astoria (that was in 1989, with Tad and Mudhoney), but it was their biggest headlining UK show. Cobain chose Captain America to open (frontman Eugene Kelly was in Cobain's beloved Vaselines), but heaven only knows what the twee Television Personalities were doing on the same bill. Outside it was Bonfire Night, but Nirvana set off sonic fireworks inside; by the third song, 'Drain You', the first 50 rows were a seething pit of mosh, eventually joined by Cobain, who wriggled over ecstatic heads like a buttered eel.

PRINCE
EARL'S COURT, 15 JUNE 1992
Eleven years earlier he'd made his UK debut at a near-empty Lyceum and the tour was cancelled. Poor Prince. By 1992, though, His Purpleness was able to bring all his pomp and majesty to town for this mammoth Earl's Court residency. To accompany the release of *Diamonds and Pearls* – his last great album – he entered the stage in a gangsta car, moaned and gyrated, removed his top, and played guitar pyrotechnics and a Duke Ellington pastiche from the piano. Oh, and his New Power Generation were his tightest, funkiest outfit yet.

JEFF BUCKLEY
GARAGE, 1 SEPTEMBER 1994
Grace had just been released to ecstatic reviews, and Buckley had played the Reading Festival a few days earlier, so the Garage seemed a cautious choice of venue. It was hot and crowded (tickets were changing hands outside for upwards of £200), but the audience was held spellbound by the soaring voice of this beautiful young man. Assorted women (and a few men) were reduced to blubbering wrecks when Buckley whipped off his shirt. A rapt crowd of indie kids and older folk-jazzers wept, moshed, held hands and howled in delight.

RADIOHEAD
ROYAL FESTIVAL HALL, 1 JULY 2000
There were plenty of great Radiohead gigs before and after this – the fractious *OK Computer* performance at the Brixton Academy in 1997, the enormo-dome Earl's Court dates in 2003 – but this date became something of a divisive issue in rock history. Headlining Scott Walker's Meltdown festival, they played a few oldies but previewed ten new songs (later to materialise on *Kid A* and *Amnesiac*) that transformed them from airbrushed arena rockers into lo-fi experimentalists. After the gig fans talked long into the night, furiously debating what they'd heard.

MUSIC

Ronnie Scott

'Who's that bloke by the tree?' asked a veteran jazz writer at the first Capital Jazz Festival. Everybody squinted against the afternoon sun; nobody knew. The bloke was Ronnie Scott, but nobody had ever seen him by daylight before. Similarly, John Fordham's fine study of the life of the famous saxophone-playing club-owner, *Let's Join Hands and Contact the Living*, is liable to disorientate all who know Ronnie as a tower of reticence defended against personal intrusion and high seriousness by a moat of old jokes. Fordham's Ronnie comes disguised in candour.

Behind the familiar public image is a complicated, emotional and sensitive man, preyed upon by restlessness, lassitude, dissatisfaction and depression. Most comics give themselves introspective hell, most jazz musicians are harassed by the unattainable sound and solo, and Ronnie Scott combines both afflictions with the additional burden of the Diaspora, which comes in the Family Size. The women in his life who have put up with the unsocial hours and the unpredictability have all been unsaddled at the water-jump of domesticity. Ronnie behind a lawn mower was never a shot on the board. His dance band saxophonist father, Jock, who divorced Ronnie's mother when Ronnie was four, was much the same.

The East End Jewish background explains a lot. Ronnie's autobiography with Mike Hennessey, *Some of My Best Friends are Blues*, is positively jocund – 'I was born in a room over a Jewish pub in the East End called the Kosher Horses' – in comparison with Fordham's anatomy of family and kinship. There was no shortage of dreaming uncles who gambled on the horses, or played violin for bar mitzvahs and weddings. The fierce sense of loyalty, instinctive generosity and – unusually in a creative artist – conviction that the world does not owe anybody a living, date back to this period.

Ronnie came by jazz the hard way. The first British modernists started out with an enormous inferiority complex in the face of American supremacy. They couldn't have chosen a more exacting style than bebop, which remains the three-dimensional chess of improvised music. Ronnie's lot pored endlessly over the handful of 78s and acetates that crossed the Atlantic, reliant upon trumpeter-pianist Denis Rose's laborious transcriptions, hanging out with jazz GIs like

Art Pepper, who was an improbable MP at Marlborough Street Jail, and finally signing on with Geraldo's Navy to play on the liners and cop the bop for themselves on 52nd Street. That first impression of New York's clubs in their late '40s bebop heyday planted the dream in Ronnie's head that one day he would have his own joint where Londoners could hear this astonishing music live.

In its short life, Club Eleven, a tatty basement in Windmill Street, became the crucible for our native beboppers, transferring to Carnaby Street and thence to the magistrates' court on a team-handed marijuana rap. 'What is bebop?' asked the magistrate. 'It's a queer form of modern dancing. A negro jive,' replied the Chief Inspector. Nor did the

action, they were really something to see, cigarettes parked under the rods of the Mark VIs, tearing through the changes, drenching each other with fast artistry and adrenalin. Modern jazz audiences modelled themselves on the coolly elegant Ronnie, sporting bumfreezer Italian suits, tab collars and flat barnets from Maison Albert – 'The College Boy and a packet of three, please, Tosca' – in Old Compton Street. Regent Shoes, next to the club, sold nib-like winkle-pickers. In his time, Ronnie has pioneered both the Harvard jumper with white piping and the lighter on a neck cord.

'Bebop remains the three-dimensional chess of improvised music.'

When the Jazz Couriers broke up in 1959, Ronnie went into partnership with Pete King – 'a laconic, squat, deceptively ponderous man with the demeanour of a fight referee' – and took the big gamble. Ronnie Scott's Club in Gerrard Street charged one-and-sixpence to members, half a crown to non-members, and presented the best of British bebop. You could slip your moorings listening to Ronnie, Tubby, Peter King, Joe Harriott, Dizzy Reece, Jimmy Deuchar, Don Rendell, Phil Seaman and the house pianist, Stan Tracey. It wasn't until two years in that the club succeeded in negotiating Musicians' Union strictures to bring over the first American guest, tenorman Zoot Sims.

The stream of American legends that followed Zoot into Ronnie Scott's supply the biographer with a wealth of anecdotes. Rahsaan Roland Kirk blowing on, impervious to a police raid; Sonny Rollins gesticulating at his dressing room mirror and repeating, 'I am Pierre the Frenchman'. Dizzy Gillespie, Getz, Dexter Gordon, Art Blakey, Ornette Coleman, Cecil Taylor – all in their different ways have shown how they embody their music, besides bursting the spirit's slumber six nights a week.

And Ronnie's reaction to John Fordham's biographical psychoanalysis? Was he happy with this portrait of a impulsively romantic malcontent? 'That's how it is,' he says heavily, like someone with a sitting tenant. 'It's strange to read your life story and see that's how you appear to others. He's captured the atmosphere pretty well, but you can't get the motivation. It crystallises things that seemed all messy edges at the time. Anyway – are you coming down to the club to hear Phil Woods?'

MUSIC

general public seem much better informed. Chris Barber may have had a point when he wondered whether the average British punter wasn't really a Max Bygraves fan at heart. Dance band leaders took a dim view of the young insurrectionaries seething behind their bow ties in the sections, and sackings were frequent. *Melody Maker* bemoaned the takeover of the music business by 'rainbow-tied, overdressed, super-padded, loud-talking and queerly tonsured youths'. Denominationalism, that typically British disease, divided the tiny jazz scene into Modernists and Traddies.

In 1957, Ronnie – a rallying point for disaffected disciples of Bird – teamed up with fellow tenorman Tubby Hayes for the legendary Jazz Couriers. In

Ronnie Scott outside his Frith Street club, in 1979.

Original review by Brian Case. Ronnie Scott died on 23 December 1996, but the club he founded still hosts major jazz acts at 47 Frith Street, W1.

MUSIC

Lemmy

Lemmy performing in Hackney, 1982.

The gnarled, ravaged figure of Ian 'Lemmy' Kilminster is a familiar sight on the streets of West London. Resembling the archetypal villainous Portobello Road dealer in his grime-encrusted jeans, battered black leather jacket, cowboy boots and matted shoulder-length hair, he looks the kind of person who'd sell you a lump of black rubber shoe heel as hash. At 36, this bedraggled figure is an unlikely rock star. He is as old as, if not older than the fathers of many of his fans – he even has a 15-year-old son – but he is also the singer and bassist of Motörhead, the power trio whose last LP, *No Sleep 'til Hammersmith*, went straight into the charts at number one last summer.

On Saturday evening I spend with him roaming West London pubs, a good portion of my time is spent propping up one-armed bandits as Lemmy rapidly loses all the money he has on him. Lemmy is a Space Invaders addict too, the machines in his favourite haunts inevitably displaying his initials as top scorer. His love of such machines is entirely logical: speed freaks often need something to do with their hands to keep them occupied. The other two group members groan as they talk about Lemmy at the end of week-long speed binges coming home and taking apart household appliances in order to 'mend' them.

The current Motörhead line-up was finalised in March 1976: Lemmy, guitarist Fast Eddie Clarke and drummer Phil(thy Animal) Taylor. Notwithstanding Lemmy's astutely self-publicising claims that the group would be so horrible 'that when we move in next door the grass on your lawn will die', it was initially near-impossible for Motörhead to secure live work. United Artists refused to release the LP they had paid for the band to record – until the group had moved on and were enjoying the first fruits of their success on the Bronze label. Ultimately, it was *because* of this rejection by the rock establishment that they rose to their current status on a groundswell of grassroots support.

Sitting on the sofa of the group's rented Battersea house, Philthy Animal wriggles uncomfortably as a result of a recent operation for the removal of anal warts. 'You hear a lot of good things and a lot of bad things about Lemmy,' he says, 'and most of them are true. He is a cunt, he is a bastard, he does knock other people's chicks off. But he's also incredibly funny: every time you go out with him, it's a memorable experience.'

'Yet he does borrow money off people and rip them off,' he continues, reminding me that the origin of Lemmy's name lay in his incessant requests to 'Lemme a fiver'. 'In the days when he used to sell speed, you could guarantee if he sold you a gram it was probably half a gram. He's very good at making you feel guilty. He's definitely got the gift of the gab.' Despite a reputation for being financially tight, however, he insists that the group's money be ploughed back into lavish stage-shows and financially disastrous touring. 'All the money goes back into the pockets of the people from whom it was stolen originally,' he says, giving a dry chuckle as he loses another fiver's worth of change in a Nudge machine.

'The biggest buzz I've ever got,' he adds, 'is not with a roll of banknotes or a pocket calculator. The biggest buzz I've ever got is screwing and going on stage, in varying orders, depending on what I'm going to do next.

'I don't see how you can get sick of enjoying yourself – I haven't so far, and I'm damn sure I resent anyone who tells me I should. Just have a good time and don't hurt anyone else doing it.'

Original interview by Chris Salewicz. Lemmy continues to tour and release albums with a new Motörhead line-up.

Pirate radio By Nick Coleman

It sounds like a dangerously Elmsian thing to say, but I sometimes feel that the only *serious* fun I've ever had was being involved in pirate radio: DBC, the great and glorious Dread Broadcasting Corporation. It wasn't the first pirate ever to needle the airwaves with worthwhile noise, but it was certainly, in its time, the most original: it was the bass-heavy home of the 'dread outta control'.

I didn't join until 1984, when DBC reopened on a daily basis after three years of regular harassment at the hands of the Grey Men with Halitosis; but even then it still had the feeling of being wicked and wild. The reason was that DBC was not about making money, careers or bringing about the fall of Babylon, but about being *heard*. I am white with a middle-class accent, so I would have sounded absurd on a black-controlled radio station dubbing up a house-style heavy roots session in the wee small hours, but I did a fairly acceptable two-hour jazz programme, which suited my pretensions at the time.

What I never worked out, however, was why it was always *my* programme that got shafted whenever the Grey Men and their devilish transmitter-melting breath slithered across the rooftops of Notting Hill. Could it really have been my back-to-back Jackie McLean Blue Notes squealing like a stuck pig rather too close to Radio Two? Or was my plummy diction the easiest to track with their little antennae, or whatever those unspeakable gantries were beneath their soiled anoraks? Maybe I was just a crap DJ and deserved it.

Whatever, I have never felt such animate ease as when I used to come off my trolley with Dr Jackle and the posse in Kilburn High Road. And what has DBC done for the rest of the world? Well, there's the Ranking Miss P, for starters, some rather good T-shirts and a whole nation of pirate radio stations needling up the airwaves with worthwhile noise.

Nick Coleman is a writer and broadcaster.

THE (ILLEGIT) SOUNDS OF THE '70S

A selection from *Time Out*'s pirate radio special, 23.3.1979.

AW/MW

AMY
Inventive community-access station for six north London boroughs.
Celebration
Album/rock format based on American FM style. West/north-west London.
Edge City
1960s music plus New Wave.
Floss
Soft and heavy rock and news. North London.
Jackie
The Radio One of pirates, based in Kingston/south London.
North London Radio
Popular top 40-type shows.
Radio City
Pure, classic rock 'n' roll.

Telstar One
London's only semi-permanent pirate, with ultra-informal presentation. Note that it may move frequency.
Weekend Music Radio
South London, pop.

VHF/FM

Invicta
Soul over London. Very professional.

Radio Free London
Rock/album-oriented. Claims link with original land-based pirate; after several raids, back since February 1978.
Telstar South
1960-74 golden oldies – all requests. Signal sometimes Dolby mono.
Thameside
Very slick pop/rock with competitions. Highly regarded, consistent;

the nearest we have to US-FM presentation.
Uptown
Intelligent rock station based in west London.
West London
Pop/album station.

Shortwave

Corsair
South-west London. Noisy programmes with lots of Free Radio propaganda. Leftish.

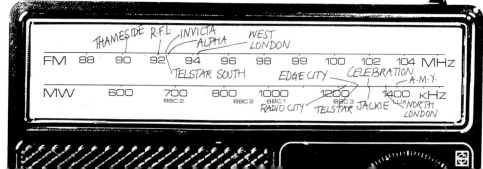

MUSIC

Capital tunes

London has inspired some of pop's most enduring masterpieces: songs that have reflected and affected our cultural landscape over the past 40 years.

1

Albion
Babyshambles
Pete Doherty dreams of grabbing his gal and escaping to places like Deptford and Catford.

2

A13, Trunk Road to the Sea
Billy Bragg
Bobby Troupe's iconic song '(Get Your Kicks On) Route 66' is transplanted to Essex.

3

Born Slippy
Underworld
A cry for help from the bottom of a glass for the Stella generation.

4

Cockney Translation
Smiley Culture
David 'Smiley Culture' Emmanuel's satirical Jamaican-English-London-English dictionary, set to a dancehall rhythm.

5

Down in the Tube Station at Midnight
The Jam
According to the Jam's Bruce Foxton: 'Paul Weller described it as a short television play transposed into a three-minute pop song.'

6

For Tomorrow
Blur
'It's about being lost on the Westway… it's a romantic thing, it's hopeful,' explained Damon Albarn.

7

Gertcha!
Chas & Dave
'It was a phrase we remembered from childhood, something yer dad would say before he slapped you one. It was part of what we called "rockney".' Chas Hodges

8

God Save the Queen
Sex Pistols
One of the most lucid, perfectly pitched and downright savage pop singles ever recorded.

9

Has It Come to This?
The Streets
Hanging around McDonald's never sounded so good.

10

Herculean
The Good, the Bad and the Queen
Damon Albarn and Paul Simonon's slow-burning hymn to London's endless variety.

11

I Luv U
Dizzee Rascal
A grim tale of teenage pregnancy set to a barrage of bleeps, ringtones and a monstrous, grinding bassline.

12

K Hole
Ali Love
'It's a song about London wrongness. You go out on one side on Friday and end up on the other side by Sunday night and don't know where you are.' Ali Love

13

Kidz
Plan B
'I know violence is exciting and all that shit, but at the end of the day, it's not right. There is no excuse for being a cunt.' Plan B

14

LDN
Lily Allen
Exploiting the arrhythmic cadences of London speech, Allen comes off like a post-punk Marie Lloyd.

15

London
The Smiths
A *Billy Liar*-esque relocation melodrama.

16

London Belongs to Me
Saint Etienne
'What really inspired the song was just the rush of excitement when you first move to London and get a flat of your own.' Bob Stanley.

17

London Town
Light of the World
Summery Brit-funk anthem from 1980, popularised by Tony Blackburn on his seminal Radio London soul show.

18

London's Burning
The Clash
'I was walking around a lot in west London, and "London's Burning" came to me all at once.' Joe Strummer

19

Mile End
Pulp
Documenting a traumatic stay in a piss-sodden towerblock in the East End, this is one of Jarvis Cocker's funniest and best-observed songs.

20

Oh Happy Day
Spiritualized
'London's just got it. It's the only city where the good, the bad and the ugly hit up against each other.' Jason Pierce, Spiritualized

21

Peter the Painter
Ian Dury
'I had a show at the Tate in 1983 and I asked Ian to write the theme music for it.' Peter Blake

22

Primrose Hill
John & Beverly Martyn
Captures the joy of a summer's evening spent lolling around on the hill.

23

Punky Reggae Party
Bob Marley
The song that cemented the kinship between punk and reggae.

24

A Rainy Night in Soho
The Pogues
If you ever want to wallow in boozy heartbreak, Soho's the place – which is why this waltzing lament makes so muchsense.

25

Sheila
Jamie T
'There's something kind of sad about the way John Betjeman talks about London in the verse that I sample on "Sheila".' Jamie T

The London Sinfonietta

The London Sinfonietta was set up in 1968 by a group of former music students, including Nicholas Snowman, who became the manager, and David Atherton, who was the conductor. They decided to bring together the best London musicians to play new music, as well as music of the 20th century more broadly, which at that time was played rather badly.

Its first concert, in 1968, took place at the Queen Elizabeth Hall, which had only just opened and was regarded as the venue for new and exciting work. The programme included *The Whale*, a newly commissioned cantata by John Taverner. This piece was subsequently recorded for the Apple record label, and featured Ringo Starr, who was roped in to bellow into a loud hailer.

Commissioning new work has always been the lifeblood of the Sinfonietta. It has commissioned many pieces now regarded as canonical, from Stockhausen to Birtwistle – giants of 20th-century music with whom the ensemble maintained close links. Stockhausen, for example, toured with the Sinfonietta, and collaborated on a piece called *Ylem* in the early 1970s. And Luciano Berio was also very closely associated with the company. Together with the Sinfonietta, these avant-garde giants helped put contemporary music on the map in this country.

The Sinfonietta has always gone in for big ideas: in 1973, it mounted a Schoenberg festival, followed by festivals devoted to Webern and Stravinsky. This was part of an attempt to reclaim the musical repertoire of the 20th century.

Until the founding of the Sinfonietta, it was very difficult to hear that music in London. And even today, although there are a number of groups playing contemporary music, people still rely on the Sinfonietta to hear large-scale works from the recent past, such as Berio's *Labyrinthus 2* or Ligeti's *Chamber Concerto*.

The London Sinfonietta has provided a model that has since been adopted by groups elsewhere in the country, as well as abroad; Pierre Boulez followed the blueprint laid down by the Sinfonietta when he founded the Ensemble InterContemporain in France.

Central to the Sinfonietta's mission has been the attempt to place modern music in a broad cultural context. The ensemble has worked with visual artists and film makers, and has also collaborated with Warp Records, putting music by Aphex Twin and Squarepusher alongside Ligeti. This was not about cross-over, or mixing genres, but about making connections. The Sinfonietta may have left the classical music ghetto behind in order to reach much larger audiences, but it has never compromised.

Gillian Moore was Artistic Director of the London Sinfonietta between 1998 and 2006.

MUSIC

Elvis Costello

'Because I don't like giving interviews, and I don't give many, people think that I'm a reticent bastard.'

If there is a key to Elvis Costello's public character, it lies in a tangle of contradictions. He is a rock star yet to achieve stardom. He rode to fame on the back of the punk movement, but was never punk. He is the most original and astringent songwriter Britain has produced in a decade, yet his biggest hit to date, 'Oliver's Army', is a blatant steal from ABBA's 'Dancing Queen', a soft-centred pop tune into which, typically, he injected a grim lyric about 'white nigger' army recruits. He is a public figure about whom little is known, and although not exactly a prima donna, he treats the rock press with contempt. It repays him by reviewing his records with tireless enthusiasm. 'I never think about rock,' this stunning rock performer announces with asperity, 'I never think about it at all.'

Once we're settled in a dimly lit café, Costello is relaxed but serious, anxious that he should do himself justice. 'Because I don't like giving interviews and I don't give many, people think that I'm a reticent bastard. On the contrary, nothing could be further from the truth,' he says. Meeting Costello, you're immediately struck by just how much he lacks the cosmetic sheen of the pop star. He is chatty and friendly, unassuming and, surprisingly, totally devoid of charisma.

Costello discovered his musical style with the arrival of punk, writing the classic 'Watching the Detectives' after listening to the first Clash album for 36 hours straight in the summer of 1977. 'Punk was a one-off. It's never going to happen like that again. You can't jump out on people like that twice, they'll always be ready for it the next time. It was inevitable that the business was going to sit back, let punk burn itself out, and then absorb it and repackage it. It doesn't mean it wasn't great while it happened.'

With the 1978 release of *This Year's Model*, one of the most savage rock records ever cut, Costello was set to become a surprise rock superstar. His LP sold over a million copies and began to evoke a fiercely enthusiastic response in America. But then – early in 1979, after a performance in Columbus, Ohio – he became involved in a bar-room brawl with members of the Stephen Stills Band. Drunk and peevish, he launched an attack on America in general and, in particular, on the tendency for black music to ghettoise itself. This vigorous anti-NF campaigner and supporter of Rock Against Racism suddenly found it within himself to call Ray Charles 'a blind, ignorant nigger'.

The story leaked to a gleeful press at a time when Costello's anti-journalist campaign was reaching its peak (Jake Riviera – Costello's manager – and his camp-following goons were stomping on journalists backstage and ripping film from cameras). The irony was irresistible: this radical had revealed himself as nothing more than a poseur, a good old-fashioned racist, right? Costello, hitherto regarded as tame, had committed an act of genuine outrage. There was a torrent of

It's *my* guitar, OK?
Left, Costello in 1990.

publicity – all of it bad. His records were pulled off playlists and he received scores of death threats. The tour ended with a beleaguered and defensive Costello surrounded by armed bodyguards.

It wasn't until last summer, when *Imperial Bedroom* was released and Greil Marcus wrote an interview for *Rolling Stone* with the cover-line 'Elvis Costello Repents', that he regained the commercial ground he had lost. He told Greil Marcus: 'What it was about was that I said the most outrageous thing I could possibly say to them – that I *knew*, in my drunken logic, would anger them the most.' A somewhat lame try at excusing himself, you may think. He didn't *mean* it; after all, Costello loves black music and his knowledge of it is all but encyclopaedic. Yet it was perhaps the inevitable result of a pose that was venomous, angry and always so self-righteous.

He still tiptoes around the subject. 'I've explained it as best I could, and I don't choose to discuss it any further… It can outweigh everything I do and that makes my whole career seem pointless.'

Costello's career lost momentum. He recorded *Get Happy!!* (title ironic, of course), a version of a Motown album which, he admits, was no sort of record at all, and then *Trust*, a singer's showcase album that seemed merely to be going through the motions. Having boxed himself in, his solution was perhaps inevitable: a quantum leap in image. He donned a pair of pointed boots, wrapped a string tie around his neck, acquired a guitar with 'ELVIS COSTELLO' inlaid in mother of pearl on the fretboard and departed for Nashville, Tennessee, where he made a record in the unfashionable country and western genre. 'I really meant *Almost Blue*. A very sad and depressed record. It's all in the sound of the voice. That's what a lot of people missed – they just saw the boots and tie.'

The record flopped in the US, but did well over here. More important, Costello revealed the quality that he considers most important in pop music: emotion. 'A good song must hit a strong vein of feeling. I think that's all it is, it's just whether it strikes some emotional thing that resonates on, that you can always pick up on.'

Changing styles, Costello has managed to keep himself, and his public, interested. Sometimes you can't help feeling that his compendious knowledge of musical style, allied to a cunning tendency to lift whatever he fancies from the current trend, gets in the way of what he might achieve. Perhaps it's an enigma he doesn't wish to solve. After all, his achievement is already considerable.

So, one last question: what is it to be famous? He smiles. 'There's such a lot of fuss being made about nothing, you know. Somebody who can rhyme a few words and come up with the odd pun. It doesn't seem like such a big deal to me. But it's my life.'

Original interview by Richard Rayner. Elvis Costello continues to write and record music in many genres.

MUSIC

Hunger artists

Rock has given up innovation, but London's indigenous dance music continues to look to the future.

By Mark Fisher

There is a moment in Alfonso Cuarón's 2006 film *Children of Men* when Kode9 and the Spaceape's 'Backward' can be heard playing. The conjunction is eerily apt: *Children of Men* was a film about a London that has lost any sense of the future. 'Backward', too, is about the inability to move forward. With its echoes of jungle, dub and spaghetti western soundtracks, Kode9's sound recognisably belongs to what music writer Simon Reynolds has called 'the hardcore continuum': the matrix of musics that came out of rave, jungle and garage. London – or, more specifically, the working-class and black cultures of London – has always been central to this continuum, which in the '90s was in a state of perpetual renewal. It seemed to display a self-correcting collective intelligence: jungle's darkness arose as a reaction to the fluorescent euphoria of rave; and when the psychedelic ballistics of early jungle subsided into the moodiness and calcified beats of techstep, R&B-flavoured speed garage arrived to lift the mood. But, in the past decade, this process has slowed down, and the best music has been preoccupied by the problem of inertia.

In the late '90s and early noughties, it was garage that was dominant. It was a broad church: at one pole were duelling MCs, at the other, a diffuse, slinky eroticism. Both modes of garage yielded chart success – Shanks and Bigfoot's 'Sweet Like Chocolate' and So Solid Crew's '21 Seconds' reached number one at the turn of the millennium. But, instead of being the UK answer to hip hop that had long been anticipated, the success of So Solid Crew and their compatriots Oxide and Neutrino proved to be short-lived. With its samples from BBC1's *Casualty* and Guy Ritchie's *Lock, Stock and Two Smoking Barrels*, Oxide and Neutrino's

'Bound 4 da Reload' in 2000 was another number one, but it served as a recapitulation of the '90s, rather than offering any clues as to what would happen in the coming decade. In fact, the fetishisation of violence that emerged in tracks like 'Bound 4 da Reload' would contribute to the eventual decline of garage, as club after club went under due to increased police regulation. The hardcore continuum was forced to retreat back into the underground.

As the decade developed, garage effectively split into two distinct currents: grime was severed from the flow of the dancefloor and dominated by the MC, while dubstep was centred on 'bass science'. Both scenes were concentrated in particular areas of London. Grime was rooted in the East End. Often crudely produced on games consoles, grime tracks were marked by angularity and a machine-like coldness. Dubstep, associated with south London, was defined by a kind of coagulated bass flow and a return to the heavily treated synthetic bass that had been one of the most distinctive features of jungle.

One voice stood out from the grime scene's feral war of all against all: the cockney twang of Dizzee Rascal, the most accomplished MC in the Roll Deep crew. Dizzee's East End vocals broadened out from the MC staples of braggadocio and hype to express a whole range of affective states: vulnerability, ennui, depression, a touch of petulance. His debut album, *Boy in da Corner* (2003), bears comparison with Joy Division's *Unknown Pleasures* or Nirvana's *Nevermind* in the way that it focuses the dejection of an era through a very particular geographical space. Dizzee's equivalent of Joy Division's Manchester or Nirvana's Seattle was the Bow estate in which

Applying the bass pressure: leading dubstep producer Oliver Jones, aka Skream.

he was born and raised. *Boy in da Corner* takes us on a tour of estates where practically every home is broken, where teenage pregnancy spoils lives before they have started, where betrayal, disappointment, casual violence and police harassment are treated as background noise, blankly reported rather than railed against.

The quasi-industrial intensity of his breakthrough single, 'I Luv U', which recalled the pulverising kick drum-driven sound of Dutch gabba rather than any garage precedents, was a misleading introduction to Dizzee Rascal's music, which was otherwise subdued, mechanical and melancholic. *Boy in da Corner*'s closing track, 'Sittin' Here', was more typical of the album's mood: at only 18, Dizzee already feels that his best years are behind him; paralysed and lethargic, he is incapable of action or movement, and craves only sedation. To date, grime has not turned out anything else that can match power of *Boy in da Corner* – even Dizzee could not follow it up himself, as if the potency of his rhymes and rhythms depended on the very sense of impotence that success has blunted.

'One voice stood out from the grime scene's feral war of all against all: the cockney twang of Dizzee Rascal.'

Although dubstep is focused on the dancefloor in a way that grime is not, it is scarcely any more effervescent. In fact, dubstep's sound could be characterised as a kind of seething inertia. Where original Jamaican dub was all about the art of disappearing the voice – you would hear the voice being etherealised into vapour trails before your very ears – in much dubstep, the vocal is removed altogether. This can lead to a certain flatness, a lack of depth of field, in the sound. But dubstep is alchemically transformed when heard in club spaces like Fwd in Shoreditch and DMZ in Brixton. Here, the waves of sub-bass constitute what Kode9 has called a compulsive 'bass magnet'. Bass becomes an environment that is not oppressive, but curiously lulling. The rise of skunk – a specially

> *'Boy in da Corner takes us on a tour of estates where practically every home is broken.'*

bred, intensely strong strain of catatonia-inducing cannabis – in certain areas of London's drug culture in the past few years has its own story to tell about the capital's musical developments this decade. The best dubstep, such as Skream's 'Request Line', mitigates the bass pressure with some high-end flitting sounds – the dregs of ecstasy, perhaps, in a scene otherwise given over to skunkanoid sluggishness.

Kode9 has been at the heart of the dubstep scene, but his collaboration with the MC Spaceape sets him at odds with the genre's taste for the instrumental. (Kode9's extensive use of Spaceape on his mix for *Dubstep Allstars: Volume 3* was a statement of intent that annoyed many so-called dubstep purists.) Kode9 and Spaceape's parched, beatless, versions of Prince's 'Sign 'O' the Times' and the Specials' 'Ghost Town' sounded like the hardcore continuum on a life-support system, its vital signs barely flickering. Their album *Memories of the Future* felt weighed down by an oppressive hydroponic humidity. JG Ballard's novel *Drowned World* has always been a touchstone for Kode9, and, as the evidence about global warming has become irrefutable, Ballard's vision of an inundated London has ceased to look like science fiction and become a plausible speculation about city's future.

Kode9's label Hyperdub released dubstep's answer to *Boy in da Corner*, the self-titled debut LP by Burial. *Burial* was another indication that the best London music in the first decade of the new millennium was haunted by the failure of the future to arrive. Burial's patch is the 'South London Boroughs' that provided the title of his first EP. It is populated by ravers who cannot adjust to the end of the dream they once lived, drawn back to the sites of collective bliss only

to find them abandoned or redeveloped. With its mottled bass and skittery, wind-blown beats and yearning vocal samples, Burial's music sounds like spectral jungle. The track title 'Gutted' epitomises the sense of desolation – as much architectural as emotional – that prevails in his tunes. Burial's London – sketched at least as vividly on his second LP, *Untrue*, as on his debut – is a city overcome by dereliction and dilapidation. Burial stalks the railway sidings and night buses that exist beyond the PR and CGI façade of London, city of international business. In an age of transnational capital, you might expect Burial's disconsolate meditations on very specific areas of London to have only local appeal; but the malaise to which Burial's tracks give voice is by no means limited to London, and his music has touched an international audience.

Planetary capital breeds its own psychopathologies as surely as it builds multinational brands. While rock has capitulated to retrospection, Burial shows that the hunger for the future in London's dance music scenes is still insatiable. In some ways, for the moment, it is only the hunger that remains.

Above, DMZ club night at Mass in Brixton. Left, Kode9 and Spaceape wait for the future to arrive.

Mark Fisher is Acting Deputy Editor of *The Wire* magazine and a visiting fellow at Goldsmiths, University of London.

HEDONISM INTRODUCTION
SEX CITYSCAPE FASHION
SOCIETY SHOPPING COMEDY
DRAMA PROTEST & POLITICS
VISUAL ARTS PERFORMANCE
LITERATURE GANGS OPINION
COCKNEYS BARS ON SCREEN
DANCE MUSIC TELEVISION
BUILDINGS CLUBS **NIGHTLIFE**
SPORT & FITNESS MEMORIES
STYLE FOOD & DRINK GIGS
CONSUME RIOTS REFERENCE

The boy from the

From the Blitz and Chaguaramas to the Wag and the Fridge: it's all in a night in the life of London.

By Robert Elms

The city was broken and the night was shut. London in the early '70s was shrouded in a clattering armour of corrugated iron, a rusting curtain thrown around years of neglect and decay, unloved and unlovely, vast swathes of the centre all but abandoned. Early closing, dimly lit, near silent, surreptitious, censorious and shabby. The inner city had been eviscerated by urban blight and flight, a place of nightlife where the night had no life. It was great.

The '60s may well have been swinging, although most of the fun was had by a small coterie of well-off, well-connected socialites with a pass to the Chelsea flower power show. There was also the Soho mod scene, based around legendary haunts like the Scene and Tiles, used by older brothers and uncles to taunt us young, would-be hipsters. But by the time I first emerged into the dark as a desirous teenager from a north London council estate, the party decade had succumbed to a severe hangover, and the night was hushed. Pubs closed in the middle of the day, and then again at 10.30pm, bars were only found in American movies, clubs were virtually non-existent, save a few sticky-carpet discos and Joan Collins jet-trash joints. Restaurants specialised in overpriced stodge for overweight businessmen. No late licences, no night buses, few cabs.

On the surface, London in 1973 was like Bulgaria on a particularly grim night. But this has always been a city where the best things lurk below the surface, hidden away, down the stairs, out the back, through the alley or up in the garret. Back then, if you knew where to look, there was a genuine underground, a thriving counterculture. Now it's an over-the-counter culture, as we've opened up and blossomed out into this slick, whatever-you-want, designer cool, 24/7 consumerist town. But back in the darkened distance of '70s London, you had to work hard to find things, and they were often in the most unlikely places.

Finchley, Fulham, Archway, West Ken, Kentish Town, Hammersmith; none of those are areas you would normally associate with revelry, but back in the day (or more pertinently the night), pub rock was the big gig in town, and the best

Visage strike a pose outside the Blitz club in Covent Garden in 1978.

rock 'n' roll pubs were often in residential areas outside the deserted centre. The Tally Ho, the Nashville, the Red Cow, the Greyhound… the list of musty old boozers enlivened by scruffy bands playing ragged R 'n' B and R 'n' R is long and memorable. Most nights out consisted of a tortuous cross-town tube ride to zone two, a pint or three in a back room, and a sweaty set from the Ducks Deluxe or Brinsley Schwarz. But if you think that, in one week back then, you could have seen Ian Dury, Nick Lowe and Joe Strummer for about 50p a time, it wasn't a bad time in which to be a music-mad kid first exploring his city. And come closing time, there may well have been afters, a lock-in with lights dimmed and a conspiratorial glow in the air.

Dancing, though, was a different matter. Discovering the considerable thrill of donning flat-soled shoes with peg trousers and a wedge haircut, the standard uniform for a mid '70s funkateer, meant I was forced to discover parts of the metropolis I never knew existed. A map of the nocturnal hotspots of greater London in the mid '70s would have been a blank until you got to the outer fringes of the city. A second-hand Cortina became the ultimate fashion accessory, because you needed a car to get to the Lacy Lady and Room at the Top in Ilford, or even out to Canvey Island for the famed Goldmine. For one wild and funky year, 1975, Essex became the unlikely epicentre of nocturnal cavorting. Kids from all parts of London crowded into their cars, or even hired coaches to ferry them to these otherwise unremarkable suburban discos, where on a Friday and Saturday, DJs like Chris Hill and Greg Edwards would make the boondocks boom with the latest imported American sides.

If a night of Brass Construction, Lonnie Liston Smith and acres of white hosiery in the wastelands of the far east was a treat, the emergence of a hipper and considerably nearer scene in the alleys of the old tenderloin was very nearly heaven. Actually, back in late 1975 – the long, hot summer just around the corner – Heaven was known as the Global Village, a brand new nightclub that opened under the arches by Charing Cross station, and by far the swankiest of a series of inner-London venues that, on a specific night, attracted the best dancers, the sharpest dressers, the most all-round righteous urban kiddies. Global Village on a Friday, the 100 Club on Saturday and, best of all, Crackers any time you could get in. Crackers, a suitably nondescript, subterranean dive on the corner of Dean Street, was where the elite feet, black and white, male and female, straight and gay, went to dazzle. Crowded, sweaty, arch and oozing adolescent cool.

'Steve Strange was Il Duce of the Door, Boy George was the cloakroom girl, and Kraftwerk, Giorgio Moroder and early Human League provided the soundtrack.'

The thrill of first swaggering into Soho – traditionally London's juiciest tenderloin, but by then a largely forgotten enclave where a few seedy, mackintoshed men followed the lure of red lights – attired to the nines, heading for the hottest basement this side of hell, was one of the most potent of my entire youth. I was a skinny, ginger, Laurence Corner version of Brian Ferry in his GI Joe phase, all epaulettes and acne, yet somehow I knew that this was where the night belonged. This was to become our W1 wonderland.

The spiky ones

1976 is one of the pivotal years in the nocturnal history of postwar London. This was when the '60s suddenly seemed like ancient history, and the future (or was it No Future?) started to rip. The night began at lunchtime on the King's Road, Chelsea, then still free from chain stores and gastropubs, as a succession of tribal youngers would gather to preen, pose and parade in their increasingly outlandish finery while the Hoorays looked on with Home Counties disdain. Shops like Acme Attractions, Johnsons and a wonky little place up at World's End called Let It Rock (later Sex) were a mecca for competing cults. Teddy boys with their lurid socks and sideburns, soul boys,

all wedge haircuts and bowling walks, Bowie boys, angular, Thin White Dukes, and this shocking new mob, of boys and girls, as yet without a tribal moniker, who had taken to ripping up and splattering their gear and their hair. All these trouser tribes would head west to strut the street. Out of this bubbling, primordial teenage soup came the explosion.

The Roxy in Covent Garden, then a tumbleweed barrio of abandoned market buildings and forgotten warehouses, was the most famous of the trailblazing punk clubs, where three-chord anarchists changed the world. But, in fact, it was a seedy leather-boy disco called Chaguaramas, where the Sex-clad Bromley contingent could sport its shocking apparel in safety, long before it was taken over by the noisy new bands. Equally, Louise's, a tiny lesbian hangout on Poland Street was the best place at which to rub shoulders and other body parts with Johnny Lydon and Siouxsie Sioux, before either of them was even in a group. Punk may have been the hard rocking sound of the Westway, but actually it emerged in the subterranean, invert discos of the West End.

Punk exploded in London and New York simultaneously because both cities were all but bankrupt. Cheap rents, squats, empty industrial spaces, failing clubs… The young and feral had the nocturnal freedom of the inner city because nobody else wanted it. The Lower East Side and the West End both changed as a result of the attention drawn to them by the spiky ones. The years that followed would be the story of these adolescent pioneers colonising the night, and thereby inadvertently reviving once moribund metropolises. Notting Hill had been home to backstreet blues and reggae parties from the time

From left, punks gathering outside the Roxy in 1978; Boy George (and friend) at the Blitz in 1980. Right, Trojan, Nicola and Leigh Bowery at Taboo in 1985.

my parents lived there, but it soon became polished up by poshos wanting a slice of urban living. That's the story time and again, when seedy neighbourhoods get discovered by the vampires, they become cool, so the rents rise, the corporate suits move in and the hipsters move on. Not so much gentrification as trendification. And it always starts after dark.

Punk's cacophonous pyrotechnics lit up the city, but it was too brief a self-immolation to really change much, and by 1978-79, London was lying dormant again. But as ever, things were festering away nicely. This was a particularly torrid time to be out on the streets, the winter of our urban discontent, as rubbish piled up, the dead went unburied and rats roamed the gutters. So did we. Little peacock clusters of the wilfully overdressed hugging the shadows so as not to be glimpsed by a still Neanderthal majority who had little truck with dandy poseurs. Our one night was Tuesday, originally at Billy's, a tiny haunt beneath a brothel on the corner of Dean Street, and then most famously at the Blitz, a dodgy, themed wine bar in Covent Garden, where Steve Strange was Il Duce of the Door, Boy George was the cloakroom girl, and Kraftwerk, Giorgio Moroder and early Human League provided the suitably electronic, Teutonic soundtrack. Hedonistic, narcissistic, overtly elitist and destined to set the nocturnal template for the next decade, the Blitz and its glittering ragbag of alumni was the club that really heralded the 1980s.

Materialistic, hedonistic, solipsistic, Thatcherite and cruel: the '80s were all of those. It was also a great decade in which to be on the guest list. London was dragged from its Rip Van Winkle snooze by a succession of youth crazes that started with the giro-financed fabulousness of the Blitz kids and ended with the all-conquering bpm frenzy of the rave scene. It was in 1979 that I first went to a warehouse party, as a gang of piratical soul boys broke into the then derelict Butler's Wharf by Tower Bridge, installed a sound system, and held a weekend-long shebeen amid the post-industrial

detritus of what is now a chic collection of riverside apartments and restaurants.

Every struggling club, venue, disused factory and abandoned warehouse was taken over by a bizarrely attired teenage entrepreneur appealing to the ever-expanding menu of styles and sounds. Rockabilly, jazz, goth, funk, hip hop… By about 1983, London was alive from Soho to Portobello with a torrent of trends, a frenzy of flyers and rumours. The tenderloin was now also home to the first stirrings of the gay village, as attitudes to diversity changed, and a slew of cool new restaurants like the Soho Brasserie, whose opening on Old Compton Street heralded the start of the trendy dining craze. Meanwhile, just around the corner on Dean Street, a bunch of media movers were plotting to start London's first swish, post-modern members club named after Groucho Marx. Design, which had once been something slightly distasteful that the French did, was now de rigueur. The decade was in full flow.

The Wag Club on Wardour Street, the Fridge in Brixton, the Camden Palace – these were some of the more lasting shrines to '80s hedonistic excess, with queues regularly snaking outside. But they were all blown away by a few smiley faces in a tiny gym in Bermondsey. Shoom, with Danny Rampling bringing that banging Balaeric beat from Ibiza to SE1, was the start of the acid house craze, which almost overnight would homogenise a once wildly varied scene.

Hippy time again

A potent combination of ecstasy, repetitive beats and baggy lilac clothing produced a seismic shift in the nocturnal geography of the city. Suddenly, all those hip, inner-city clubs were so last decade, as a new generation of revellers rejected natty

From left, Johnny Rotten and the Sex Pistols play the 100 Club in 1976; Koko, formerly the Camden Palais.

urban elitism in favour of vast, loved-up raves in muddy fields beyond the M25. It was hippy time again. As a Gaultier wearing, *Face*-writing, Soho thirty-something, I knew my time was up. I was beyond playing hide and seek with the police in Farmer Giles territory, and hated the huge new superclubs, like Ministry of Sound, that sprang up to provide an inner-city equivalent of the rustic rave experience, corporate cash-ins where you could buy the T-shirt and the CD.

Clubbing, with a strict four-four beat, was the dominant youth culture of the '90s. But there was also the pop revival, with Cool Britannia and its capital, home to a slew of groovy bands hanging out in grotty pubs, while a host of shiny designer bars and swish members' clubs sprang up to cater for those old souls like me who wanted a more chilled evening out. Restaurants of every kind had transformed the culinary reputation of the city, and after the Eagle in Farringdon Road found a formula to flog foccacia and fava beans alongside pints of bitter, there was a gastropub on every block. Laughter was also served up on a plate, in pubs and clubs where pissed-up punters heckled comics desperately searching for a TV show. Stand-up as entertainment for those who barely could.

The millennium saw us all party like it was 1999, and then it wasn't. A new century witnesses a new London, confident, affluent and cool, though I no longer see much of life after dark. Bands are big again, a contemporary twist on pub rock, as boys with guitars hold sway in grungy boozers on the Holloway Road or in Bethnal Green. There are scenes like grime and dubstep, new rave and gabba, which I've only read about in magazines. I've definitely experienced the eastward shift of the city, with Hoxton and Brick Lane – once wastelands with boarded-up buildings and braziers burning in the street – now awash with statement haircuts and louche hangouts. Dear old Soho is no longer anybody's secret, and Covent Garden has been handed over almost entirely now to the tourists.

Nocturnal London has expanded in every sense: 24-hour licensing, all-night buses, after-hours clubs, the once tiny scene reaching out to cover parts of the city that were irretrievably lost. When you hear that a cool new bar or club has opened in Deptford or Poplar, you no longer think it's a mistake. London, lauded from every side, is no longer a failed state of a town, it's a buzzing, brilliant city where every taste is catered for and every night is alive. But I sometimes wonder if, in becoming such a success, it has lost some of the edgy subterranean energy and gutter creativity of the dark years. It seemed like it was more fun back then, because you had to put in more effort. Maybe, of course, I'm just too old.

Robert Elms is a writer and broadcaster. He wrote a column for *Time Out* from 2002 to 2004.

TIMELINE

1973
Dingwalls opens at Camden Lock, a new kind of venue where you can eat, drink and be entertained in comfortable surroundings.

1976
Many gay/soul boy clubs become live punk venues. Chaguaramas becomes the Roxy, which lasts just three hectic months and hosts an infamous Sex Pistols gig.

1978
Roller-disco takes over the Empire Discotheque in Leicester Square, Camden's Electric Ballroom and Glades (now Heaven) in Charing Cross.

1979
DJ Rusty Egan and Steve Strange (later of Visage) open Bowie-inspired night, Club For Heroes, at Billy's. 'A good night at Billy's was like a Hieronymous Bosch painting,' recalls photographer Derek Ridgers.

1980
New gay venue Heaven opens under the arches at Charing Cross. It helps bring gay nightlife into the mainstream.

1982
The Wag opens on Wardour Street, and the new underground sound is New York's electro funk, aka hip hop.

1983
The first regular warehouse parties, such as the Dirtbox and Circus, take nightlife into disused factories and garages.

Peter Stringfellow opens the Hippodrome on Leicester Square.

1986
Taboo, the ultimate in decadence, runs for a year on Leicester Square, hosted by Leigh Bowery.

Café de Paris, one of London's most historical and stylish venues, reopens to trendy clubbers, causing huge queues. Even Tina Turner is asked to pay.

1988
Smiley culture sweeps London, but attracts shock-horror headlines due to the widespread use of ecstasy.

1989
Orbital raves in the countryside around the new M25 attract crowds of up to 20,000, leading to calls for tougher policing and outright bans.

1990
Turnmills in Clerkenwell is the first UK venue to get a 24-hour music and dance licence. Other venues extend their opening hours from 3am to 6am, although the alcohol licence hours remains the same. Pubs may now stay open all afternoon, and until 3pm on Sundays.

1991
The Ministry of Sound opens at Elephant & Castle. One of the UK's first superclubs, it plays a central part in the house music scene.

1995
Private members' club Soho House opens on Greek Street, catering to a film, arts and media crowd.

2002
Ibiza's most famous club, Pacha, brings glitz and glamour to Victoria bus terminus.

2008
Much-loved Clerkenwell club Turnmills closes after 23 years, to make way for an office development.

A bluffer's guide to cabaret

What is it? A type of entertainment combining song, dance and theatre, usually staged in a nightclub environment. The term is a French word for café, which derives from the Middle Dutch *cabret*, through the Old North French *camberette*, and from the Late Latin *camera*. The world basically means 'small room'. The first cabaret was opened in Montmartre, Paris, in 1881. German cabaret appeared at the turn of the 20th century, and found its heyday in the 1920s and '30s.

The experience The idea of cabaret being cool takes a bit of getting used to. Until recently, I'd presumed it to be the live entertainment equivalent of *The Generation Game* or 'The Birdie Song', a half-forgotten end-of-the-pier affair involving forced grins, musty moustaches and spangly assistants. That or lap-dancing with better PR. But no: according to Simone Baird, *Time Out*'s

alternative nightlife guru, cabaret is one of the fastest growing scenes around, with many of the city's hottest tickets offering entry to a red-and-black retro wonderland where 'sexy' and 'fun' are the boxes to tick.

In less time than it takes to lace a corset, Simone had set me up with a broad tasting menu of what the scene has to offer. First up was a Friday night in Bethnal Green to see current cabaret darlings the Puppini Sisters, whose faux-'40s close harmonising has already got their card marked for crossover success. 'You're lucky to be seeing them in such an intimate venue,' Simone assured me. 'It's been sold out for ages.' Hidden in a converted industrial building down an alley off Cambridge Heath Road, Bistrotheque was disarmingly classy inside, with Victorian-style etched glass and ornamental carvings in the bar, and a cosy but classy performance space. The Sisters put on a

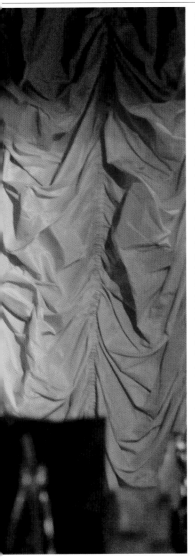

storming act, cooing their way through standards trad and modern and getting the audience eating out of their slinkily-gloved hands. Personally, I like my entertainment with a little more bite, but the pastiche was spot-on, and the girls' perky, nudge-nudge charm a perfect fit for the relaxed, intimate space.

From there it was a short stumble to the Bethnal Green Working Men's Club, off Green Road. I'd heard this was the current place to be, a feeling most of the crowd seemed to share. They'd certainly made the effort: chaps in hats and girls in pearls were the order of the day, with waistcoats and corsets by the cupboard-full. As someone who's never been told off for overdressing, I felt a bit shabby in my T-shirt and jeans, but it was no big deal because the mood was so friendly, thanks perhaps to the cheap bar, the singalong feel of the upbeat playlist – lots of vintage rock 'n' roll, New Romantic tunes and recent guitar rock – and the vaguely mischievous air of kids let loose in their grandparents' wardrobes and jewellery boxes. (The bouncer was still a bit of a prick, but a prick in a tweedy jacket…)

The other two events on my cabaret calendar were closer to the compère-introduces-varied-bill-of-fare template I'd imagined, and both were somewhat mixed bags. The Sunday Night Cabaret Spectacular at Too2Much, in the heart of Paul Raymond-land, was certainly well suited to the plush, tiered performance-bar surroundings, and made for a suitably laid-back end to the weekend. But the acts themselves didn't make a great impression: sarky stand-up Mary Bourke did a grand job, and Aussie co-host Amanda Symmons had a nicely barbed sick-of-London number, but otherwise the singers were a bit ordinary. Meanwhile, burlesque – cabaret's naughty sister – was represented by a frankly baffling drag king striptease that ended with flaming nipple-tassles.

Last was the regular Wednesday night Cabaret Salon at the Volupté Lounge, off Fetter Lane, perhaps the swankiest of the venues. ('Is that what you're wearing?' Simone sighed when she clocked that day's T-shirt-and-jeans ensemble.) Bypassing the ground-floor cocktail bar, the plush downstairs performance space turned out to be geared more towards dining than drinking, with a young professional-looking party and a few older couples. The opening act – an unengaging guitar-strummer who seemed to love himself enough for the whole room – went on far too long, but others worked the room well, including the wittily deadpan Miss Tallulah Mockingbird, whose way with feathers gave me faith in burlesque. Singer Jessie Pie meanwhile nailed precisely the right balance of sexy and fun, with a distinctly disciplinarian set that ended up feeling like a dirty joke shared with the audience. I don't know if it's art, but it sure ain't *The Generation Game*.

What to say 'The elegance of the Puppini Sisters obviously references the 1940s, but also harks back to Yvette Guilbert or Jane Avril in their performances at the Moulin Rouge in the late 19th century.'

What not to say 'Is she going to take her kit off, or what?'

Original report by Ben Walters.

Memory bank

Immodesty Blaize on Lady Luck

I still remember the early Lady Luck days, around six or seven years ago: every Friday, underneath a chavvy Euston strip bar. You went down into the basement and straight into an amazing time-capsule, draped in red velvet and spinning glitterballs. The women looked exquisite in huge prom dresses, or '40s gowns or bouffants. Even the men looked amazing, in zoot suits, fedoras, spats, or Teds and Rockers gear. I'd sit up with my friends the night before, excitedly planning flouncy creations. We often sewed things especially, or searched out vintage finds.

At Lady Luck you could actually dance in couples, which wasn't really happening in other clubs – you could partner up for a jitterbug, some swing, or a good old smoochy prom number. People even asked for a dance the proper old-fashioned way! In fact, it was just like going to a prom in your front room, cosy and far away from the outside world. The music was top-class; DJs El Nino and Jake Vegas played everything: Tom Waits, Little Richard, Sinatra. Add the ferocious cocktails and the dancefloor went absolutely mental every week.

What made it even more kooky was that you shared the Ladies with the strippers from upstairs. You'd see a '40s pencil-skirted, fur-clad vixen with a pill box hat standing at the mirror beside a neon yellow Lycra-clad pole dancer, sharing a red lipstick between them. Sometimes the DJs would bring down one of the girls from upstairs to perform an impromptu striptease, or you'd get an interlude from, say, Son of Dave. That was a special, golden time, and Lady Luck was the real forerunner of the retro, glam, dress-up clubs of today.

Immodesty Blaize is a burlesque performer.

Crazy days

Grooves, raves and party smarties down the decades.

NIGHTLIFE

Acid rock

1960s

Rockers take acid and get lost in music. The results are unlistenable to everyone else.

Disco

1970s

Middle-class men dress as pimp-daddies, doing the moves from *Saturday Night Fever*; girls wear afro wigs and dubiously short shorts – the effects of D-I-S-C-O live on.

Punk

1976

Pogo! The Sex Pistols! Vivienne Westwood! Notable punk club the Roxy lasted just three months in '76, with Don Letts dropping plenty of reggae because there weren't enough punk records to play.

New Romantics

1979-82

Steve Strange and Rusty Egan were the faces behind many of the clubs that later epitomised the New Romantic scene: Fame (better known as A Club For Heroes) at Billy's in 1979; Blitz (1979-80) in a Covent Garden wine bar; the Camden Palace in 1982. Whether as pierrots in thick pan-stick, Edwardian dandies in crushed velvet, or futuristic space cadets in *Blake's 7* outfits, the Bowie fans, transvestites, skinheads and ex-soul boys always looked outrageous. Bowie's 'Ashes To Ashes' video was inspired by a visit he made to the club.

Goth

1982

Goth was what happened when disenchanted post-punks and New Romantics met, shared their love of records by the Cramps, the Gun Club and the Cure, wore an unfeasible amount of eyeliner and more black fabric than a state funeral. Cue jerky 'freeze frame' dancing at clubs like the Batcave, the Kit Kat Club and Astral Flight.

Taboo

1985-1986

Intensely hedonistic and all too brief, just like the legendary performance artist who organised it. Leigh Bowery's Taboo ran every Thursday in Leicester Square for just one year of polysexual posing to eclectic trash disco. Intimidating in the extreme (doorwhore Marc Golding was fond of holding up a mirror and sighing: 'Well, would *you* let you in?'), it closed after Bowery's on/off boyfriend Trojan and Golding died of drug overdoses.

Flare groove

1987

Rare groove mixed with fresh hip hop, whatever Prince was releasing, and a relishing crowd who rocked a Blaxsploitation look.

Acid house

Summers of 1987-89

Famously, four DJs went to Ibiza, took drugs and, upon returning, recreated the Balearic vibe in sports halls and warehouses. The 1980s obsession for dressing up-up-up was ditched in favour of comfy Kickers, baggy jeans and baggier hoodies all round. Posing and acting superior gave way to ecstasy hugs with strangers.

Acid jazz

1989-1990

Played at Talking Loud, Saying Something (the club hosted by DJ Gilles Peterson). It spawned a million unfortunate beard stylings, and briefly brought wobbly-legged jazz dancing back into vogue.

Funki Dreds

1985-1990

Soul II Soul Sound-system aimed to reflect London's cultural make-up, poppy enough for white kids but soulful enough for West Indians. It brought a warehouse style and genuine multicultural crowd to the Africa Centre in Covent Garden every Sunday. Prominent Dred Jazzi B recently received an OBE.

Happy hardcore

1991-92

The acid house beats sped up, as did the drugs. Ravers started to wear all the colours of the day-glo rainbow and do the 'big fish, little fish, cardboard boxes' dance. Massive barn-like raves on light-industrial estates offered '17 arenas! 256 DJs! 1,000,000,000,00 MCs!' on their flyers, and the police did their best to shut them down.

Drum 'n' bass

1995-1996

A musical genre to call our own. Rave break beats morphed into jungle: heavy, bass-driven music with nimble MCs. Grooverider & Fabio's Rage at Heaven (1991) would cement the scene, but it wasn't until the middle of the 1990s that D&B (as jungle became known, once everyone had stopped insisting that there was a difference) became the coolest thing in town. Goldie's legendary Metalheadz was every Sunday at the Blue Note on Hoxton

---

Memory bank

Goldie on Metalheadz at the Blue Note

I started the club back in about '96, because I felt that no one had really done a Sunday night, apart from the old jazzers many years before, and I wanted to have a place that was for more cutting-edge music. It was great, because they used to have a jazz session in the afternoon – in the old Blue Note tradition – and people used to stay on and have a good old knees-up. I wanted a place where there was a family of people, and you left your ego at the door.

I meet people now from the strangest walks of life, and a lot of them tell me they used to go there. The Blue Note was a melting pot of ideas: sure, it was about the experience of being there, but it was also about the queue around the corner to get in, about being in the car on the way home, talking about tunes… If you went early enough, there was food upstairs, there were board games, so you could have a bit of a chill-out.

Probably my best moment ever was taking my gold disc down there, bringing it back 'home', if you like; I stopped the music, put the lights on and thanked everyone – especially Fabio and Grooverider – for making it all possible. If you set the right tone in any environment, that vibration will go through people, and that's what Metalheadz was all about. The one thing Metalheadz always stood for was the big 'I' – integrity.

Square, back when there was nothing else in the area, and the bass in the basement made your trousers stand to attention.

Britpop

1995-1996

Indie for Londoners who didn't want to look like a grunge scruff-bag. Blow Up started in 1993 and was the breeding ground of the Britpop sound. Full of sharp-suited music types (Blur and Jarvis Cocker were regulars), it was dubbed 'The Club that Changed the World' at Britpop's zenith in 1995.

Asian underground

1995-98

British Asians became super-cool in 1997 thanks to Talvin Singh's compilation *Anokha – Soundz of the Asian Underground*. Countless comedy sing-along moments were had thanks to Fatboy Slim's remix in the same year of Cornershop's 'Brimful of Asha'.

UK garage

1996

Much hyped by the *Face*, in fact, UK garage was never quite as crossover popular as everybody made out at the time.

Handbag house

Mid 1990s

Glitzy, spangly, very accessible house music for glamorous and dressed-up girls. So called, of course, because they danced in high heels around their handbags.

Trade

Mid '90s

When most Londoners were flicking through the Sunday papers, Trade babies – as they were known – were hitting the dancefloor of this all-day hard house debauch-athon. Buff, topless gay men, girls in bikini tops, all-night ravers: they partied hard and fast.

Heavenly Social

1994

For six blisteringly hedonistic months in 1994, Sunday evenings at the Albany in central London spawned the big beat sound that would prove so popular in Brighton. Rings of amyl were burned on the dancefloor, and people danced on speaker stacks to the Dust Brothers, later known as the Chemical Brothers.

Trance

1998

Electronic music to wave your hands in lasers to, taken awfully seriously in Germany. Didn't work so well without a gutful of drugs.

Electroclash

2002

Just when you thought dance music was dead, a couple of midweek clubs in London created a phenomenon. Erol Alkan's Trash, every Monday at the End, and Nag Nag Nag, every Wednesday at the Ghetto with resident spinners Jo Jo de Freq and Jonny Slut, threw electronic classics, guitar records and 1980s classics into the mix, and came up

with what was called electroclash. Essential record? Tiga's 'Sun-glasses at Night'. What followed was an initially amusing but very soon tiring deluge of mash-up records.

Vintage

2004

Swing and sleazy jazz clubs like the Rakehell's Revels at the Café Royal and El Nino's ongoing Lady Luck gave hip cats and corset-wearing girls a place to pose. Supplies of red lipstick ran very low, and grandparents' wardrobes were ransacked.

Nu-rave

2006

Eighteen-year-olds in Dalston wearing every trend from the 1980s at once. A fashion-led fad that was as hilarious as it was popular for a few weeks over the summer.

Boombox

2006

The Blitz of a new generation? Pretty young things railed against each other to create the most extreme and over-the-top look. Butternut squash? Strap it to your head. Length of gardening hose? It's a necklace. Ran every Sunday in Hoxton. Of course.

Dubstep

2007-8

Grime without the nonsensical jibber-jabber shouted over the top. Not surprisingly, a lot more popular than regular grime.

Compiled by Simone Baird.

DANNY RAMPLING on Shoom and the acid house scene

Before acid house, I was aspiring to be a DJ, and there was just no way in. No matter how many doors I knocked on and how many people I hung out with who were in the music business, there just weren't any openings. The rare groove and hip hop scenes in south London, where I came from, had become very dull and were crying out for change.

Acid house was a breath of fresh air in '87 – it was like when punk arrived. Within the space of about six months, everything changed. Certain people resisted it. I can still see the looks of horror on their faces: 'What's happening to our friend?' London really shaped the acid house scene, and it was so rebellious. It was all built on word of mouth too, whereas now – in terms of creating youth culture – everything's over before it's begun. The energy of the people who came together in acid house attracted all walks of life: black, white, gay, straight, high society, the middle class, the unemployed, everyone… There was a small clique of people doing their thing, and then all of a sudden, we burst on to the scene with this music from hell!

We used to have Leigh Bowery at Shoom, and people like Neville and Spike, who were leading club promoters at the time – they were all drawn to this basement in Southwark. The first night was in November 1987, and we all knew acid house was going to explode. Anyone who had any contact with it knew it was going to have a major impact on youth culture. Every night of the week there was something happening, and London became a village. All of these unique and individual characters came together, and so many strong friendships were forged that last to this day. That's quite remarkable, and something to be treasured. I'm filled with gratitude to have helped shape that movement.

NIGHTLIFE

I bet we looked good on the dancefloor

A photographic bop through the past two decades of London club land, a wild world of colourful characters and bold beats. A world that is constantly reinventing itself. A world that never, ever stands still.

By Dave Swindells

DJ Mark Moore at Sacrosanct, Shaftesbury's, 1987.

A typically anarchic Mutoid Waste party, held in a King's Cross warehouse, 1988.

Norman Jay DJs at the Carwash warehouse disco party, 1988.

Dawn rises in a field near East Grinstead at a Boys Own Party, 1989.

P-funk fans and rare groovers at the Wag, 1987.

Glamour goths at the Embassy, 1985.

Café de Paris, 1987.

Gyroscopes, along with bouncy castles and other fairground attractions, became a regular feature at raves in 1988.

The summer of the Orbital rave: 5am at a World Dance rave, near East Grinstead, 1989.

DJ Jazzy Q of Soul II Soul at the Fridge, 1989.

Indie kids work the baggy look at a Charlatans gig, 1990.

Tasty Tim and Maur Valance at Kinky Gerlinky, 1990.

Chilling out with some ambient house at the Hippodrome, 1991.

The Pussy Posse Party, Bagleys, 1991.

Club host Phillip Sallon at the Mud Club, Saturdays at Bagleys, 1995.

Goldie hits the decks for Metalheadz at the Blue Note, 1996.

Twice as Nice at the Colosseum. One of the club's dancers flaunts it in the UK garage room, 1999.

Russian hostess Lotta at Kash Point, 2003.

A youthful Gilles Peterson (left) with Femi and Patrick Forge at Dingwalls' final Sunday Session, 1991.

Asian cool at a bhangra event, Le Palais, Hammersmith, 1992.

Fabric, one of London's new generation of megaclubs, 1999.

Move at the Ministry of Sound, 1999.

Bastard Batty Bass at the Star of Bethnal Green, 2008.

Dave Swindells has been *Time Out*'s nightlife editor since 1986, and has been photographing the scene since the early '80s.

Alternative Miss World

For the past 16 years, avant-garde sculptor Andrew Logan has been throwing London's biggest and most outrageous party: the Alternative Miss World contest, a rude and ritzy trash exhibitionists' bash, where men, women and others slip into their gladdest of rags and fight to become the underground Belle with the Balls.

NIGHTLIFE

The first one was in my studio in Hackney in 1972. I'm a great lover of parties – giving parties – and I'd just been to Crufts dog show and I found that rather inspiring – all these little dogs trotting up and down. About 100 people came, all my friends. At that one there was really no difference between the people who entered and the audience. I suppose in a way that was my ideal. Then it was all outrageous. Funnily enough, it still is, come to think of it.

The following year, we'd had such a good time, we said let's do it again. Bowie was asked as a judge, and he arrived in this huge limo, but he couldn't get in. It was only a small studio and people were climbing over back gardens, climbing in the windows, hanging off everything… It was like a bus in India. Anyway, David drove off, but his wife Angie was a judge. So was David Hockney. Miss Holland Park Walk won: Eric Roberts, a black man. It was a shock to everyone.

In '75 we'd moved to Butlers Wharf by London Bridge. That's when the lights went out – someone tripped over the cable and the entire place was thrown into mayhem. The men on the door taking money – thugs, basically – wound up getting blow

jobs on the stairs. Mayhem! And Molly Parkin, the compère, she got thrown in the pool. She'd been very aggressive with the audience all evening. Pre-punk, remember? Vivienne (Westwood) and Malcolm (McLaren) were there with their entourage. I remember the outfits were all ripped, safety pins everywhere, very aggressive. Malcolm was just forming the Sex Pistols then. The following year, in Butler's Wharf, they played their first gig, and we all ran away and hid in a corner.

The '78 event was held in a circus tent on Clapham Common. I'd always loved going to the circus. The judges were in lion's cages, I loved that. That one was filmed by Richard Gayor, who at the time was very interested in disappearing tribes and disappearing civilisations, and I always thought I was something of that genre really. I suppose the climax was when the Alternative Miss World was crowned. That was Stevie Hughes, Miss Linda Carriage – extraordinary looking, you couldn't quite believe it was a man. Anyway, we had a donkey as the throne. I had thought I'd like an elephant, but I couldn't get hold of one – and the donkey fell off the stage into the contestants and Miss Carriage went flying…

A contestant on the catwalk at Alternative Miss World 1991.

Memory bank

Jonny Woo on the Bricklayer's Arms in the summer of 1997

I moved to London from college in Birmingham in 1996, and folded jumpers daily in a Regent Street store. I escaped every Friday night to the London Apprentice, the local gay club, which had the city's busiest toilet. There had to be more to life than this. My mate Julie had just got a job round the corner. 'I've found this really mad

pub!' she said in a broad Brummy twang. 'It's owned by this woman called Vicky, and there is this guy called Pablo. It's called the Bricklayer's Arms.' I had to find this 'mad' pub.

The Bricklayer's didn't open at the weekend. It was packed full of kids with scruffy hair and oversized specs knocking back shots. I wanted in on the party.

I got a job working a massively understaffed bar during the summer of 1997, which just got busier and busier. Katie Grand and Giles Deacon drank tequila and orange. Fee Doran (stylist Miss Jones) spun weird music and invented the Shoreditch look, which would remain for the next decade. JJ (Noki) told me dirty stories behind the bar.

Me and Julie did a pub quiz, and for one summer's day party, Vicky decided to cover

the floor of the entire pub in real turf. I think I only worked there for six months. It was the summer and every weekend there were at least five warehouse parties; Charlotte Road was blocked by kids on booze and drugs. I loved it; it was messy and it was perfect.

There was nothing else in Shoreditch really, just fantastic anarchy. Then, at some point, someone in the press decided to tell the rest of London that Shoreditch was fashionable.

A lot of the old faces have moved on. Julie has two kids in Tunbridge Wells. Others stayed, Pablo opened Bistrotheque seven years later. The expensive warehouses are now owned by rich architects, and Vicky has sold the Bricklayer's. I moved to NYC, returning in 2003. A major spell was cast that summer, because I still love Shoreditch. It's my home.

Jonny Woo is an alternative drag queen.

In '81 I really got ambitious. I thought, I've done the circus tent, I'll do a Cecil B De Mille now – huge. So I hired the Grand Hall at Olympia. The catwalk was 250 feet long and 15 feet wide – it was like a little road. And we had huge things made, a ferris wheel at one end, and basically we lost £20,000. And that was my Cecil B De Mille. Mind you, he must have lost money as well.

Four years later, we're treading very carefully now. I was very nervous about the money, so I decided to go legit, with a stage and so on, at the Brixton Academy. That was the year the robot won. Bruce Lacey, he'd entered his wife year after year, then they divorced, and he entered this robot that won. Very embarrassing. I think she felt a bit miffed.

The next year was Chislehurst Caves – a real underground event. But the people who had hired the caves just didn't have a licence for events like ours, and two days before the event they said no. It was the time of the AIDS scare, and the local paper was running stories about AIDS in the caves and so on. Anyway, the Brixton Academy stepped in again. Jenny Runacre (the actress) won, the first woman to do so. Mind you, she deserved to, she'd been entering since the first one, poor thing.

I'm planning the next one in 1990. By then there'll be a whole new generation, which will make it all different again. I think the next one should have the theme of 'air' – an outdoor event on Sunday afternoon. Which for all those nightclubbers should be rather a shock.

NIGHTLIFE

Memory bank
Oliver Peyton on dressing up and going out

I have many memories of going out when I would come over to London from Ireland in the mid 1970s: Thin Lizzy at the Hammersmith Odeon (the ticket cost me £12 from a tout, which to me was like a mortgage), the Clash, Joy Division at the Lyceum… There was a period of time from the mid '70s to mid '80s when going out in London meant counterculture. When I went to some of the places, people were dressed in amazing ways. I remember a girl called Scarlett, who used to run Cha Cha's (a precursor of Heaven), Leigh Bowery in his outrageous outfits, and an underground club called Circus. London for me, as a young Irish person, was an amazing thing. It formed me as a person. I really do feel that young people need to be involved in going out and dressing up.

I was never into cross-dressing, but I am a bit of a clothes horse. Part of the whole punk thing was the gear. It was a symbol of your tribe. I remember my mum once burned one of my Seditionary T-shirts because she said it was obscene. To be honest, it probably was, but I was very upset: it cost me a fortune. After punk, and new wave, the New Romantics came along at just the right time for me.

In the 1980s I ran a nightclub in Tottenham Court Road. One night I went along to Shoom, when Danny Rampling was on. I remember seeing something I'd never seen before: everybody wearing ponchos, and dry ice everywhere. After Shoom, it was the beginning of the end. House music became popularised, and all those warehouse parties and out-of-town raves capitalised on it. Once it was possible to take 100 grand or more a night, it became just another commercial enterprise.

Now a lot of the night clubs are just another marketing tool for a brand. I feel it's a bit depressing, but maybe that's because I'm old.

Oliver Peyton co-owns a number of restaurants, including the National Dining Rooms, Inn The Park and the Peyton & Byrne chain of cafés-cum-bakeries.

London boasts round-the-clock drinking and clubs that don't even open till 4am, but it wasn't always so.

By Lisa Mullen

Staying up past

Britain's Edwardian licensing laws have always grated on Londoners. Historically, the capital evolved into an all-night city as an inevitable expression of its mercantile DNA; its taverns, coffee houses and music halls would never be closed as long as there were paying customers still walking through the door. Jeffrey Bernard, perhaps not wholly disinterested as a commentator, summed it up for *Time Out* in 1982: 'The trouble with this country is that people don't drink enough,' he stated. 'I mean, look at the period 1790-1815: the English had a reputation for being a load of arseholed drunks. Everybody went round pissed all day. And look what they achieved: Waterloo, Trafalgar, the Nile.' The libertarian imperative survived Puritanism

and Victorian values, but World War I changed all that. The 11pm curfew introduced in 1915 may have been designed to shore up the war effort by preventing hangovers among factory workers, but its intrinsic class snobbery – rich men's playgrounds, the casinos and private clubs were not affected by the laws – clearly appealed to subsequent generations of those in power. The masses should not, they felt, be out and about at all hours causing trouble and making a noise. They should be tucked up in bed at a sensible hour, ready for work.

In reality, though, it only ever worked like that in the suburbs and provinces. Restrictions on the sale of alcohol certainly had an impact on late-night London, but only by encouraging exactly

our bedtime

the kind of subculture that was to prove definitive of the city's vibrancy and mercurial adaptability. When time was called, Londoners found another way. They went clubbing. They set up dodgy drinking clubs or got creative with legal loopholes. They sneaked into hotels and organised lock-ins and took up gambling. Still, London hated being babied by the state in this way. Put simply, it was embarrassing.

From its earliest days, *Time Out* has lobbied for London's right to stay up past its bedtime. In 1971, a guide to all-night London was written for the magazine by Jeremy Beadle, who included a list of two late-night chemists, a dozen or so 24-hour lavatories and the crucial pre-cashpoint-era tip that 'if you have a Giro account you can cash cheques at

London nightlife, 21st-century style: the queue outside the 333 club in Hoxton.

the all-night PO in Trafalgar Square'. Tellingly, his listings excluded strip clubs and gambling dens, 'because their habitués know them anyway'. He painted a vivid picture of the city after hours: 'You will often find the whole side of [a] theatre open, a yawning wound through which sets and props can be carried to waiting vans… Police panda cars patrol the streets… There is always the river.'

Pickings were nevertheless decidedly slim for the would-be reveller at this point in history: 'It is important to remember that after midnight,' he warned, 'if business is slow at discotheques and restaurants, the management will close them, regardless of official opening hours.' Food choices were limited to kerbside stalls ('food is generally poor but cheap… most people who use them are friendly and chatty, full of dirty jokes and well-worn tales'), all-night cafés like Mick's on Fleet Street (full of journalists) and the emerging breed of what were called 'production food' chains ('certain Wimpys have direction from head office to refuse service to unaccompanied women after midnight, because they might be prostitutes').

Discos did a good trade after the pubs closed, charging on-the-spot membership (despite a widely ignored law stating that there should be a 48-hour interval between joining and admission), and profiting from food sales too. But Beadle couldn't find much in the way of live music to excite him: 'Most of the musicians take their music very seriously and like to be listened to in almost "concert form". Many people in the audience, however, are out for a leap, and become a constant irritation to both the musicians and their admirers.'

Things had not improved much by 1981. 'By 3am most of the clubs have closed and the London night is a great blank plain dotted with small pockets of activity,' Paul Charman wrote in his guide, noting that even the 'hostess' clubs were subject to this curfew: 'Any pretence of eroticism is dispelled at 3am sharp as the bar shutters slam down and the women troop off to dress.'

Throughout the 1980s, nightclubs were the new winners on the late-night scene, though venue owners who really just wanted to run a bar were starting to complain more vocally about the onerous conditions placed on a post-11pm licence. Alcohol, the law stated, could only be provided as an 'ancillary' service beside 'a substantial meal and/or live entertainment'. Club entrepreneur Lenny Bloom summed up the general feeling: 'Without the law, the situation would be much more open, and you wouldn't have that shoddy, ripped-off feeling,' he commented.

'It wasn't until 2005 that the licensing laws were properly revised, and 24-hour drinking became a possibility.'

Time Out's 1981 guide had a few new tips about where to get a drink after hours: taxi drivers were apparently the people to ask about 'hotels that have dispensing machines selling miniature bottles of alcohol'; and early-morning market pubs were also mentioned, though 'most discourage people who are not connected with the market'. The feature ended with a paean to the new Xclusiv Club on Margaret Street: 'Glass dancefloor, giant video, 300-bulb lighting system, waterfall fountains… is this the future?'

A Keep London Open campaign the following year pressed for a relaxation of the West End's

Soho's Freedom bar/club gets its message across.

licensing laws, and in 1988 declared a partial victory – 'The end of Time' – when pubs were finally allowed to stay open all afternoon. But it wasn't until 2005 that the law was properly revised, and 24-hour drinking became a possibility.

So did it matter? Was London scarred by 90 years of prohibition? Arguably, the sense of transgression that came with being up all night added a crucial frisson to the experience. At chucking-out time, the quest was on to find something to do, even if it was simply an inebriated walk down to Chelsea for an inedible burger from a street stall, or the challenge of walking into the West London Air Terminal on Cromwell Road and pretending to be a passenger in order to gain access to the Grill & Griddle. How many Londoners were forced to experiment with new experiences, just for want of anything better to do? How many met people, heard music, created trends that they would never have encountered otherwise? Of course, it's easy to be nostalgic about someone else's inconvenience. But perhaps what doesn't kill a city's nightlife makes it stronger.

HEDONISM INTRODUCTION
SEX CITYSCAPE FASHION
SOCIETY SHOPPING COMEDY
DRAMA PROTEST & POLITICS
VISUAL ARTS PERFORMANCE
LITERATURE GANGS OPINION
COCKNEYS BARS ON SCREEN
DANCE MUSIC TELEVISION
BUILDINGS CLUBS NIGHTLIFE
SPORT & FITNESS MEMORIES
STYLE FOOD & DRINK GIGS
CONSUME RIOTS REFERENCE

The view
from the terraces

Football's recent history can be measured out by the oscillating fortunes of Chelsea and Wimbledon, but which model will it follow for its future?

By Peter Watts

It's 1991, and after queuing for an hour to get in, and then waiting another hour for the match to start, I'm starting to wonder whether it was worth the effort and £8 entrance fee: Chelsea are losing 2-1 to Wimbledon at Plough Lane, the latter's cramped, tumbledown stadium near Wimbledon dog track. The view from the away terrace is terrible for the top division, you can barely make out the top of the crossbar in the goalmouth beneath you, but as Chelsea's Gordon Durie turns and scores, the surge from celebrating fans pushes me down the terrace and twirls me back to front. My leg catches on the vertical support of a crush barrier and twists around, creating a huge purple bruise that I proudly show off at school on Monday.

Abruptly, the celebrations end. The linesman's flag is raised. He has disallowed the goal, and there's no action replay to show why. The Wimbledon fans jeer, Chelsea lose, I nurse my wound. Chelsea finish the season 11th; Wimbledon come sixth. Nearly breaking my leg celebrating a disallowed goal is one of the few memorable moments from a dismal season that ended with a 7-0 defeat at Nottingham Forest.

If you told that story to a 15-year-old football supporter from 1968 or one from 2008, it is difficult to guess who would be more surprised. Football has undergone extraordinary changes over the past 40 years, transformations encapsulated in the oscillating fortunes of Chelsea and Wimbledon. In 1968, Chelsea were the most fashionable team in the land: young, vibrant, popular, stylish and successful. Conversely, few had heard of Wimbledon, an amateur outfit stuck in the Southern League. Forty years later, and after plenty of ups and downs and a period when Wimbledon habitually outperformed their rivals, Chelsea are once again one of the biggest clubs in the country. But terraces have gone, Plough Lane has gone – hell, even Wimbledon have gone, a stellar rise through the leagues ending in ignominy when they were split into two, with one ersatz version playing league football in Milton Keynes and the other back in non-league, playing in front of 3,000 in Kingston.

Teens and hooligans

The only way to really grasp these changes is to look at them chronologically. In 1968, football was riding the crest of the postwar wave and attracting huge crowds. However, two trends were emerging that would distinguish 1960s football from its forebears. The first was the transformation of footballers into celebrities, a result of the abolition of the minimum wage in 1961 and the introduction of regular televised matches. Manchester United's George Best was the poster boy for football as the

Police hold back fans at the Clock End of the old Highbury Stadium, 1980.

new cool, but it was a role manfully shouldered by King's Road carousers such as Peter Osgood, Charlie Cooke, David Webb and Tommy Baldwin.

The other factor was the appearance of a distinctive youth culture in the late 1950s; teenagers had the freedom and cash to go to games at home and, crucially, away, where bonds were forged and rivalries cemented. In 'Football Gangs', a landmark piece published in *Time Out* in 1972, Chris Lightbown explained what this meant, as kids claimed the terrace behind each goal as 'the End', to be protected from intruders at all costs, vocally and physically.

But football hooliganism was still not seen as a major threat: drinking was still allowed on terraces, and there was no segregation. But things worsened as the '70s progressed, and the fortunes of the four major London clubs – Arsenal, Chelsea, Spurs and West Ham – similarly plummeted. Arsenal won the Double in 1971 and then went missing; Chelsea were relegated, promoted and relegated again as they stumbled towards insolvency; Spurs went down and up; West Ham beat Fulham in the 1975 FA Cup final, then went down and stayed down. In 1975, Queen's Park Rangers were London's highest placed club; they came 11th. The backdrop was even uglier. Hooliganism, especially at Chelsea, West Ham and Millwall, was destroying the game from the inside, driving away crowds and investment, turning stadiums into barbed-wire police states. On the pitch, England failed to qualify for two successive World Cups as the game faced a talent-drain, despite an extraordinary record in the European Cup that saw English clubs win the trophy seven times in eight seasons between 1976 and 1984.

The result was an increasingly unpopular national sport. Chelsea's crowd drained from 40,342 at the start of the decade to 24,782 at the end; the First Division average went from 32,074 to 27,428 over the same period, and continued declining into the early 1990s. In 1974, *Time Out*'s then Sports Editor Peter Ball thought he'd spotted the problem: 'In the last 20 years, football has been taken away from its natural community, commercialised and given the worst trappings of Hollywood by the media. Is it any wonder that the kids, whose dads used to live next door to the local players, feel alienated?'

The upside of this was that it levelled the playing field and allowed smaller clubs to move into the vacuum. Wimbledon joined the football league in 1977 and began a staggering rampage up the tables that saw them in the First Division within a decade. Crystal Palace were dubbed the Team of the '80s as they briefly topped the First Division in 1980; Watford powered into the First Division and reached the FA Cup final in 1984; even Leyton Orient reached the FA Cup semi-finals in 1979.

But part of the climate that allowed them to prosper was the stunning primitiveness of the

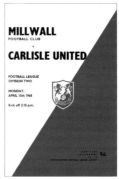

English game. Excluding Liverpool, who ruled the era with Stalinist ruthlessness but considerably more efficiency, English football was technically and tactically stale. Most teams were built on the idea of ten grafters and a crafter – Hoddle at Spurs, Wilkins at Chelsea, Brooking at West Ham and Brady at Arsenal. Peter Ball dissected England's failure in the 1980 European Championships and came up with some familiar problems: 'The English game… does not enhance the development of techniques, nor of flair players, who tend to be regarded with suspicion. The history of English football is littered with names whose vision and skills have failed to tell over the long haul of the English seasons, and have, in the end, lapsed into a sullen and possibly embittered disenchantment.'

One way to get round this was to recruit foreign players, which Tottenham did in 1978 when they signed the Argentines Ossie Ardiles and Ricky Villa, but for the most part the English league was suffocatingly insular. And often it was just plain racist. All the London clubs suffered problems with bigots, but Chelsea, West Ham and Millwall had the worst of them, with the National Front openly recruiting outside grounds. Whereas West Ham first fielded black players in the 1960s and Millwall in the 1970s, Chelsea did not take the plunge until 1982, and when Paul Cannoville made his debut, a significant proportion of the Chelsea fans walked out. It was only under chairman Ken Bates, who had bought the bankrupt club for £1, that a battle to reclaim the club from the racists was staged.

Fanzines and books

Chelsea weren't the only club to suffer financial problems, as property developers started eyeing up the valuable tracts of land the half-empty and decaying stadiums occupied. By 1985, Charlton's average attendance dropped to 5,000, and the club could no longer afford to stay in its home ground, the Valley, so moved in with Crystal Palace. Two years later, Fulham and QPR fought a sustained battle against David Bulstrode, a developer who wanted to merge the clubs into Fulham Park Rangers and turn Craven Cottage into flats, and Stamford Bridge was threatened by Cabra Estates until Bates secured the freehold.

This turbulence had a positive effect on supporters, who suddenly began to take a more constructive approach. A fanzine movement sprang up, allowing supporters, previously cast as goose-stepping, baby-eating Neanderthals, to show they had wit, intelligence and creativity, and were prepared to challenge their clubs rather than blindly support them. Every club had at least one fanzine and most had several, ranging from tatty sheets of photocopied, hand-stapled A4, to epic, glossy tomes that rivalled official programmes in expense and were considerably better value for money. Sportpages, a bookshop on the Charing

'On the pitch, football was tough, fast and tactically primitive, but it could also be unpredictable and exciting.'

Cross Road with hundreds of fanzines strewn across the floor in giddy piles, became a rallying point for supporters in London.

The early days of the fanzine movement even engendered a brief flowering of camaraderie among rival supporters, at least until antagonistic, insular publications such as Manchester United's *Red Issue* turned up to revel in their own divisive nastiness, hastening the demise of supporter solidarity and heralding the tediously partisan commentary of many of today's football bloggers. Nick Brown, editor of the *Chelsea Independent*, recalls: 'The early *Chelsea Independent*s, like all fanzines, brought fans back to football and allowed supporters to air their views, where otherwise they would have been ignored. The *Independent* could also challenge the club on the serious issues of racism, policing, pricing and ticket arrangements.' At some clubs, enfranchised supporters went a step further. In 1990, Charlton fans formed the Valley Party and secured 11 per cent of the vote in Greenwich local elections on a platform of getting the club back to their old home. Charlton returned to the Valley two years later.

The 1980s had been a terrible decade, but the fun was returning to football. This was a good time

Chelsea's Peter Osgood outsmarts Manchester United's George Best at Stamford Bridge, 1968.

to be a football supporter. Terraces meant cheap tickets, and few games were televised, meaning the 3pm Saturday afternoon kick-off still dominated. Grounds were vast, so matches rarely sold out, allowing the promiscuous supporter to pick and choose a fixture on a Saturday morning.

The cost of the improvements had been huge, though. Wooden stands were phased out after an inferno at Bradford killed 56 in 1985; that same year, a riot involving Liverpool supporters in the Heysel Stadium, Brussels, caused the deaths of 39 Italians and led to improved policing and serious sentences for hooligans; perimeter fences came down after 96 caged Liverpool fans were crushed to death at Sheffield Wednesday's Hillsborough stadium in 1989. Hooligans were still rife, but cameras in stadiums forced them on to the streets, where the anarchic gangs of the '70s became quasi-military groups, adopting names like the Bushwhackers (Millwall) and Headhunters (Chelsea) as they engaged in pre-arranged meetings far away from normal supporters.

On the pitch, football was tough, fast and tactically primitive, but it could also be unpredictable and exciting. Wimbledon's ragtag bunch of hodcarriers and hoofers rough-and-tumbled their way into the First Division, where they terrified the elite and won the FA Cup against Liverpool in 1988 – a formidable achievement for a club with attendances of barely 10,000. Arsenal, scarcely more sophisticated, secured an astonishing league title on goal difference a year later (their first since 1971), when they beat Liverpool 2-0 at Anfield, with the crucial second

goal coming in the last minute of the last game of the season. West Ham and Tottenham favoured a more sophisticated style of football, but had little to show for it, and threadbare Chelsea continued to switch between the top two divisions.

As the visible threat of hooliganism eroded, attendances rose, boosted by England's unexpectedly successful World Cup campaign of 1990, headed by the Tottenham duo of Gary Lineker and Paul Gascoigne. Which made Nick Hornby's timing all the more fortuitous. *Fever Pitch*, his solipsistic account of the trauma of supporting one of the country's most successful teams, was an astonishing success, devoured by 'people who don't usually read books'. Published in 1992, it told the story of Hornby's life, measured out in Arsenal fixtures, and its acceptance by serious critics marked the first significant step in football's long march towards gentrification.

The same critics didn't have much time for another Arsenal fan, Colin Ward, who, equally significantly and just as unwittingly, had written a eulogy for the old guard three years previously with *Steaming In*, a fan's eye view of terrace culture since the early 1970s. Tough, self-confident and witty, where *Fever Pitch* was reserved, self-analytical and witty, *Steaming In* was the first book written by a former hooligan and remains the only one worth reading. But Ward was already a dinosaur. The Taylor Report, commissioned after the Hillsborough disaster, called for all-seater stadiums, and the great terraced Ends up and down the country were broken up and sold, piece by piece, back to the fans via the club shop. Some clubs simply couldn't afford to pay the builders: Wimbledon said farewell to ramshackle Plough Lane and moved in with Crystal Palace.

Money talks

Football was fashionable; greed was next. The richest English clubs had long agitated for a 'super league', which would essentially see their income ringfenced from the rest of the football league, and in 1992 they got their wish: the Premier League was financed by an astonishing £190m broadcasting deal with Rupert Murdoch's Sky that saw an unprecedented 60 fixtures screened live each season. Pundits were flabbergasted. Andrew Shields, *Time Out*'s Sports Editor, argued that an elite league would last 'two seasons, three at most' and that fans would refuse to pay ever-rising ticket prices. 'The boredom factor will be hugely influential,' he predicted.

That's not quite how it worked out.

In fairness, few people anticipated the explosion of interest and wealth that came with the Premier League, as more games were televised each season and clubs' revenue increased accordingly. Put simply, demand exceeded supply: clubs had to reduce capacity when they converted terracing into seats, but as attendances were increasing they were able to charge more for entry. With TV revenue also rising, clubs were suddenly richer than ever before and could compete with the Italian and Spanish leagues for the best, most exciting players, raising standards, increasing demand, feeding the whale. The smaller clubs struggled to compete, while others spent rashly to keep up with the giants, now led by Manchester United, a commercial juggernaut masquerading as a football club.

The football-going experience was much changed, as ticket prices forced out young and poorer supporters, diluting the atmosphere and deadening the camaraderie. In 1972, Chris

The changing face of football: the Emirates Stadium opened in 2006 and has a capacity of more than 60,000.

Lightbown had said that Chelsea's Shed 'sounded like London's answer to the Kop', but by 2002, Stamford Bridge was more regularly likened to the nearby cemetery. Under Bates, Chelsea charged the highest prices in the country, and the new money paid for superstars such as Gianfranco Zola, Ruud Gullit and Marcel Desailly, who brought unexpected success to the club, who suddenly found themselves fashionable once more.

Arsenal were also in the ascendancy, French manager Arsene Wenger transforming the culture of the club by embracing a cosmopolitan recruiting policy and producing teams of mesmerising beauty, allowing Arsenal, who had attracted barely 18,000 for a game at the start of the '90s, to build a stadium for 60,000 a decade later. The smaller London clubs fared less well. QPR were runners-up in the First Division in 1976, Watford came second in 1983 and Crystal Palace third in 1991, but those days were over, as the behemoths of English football flexed their financial muscle.

Wimbledon suffered most of all when the Football League shamefully allowed their owners to move the club wholesale to Milton Keynes. Wimbledon supporters, outraged and emboldened, promptly formed their own club, AFC Wimbledon, with a policy of fan ownership and an adherence to what were seen as pre-Premier League principles.

Modern football's alternative model to AFC Wimbledon began just across the river. Fulham had started the trend of rich benefactors bankrolling astonishing success when Harrods owner Mohamed Al Fayed bought Fourth Division Fulham in 1997 and had them in the Premier League by 2001. The ante was upped by neighbours Chelsea in 2003, when Russian oligarch Roman Abramovich pounced on a club that had overspent on their way to become one of the success stories of the Premier League and were in dire need of financing. Over five years, Abramovich, said to be worth £11.7bn, invested £500m on players, wages and facilities, and Chelsea suddenly joined the European elite, although the road was rarely less than bumpy. If Peter Ball's 'kids' were alienated from players in 1974, they are living on a different planet in 2008, as ticket prices nudge £50, the amount some players earn in five minutes.

Few think that such levels of expenditure are healthy, and many question whether it is sustainable, as football threatens to become the game that ate itself. Football has faced bigger crises over the past four decades and survived, but the time might soon come when supporters have to decide whether they want the future of their sport, let alone their clubs, to take the form of AFC Wimbledon or FC Chelski.

Peter Watts is *Time Out's* staff writer, and a lifelong Chelsea fan.

TIMELINE

1968
Arsenal, Chelsea, Fulham, Tottenham Hotspur and West Ham United all compete in England's top football division. Four decades later, the same five clubs are again London's teams in the Premier League.

1974
Twenty-five-year-old Australian Michael O'Brien becomes the first known streaker at a major sporting event, when he runs naked on to the pitch at an England-France rugby international at Twickenham.

1979
Debbie Moore opens Pineapple Dance Studios in a former pineapple warehouse in Covent Garden.

1980
Wandsworth boy Frank Bruno becomes the youngest ever ABA Heavyweight Champion, aged just 18, and launches his professional career with 21 consecutive wins by knockout.

Bjorn Borg wins the men's singles title at Wimbledon for the fifth year in a row. He loses the 1981 final to John McEnroe.

1981
The first London Marathon is held. Decades of ridiculous outfits follow.

1982
Jane Fonda's Workout Book and the original *Jane Fonda Workout* video are released as aerobics grapevines into London.

1988
Wimbledon FC surprise the football world and win the FA Cup by defeating the favourites, Liverpool.

1993
Lennox Lewis becomes WBC Heavyweight Champion of the World. The 6ft 5in boxer, born in West Ham, beat Mike Tyson and Evander Holyfield in a hugely successful career.

1995
Frank Bruno wins the WBC Heavyweight title by beating Oliver McCall at Wembley Stadium.

1996
England host the UEFA European Football Championships. Catchy anthem 'Three Lions' reaches number one in the charts.

1998
Arsenal win the Premier League and the FA Cup. Arsene Wenger is the first foreign manager to achieve the domestic double.

2001
Plenty of old buffers spill their G&Ts when the futuristic, pod-like Media Centre, designed by Future Systems, changes the look of Lord's cricket ground.

2003
Russian billionaire Roman Abramovich buys Chelsea FC and then sets about buying them an entirely new team.

2004
Cambridge and Oxford compete for the 150th annual Varsity Boat Race on the Thames. Cambridge wins.

2005
London wins the bid to host the 2012 Olympic Games. And England defeat Australia 2-1 over five Tests – clinching the series at the Oval – to win the Ashes for the first time in 16 years.

2007
The All England Lawn Tennis Club announces that for the first time male and female competitors at Wimbledon will receive equal winnings.

Arsenal's new Emirates Stadium opens. The old Highbury ground is sold, to be converted into luxury flats.

The new Wembley Stadium, designed by architects HOK Sport and Foster and Partners, opens late and over-budget. The 436ft high steel arch over the stadium can be seen across London.

2008
Paul Gascoigne, former golden boy of English football and Spurs hero, is sectioned.

Walthamstow Stadium, which has been hosting greyound racing since 1933, announces it is to close.

SPORT & FITNESS

Football gangs

SPORT & FITNESS

To get an idea of the North-Bank West Ham, visualise Alf Garnett, and multiply by 5,000. They are, by turn, witty, courageous, cowardly, bigoted, loyal, friendly, insular, open, honest and prejudiced. What other End would sing: 'We shall not be moved' as '… just like the team that is going to win fuck-all, we shall not be moved?' It happened at West Ham two years ago. What other End would take 4,000 to Stoke for a League game, fight for the End, split for the pub before half-time, and jog back home and south like honky kings, having heard that they had lost the match 2-1? West Ham, August 1968.

Which is to say that there is a lot more colour on the North Bank at Upton Park than just the claret and blue scarves of the supporters. The North Bank has shown fantastic loyalty to a team that, at the beginning of the decade, was promising to emerge as one of the teams of its time, but which went on to achieve practically nothing. One thing that is keeping them there is the nature of some of the players on the field; it is said that when West Ham were fighting Coventry at Coventry station last year, Billy Bonds and the inevitable Harry Rednapp came along to lend a hand.

The other thing that is keeping them there, of course, is the family-type loyalty that has always surrounded West Ham. As the character of the East End is muffled in high-rise flats, loyalty to West Ham is one of the few ways that the East End culture can live on. (This attachment even holds for the 'overspill' towns made up of Londoners. West Ham supporters shunted out to the new towns keep making the long journey back to London; other teams' supporters gradually fade away or lose interest.)

The family aspect extends as far as the leadership of the North Bank; West Ham is anarchic. It has to be, as it has always been made of set gangs, which would accept no overall leader. Hence the lack of a Johnny High or Eccles. And hence the massive turnouts at local derbys, particularly with Arsenal, when, although the team had been going through a bad patch, the gangs have been able to call on massive reserves that are usually uninterested in the football. (The seven lorry-loads of Barking/Ilford gangs that turned up at Highbury in April 1969 are a classic example.)

But with the power of the gangs fading in the past two years, and with several gangs pulling out en masse, a rough sort of leadership has come to be accepted on the Bank. Even so, a family assumed the mantle of leadership, rather than any individual Cooper (Barking). Even little Mel Cooper, 15, has a squad of 15-year-old bodyguards. Ilford's Johnny Williams and the notorious Rollo, of fuck-in-the-stands fame, are accepted as leaders, but carry little territorial clout. (NB: The family ethos does not stop there; Rednapp, Taylor and Ayris are all know to have cousins on the North Bank.)

The North Bank really started in 1966 – late for a London club. One might say that the post-Mod influx of violence into football in the other clubs

'The club was forced to ban banners in 1967 as they were being used almost solely for weapons.'

took until then to match the built-in hardness of the East End. But once the fashion reached West Ham, it was adopted with no holds barred, and the club was forced to ban banners in 1967 when they were being used almost solely for weapons. This was the year of the North Bank's baptism of fire; the final match of the season when the visitors were the Championship winners Manchester United, whose Stretford End rained bottles on the North Bank almost at will. Starting from here, the gangs, and in particular Barking and Whitechapel, made a concerted effort to keep the North Bank free. And

Police grapple with fans at Upton Park as Manchester United visit West Ham.

apart from a shock taking by Chelsea in 1968, they have, by and large, been successful. Until the present day, when the form of the team is starting to reach new heights of eccentricity, which must affect even the most loyal of supporter. And everyone is concerned with the event, which is at the back of the minds of all London football underground: 1972 – Millwall down the road, and south of the water from West Ham – coming into the First Division.

Original feature by Chris Lightbown.

The role of the guvnor

Ever since Herbert Chapman led Arsenal to two league titles in the 1930s, London's football clubs have preferred to have vivid personalities rather than dour technocrats at the helm. Here are some examples.

Jose Mourinho has a great handshake. Believe me, it's only when you're on the receiving end that you really appreciate just how powerful a weapon it is. The secret, like most of the 42-year-old's finely honed man-management techniques, is all in the detail.

Here's how it works. As we're being introduced, Mourinho leans back, closes one eye and squints, as if sizing me up. A mock scowl registers on his face, but just as I'm beginning to smell trouble, it instantly dissolves into a smirk that suggests I've more than met with his approval. At the same time, his hand sweeps down from a height somewhere near his right shoulder and, while he maintains eye contact, grasps mine firmly and swings it matily from right to left. The grip is only released when he slowly confirms my name as if welcoming me into his secret brotherhood. It's warm, endearing and effortlessly disarming.

Those who have met Bill Clinton talk of his knack of making them feel that they're the most important person in the world. Mourinho's the same. I may have been wrong, but despite his more pressing Premiership engagements, I got the distinct impression that there was nowhere else the world's most sought-after manager would rather have been than sitting with a heavily perspiring QPR fan, armed only with a dictaphone and six long years of hardened, bitter envy.

Do you feel like a true Londoner yet, or still like a visitor? It's incredible. In just one year, everything in London has become so familiar to me. That and the fact that my family and I were received with such open arms means I've always felt like a Londoner from day one.

Has John Terry taught you any cockney rhyming slang? Yes I've started to understand a little bit. Like apples and pears, yes?

What are your favourite London locations? I like Hyde Park very much. The kids love it there, and we don't get bothered. So the kids ride their bikes and we feed the ducks.

Have you visited the thriving Portuguese community in Stockwell? I've been once or twice for shopping. The supermarkets are

SPORT & FITNESS

Wembley Stadium

Until their demolition in 2003, the 126-foot high Wembley twin towers had been seen as beacons by legions of football fans starting their walk up Wembley Way. The stadium was constructed in 300 days for £750,000 by architects Sir John Simpson and Maxwell Ayerton, and the engineer Sir Owen Williams. Built to host the British Empire Exhibition in 1924, Wembley Stadium was first known as the Empire Stadium and intended to be knocked down immediately after the exhibition. Instead, it remained and was regularly updated and improved, with floodlights added in 1955, and the electronic scoreboard and all-encircling roof in 1963, at a cost of £500,000.

Bolton Wanderers and West Ham United contested the 1923 FA Cup final, the first football match to be played at Wembley. The FA did not allocate tickets for the game, so an estimated 200,000 people crammed into the stadium, making it the highest attendance ever recorded at the ground. The match has since become known as the 'White Horse Final', after mounted police, including PC George Scorey and his white horse Billie, had to push spectators back from the pitch and into the stands to enable the match to begin.

Things have gone more smoothly since. Wembley highlights include England's first and only World Cup victory in 1966, as they defeated West Germany; Manchester United (including the Busby Babes) beating Benfica 4-0 in the European Cup final; and England stuffing Holland 4-0 at Euro 1996. Dietmar Hamann scored the last ever goal at the old Wembley Stadium, when arch-rivals Germany beat England 1-0 in a World Cup qualifier. Wembley has also hosted the 1948 Olympics, greyhound racing, motorcycle speedway, numerous music concerts and Evel Knievel's failed but spectacular attempt to jump over 13 buses on a motorbike.

But the stadium clearly didn't have the capacity or the facilities the events demanded. In 1999, Tony Banks, then Sports Minister, denounced Wembley Stadium as a 'disgrace', and dismissed the ferrous-concrete towers as 'just a couple of add-ons'. The new Wembley, which opened in March 2007, has a capacity of 90,000, and was designed by Foster and Partners with HOK Sport. Costing £798m, it took more than six years to complete, and finished more than a year and a half behind schedule. The 436-foot high arch that supports the roof is more than three times the height of the original towers, and on a clear day can be seen from 13 miles away in Canary Wharf. *John Sunyer*

Jose Mourinho managed Chelsea from 2004 to 2007, winning the Premier League twice, the League Cup twice and the FA Cup once.

good and we can get things from Portugal there that the kids really like.

Have you tried English wine? No!

What about English beer? No, I don't drink any beer. I've only been to a pub once and that was to get cigarettes for my wife at 11.30 in the evening. I prefer bars for sitting and drinking tea or coffee. Oriel in Sloane Square is the closest I come to a pub.

How do you get on with Chelsea chairman Roman Abramovich? We get on well and we understand each other very well. He loves his friends, his family and his football, and I'm here to make his dreams come true on the pitch. He invited me for a week's holiday on his yacht, touring around the South of France and Sardinia.

Who's the greatest player you've ever seen? Ronaldo in 1996. I saw Maradona, Eusebio, Zidane and Gullit, but I never saw anyone to rival Ronaldo in 1996. Every day I worked with him I was constantly amazed at the things he could do, like scoring goals by beating five opponents on a 50-metre run. I've still never seen anything like it.

Will you encourage your son to become a professional footballer? No. It will be entirely up to him. He loves football, he plays well and has a great left foot. For his age, he's fantastic, but I never play football with him or take him into the garden for a kickabout. I go home and ask, 'What do you want to do?' Every time his answer is either skating or tennis. So of, course, that's what we have to do.

Finally, you speak several languages and have an enviable record of success. Is there anything you're useless at? Things at home [mimes hammering a nail]. DIY. I am a disgrace at that. I cannot mend a tap, I cannot even change a lightbulb. I am hopeless. A zero. A disgrace! My wife does it all, and when she can't, she has the number of a man who can.

Interview by Graham Wray.

SPORT & FITNESS

The fans of Watford have faith in their chairman, Elton John, and Graham Taylor, the manager he appointed in June, 1977. For these two have wrought a miracle, transforming a down-at-heel Fourth Division outfit into a well-run First Division operation at a time when the sport is contracting, reeling from years of profligate spending and bad financial management.

Taylor was phlegmatic about the team's fortunes – or lack of them. 'The ball hits the post, it goes in, we win, so I'm a good manager. The ball hits the same post, it stays out, so I'm a bad manager. Let's just get the whole thing in perspective. If we've managed to lose properly, with some dignity, this little run we've had may be one of the best things yet for us. We'll cope with our next period of winning far better way than we might've done.'

This is typical of Taylor's very 'moral' attitude, formed as much by his days at Scunthorpe Grammar as by the hard realities of a relatively undistinguished playing career. Unfashionable qualities like honesty and loyalty are often to the fore in his conversation.

Fans, he thinks, miss off-the-field standards reflected in the simple differences he found managing Watford in the Second and then First Division. No longer, he says, does the player drink in his local. He goes to nightclubs. The fan stays in the pub with his pint. And as for the proliferating formations of the modern game: 'I mean, the fact that someone's spent 30 years on the terraces, he must know something about the game! In the main, he's not daft… And he's got to be entertained. *Of course* he doesn't understand the modern game, 'cos a lot of us don't bloody well understand it. We've lost our way.'

'I think we can grace the occasion,' says Queens Park Rangers manager Terry Venables of Saturday's FA Cup Final. 'I hope we do.' If so, then Venables's team will have done him a favour. For, incredible as it would have seemed two and a half years ago, Venables's image as the shining light of English football has come in for suspicion.

Thirty months ago, Crystal Palace were challenging at the top of Division One in their first season back in the top flight, and their shrewd, bubbling young manager was pointing the way forward for English football. If you did the right things, worked on developing young players' technique and added your own sharp tactical brain into the mix, there was no reason why English teams couldn't play like the Continent's finest.

Of course, the team could not sustain the form, and by the end of the season had slipped back to 13th. But it was still a testimony to Venables's genuine talents as a coach that he had taken an ordinary team so far. But the following season, things changed. The side started badly. Venables later resigned and joined QPR.

Venables is readily roused by slurs on London football, and particularly on the character of London footballers. QPR's and Spurs' presence in this year's cup final, the second time in three years that two London clubs have contested the final, has provided him with ammunition, and he has used it with relish. 'Well, if you're attacked, you've got to have a go back,' he says characteristically.

Very characteristically, in fact, for, as a fellow London manager remarked: 'What you've got to understand about Terry is that he likes to think he's very sophisticated, but deep down there's a good old East London backstreet scrapper.' Less brash

> 'Venables is readily roused by slurs on London football, and particularly on the character of London footballers.'

and much more modest than his image sometimes suggests, he has a great talent for putting across strong criticisms without upsetting people or provoking big headlines. He is a man of substance in all respects. His idealism about the game, his belief in skill, his belief that English football has to be open to new ideas and new approaches, is undoubtedly genuine, and his teams bear it out.

Nevertheless there are doubters. As one solid pro of impeccable judgement put it: 'Terry? Well, all that Crystal Palace and QPR thing, it's not to my taste. It's a bit flash, a bit spivvy. I don't think, in the end, people like that come out on top.'

Interview by Geoff Brown.

Interview by Peter Ball.

London Marathon

The organisers claim the London Marathon is the world's biggest annual fundraising event, with an impressive £315m raised for charity since its inception as an annual event in 1981. That year, the men's race ended in a dead heat when Dick Beardsley and Inge Simonsen famously held hands as they crossed the line in two hours, 11 minutes and 48 seconds.

The first London Marathon actually took place in 1908, when the city first hosted the Olympic Games. Thousands congregated on the capital's pavements to share the fascination of watching humans push themselves to complete exhaustion. On this occasion, Italian runner Dorando Pietri won, helped back to his feet after collapsing five times on his way to victory. After being disqualified for receiving assistance during the race, Pietri said: 'I am not the marathon winner. Instead, as the English say, I am the one who won and lost victory.'

Since 1981, more than 700,000 people have completed the 26-mile race around London's streets, with the number of applicants always exceeding the number of places. In 1981, there were 20,000 applicants and 6,255 participants; in 2008 the event attracted 80,500 applicants, with 34,497 finishing the race.

The marathon course stretches from Greenwich Park to the Mall, via Woolwich and the Isle of Dogs, past famous landmarks such as the Tower of London, Buckingham Palace and Big Ben.

Kenya's Martin Lel has won the men's race three times (2005, 2007 and 2008) and holds the course record of two hours, five minutes and 15 seconds. The UK's Paula Radcliffe holds the woman's course record, clocking two hours, 15 minutes and 25 seconds in 2003.

Among the illustrious list of participants are the group of fun-runners known as the 'Ever Presents', who have completed each race since 1981. Although no match for professional runners, Buster Martin is the London Marathon's oldest competitor at 101 years old, completing the race in approximately ten hours.

SPORT & FITNESS

Show dem we culture!

In *Beyond a Boundary*, his imperishable study of the game in the Caribbean, CLR James wrote that cricket 'is fundamentally unthinkable outside of the context of British colonial rule.' The cricket field is a 'stage on which selected individuals play representative roles… charged with social significance.' Rarely can the truth of this analysis have been more vividly demonstrated than at the Oval over five sweltering days in August 1976.

Shortly before that summer's Test series against the West Indies began, England's South African-born captain Tony Greig had given an interview to the BBC. Clive Lloyd's touring side, he reckoned, weren't all they were cracked up to be: 'These guys, if they get on top, they are magnificent cricketers, but if they're down, they grovel, and I intend… to make them grovel.' He would soon have cause to regret this provocation.

West Indian anger at Greig's crassly inflammatory remarks was sublimated in the destructive brilliance of Vivian Richards' batting and the unrelenting ferocity of a fast-bowling triumvirate led by the 22-year-old Jamaican Michael Holding. By the time they arrived at the Oval, the West Indies led 2-0, the ageing yeomen of the English middle-order having taken a fearful short-pitched pummelling at

Positive vibrations: a fan celebrates yet another wicket down for the West Indians at the Oval Test match in 1976.

Old Trafford and England's bowlers having been flayed to all parts at Headingley.

Each of the previous Tests had attracted large numbers of West Indian spectators. But at the Oval, just up the road from Brixton, the crowds were bigger than ever. The bank of seats in front of the Archbishop Tenison's School was transformed into a corner of the Caribbean for the duration of the game. West Indian bowlers approached the crease accompanied by a din of rattling cans and empty bottles, and the fall of each English wicket was greeted with a delirious pitch invasion – none more delirious than that which followed Holding's dismissal of Greig for one run in the second innings. Holding finished the match with 14 wickets, a remarkable performance overshadowed by Richards' magisterial 291 in the first innings.

Indeed, it was the glowering, immaculate Richards who most completely embodied the spirit of self-assertion which that Test series had awakened in West Indians in Britain. According to the black activist Darcus Howe, West Indian cricket had never had 'such an intense social reflection. We felt stronger.' Two weeks later, black youths tested their strength at the Notting Hill Carnival, which ended with the police being forced to flee down Portobello Road under a hail of missiles.

A night at the dogs

Greyhound racing is just next door. The dogs are running every night in London, usually in vast and almost deserted stadia like Wembley and White City; performing only to a minute band of greyhound fixers (about 6,000 for an average night at Wembley), the men who just can't stay away. The dogs have all but had it as a pastime for the masses.

It's a real shame. The discovery that the dogs are exciting and beautiful to watch, and that a meeting is a funny and thrilling occasion, may have come too late for the jaded spirit that seeks it out. Which is not to say that greyhound racing ought to be saved merely because it is surely going to vanish – but simply that we ought to know what we are missing, and about to lose.

We went as strangers to Hendon Stadium (on the North Circular) for an afternoon meeting, fearful of being rooked. About 200 men are queuing outside the gates waiting to go in. A man is selling the *Sporting Life*, the ever extending daily Talmud of the leisured gents. The paper costs five pence. You offer the man a pound and he sizes you up in the second that it takes him to get the greenie out of your hand. 'Look,' he says, 'I can see you boys haven't got much to lose. So you don't want to lose. Right? Right. Now look here.' He opens the racing card and stabs his finger on the page at a dog's name. 'In the first race, that one'll home ahead and,' another stab, 'That one'll follow him home. All right? Right. So now you've paid for your day and you're in no hurry. Take a rest. Have a drink. Don't bother about the second and third races. They're a load of rubbish. Now, in the fourth. Look,' he stopped suddenly, glanced conspiratorially around him and fished in his pocket to draw out a plain brown envelope with a note inside. On the note were the written names of two dogs, 'I can see you're all right. Don't spread this around. But those two are certainties for the fourth and fifth. Okay?'

'Right,' he said, 'that's a bob for your paper and, well, I don't want to take your money, let's say two bob each for you and your mate for the information. Don't thank me now. Thank me after racing and have a nice time.' The word 'sucker' silently formed in the word bubble over his head.

Down to the track side. Six furtive dogs were being paraded by six scruffy handlers. All eyes were on the bookies' boards and on the constantly changing odds. The odds move at a tremendous rate, all changes reflecting the amounts of money wagered on each dog. The favourite is always the dog that has had the most money laid on it. The worst dog in the race would be favourite if all the mugs in London gathered to put their money on it. In this case, only

one mug had chosen to throw away his money. I sat and watched the odds lengthening against my dog. 'If they reach 100/1 I stand to win £5 when it crosses that line,' I thought, as the dogs were stuffed into the metal box of traps at the start of the track.

The six flaps of the traps flew open. Five dogs rocketed out at tremendous speed and set off in hot pursuit of the hare. A sixth greyhound lumbered from its trap and began to clip-clop a lazy gait around the track. The whole race was over in less than 30 seconds, the lead dogs craning and straining their flashing way across the line in a tight, blurring pack. The pack were going so fast that they burst through the arms of their handlers who were waiting to catch them on the bend after

the finish. The sixth dog, my dog, my four bob's worth, took one look at the handlers, wagged its tail, yawned and sat down.

The afternoon went on in this manner. For the fourth race I smiled grimly at the idea of putting any money on the dog that the newspaper salesman had suggested. It won by a street.

To my left was the archetypal racing man. A crisp navy blue blazer, light blue shirt and lighter blue trousers. A manicure, tightly cut black hair, king-size fags and a bundle of notes in his jacket pocket that must have made £150 in tenners alone. Somebody knew how to play this game for sure. I was leaving the stadium about 30 bob down, morose and humiliated.

Original report by Neil Lyndon. In 1971, London had 30 greyhound stadiums, with Catford, Clapton, Hackney, Harringay, Stamford Bridge, Walthamstow, Wembley, West Ham and White City among the more famous. Only Wimbledon and out-of-town Crayford and Romford remain.

SPORT & FITNESS

The last prizefighter

Roy 'Pretty Boy' Shaw spends every Sunday lunch at the Seven Kings, a rambling, two-storey pub out along the Romford Road. The Kings is a boxing pub, and in its main bar stands a full-size boxing ring where the young knights of Ilford and Romford and Chadwell Heath can, after a few midday pints, strip to the waist, pull on a pair of gloves and cover each other with blood and vomit before returning home to *Match of the Day*.

There are other attractions: a comedian with a seamless stream of black and blue jokes (this is white man's country out here); and a stripper who lies on her back on the canvas between bouts and opens her legs in 4/4 time at the surrounding tables. But like the roasts upstairs in the Carvery guttering on their serving trays, Sunday lunch at the Kings is about muscle and blood.

Roy Shaw sits with his manager, Joe Carrington, at the best table in the house, surrounded by Joe's 'prospects': hard young men from Essex and the East End with muscular necks and huge hands. Although at 5ft 9in he is one of the smallest there, Shaw makes them all look like children. It is not just the generation gap, although there is a world of difference between a face that has spent ten years behind bars and one that is fresh out of a comprehensive.

Throughout the afternoon his table draws a constant trickle of visitors: friends, acquaintances, up-and-comers all squeeze their way through the furniture to shake his hand, punch his bicep, wish him well. From the stage the comedian refers constantly to him, his manager and his impending bout. Behind his seat a knot of older regulars congregates. In the Kings at Sunday lunch, Roy Shaw is obviously the guvnor.

Unhappily, this particular Sunday he is little impressed by the performance. 'You call these tough fights?' he snorts, as the last young hopeful throws in the towel. Today's fighters have it too easy, he says, fighting if they want to, not fighting if they don't. 'My own boy, I took him to an amateur club and I saw him spar, and there was so much natural ability, but, shame for me, he's not interested. Took him down the club, paid his membership, but you can't force him to like it. He wanted to do that soppy kung-fu stuff. Now he's just messin' about. Skinhead,' he laughs.

'Before, fighters had to fight to get the money to support theirselves and their families, and it pulled that little bit extra out of 'em'.

So was that how he got to be London's Number One (as it says on the flyposter), by boxing his way up off the breadline?

'Me? Nah. I was an amateur. I got money in from robbin' banks.'

Roy Shaw was born in Stepney in 1936. In those days, Stepney kids either fought or went to the wall, and Shaw was fighting almost as soon as he was walking. 'Me dad taught me. He was a good fighter – not a champion, a tough 'un, a hard man – and he taught me.'

He immediately developed a taste for the sport. By the age of ten – the year his father was killed in a motorcycle crash – he was a member of the amateur club Stepney St Georges.

'I lived boxing. I never went out with birds or nothing. All I done was box and train, day and night. Me mum'd put on the television and I'd be upstairs doin' sit-ups or shadow boxing. I loved it. I fought me way through the Schoolboys, got to the finals of the ABAs, got to the finals of the ABC of Great Britain. I had a good amateur career.'

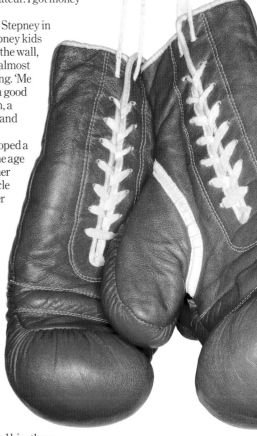

His first robbery earned him three years in a Borstal in Wales, but he soon escaped. 'We just bashed up the Borstal doctor and nicked his car, I'm afraid. I was a naughty boy.' After that he travelled across the country with the fairground boxing booths before deciding to turn pro under the name Roy West.

'I was a pretty good prospect,' recalls Shaw with pride. 'Mickey Duff, now the country's top promoter and the godfather of licensed British boxing, thought I was the dog's dinner. He reckoned I was another little Marciano.'

Shaw had ten fights as a professional – ten fights, ten wins and six KOs. And he was still in his early 20s. 'Things were going quite good,' he recalls. 'There wasn't a lot of middleweights around at that particular time, so I think I would've done well. But then I got captured. I had a fight in a dance hall – Tiffany's in Ilford – on Christmas Eve and they nicked me from the time I escaped from Borstal. They give me three years and that was that.'

The arrest stopped Shaw's boxing career cold. On his release he was judged persona non grata by the Boxing Board of Control, and refused a licence. 'So then I went right off the rails – thieving and robbin' banks and bank vans.' His biggest haul was £90,000 from a bank robbery van in Kent. It was also his last. Someone grassed ('Put his name in the paper, Roy,' urges Joe Carrington) and three weeks later he was arrested.

He and two other defendants each got 15 years. 'Nowadays,' reflects Shaw, '15 years is accepted pretty much as a normal sentence, but we was the first to start gettin' the big ones. It shook you up a bit hearin' 15 years, but I was only young, and I ain't bein' big-headed, but it didn't bother me too much. You shut off your outside contacts and that is your life, inside.'

The last major bare-knuckle bout fought on English soil took place at Farnborough in 1860, when Tom Sayers and the American champion John Camel Heenan battered each other into oblivion in two hours and 20 minutes. Seven years later, a Cambridge undergraduate drew up a boxing code under the patronage of the eighth Marquis of Queensbury, and the bare-knuckling era ended. Less than two years after his release from prison, Shaw picked up where Sayers and Heenan had left off.

'I was runnin' a bit short of cash, and they said, "You're pretty fit, why don't you go over and have a fight with some of the gypsies?" The pikeys have their meetin's every year and bet money on each other – you know, "I'll have five grand my son can beat your son" type of thing – and you can go down there and challenge any of 'em and earn yourself a few bob.' At that time, the acknowledged king of the gypsies was a barrel-chested ex-con named Donny 'the Bull' Adams, and he accepted Shaw's challenge. 'It was like a prestige thing,' remembers Shaw. 'He was the Daddy in the nicks and the Daddy of all the gypsies, and I thought I was the Daddy of the nicks. It was a personality clash sort of thing.'

Shaw flattened Adams within 30 seconds, the crowd – 'More familiar to viewers of *Police 5* than *Grandstand*', as one writer tactfully put it – invaded the ring for a rapturous all-in brawl, and 'bootleg boxing' was born.

Overnight, Shaw was elevated to the role of an East End Billy the Kid, picking off challengers like a gunslinger: Terry Hollingsworth (first round), Lenny McLean, so big they couldn't find a pair of gloves to fit him (fourth round), an Irish champion whose name no one can remember (third round). He became an East End celebrity: 'I got people comin' up for autographs and people along the street, you could see 'em pointin'.' And his stock as a club bouncer soared: 'I was lookin' after trouble houses and not gettin' no trouble.'

Gene Hackman, the actor, was so impressed by his performance against Lenny McLean that he helped arrange a fight between Shaw and an American pro named Ron 'the Butcher' Stander. 'Who's this Roy Shaw, anyway?' Stander kept asking between drinks. He found out when a blow that landed somewhere between his kneecap and his navel folded him up before the end of the first.

Tonight there's the weighty matter of Lew 'Wild Thing' Yates to be settled. At 18 stone in his socks, and with a face covered in shaggy black beard, Yates, 'Liverpool's Hard Man', resembles no one so much as Bluto, the bully from the Popeye strip. Also a bouncer, he's been waiting five years for his shot at Shaw, and he radiates confidence. In 50 amateur fights he's never been stopped.

The fight is in what used to be Tiffany's at Ilford, the same Tiffany's where Shaw was arrested on the dancefloor two decades ago. All 1,100 seats in the place have been booked for weeks; the manager reckons he could have sold the place twice over.

Lew Yates is first into the ring in a blue silk dressing gown. He is the perfect villain: vast belly covering the Everlast buckle on his trunks; his pale back mottled with boils and pimples. Shaw follows, to the sound of Gary Glitter's 'Come On, Come On' and the roar of the faithful. He is wearing a white towelling dressing gown with 'Mean Machine' stencilled on the back. Beside Yates he looks a dwarf. Both avoid each other's eyes.

There is an awful fascination about a Roy Shaw fight – the same fascination that makes people slow down to look at motorway wrecks. As soon as the bell sounds, he is on Yates like a bulldog, hammering him on to his knees within 30 seconds. Stunned, Yates takes the count, and then manages to hold on to the end, just.

'Was that how he got to be London's Number One, by boxing his way up off the breadline?' "Me? Nah. I got money in from robbin' banks."'

In the second round, he catches Shaw with several huge shots to the head. Then he changes tack and tries to crush him against the ropes. In the third, Shaw goes for the eyes and Yate's face comes apart. The lasting image is of Yates slumped on one knee against the bottom rope, his face covered in blood, one red Gorgon's eye staring balefully out at the roaring crowd. He does not come out for the fourth.

Original report by Don Ateyo.

Let's get physical

From the Lycra and legwarmers of the '80s…

By Andrew Shields

Keeping your balance: on skates in the '80s, and, above right, on the mats in the '90s.

SPORT & FITNESS

In October 1981, Olivia Newton-John's 'Physical' hit the top ten. The accompanying video caused a sensation, with its clutch of flabby blokes transformed into muscular hunks while Olivia strutted about a fitness club in slinky leotard and headband. The following year, *Jane Fonda's Workout Book* and the original *Jane Fonda's Workout* video were released in Britain, and the phenomenon known as aerobics grapevined its way across the Atlantic. Fonda didn't invent the word 'aerobics' (that was Kenneth Cooper, an American doctor who advocated a move away from disease treatment to disease prevention through aerobic exercise). However, she was the inspiration behind classes springing up at the Fitness Centre in Covent Garden, Seymour Hall near Marble Arch, Central YMCA off Tottenham Court Road, and stalwart dance venues such as Dance Attic in Fulham, Danceworks off Bond Street, and Covent Garden's Pineapple Studios. The combination of beat-heavy music and repetitive, high-impact moves – choreography back then was minimal – was an instant hit.

Soon, aerobics instructors such as Bridget Woods at the Fitness Centre, Dawn Jamieson at Seymour Hall and Jamie 'Fat Busters' Addicoat had attained guru-like status, their classes packed with sweat-stained adherents. The message they proclaimed to out-of-condition Londoners was one of empowerment: you didn't have to be 'sporty' to join in. Anyone, no matter what their age, shape or level of fitness, was welcome. Lycra and legwarmers were de rigueur.

By far the most controversial (and later discredited) aspect of Fonda's book was 'the burn'. She, and many of those motivated by her, pressed on through pain in the belief that it was the only way to leap across the threshold of fitness. In fact, it proved merely to be a hobble into the doctor's surgery, as joints were wrenched, and tendons and ligaments torn by grindingly tough routines that had yet to benefit from the application of exercise science. After all, most teachers were making it up as they went along.

In September 1983, a sports scientist went undercover to sample 30 classes around the capital. His verdict was damning: 'Given the generally low level of expertise shown by many self-styled aerobics instructors, I can confidently predict that, at best, many of those sweating and straining in their bright leotards are gaining no benefit at all, while at worst many face the prospect of immediate, or long-term, injuries.' It was to be another three years before the first book on the subject, *The YMCA Guide to Exercise to Music*, was published. Central YMCA became the focus for research into safe and effective teaching, and launched a formal qualification in 1987.

The aerobics boom saw 'Mad Lizzie' Webb, the Green Goddess and Mr Motivator carve high-profile TV careers as the knee lift repeater, spotty dog and box step entered the lexicon. Though the routines of that era now seem dated and sometimes positively dangerous, it would be wrong to forget the spirit in which they were conceived. 'Like me,' wrote Fonda, 'you may never have thought of yourself as an athletic sort of person. You were an observer. Sitting it out. I don't want to be a bystander any more. I want to participate, not necessarily to achieve excellence, but just to have fun.' The fitness industry has moved on, but that sentiment is no less valid.

...to the tree posture of the '90s and beyond.

London's fitness boom of the late 1980s was Thatcherite Britain in microcosm: aggressive, pumping and look-at-me. Nowhere typified this image more than the Barbican Health & Fitness Club, where many of the City's loadsamoneys worked out. Clad in vivid red, chrome and neon, with Reuters screens flashing the latest share prices, this disco with treadmills was run by an American former bodybuilder with an intense stare and a vice-like handshake. Here, the quality of a workout was subsumed by quantity. How many classes! How many repetitions!! How much poundage on that goddam bar!!! If you slackened, one machine even had a sergeant major voice on a tape loop to kick your lazy butt back into action.

The mindlessly mechanical approach encouraged by many such clubs of that era brought plenty of bad press. Type 'A' personalities refusing to take rest days and hobbling to the gym when injured spawned the phenomenon of 'exercise addiction'. A reaction was inevitable.

It suddenly seemed self-defeating to spend 40 minutes pounding the treadmill in a sweaty bunker when fresh air and sunshine were but a stride away. The clubs themselves were compelled to rethink their strategy: it was no longer acceptable to provide a weights room and an unvarying schedule of high-impact aerobics classes, and demand a four-figure sum for the privilege of (usually corporate) membership. The 1990s brought a spate of closures as London's fitness industry contracted and professionalised.

It's now difficult to find a club that does not feature yoga or Pilates on its programme. Yet only 20 years ago these were still esoteric pursuits, known only to a small band of initiates and undiscovered by the media. The 1989 edition of *Time Out's Sport, Health & Fitness in London* guide listed a mere nine yoga centres. Of these, the venerable Iyengar Institute is still operating in Maida Vale, and Notting Hill's Sivananda Centre, set up by Swami Vishnu-Devananda, has moved to Putney but still functions as an ashram for yogis seeking an authentic spiritual vibe.

Pilates? The 1989 guide mentioned just six teachers, including Alan Herdman, who brought the technique to London, and ex-Rambert dancer Dreas Reyneke, whose Notting Hill studio attracted its share of low-key celebrities long before stars such as Hugh Grant and Madonna started shouting about their 'girdle of strength'.

Inside two decades, both disciplines have become part of the exercise mainstream – guided by the shrewd business brains behind some of Europe's most innovative venues. In 2000, Triyoga opened in Primrose Hill, replacing yoga's mung-bean reputation with a sleek, glamorous image tailored to the Gwyneths and Sadies living nearby. Among its founders were lawyer Jonathan Sattin and Tina Gaudoin, one-time deputy editor of *Tatler* and senior writer at American *Vogue*. The Life Centre in Notting Hill has also been instrumental in turning yoga from hippy to hip, thanks to the acumen of bankers Elizabeth Stanley and Christine Letter.

A betrayal by those who once trekked to India to sit at the feet of their guru? Yoga and Pilates may have their share of Uggs-wearing bandwagon-jumpers – anyone for a DVD fronted by Geri Halliwell or Linda Barker? – yet the London gym scene is infinitely richer for their popularity. We have finally begun to learn that true fitness has little to do with press-ups and circuit training, but more with harmony between body, mind and spirit.

Andrew Shields has been Sports Editor of *Time Out* since 1990.

Skateboarding

A writer friend of mine was once approached by a bloke in a pub, who suggested he do something about the craze. 'Which particular craze do you mean?' he asked. 'Roller-skating? Hula hoops? That sort of thing?'

'Nah, nah', said the bloke. 'Not that sorta craze – the Krays, Ron and Reggie!' My friend made an excuse and left.

I was tempted to do exactly the same when the idea of a feature on the current skateboard craze was suggested. A natural distaste for Americana was compounded by a distinct feeling of being not so much on a bandwagon as a good hundred yards behind it.

So it was with ill grace that I set off for the Hammersmith Assembly Rooms on a dreary Monday evening, for the inaugural meeting of the Pro-Am Skateboard Association of Great Britain, at which, I had been assured, I would meet 'all the cats that matter'. Arriving outside the Hall, I saw over 100 of the 'cats' milling around on the forecourt. Some were paddling idly up and down on their boards, others exchanged info on the latest skating areas discovered. By far the majority, however, were huddled around what I initially suspected was the unfortunate victim of mass mugging. It turned out he was a radio reporter with a tape recorder.

By now, I'd also become uncomfortably aware that, at 25, I was at least ten years older than anybody else around me. An impulse to retreat to my own generation was arrested by the arrival of my contact, an American teenager named Trey Casimir. 'Hi, you must be Stan Hey, right?' 'How did you know?' I asked. 'Well', he said coolly, 'You're the only old guy around here, and you've got a briefcase.' I surveyed the mob with evident unease. Trey caught my look. 'We're a real bunch of hooligans, huh?' he said reassuringly.

Trey had advertised in *Time Out*'s Sportsboard section for 'empty, round-bottomed swimming pools, empty cemented reservoirs, or banks' where he and his fellow skateboarders could practice. 'Get many calls?' I asked. 'Oh, er, one, to be exact.'

It's perhaps ironic that surfing should have spawned the ultimate urban sport, an activity that needs no fields, no water, just a strip of concrete or a tarmac slope. And yet, despite its generally soulless context, the essence of the sport is very much improvisation. I guessed as much when on a visit to the South Bank, a clutch of skateboarders were busy forming a slalom run with a dozen empty Coke cans.

I'd been told to ask for Tim the Australian, who was deemed a 'hot' skater who talked 'straight

shit'. Unfortunately Tim wasn't around. Nor was 'Crazy Simon'. 'He broke his board and went home,' I was informed. With my two intros blown, I decided it was best to sit back and watch.

The centre of the action appeared to be underneath a concourse to the left of the Royal Festival Hall. There, a large paved area sweeps up into a three-sided bank, and a seemingly endless stream of kids was hurtling up to the bank, riding it, and turning back down and away. The favoured stunt seemed to be the kick-turn, swivelling the board round on the rear wheels just as it stalls at the top of the slope. One or two were trying spins ('Don't call 'em spins, they're 360s'), while others were riding along the top edge of the bank, crouched down and holding their boards ('carving').

It was an impressive display. Only the flashier skaters seemed to be wearing safety gear (helmets, gloves, knee and elbow pads). I spotted one kid wearing his mum's best sheepskin mittens; another sporting his dad's racy, black leather driving gloves. The thinking about safety gear seems to be that once you've hurt yourself, you'll

Concrete heaven: the South Bank undercroft, above, and Bay Sixty 6 skate park under the Westway, right.

bother to wear it. For one lad there, it had taken a broken arm to do the convincing.

Many of the better skaters have been enlisted into teams by skateboard manufacturers. Given free boards and equipment, they're required to skate demos for their masters as well as plug their boards around the various runs. Rivalry has become intense with one team sabotaging another by throwing refuse under their wheels during a run.

In the main, however, it seems a friendly clan. When they're not riding, they're talking boards or wheels, with a mystique that's almost Masonic. Before long a G&S Fibreflex (an ace board) or a Bennett Truck (an ace axle) begin to sound like the Holy Grail.

The other big topic is, of course, places to skate. Often it's a car park left empty at weekends or a quiet street with a tempting slope. Many even hitch to Weymouth, where there's a bona fide skate park. I asked a young American if he was disappointed with the lack of facilities. 'No, not really. I don't mind as long as I've got somewhere. This place has got plenty of curves, and it's fun.'

Original article by Stan Hey.

'The ultimate urban sport: an activity that needs no fields, no water, just a strip of concrete or a tarmac slope.'

Going for gold

The 2012 Olympics could be the greatest sporting event ever to come to London. But with it comes a huge responsibility: to the 10,000 people expected to compete, to the schoolchildren encouraged to take up sport, to the communities displaced by the building work, and to the future of the city once the games have ended. **By Rebecca Taylor**

For centuries, the lower Lea Valley area of east London (situated on the cusp of Newham, Waltham Forest and Tower Hamlets boroughs) has been the dumping ground for industrial waste and scrap. Although within spitting distance of the city, it has some of the most deprived areas in the UK, with high unemployment, overcrowded housing and poor infrastructure. The land around the industrial estates undoubtedly has a bleak and untamed beauty, but much of the soil is contaminated and clogged with rubbish. Small wonder, then, that when the idea of staging the Olympics in this bedraggled patch of London was mooted, it was hailed as the chance for massive investment and regeneration in the area.

Today, that vision is coming to life in the form of cranes, bulldozers and scaffolding that have presided over the landscape since the summer of 2007, when the first building work on the Games got underway. It represents one of the largest planning applications in European history: a 15-volume, 10,000-page document outlining one of the largest urban parks to be built in the past 150 years. But what legacy will it leave for the residents of east London – and how has it affected the communities whose lives have already been changed forever as development continues?

The legacy package is impressive: more than £17bn has been pledged for transport projects, up to 50,000 new jobs have been promised, £11m will go to fund skills training, and 30,000 new homes are planned for the area. It's a grand and shimmering vision for the future – but the reality for some of the area's residents has, so far, not been so rosy.

The gypsies

Overshadowed by an enormous electricity pylon, the Clays Lane travellers' site in Stratford was never the most salubrious of addresses, but for the English Romany gypsies who had lived there since 1971, it was home. In April 2008, the gypsies and travellers were relocated to new plots, as Clays

Lane, along with a nearby site for Irish travellers in Waterden Crescent, Hackney, were earmarked by the London Development Agency (the LDA, which is overseeing the Games development legacy) for Olympic land.

It was the end of an era for many of the families. 'A hundred years ago, this area was thriving with gypsies,' says Tracie Giles, 34, who has lived on Clays Lane for much of her life. 'My parents travelled all over the country until they met and married on Clays Lane in 1972. The first 11 years of my life we travelled, usually in Essex and Kent, but always coming back to London in the winter. We travelled in a Vickers caravan, which was chromed and streamlined and very grand.'

Many of the community are bitterly disappointed with the new site, which, although close to Clays Lane, is surrounded on all sides by busy roads and has a nightclub next to its entrance. 'There are too many cars, too much noise and congestion. On weekend nights it can go on until 3am,' says Giles. 'We feel badly let down. We have written to local politicians to say, "You are talking about 15 families who have been here for more than 35 years – they are residents of the borough, they pay rent and council tax" – but because we are an ethnic group, they just sweep us to one side, like we don't matter.'

The Irish travellers have fared better. Their relocation has split the original community into three, but the new facilities are superior to their original site, and include the first 'group housing in Britain': families live in bungalows with a space alongside for the caravans.

The gardeners

Squeezed between a bus depot and a food factory, the Manor Gardening Society Allotments in Waterden Road were a burst of nature amid the bleak industrial surroundings. For more than 100 years, generations of gardeners had tended their plants on this site of more than 80 allotments, growing flowers, vegetables and fruit in an area that was categorised in a London Assembly report as a fresh food 'desert'. But the land the allotments sit on will be turned into a concourse for a walkway that will link the Games' facilities.

'It was an island of paradise next to the industrial sites. There was no acknowledgement that people who gardened there all their lives could have had some beneficial input in the plans,' said Sam Clark, the proprietor of Moro, who had an allotment on the site for six years.

'In the 16 years I was there, I grew a fig tree, peach tree, grape vines and an olive tree,' said 64-year-old Hassan Ali. 'I brought my grandchilden and showed them how to grow tomatoes and strawberries. On Sundays, we made barbecues. Once they bulldoze over it, our story is gone.'

In September 2007, the last of the gardeners harvested their crops. By November, they had been

Poplar resident, and Olympic hopeful in the 400m hurdles, 18-year-old Perri Shakes-Drayton.

Sebastian Coe
Chairman of the London Organising Committee of the Olympic Games

'When, 30 years ago, those of us involved in sport were trying to point out that London was a Third World city in terms of sporting facilities, people just sat on their hands and didn't do anything. We are now being asked about participation by people who wouldn't have crossed the road to support those causes previously.

'The number one legacy of the Games, indisputably, will be proper facilities that communities can use. I'm not talking about the Wimbledons or Wembleys. I'm talking about facilities where people can train and develop the next generation. It's a joke that London only has one 50m swimming pool; it's a joke that London has survived with the circa 1960s track and field facilities at Crystal Palace.

'If you look at rates of health-related activity, you have pockets that are really unresponsive to that, pockets of deprivation and pockets of ill-health. The Games will raise those rates of activity. The boroughs are already responding with programmes of sporting inclusion.

'The other issue is that the Games is a focus of creativity, so the Olympic cultural festival that will kick off in 2008, when the Mayor brings the flag back to London from Beijing, is very important for us.

'We have a commitment from the Mayor to fund the legacy to the tune of £10m a year. The venues are designed so that they won't be white elephants. If you look at the design of the Olympic athletics stadium, as much thought is being put into its legacy as what it looks like.'

Interviewed by Rebecca Taylor 25.7.2007.

moved to a new site on Marsh Lane. Pictures of the new site, taken in spring 2008, show stretches of muddy, water-logged plots. Traffic thunders by on the busy Orient Way road. Gardeners report that heavy rain leaves pools of water on the plots, and that plants grown in these conditions are likely to die. The gardeners have been promised new plots after the Games, but it will be no easy task to relocate them for a second time.

The cyclists

One of the bitterest fights over the Olympic development plans has come from the most unlikely of quarters: cyclists. The Eastway cycling circuit in Stratford had been a national cycle sports centre, where top cyclists Bradley Wiggins and Eddie Merckx trained and competed. It was closed in 2007, and the cyclists' facilities were relocated to Hog Hill in Redbridge after a long battle with the LDA to find an adequate alternative. But what has really left cyclists fuming is the legacy facility that will serve them when they return to their original site after the Games. In the 2005 Olympic bid, the cyclists were promised a £22m VeloPark that would be 'a unique, world-class venue for all disciplines and levels of cycling'.

The VeloPark has been shrinking ever since, as the LDA has to recoup costs for the Games by setting aside Olympic land that will eventually be sold off to developers. In the latest plans, the VeloPark had been reduced from the promised 34 hectares to just ten. The mountain biking track will be only 950 metres long, instead of the 3.5 kilometres needed to host regional or national competitions. Meanwhile, an existing road circuit for cycle speedway has been reduced to a narrow strip either side of the busy A12 and over a motorway bridge. 'The legacy was the jewel in the crown of the bid. They said there would be major benefits for those who do sport in London,' said Michael Humphreys, of the Eastway Users Group, which has been fighting the latest proposals. 'Instead, there is mediocre provision for a road circuit and no off-road provision. We will have lost an important facility where we were able to guarantee provision of world-class facilities.'

The homeless

On 23 July 2007, the residents of the Clays Lane housing estate in Stratford left their homes for the last time. Once a vibrant community of 450 people, with its own café, community hall and advice centre, the estate is now a huge dirt pile as bulldozers have moved in to create space for the Olympic Village. Set up in the 1980s to address the lack of housing for young single people, Clays Lane was the largest purpose-built housing co-operative in Europe. By the time builders moved in, the place resembled a boarded-up ghost town,

'One of the bitterest fights over the Olympics development plans has come from the most unlikely of quarters: cyclists.'

but around 15 residents held out until the end.

Ed Doherty, 34, who lived at Clays Lane for ten years, was one of the last to leave. 'This has been a unique place. We'll never see the likes of this kind of community in London again,' said Doherty, who had decided to move out of London to a flat in Brighton. 'We lived in blocks arranged around a courtyard, with communal bathrooms and kitchens. It was like living in a big family. Lots of artists and musicians lived here, and the atmosphere was very creative.

'In the '90s, there were free parties, with DJs and performers. Sometimes over 1,000 people attended, and the party would spill over on to the Eastway cycle track next door. On the day London won the Olympics, I was just surprised. How could this place that I'd lived in for so many years be turned into a new development so quickly? The LDA presented the move as something positive, whereby residents were offered self-contained flats. The point is that many people chose to live here because we want to live communally. We also had low rents, which we will see double in our new places. It's terribly sad to leave. It's been a place of great memories.'

A few days later, Doherty moved his life belongings out in a white mini-van and headed off to a new life in Brighton.

The pace of change already made to the area is astounding; when the International Olympic Committee visited the site in May 2008, they expressed surprise that so much of the building work was already underway. The scale of such a project means it is inevitable that communities are affected, and not always in ways they consider beneficial.

But there are some bright spots that could point to a more optimistic outcome for local communities. 'The Olympics is already making a positive impact. The Mile End track has been refurbished and now puts on more events for local children, and lots more children have joined the athletics club. Children around my estate who were never active at all are getting into sport. I'm excited about it,' says Perri Shakes Drayton, an 18-year-old from Tower Hamlets who is a potential 2012 Olympic hurdler.

If the area can be re-energised through investment and infastructure, then it could dramatically improve the lives of many of the people growing up there now, creating a vibrant new part of London and opening up more opportunities than it destroys – and that really would be a legacy to be proud of.

Celebrity
will eat itself

For decades, a parade of fashionably dressed, media-hyped restaurants has excited London's chattering classes, but the cooking hasn't always merited the attention.

By Jonathan Meades

One of the more telling images of the Blair years was of the multipartite motorcade it took to get this most Bourbonish of British prime ministers and the then French president Jacques Chirac from Downing Street to the absurdly overhyped Nobu at Hyde Park Corner. The choice of restaurant was symptomatic of New Labour. Flashy, deracinated, Japanese-Peruvian cooking with the inevitable wretched 'twist'. In other words, more spin than essence. A sort of fashion item.

Shortly before, Sir Terence Conran, hardly a disinterested party, had declared that London was something called 'the restaurant capital of the world'. And ever since, a jingoistic army of coke-brained PRs, characterfully moronic telly chefs, gormless food writers and ignorantly incurious restaurant reviewers has trumpeted London's triumph to a staunchly credulous public.

This is hardly surprising. England is, after all, world leader in self-delusion (see World Cups passim). Among the many enthusiastically peddled and eagerly received ideas that have become articles of gastronomic faith is the one that states that before becoming the restaurant capital of the world, London was the restaurant sump of the world.

Of course, were one to judge London *restauration* in 1968 by the year's most effortfully cool, most tiresomely hip, most groovily 'underground' restaurant, that particular article of gastronomic faith would be validated. The macrobiotic restaurant Seed in a Paddington basement was a demonstration that hideous cooking is no barrier to a restaurant's success in London: brown rice, leaden bread, pastry like wood pulp, lentils, chick peas, unidentifiable stewed vegetables, the liberal use of tahini. And loud music – which was, in those days, seldom heard in restaurants. The customers, all in their twenties, were hippyish pop musicians, 'alternative' entrepreneurs, full-time beautiful

people – members of a small, sartorially exotic tribe that today is taken as representative of the age. It wasn't. Nor, mercifully, was Seed itself. It lasted for less than two years: but the anti-gastronomic craze it fomented did not die with it. Some of the imitators it spawned, such as Oodles in James Street, W1, and Manna in Chalk Farm, astonishingly survived. And self-righteous, proselytising vegetarians were to become as dismal a feature of the early '70s as Fry boots and soft rock.

Equally atypical but entirely worthwhile, and, in time, vastly more influential, Le Gavroche, then in Lower Sloane Street, celebrated its first birthday in 1968. The Roux brothers aspired to and achieved a level of cooking that had not been seen in Britain since the days of Escoffier. Le Gavroche was a plutocrat's playground. Gourmets on a budget had to satisfy themselves with the earthily Burgundian produce sold at their neighbouring charcuterie Le Cochon Rose.

Among the shop's customers was Elizabeth David, who lived nearby, and whose books on French rustic and regional cooking had, throughout the '60s, inspired countless bistros. Several thousand were to be found in SW1, SW3, SW5, SW7, and SW10: Casserole, Le Matelot, Chanterelle, Parkes, Le Carosse, Au Père de Nico, Casse-Croûte, La Poule au Pot, Le Rêve, Provans, Sans Souci, the Spot… The owners tended to be louche boozers, the chefs keen amateurs, the members of staff decorative. No owner was loucher than Nick Clark. No member of staff more decorative than the young Fay Coventry, later to become better known as Fay Maschler, revered restaurant critic of the *Evening Standard*.

Nick's Diner was frequented by people too old and too urbane to be fully fledged beautiful people: model Pauline Stone, Jane Kasmin, actor Laurence Harvey, colourful conman 'Dandy Kim' Caborn-Waterfield, Suna Portman, and Bond set designer

Time Out's first Eating Guide, published in 1982. Right, Michel (left) and Albert Roux, of Le Gavroche, in 1967.

'Britain's preposterous urge
to divest itself of its own
cooking was already
apparent in the late '60s.'

Ken Adam, loosely grouped as the 'Chelsea Set'. The cooking was OK. But – plus ça change – the prices were three times those one would pay in Paris where – plus ça change, again – what was considered everyday was reckoned exceptional in London. Mrs David was a collector of vernacular recipes just as, say, Cecil Sharp had been a collector of folk songs. To collect is not to instruct. Her sources were peasant housewives who knew a few recipes by heart, and highly trained chefs who often came from peasant backgrounds. London amateurs had neither of these advantages. Further, they seldom had access to appropriate ingredients. London bistro cooking was as much characterised by approximation as it was by francophilia.

Britain's preposterous urge to divest itself of its own cooking was already apparent in the late '60s. But there still existed a gamut of restaurants that specialised in dishes that today possess the exoticism of the unattainable: boiled beef, dumplings and carrots; jugged hare; kedgeree; steak and kidney pudding; Irish stew; mutton with caper sauce; fish pie, and so on. At the Hungry Horse on the Fulham Road such dishes would be washed down with black velvet and followed by syllabub. The main restaurant was in a basement entered through a gated courtyard. Upstairs, with a narrow frontage to the street and a simplified menu, was the Pie Shop, from whose counter the rapid changes overtaking that stretch of road now known as the Beach might be observed. Just down the road was Baghdad House, whose basement was all carpeted walls, low brass tables, cushions and pouffes where slumped King's Roadies smoked joints. That the Iraqi cooking was delightful was a bit of an irrelevance. And by 1972, that all-purpose Middle-Eastern tat was so hopelessly yesterday.

That year the Beach was home to Parson's (spaghetti, but more American than Italian), the Great American Disaster (burgers), Small's Café (American, vaguely diner-ish) and the Last Resort (American, vaguely film noir-ish). In Kensington Church Street, Tommy Roberts, who, more than anyone, invented glam rock, opened an expanded version of his garish King's Road shop Mr Freedom (velvet dungarees, satin trousers, pornographic enamel brooches, appliqué T-shirts). It included a joyfully plastic diner called Mr Feed'em. This obsession with ersatz Americana could lead to only one outcome, the arrival of the all too real thing. Woolwich is a tough, former garrison town,

From top, chefs through the decades: Peter Langan, Anton Mosimann, Ruth Rogers (left) and Rose Gray.

which belongs more to north Kent than to London. McDonald's opened its first British branch there in 1974.

The Mediterranean love affair

1974 also saw the closure of Schmidt's. This Charlotte Street institution seated over 500 customers, had spectacularly rude waiters, and felt like a relic of a distant era – which, indeed, it was. Although it offered 'tomato soup (Heinz)', most of its German dishes were well made, abundantly portioned and very cheap. Schmidt's demise was a pointer. It signalled that time was up for London's central, northern and eastern European restaurants: Maurer's, Marynka, Polonia, Silver Spur, Luba's, Cresta, La Tertulia, Dania, Csarda, Old Russia, Cosmo, Dorice, the Berlin Room, Le Mignon, Chez Kristof, Isow's, Edelweiss, the Nosh Bar, the Hendon Grill, Blooms…

None of these establishments was able to satisfy the new British taste for climatically unsuitable and unsustainable cooking first experienced through increasingly cheap foreign travel. It was a sort of holiday romance that didn't wither. Britain fell for food it couldn't grow. The last thing it wanted was Germanic cooking that reminded it of its own, which it was hurriedly burying. It craved dishes from southern Europe and the Middle East, from the Indian subcontinent, from north Africa, China and Japan, from anywhere hot.

By the early '70s, tandoors were starting to appear, and Indian restaurants were beginning to dispense with flock walls (save in sitcoms). Similarly, Italian restaurants were dispensing with Chianti bottles slung from the ceiling (save in sitcoms). Chinatown, not yet so called, was taking shape, an exclusively Cantonese shape – although London already had a Peking-style restaurant: the former chef of the Chinese embassy, preferring NW10 to Mao's murderous dictatorship, had defected to open Kuo Wan in Willesden High Street.

The first *Michelin* guide to London appeared in 1974. It began as it would continue, rewarding preciousness, chi-chi and fussy neophilia while at times failing to distinguish between aspiration and achievement. The main people who take any notice of the pompous compendium are chefs. Which is unfortunate: the influence it has had on British cooking has been baleful. *Time Out* published its first restaurant guide, *Eating Out in London,* in 1982. There were,

FOOD & DRINK

of course, well-established guides – the less than sybaritic *Good Food Guide* and those of Egon Ronay's organisation. But neither of these annual offerings reached any but the converted: indeed, the *Good Food Guide* called its correspondents, from whose reports it was compiled, 'members of the Good Food Club'. Newspapers and magazines regarded food and cooking as peripheral activities at best: to be relegated to what were called 'the women's pages'. Elizabeth David's accounts of her battles with assorted editorial harridans indicate the era's depths of ignorance and despisal. Restaurants were seldom reviewed. And when they were, it was usually undertaken as a perk for people who not only knew nothing, but were,

After the success of Chinatown (top), Londoners developed a taste for dishes from Vietnam, Japan and Korea.

astonishingly, proud to own up to it. No one would appoint a cricket correspondent who didn't understand the lbw law, but a restaurant reviewer who believes, for instance, that sweetbreads are testicles seemed entirely admissible – and still is, sadly. A newspaper executive once justified this to me by claiming that since restaurants were 'democratic', anyone could have an opinion.

But a new generation of food writers such as Fay Maschler, who won a competition inn 1972 to replace Quentin Crewe as reviewer for the *Evening Standard*, began using measured populism to take restaurants out of the gastro-ghetto and open up a hitherto exclusive subject to readers who had believed themselves uninterested. Every paper and

The new breed of
London restaurant:
St John, in Smithfield.

magazine in Britain now has a restaurant reviewer – who is often subjected to ill-conceived editorial pressure to cover new restaurants when they open, as though they were plays or films, a strategy that only exacerbates their ephemerality.

During the '70s, some writers started to champion restaurants outside the franglais hegemony beloved of the guides, restaurants that were overlooked or routinely derided as serving mere fuel for the impecunious. Previously specialised subcontinental restaurants – the excellent Sri Lanka in Earl's Court, for instance – had received no publicity whatsoever, nor did Cypriot cafés such as the glorious Koritsas opposite Camden Town station. Today, Turkish outfits in Harringay, Vietnamese soup kitchens in Shoreditch, Kurdish community centres in Stoke Newington, Korean cafeterias in New Malden, and Ugandan Asian joints in Tooting are known outside the populations and localities they initially served.

Fish and chips, 'the national dish', is actually Sephardi, and was unknown in London before the 1850s; the long-held conception of Italian cooking as predominantly pasta, tomato and pizza was due to the majority of Italians in the UK having come from the south, where those foods are commonplace. The history of this city's *restauration* has always been determined as much by successive waves of immigration as it has been by fads. But the two are strangely separate. Fashion has its own independent motor, it doesn't reflect demographic shifts. If one considers the restaurants that have been most in vogue over the past 40 years, they suggest that London is predominantly monocultural. They further suggest that culinary indifference is no obstacle to mainstream fashionability.

It's hard to imagine that people ever went to Langan's Brasserie primarily for the cooking. It had other attractions: Peter Langan was a shambolic, champagne-fuelled figure in a white suit whose trousers reached his chest. This was a restaurateur who gave an new meaning to *le patron mange ici* by metaphorically performing cunnilingus on privileged guests. Customers might expect to see celebrity weather girls, top sideburns, actors whose name was on the tip of their tongue, major stars such as Gareth Hunt and Jane Seymour. The excitement was tremendous. And then there was the look of the place: early 20th-century paintings (chosen by Brian Sewell), formally dressed waiters, velvet banquettes, sumptuous lavatories. It was brash, opulent, glamorous, loud. It opened in 1976, remained a hot ticket for almost a decade, and is still a bridge-and-tunnel favourite; such longevity is unusual in London. Langan's cast aside the intimacy and home-made decor that had characterised bistros. The restaurants that set themselves up as rivals to Langan's, most notably Le Caprice, were professional, polished and shouted about their design.

Small portions, big plates

La Nouvelle Cuisine was a term coined in 1972 by the journalists and self-publicists Henri Gault and Christian Millau. It was simply a label for an already widespread tendency of French haute cuisine to eschew restaurant conventions and adopt lighter preparations that owed something to rarified domestic practice. The new craze, half digested and widely misunderstood, spread throughout France. It initially arrived in Britain in the late '70s in the form of books. Bocuse, the Troisgros brothers, grinning Roger Vergé, Didier Trouduc and dozens of others jumped on the bandwagon.

Their example was eagerly followed in London. And eagerly traduced. In unskilled British hands, nouvelle cuisine became a set of clichés. Miserable portions, unrecognisable vegetables, sauces so over-elaborated that they tasted industrial – all arranged on huge plates by persons who believed themselves to be Miró, but who actually had the visual acuity of a Chingford flower arranger. So far, so preposterous. But as well as adopting its hackneyed idioms, London also succumbed to nouvelle cuisine's cult of the chef.

With very few exceptions, chefs had hitherto been invisible, unknown by the general public. The popular conception of a chef was someone like Anthony Burgess's aitch-dropping, heavy drinking Arry in *Inside Mr Enderby*. Arry, of the Conway Hotel in a phenomenally seedy Hove, attempts to woo Thelma Walpole by sending up to her room stewed tripe, eels and reams of verse which FX Enderby has composed on his behalf. If only the actuality had turned out to be as engaging as Arry…

The mediation of chefs was, and remains, notable for its sychophancy. Pompous, pretentious, irony-free disseminators of cracker-barrel wisdom were taken entirely at their own estimation by dim journalists whose articles crossed the boundary between consumer journalism and producer PR. This was a world away from the scholarly writing of Elizabeth David, Jane Grigson, Alan Davidson and so on. At first the idolatry was confined to those who were masters or near masters of their craft. The Roux brozzairs (Le Gavroche), Pierre Koffmann (La Tante Claire), Anton Mosimann (the Dorchester), Michael Quinn (Ritz), Guy Mouilleron (Ma Cuisine), Raymond Blanc (Le Manoir aux Quat' Saisons). And Nico Ladenis, who realised that a reputation for irascible unreasonableness was good for business, and thus created the tiresome template for Marco-Pierre White, Gordon Ramsay and a whole school of mouthy pugilists who assume that the world is interested in their playground feuds. Today, every chef is a celebrity chef, just as every model is a supermodel. A worthless subcultural industry has turned cooking into a form of light entertainment and chefs into telly 'personalities'.

There existed a marked divide between the gastronomic and the modish. Gastronomic restaurants – L'Arlequin, Le Gavroche, Chez Nico, Inigo Jones, L'Interlude de Tabaillaud, Tante Claire – tended to be stiff, formal, hushed, exclusive, socially stodgy. Modish restaurants were, supposedly, fun – save for the cooking.

Bibendum, Alastair Little, the River Café, Harvey's and Kensington Place opened within a year of each other in 1986-87. They caused an immense and unprecedented fluctuation in the complexion of London *restauration*. Formerly separate strands were threaded together. I had started a weekly column in the *Times* in the summer of 1986. The first 18 months were to prove far more exciting than the long years of satiety that followed. The keynotes were repetition, plagiarism, assembly cooking, the thwarted promise of gastropubs and the re-emergence of nouvelle cuisine, this time calling itself molecular gastronomy and pretending to be scientific. Though the culinary bar has been raised, and London of recent years has been thrilled by some truly exceptional new restaurants, for every St John or Café Anglais or Santa Maria del Buen Ayre there are dozens of empty vessels, charging the earth in order to cover the highest rents in Europe, massive start-up costs, and the exorbitant fees of derivative designers and PRs.

Jonathan Meades was food critic of the *Times* from 1986 to 2001.

TIMELINE

1968
A pint of bitter stands at one and eightpence.

1974
The first McDonald's in the UK opens in Woolwich.

1978
The Monmouth Coffee House begins roasting and retailing fresh beans at its shop on Monmouth Street.

1979
Neal's Yard Dairy opens in Covent Garden and makes fresh cheese, crème fraîche and the first Greek-style yoghurt in the UK.

1982
Billingsgate fish market, the largest in the UK, relocates to Docklands.

1983
Gerrard Street is pedestrianised to cater for the huge number of visitors that Chinatown attracts.

Sally Clarke launches her no-choice set dinner restaurant on Kensington Church Street, W8.

Rococo Chocolates is founded by Chantal Coady, introducing choccy sardines, corn-on-the-cobs and gulls' eggs.

1985
The Groucho private members' club is established in Soho by a group of publishers looking for a congenial spot for their long lunches.

Peggy Czyzak-Dannenbaum founds La Fornaia bakery, which later introduces ciabatta bread to Britain, kickstarting the gourmet bread revolution.

1986
Pret A Manger opens its first branch in Victoria.

1987
Bad-boy chef Marco Pierre White opens his first restaurant, Harvey's, in Wandsworth. His sous-chef is Gordon Ramsay.

1988
Ruth Rogers and Rose Gray launch the River Café in Hammersmith.

1991
In Farringdon, the Eagle starts serving good, freshly prepared food with its fine ales, an idea that swiftly spawns the term 'gastropub'.

1992
Alan Yau opens his first Wagamama in Bloomsbury. The noodle canteen now operates in 12 countries, with more than 30 outlets in London alone.

1998
Gordon Ramsay opens his first restaurant at 68 Royal Hospital Road. In 2001, he is awarded a third Michelin star and becomes one of only three chefs in the UK to hold this rating.

1999
Nina Planck, a fruit and vegetable farmer from Virginia, sets up the first farmers' market in the city in Islington. By 2008, farmers' markets are common across London.

2002
Jamie Oliver's Fifteen restaurant opens in Shoreditch in a blaze of publicity resulting from the TV series *Jamie's Kitchen*.

2005
Dans Le Noir opens. The restaurant serve its starters, main courses and desserts to customers kept entirely in the dark. The waiters are blind and the wine glasses unbreakable.

2006
Borough Market celebrates its 250th year as London's oldest food market.

London's longest-serving landlord, Norman Balon, calls time for good at the Coach & Horses in Soho. He began helping his parents behind the bar aged 16 in 1943 and never did any other job.

2007
Antonio Carluccio's Neal Street restaurant closes. Started by Sir Terence Conran in 1971, it was bought by Antonio and Priscilla Carluccio in 1984.

2008
The Hawley Arms burns down in the Camden fire. The 'Camden canners' mourn as their favourite watering hole goes up in flames.

On the spice trail

So-called 'Indian' food has established itself as a UK takeaway staple, but a new breed of modern Asian restaurants is introducing Londoners to a more sophisticated side of the cuisine.

T he establishment of Indian food in the UK national diet, though remarkable for its pervasiveness, should have come as no surprise. The East India Company – given a royal charter by Queen Elizabeth I in 1600 to trade exclusively with the 'East Indies' – was based in east London, and Lascars (Bengali seamen) became a common sight at the docks. By the time direct colonial rule was established in India in 1858, the British Raj was firmly ensconced, and Anglo-Indian cooking became popular among the many returned officers and merchants frequenting London's dining clubs in the 19th century. Many sahibs (and memsahibs) brought favoured servants and cooks back with them from India, and Anglo-Indian dishes are recorded in nearly all the cookbooks and menus of the time.

It wasn't until the 20th century that London saw large waves of immigration from the Indian subcontinent. The British Nationality Act of 1948 – the year following Indian Independence – made it easier for citizens of India and the new state of Pakistan to move to the UK in search of work. Many chose to work in restaurants, peddling not the sort of food actually eaten in India, but a bowdlerised version of it that fitted British ideas of 'curry'. One area where the authentic tastes were – and still are – found is Southall in Middlesex, where Punjabis settled en masse and now form the majority population. It remains the best place in which to look for the meaty, rich, complex flavours of layered spicing and the roasted meats of the tandoor oven.

Things gathered pace after the Indo-Pakistani War and the Bangladesh Liberation War in 1971, which brought a new influx of displaced settlers, with varying levels of literacy and education. Whitechapel was their favoured location, following in the footsteps of the Lascars a century earlier. Brick Lane established itself as London's main curry corridor – a destination for low prices and spicy food, rather than fine dining – during

the 1970s. The 'curry house' was born, together with jokes about 'ruby murrays', flock wallpaper, lager and phals, which still dog the popular but outmoded perception of 'Indian' restaurants. Enterprising Bangladeshis, this time in Camden, are also responsible for the cluster of South Indian vegetarian bhel poori houses in Drummond Street, behind Euston station.

Though the majority of what Londoners call 'Indian' restaurants are, in fact, run by Bangladeshis, the East African Asian population has also had a strong influence on London's culinary mores. The expulsion of more than a million from the continent in the '70s – 900,000 from Uganda under Idi Amin in 1972; another 200,000 from Kenya and Tanzania soon afterwards – brought them to Wembley. Surrounding districts and streets such as Ealing Road continue to reflect the ethnic mix of this diaspora; people whose forebears originate in Gujarat are the main group, but there are also many Pakistanis, Tamils and Punjabis. Ealing Road is at its exotic best on a Saturday, with sugar cane juice vendors, bootleg bhangra CDs and Bollywood DVDs on sale from

street vendors, and the enticing aromas of cooking from the many cafés and restaurants specialising in everything from bhajias through Bombay street food to the heat of Sri Lankan dishes.

By far the most diverse of London's Asian neighbourhoods is Tooting. An accountancy college first drew young professionals from the subcontinent as far back as the 1950s, and many liked it enough to stay. Tamils make up the majority of Asian residents today : there are around 30,000 between Colliers Wood and Tooting. Their numbers were swelled by two waves of civil war in Sri Lanka in the 1980s and '90s, but the area's restaurants remain a heterogenous mix of South Indian, East African Gujarati, Tanzanian Punjabi and, more recently, Sri Lankan.

Making the food of the subcontinent ubiquitous was one thing, but it took more recent immigrants direct from India to raise the culinary bar. The Indian new wave took off in 1990 with the opening of Chutney Mary, when Camellia Panjabi, then in charge of catering at the luxurious Taj Group of Hotels in India, decided to create a restaurant that showcased India's best cooking. Her expertise across India allowed her to handpick chefs from across the subcontinent, who she employed to recreate exciting regional dishes; Chutney Mary remains one of the best places for these and for contemporary, modern Indian cooking.

Tamarind opened in 1994, and definitively broke the link with colonialism by opting for a strikingly modern interior by designer Emily Todhunter. It led to a number of spin-offs, including Benares, set up by Tamarind's chef Atul Kochhar, now a household name since his appearance on the BBC's *Great British Menu*. Also pioneering smart, modern Indian cooking were chef Vineet Bhatia, who introduced chocolate samosas to London menus, and entrepreneur Iqbal Wahhab, who launched the Cinnamon Club dining rooms in Westminster.

Innovation continues apace and London is now seeing two new trends in its Indian food. The first is that the bigger operators, such as the Chutney Mary Group, have created spin-off low-budget canteens such as Masala Zone; Tamarind has created Imli; and Vineet Bhatia has launched Urban Turban. The other is the growth of regional Indian cooking, both on pan-Indian menus and in specialist restaurants such as the South Indian Rasa chain. It can now be said that, 60 years after the British Nationality Act brought enterprising Asians in their thousands, London's best Indian restaurants finally rival some of the best in India.

Guy Dimond has been Food & Drink Editor of *Time Out* since 1998.

Chinatown

Red and gold pagoda-style telephone boxes, large ceremonial gateways and stone lions decorate Gerrard Street, Chinatown's main drag. The surrounding cluster of Soho streets is packed with restaurants and small shops selling everything from iced grass jelly to speciality teas, and the most important ingredient in any thriving area, people.

The Chinese community now established in W1 only began moving to Soho in the 1960s. The capital's original Chinatown was in Limehouse, east London, close to the docks, but bomb damage during World War II and redevelopment plans forced the community to head west. Since then, London's Chinese population has grown steadily, from around 300 in 1914 to more than 80,000 in 2001, and rising. Eight main regional cuisines – Shandong, Cantonese, Sichuan, Jiangsu, Zhejiang, Hunan, Fujian and Anhui – are all represented in Chinatown. The most popular are Cantonese dim sum, spicy Sichuanese and Peking duck. Chicken feet and duck tongues are among the more daring specialities on offer.

A fond farewell to the London caff

By Bob Stanley

The queue for the last ever specials at the Copper Grill stretched halfway down Eldon Street by one o'clock. All bade farewell to one of London's finest caffs. The wooden banquettes, copper piping, city murals and fabulous '50s counter will all have been skipped by the time you read this. Ditto the Piccolo bar two doors down (the best Formica in town) and the Euro on Swallow Street.

The Italians are renowned conspiracy theorists. What do they make of the rapid disappearance of their great contribution to London culture, the café? My obsession with them began when I was four, with a BBC kids' programme called *Joe*, set in a transport caff (lorries! a jukebox!), and blossomed when I moved to London in the mid '80s, fuelled by Dexy's Midnight Runners's 'The Teams That Meet in Caffs', and the photo on the back of Madness's 'The Sun and the Rain'.

The green-and-white luncheon voucher called to me. Thinking I was a kind of beatnik, I planned to while away my days over frothy coffee, reading Waterhouse, Mackay and Brautigan and, with like-minded souls, plot to bring down the government. My hangouts were the Regent Milk Bar on Edgware Road, Gattopardo at King's Cross, and the Oval Platter on Charing Cross Road.

Perk life

I got hooked on cappuccino at Wrights, an Italian sandwich bar next to the London School of Economics. That cappuccino became synonymous with Godard, Dali, Marx, Freud, hours of thinking and talking. These days, like all Londoners, LSE students are spoiled for choice: coffee chains and brasseries along Kingsway, a Covent Garden saturated with pavement cafés, the National Film Theatre's newish and buzzy South Bank café (there was a time you could only get tea in red plastic teapots!), and even upmarket venues like Bank and Number One Aldwych, for a swish espresso before a morning lecture. Fifteen years ago, none of this existed. Even

ten years, ago things hadn't changed much. Then, hanging out in coffee houses like Hampstead's Coffee Cup was like indulging in a secret fetish. Others went to an office; we went for coffee.

Cool interior design, focaccia sandwiches, a choice of beers – things you take for granted today – weren't on the menu then. The local, down-to-earth Italian (of course) park café at Golders Green, surrounded by wonderfully eccentric, argumentative Jewish OAPs in animated political discussions, was my summer home from home.

There were Londoners who craved fresh air and muddy walks in the country, and there were those of us who made regular pilgrimages to Paris, not for the coffee (for that you went to Italy), but the café life. After the high-spending yuppies transformed London in the '80s, an influx of new bars and brasseries arrived in the early '90s. But the scene still lagged behind Paris. Bar Gansa in

Cafés were a haven while everything else in the city seemed to accelerate. The pace of life in a London cafe is resolutely mid 20th century. The history appealed; Soho caffs like the New Piccadilly were just about the only remnants of the area's bohemian golden age when Francis Bacon, Colin Wilson and Adam Faith could all be sitting at adjacent tables. The classic caff sees no boundary between boho, biker and office boy. It's truly cosmopolitan.

Adrian Maddox, in his essential book *Classic Cafés*, considers the quality of the food to be less significant than the curve of a coffee-cup handle or the number of chromed pipes on an espresso machine. Perhaps this explains their demise: tea and toast costs a pound, liver and bacon three quid. Anyone can afford it, which is why the customers are such a cross-section of London life. To cover the current steep rent rises, a cup of tea should cost something like two pounds. This ain't going to

The much-loved New Piccadilly on Denman Street, W1, served its last cuppa in 2007.

happen. The result is that these independent traders are being squeezed out, replaced by identikit shops from Anywhere, UK. Many café owners are now close to retirement age, and if the kids don't want to take over the business, it folds.

Happily there are exceptions: Andrew's on Grays Inn Road and Pellicci's on Bethnal Green Road have been handed down, hopefully secure for another generation. But the recently vacated Tea Rooms on Museum Street or Rendezvous on Maddox Street will be hard to replace in a brave new world of fast food and binge drinking.

It doesn't have to be like this. The Chelsea Kitchen on the King's Road has always been popular among models, media types and toffs. Likewise, the Pollo Bar on Old Compton Street is regularly rammed. There are more. People like the grub, the decor, the atmosphere.

Just before Christmas, I started working on a Channel 4 documentary on the classic West End caff [*Today's Special: Café Culture*]. It soon took on the form of archive work, capturing disappearing London, a most melancholy task. Too late, we got in touch with the Museum of London to see if they could save the interior of the Copper Grill. They could, but not at a day's notice. I rescued a salt-and-pepper set. Some consolation.

The film intended to reflect the beauty of the caff, its cheerfulness, unique architecture, classlessness, and history as the birthplace of the British teenager. Let's face it, the revolution will never begin in a Pret.

Bob Stanley is a member of Saint Etienne, whose compilation *Songs for Mario's Café* is on Discotheque.

Camden was a rare combination of café, bar and restaurant. You could eat, snack, drink alcohol or coffee, or do the whole lot. Two years of my life were spent here writing an angst-ridden book, hanging out with some of the wildest people I will probably ever meet, and forging some of my strongest friendships.

By the end of that period, London was changing. From being faithful to our chosen cafés, choice made us promiscuous. Yet a curious thing happened. After a while, we went back to old favourites like Bar Italia, the original all-night café; the Troubadour, one of the oldest and most popular coffee houses; Pâtisserie Valerie, with its unbeatable cakes and convivial atmosphere; and Golborne Road's authentic Oporto and Lisboa. A café needs exceptional character to make its mark with the non-nine-to-fivers who create a café by imprinting their character on it.

The successful new contenders have created an atmosphere of their own, invariably fusing different elements of London lifestyle. The most obvious trend is towards the internet café, where you can hang out, surf the net and get wired up on espresso. Another, and perhaps the most significant, development is the blurring of the boundary between café and bar, sometimes laced with a club atmosphere. As London's artists have wowed the world – fashion designers, Britpoppers, architects, film-makers – the creative meeting points have become bolder, more fun.

By the time the media coined the phrase 'Cool Britannia', London had not only joined its overseas counterparts in embracing coffee as part of an urban lifestyle, it had overtaken them with its uniquely varied café society.

By Lorna V. From *Time Out*, 5 August 1998.

FOOD & DRINK

A sip in time

Beer, Bradsell and bargain booze:
raise a glass to four decades of drinking .

By Michael Hodges

I n August 2006, I sat in the Spread Eagle Pub in Wandsworth with some very angry men. The pub was, and luckily still is, a London classic – a Victorian palace of etched glass and balustrades. My fellow drinkers were Young's employees: the brewers, bottlers, draymen and farriers who gave the Wandsworth brewery its distinctive beer and its distinctive heritage.

Or they had been until that morning, when, at a meeting in the brewery yard, they had been told that Young's was closing. Clearly the only thing to do was get very drunk, and although a miserable afternoon drinking bitter with men in jerkins may appear an odd way to start an assessment of London's drinking culture, the closure of Young's is in many ways the story of that culture.

Until the '60s, the majority of people in this city did their drinking – and learned to be social drinkers – in an institution that was famous throughout the world. The London pub catered for everyone and everything. Fleet Street was still the heart of the newspaper industry, and once copy was filed, whole days were lost in establishments such as Ye Olde Cheshire Cheese and El Vino. In Soho, bohemians and alcoholics shared the pleasures of wasting an afternoon in the French House or among the dishevelled patrons of the Colony Club, in a piss-up that showed all the signs of never ending.

In those pubs, Londoners drank whisky and beer, pink gins and vodka and tonics, and ate crisps. But as the '70s turned into the '80s, the London pub began to decline. Although this decline would make a lot of money for the big breweries and drink manufacturers, it actually happened for the most right-on of reasons: the new freedoms the 1960s had brought to women. As newly liberated female Londoners found their spending power increasing, they demanded something slightly more sophisticated than the light ale and fag smoke that characterised the city's pubs as much as smog had characterised its air in the 1950s.

The result was the chain: stripped-down pubs offering predominantly microwaved food and pine tables that spread over London like a rash, as old-style pubs were converted into stripped-down sheds designed for 'vertical drinking' (that is, standing up until you fell down). The style found

FOOD & DRINK

As pubs went out of fashion, so did beer, and over the past 40 years, many trends have been manufactured to meet this apparent need to abandon rational London drinks. Cider on ice, the ubiquitous spritzer, tequila slammers, bottles of Mexican lager with lime wedged in the neck, and, in the 1980s, a craze for brightly coloured cocktails: sweet concoctions of umbrella, juice and liquor called Up the Bum, Long Slow Shag or Chocolate Mind Bomb.

Then, in 1994, Dick Bradsell, a former punk rocker from the Isle of Wight, started work behind the cocktail bar at the Atlantic Bar & Grill. Dick's, named in his honour, was a one-man revolution in London drinking. Bradsell, who had worked at famous bars like the Zanzibar and the Café de Paris, foresaw the trend for bars overtaking pubs, but he rescued the cocktail from its garish nightmare. Once more, Londoners were drinking dry martinis and gin slings, but they were no longer the preserve of the well-heeled habitués of bars like the Dukes Hotel in St James (which still offers the best mixed-at-table dry martini in town).

When Bradsell opened the Player in a Soho basement in 1998, he took the new sophistication and democratised it. The Player was nominally a members' club – in reality a sop to Westminster Council's licensing department – but it was easy enough for non-members to go down the stairs and experience a bar that offered the camaraderie of the pub and a uniqueness that no chain could match. And killer cocktails. Ten years later, Bradsell's legacy has spread over all of London, even to Peckham – an area associated with gunfire rather than gin, whose Bar Story serves sensational cocktails in a railway arch.

Unfortunately, many London drinkers cannot afford to go to bars: the capital is, notoriously, the most expensive place in which to drink in the British Isles – and, apart from Scandinavia, perhaps the world. Instead, they buy discount alcohol from supermarkets, leading to an epidemic of alcohol abuse. Madly, the government's response to this problem is to put more duty on drink, forcing more people out of pubs.

It's possible that in another 40 years, there won't be any London pubs. Or, to be optimistic, those that survive and prosper – like Greenwich Meantime Brewery and its Union pub on Greenwich's Royal Hill – will offer the comfort of an All Bar One with the independently local atmosphere of an old-fashioned London pub.

And there is still a hint of old Soho around for those that care to find it. The Colony is to be closed, and the French House, suffering the attraction of being the last of its kind, is often busy beyond endurance, but if you get there in the morning, and put work out of your mind, you can still feel the frisson of pleasure that comes with knowing you will be spending the whole day drinking in London. Just for the sake of drinking.

its apogee when the Midlands brewer Mitchells & Butlers opened scores of All Bar Ones across the capital in the 1990s. They were featureless, packed and no different in atmosphere and appearance from bar to bar: suddenly London's uniqueness was no more.

Even Soho changed. The development of a gay village saw Soho's atmosphere morph from seedy self-indulgence to one of out-and-proud celebration, with the rise of gay bars like the Admiral Duncan on Old Compton Street. Arguably, the pink pound saved Soho from the chain bars, but it came at a terrible price: two people were killed and dozens more injured and disfigured when the Duncan was bombed by a homophobic extremist in 1999.

Fancy a pint? Or perhaps a cocktail would be more appropriate these days.

FOOD & DRINK

The most modern thing in Manze's pie and mash shop is the extractor fan, suspended from the ceiling and gently humming. The rest – the bevelled green tiles and wooden benches – is much as it was when the place was established more than 100 years ago.

'See over there?' says Geoff Manze, grandson of the restaurant's founder Michele Manze, gesturing over to the front window. 'That's where you used to have galvanised trays with water running through them, and the eels all slithering about!'

Geoff is a big, friendly guy, who laughs with the sort of ease you'd expect from a giant about to eat or befriend a small child. 'You'd come up to the window, say, "I'll have that one". They'd pull it out for you, and chop it up there.'

Tradition is very much the watchword at Manze's, a true family firm: Geoff's brother Graham runs the Peckham restaurant – recent recipient of a blue plaque heritage award from Southwark, as voted for by borough residents – and his other brother, Rick, the Sutton branch. The Tower Bridge restaurant, where we're sitting today, is the oldest pie and mash shop still in existence in the capital: a London legend, a last bastion of Britishness. Albeit founded by an Italian. Geoff's grandfather came over to Britain when he was three years old in 1878. The family came from the village of Ravello, on the Amalfi coast, and their plan was to sell ice-cream. That was until they arrived in the UK and realised that the ice that had seemed so appealing in sun-drenched Italy might not go down so well in rainy, industrial London. Michele Manze opened the first of his pie shops in 1902 at 87 Tower Bridge Road.

Pies weren't new in London, though. During the 1700s, an army of 'pie men' walked the streets selling their wares straight off the trays to poor families in need of a good, hot meal. In those days, the pies were always filled with eel (rather than beef), and local eel at that, caught in the Thames, sold to the pie men at Billingsgate market, and served up with vinegar, or pea and mint sauce. The first proper pie shops sprang up in London around 1850, with little stalls outside where people could buy live eels to take home and cook (presumably concussed first). Inside, there were mirrors on the walls and marble floors covered in sawdust on to which you could spit out your eel bones. The shops tended to be located near markets, mopping up trade from stallholders, dockers and factory workers.

By World War I there were 150 pie shops in London; by 1930, the Manze empire had grown to 14 pie, mash and eel shops (though all but three have since closed or been taken over). Even rationing during World War II seemed to work to the pie shops' advantage, with pie and eels an easy way to get a nutritious supper – and once the war was over, it's said that London embarked on a lengthy beer, pie and eels bender.

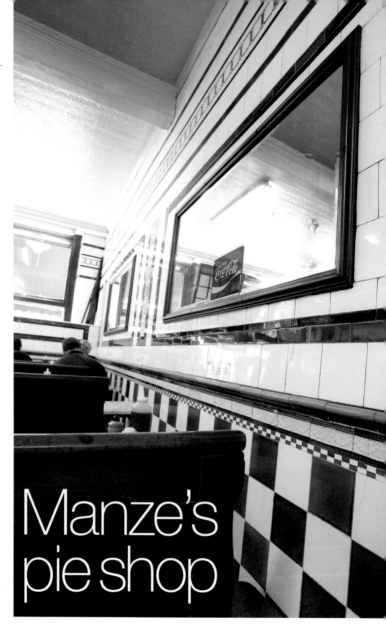

Manze's pie shop

'I think pie and mash got popular purely because you get a decent meal for very little money,' says Geoff. 'And although it was a treat to come to one of these, it was an affordable treat. Rather than go out to a fancy restaurant and spend a lot of money, come here, get a decent meal that'd fill you up all day.'

Geoff was introduced to the family business as a boy; he'd come in every Sunday with his dad, to clean out the flues on the coal-fired oven.

'When I came through the door, there was always a familiar smell, although nothing was cooking or anything like that. Every now and then, I pick up the smell and it reminds me of that …' Did he like the food as a little kid? 'I didn't. I was very fussy as a child.' And your favourite food now? 'Curry. I love curry.'

Today, Manze's is still packing them in: young, trendy couples in Camper shoes,

EAT IN		£	p
1 PIE & LIQUOR		1	65
1 PIE	1 MASH	2	30
1 PIE	2 MASH	2	95
2 PIE	1 MASH	3	45
PIE	2 MASH	4	10
EELS & MASH		3	00
JELLIED EELS		2	35
DRINKS			70

shopped-out mums with gaggles of small kids, and big blokes covered in tattoos.

'They're the same people day in, day out, and then the next generation comes along that they've brought up on it, and they've become pie and mash addicts, and they carry it on,' says Geoff.

But London's appetite for pies has been on the wane since the '50s. Rents rocketed and factories began to relocate out of town; it wasn't long until fast-food joints began to appear, and the pie shops began to close.

'We're still very threatened by all of them,' says Geoff, 'but you've gotta learn to live alongside them. You can only compete to a degree, because you're different.'

How about trendy young pie firebrands, like the Square Pie Company?

'Never heard of them,' says Geoff.

You're not worried about them invading your turf then?

'Obviously not!'

One of the most impressive aspects of Manze's, apart from the fact that you can still get a meal of two pies, a mountain of mash and a lake of liquor for £3.45, is its total resistance to modernising. The washing-up is done by hand behind the counter; the background noise is conversation and the scratch of fork on plate; and the hygiene certificate hangs about ten feet up the wall, with a mysterious

Pie and mash – but no baked beans.

splodge of food stuck to it (how it got on there is anyone's guess). And the menu, painstakingly spelled out on a peg board by the cash till, never changes: pies, mash, eels, tea, sarsaparilla.

'We did try to change it once,' says Geoff. 'We introduced baked beans, peas and sausages.' Did they catch on? 'None of them. We were throwing away more than we were selling.'

The only concession, it seems, is the vegetarian pie option. 'It did seem very odd, but we were losing out. If four people go to lunch and one's a vegetarian …'

What do you think of the vegetarian pie?

'I've never eaten one, I've got to say that. But I tried the filling, which is minced soya…' He winces.

Original article by Sophie Harris.

FOOD & DRINK

Memory bank

Nick Broomfield on Schmidts, Charlotte Street

Schmidts opened on Charlotte Street in 1901, and was a meeting place for the German community in London. A number of spies were arrested there in both wars. It looked like a German bierhall: very long, with notoriously rude waiters. It was always full, so they'd shout at you if you took too long or asked any questions about the food, which was served in a complex chit system. The food was great and pretty cheap: my mother was Czech, so I grew up with dumplings, goulash and sauerkraut. When it closed, I bought an enormous umbrella and hat rack, and a big wooden chest where all the branded cutlery was stored – I use it as a tool chest. I guess they sold up because rents were too high and Mrs Schmidt was getting too old to work.

Mrs Schmidt was an institution: very gruff, with her hair in a severe bun and a formidable moustache. She was always on the lookout for people trying to steal her salami. They were stored behind these glass counters, and when I was at film school and we were all broke, the challenge was to swipe one. If you got caught, you probably got sent to Germany in a diplomatic bag.

I was with [future director] Ben Lewin, who'd had polio when he was younger so he used crutches. We'd normally have him collapse in the middle of the room, and while everyone rushed forward, I'd reach over and try to get a salami up my sleeve. We only managed to do it once, so I don't think we contributed directly to the restaurant's closure.

There's nothing like it now. Heavy German food doesn't really fit in with today's macrobiotic yoga culture. The German community is more assimilated now, and others have taken their place.

Nick Broomfield is an award-winning film maker whose work includes Aileen: Life and Death of a Serial Killer, Ghosts and Battle for Haditha.

A health food history

FOOD & DRINK

Two hundred years ago, when left-leaning thinkers looked around the polluted urban landscape of the Industrial Revolution and began to argue that people should purify themselves through diet, they formed the Vegetarian Society to promote the simple idea that meat was the enemy. By the Edwardian era, a parallel motivation for vegetariansim had arisen, which hooked itself on to concepts of non-violence (Mahatma Gandhi was a member of the London Vegetarian Society) and other self-consciously progressive ideas – and it thrived.

Matthew Kay from Manna in Chalk Farm (one of London's oldest surviving vegetarian restaurants, founded in 1967) has researched the movement's history and discovered that as early as 1897 there were no fewer than 32 vegetarian restaurants in the capital. A 100-year-old map from the Vegetarian Society shows several eateries, including one, the Garden, that appears to be a chain.

'The image of the sandal-wearing, nut-cutlet-eating vegetarian became popular in cartoons in Punch in the 1930s and '40s,' says Kay, 'and it was people like George Bernard Shaw who were being cartooned. That image has nothing to do with the later '60s and '70s hippy influence.'

While the vegetarian movement is proud to hold up radical thinkers like Shelley, Rousseau, Shaw and Tolstoy as totems of their tribe, other carrot-juicers went over to the the dark side. 'Yes, there was a link with self-improvement and teetotalism,' says Kay, 'but on the other hand there was a link with the right, with Hitler, Wagner, the body beautiful, naturism, that whole side – the will to power, dominating the body as well as the world.'

While the first body fascists were striving for one kind of purity in the 1930s, another group was emphasising food provenance: the Soil Association. Unlike the urban and socialist vegetarian movement, organics were the preoccupation of landowners like Lady Eve Balfour, who in 1943 wrote a seminal book on the subject called *The Living Soil*. Her theories dovetailed with vogueish anti-modern ideas about tradition and authenticity, from the arts and crafts movement to Cecil Sharp's folk revivalism, but the organic movement was distinctively upper-crust. 'Which is still the case if you look at Prince Charles and his adherence to it,' adds Kay.

It was 1960s counterculture that fused grow-your-own organics with vegetarianism, drawing on eastern traditions of Hinduism and Buddhism to connect meatlessness with spiritual cleanliness. By then, dining options for London's vegetarians had shrunk. Among the stalwarts were Manna,

Cranks, 1975.

Manna, 1968.

Cranks (with branches across London), and Food for Thought on Neal Street. With its historic links to the fruit and veg trade, the Covent Garden area seemed a natural location for a meat-free outlet, and Neal's Yard continues the tradition of offering lunch options with a side order of good karma. During the hippy era, though, the fare was unexciting by modern standards. A 1967 Manna menu Kay has unearthed boasts such exotic items as avocado (a luxury at six shillings), fondue and yoghurt. 'It was a bit of a sackcloth option in the '60s,' he laughs. 'You were eating it because it was doing you so much good. There's an element of that now in organic food too; people will eat anything as long as it's organic.'

And, increasingly, that includes meat, once anathema to the hardcore ethical eater but now perfectly acceptable to many, as long as it ticks all the other boxes. According to Chris Olivant of the Vegetarian Society, which has seen its membership stagnate in the last decade, people's definition of 'untainted' food has shifted since vegetarianism's most recent heyday in the 1990s, when new-age ideas coincided with BSE-inspired meat paranoia. 'There are more options now; buying locally, buying organic, that sort of thing,' he says. 'At the same time, some people are cutting vegetarian foods from their diet because they're not sure how fairly they're traded. Soya is a case in point. People are worried it might be GM, there are health issues around eating too much soya at certain ages, and soya is grown in rainforests and so forth, plus there's the air miles. But you can virtually pick any food in the world and decide not to eat it.'

Original article by Lisa Mullen.

Gordon Ramsay

You're a big fan of the fry-up. . .
The full English breakfast, late Friday night, at Vingt-Quatre on the Fulham Road. It's the best place for it. When you've finished in the kitchen, you've been on a high for the last four hours and things have gone well – you can't go home and switch off, you've got to wind down slowly.

How often do you cook for yourself?
Never. I can't. Chefs don't cook for themselves because they graze. You are like a heifer, tasting constantly.

You must cook for somebody sometime.
Never. I don't hold dinner parties. If someone comes round, they expect fireworks and I don't want to do fireworks. Cooking's stressful and when you're home you don't want to deal with the scrutiny. Second, the oven at home is just a disgusting mess. It's laced with chicken nuggets and alphabet fucking hoola-hoops.

What will you never be able to eat/drink again?
In Australia last year, I was served what they called lambs' kidneys – they were very pale and they had all these veins running through them – pan-fried with brioche crumbs and garlic. But, in fact, they were sheep's testicles. The worst drink I ever had was absinthe. I would rather stick my tongue in a cow's backside than drink another glass of absinthe.

What do you miss about you mum's cooking?
Mum wasn't a terribly great cook. If I wanted to rekindle a relationship with my mother's cooking, I'd go and eat school dinners.

What's your most extravagant eating/drinking luxury?
1966 was a great year for vintage wine, and it was also the year I was born. So, Château Latour '66.

What would make your ideal bar, and why?
To get a great bar, ban all cigar- and pipe-smoking ponces, and have a great selection of champagne served by half a dozen of Peter Stringfellow's girls.

Delia, Nigella, or Jamie?
I'd like to have a bowl of spaghetti carbonara under the duvet with Nigella – as she is on the advert – and send Delia home to the missus. Jamie's a very talented cook and he's fun to have in the kitchen. When he worked with me, all my guys expected him to roll in at ten. But seven o'clock in the morning, he'd be bright as a berry, chirpy and ready to go.

That's very diplomatic.
I've got to be diplomatic.

Interview by Alexia Loundras, *Time Out*, 27 February 2002.
Gordon Ramsay now has a stake in 12 London restaurants.

FOOD & DRINK

For your dining pleasure

Reviews of key London restaurants from *Time Out*'s Eating & Drinking guides over the years.

FOOD & DRINK

Le Caprice

Arlington Street, SW1

1983

During the course of one recent lunchtime sitting, the tables were graced by Ian Dury, Tina Brown, Shirley Conran, Leslie Caron, Peter Blake and most of the staff of *Vogue* magazine. Stargazing aside, Le Caprice's menu is short and caters for most moods and degrees of hunger.

Saucisses d'agneau arrive prettily, accompanied by onion marmalade and a bill for a mere £4.25; the more indulgent petit carré d'agneau en croute, well seasoned and choux croute-d, adds to *l'addition* by £6.50. With a selection of vegetables that, in all honesty, are cooked for too long to justify even the nominal £1 charged for them, you can spend a tee-total lunchtime seeing and being seen for under a tenner.

L'Escargot

48 Greek Street, W1

1983

Along with Langan's, L'Escargot is one of London's most spacious and elegant places in which to eat. Downstairs is run as a brasserie and upstairs, presided over by Eleana, Bianchi's ex-maitre d', the eau de nil

and eerily lit dining room has taken over from Bianchi's as the literary world's favourite lunch spot.

Joe Allen

13 Exeter Street, WC2

1985

Joe Allen's, styled on the famous New York establishment, is about the nearest we've got to a classic American restaurant. The menu features barbecued ribs, caesar salad, an excellent chef's salad, black bean soup, chilli, chopped steak and one of the best burgers in town. Puddings, such as pecan pie, chocolate brownies and crème brulee, are of high quality and stacked with an almost ludicrous number of calories.

Service is quick, if occasionally off-hand, and Joe Allen's is always busy. One beef – why can't Mr Allen put a finned Cadillac over the door like the one over JA's in LA?

Alastair Little

49 Frith Street, W1

1986

The eponymous restaurant of the brilliant, self-taught chef Alastair Little has become a London hotspot. The decor is modern and stylish, and informality is achieved with a walk-through

kitchen. Little has been heavily influenced by Michel Guerard, the innovator of cuisine minceur, and he is especially good with fish. Outstanding dishes are warm red mullet on a bed of salad, a rich, smooth duck liver pâté served with tiny spinach leaf salad, and steamed brill accompanied by sorrel sauce. Desserts are always a blend of the exotic and the familiar: passion fruit mousse cake and colour-coded sorbets.

Clarke's

124 Kensington Church Street, W8

1986

Clarke's is firmly in the French tradition of the chef/patron-run restaurant and Sally Clarke has had great success. She charges a set price of £15 for a menu of fresh, light, French-ish food.

On the day we write, Clarke offers a chilled soup of green lentils, bacon, chillis, fresh coriander and avocado, served with deep-fried corn chips, various fish tossed together with fresh chervil and champagne, baked in wafer-thin pastry with baby potatoes and spring cabbage.

To follow, there's British cheese with oatmeal biscuits or toasted almond meringue served

layered with a lemon and yoghurt cream, passion fruit, pear, banana and papaya.

Harvey's

2 Bellevue Road, SW17

1987

The chef at Harvey's is Marco White, a fiery young Yorkshireman with an impressive CV. He considers texture, flavour and freshness more important than appearance, though his tagliatelle of oysters was prettily presented – and sublime. The set dinner menu at £15.50 gives several choices in each of two courses, and there's a smaller lunch-

time menu for £9.95. On our visit this included three main courses: roast rabbit with wild mushrooms, bavette of Scotch beef in red wine and a deliciously tender fillet of pork with a creamy tarragon sauce. The perfect dessert is Marco's terrine of fresh fruit, set in an orange jelly and decorated with brunoise of fruit and orange syrup sauce.

Kensington Place

201-205 Kensington Church Street, W8

1988

Bibendum

The management team of Nick Smallwood and Simon Slater have created a cool, glass-walled environment at Kensington Place. Chef Rowley Leigh's menu includes such delights as grilled foie gras with a sweetcorn pancake (£8), but it's not entirely composed of expensive ingredients. Mussels and spring cabbage (£3.75), roast saddle of rabbit with tomato and basil (£7.50), with the already legendary baked tamarillos to follow are all excellent.

Bibendum

Michelin Building, 81 Fulham Road, SW3

1988

Foodies eagerly awaited the opening of Sir Terence Conran's new headquarters in the Michelin Building at Brompton Cross. They they knew it was to be run by Simon Hopkinson and Joel Kissin, the winning team from Hilaire in South Ken. Hopkinson has established a reputation for consistently superb, imaginative modern French food; and Kissin runs the front of house so expertly that dishes always arrive promptly and in perfect condition.

The food is robust and satisfying, simple but not simplistic, and includes consommé, saucisson with lentils, and salade de museau (pig's snout), offal (tripes, sweetbreads and brains), and a few rarities. The dining-room, with its bold stained glass and soothing blue and

cream is elegant and comfortable. Prices are commensurate with the luxuriousness of the operation.

The River Café

Thames Wharf, Rainville Road, W6

1988

The River Café is quite simply in a different league from other Itailian restaurants in London. It looks out on to the river, has a bright and airy interior and manages to be both glamorous and comfortably informal. The food is almost rustic in its simplicity, but delicious.

Starters include wonderful Tuscan dishes rarely seen in restaurants, such as panzanella, a flavourful salad of bread, tomatoes, olive oil, capers, basil and olives; grilled peppers with capers and a superb spaghettini with fresh chilli, garlic and parsley. Main courses include butterflied grilled lamb with char-grilled aubergines. A simple salad of rocket leaves and green beans was an admirable accompaniment to the main courses.

Desserts included the best choclate cake we'd ever eaten and a meltingly delious apricot and almond tart. The red house wine from the Abruzzi area of Italy is excellent and the wines are good value, with several bottles at £11 or under. The service is efficient and unfussy yet amiable. A real treat of a place with a very indiviual and successful style of cooking.

Sketch

Quaglino's

16 Bury Street, SW1

1994

To descend the stairs of Quaglino's into the spectacular hangar of animated tables, held up with jazzily painted columns and terminating in a mirrored crustacea bar, is to feel you've arrived at the epicentre of eating out as an event.

This is Sir Terence Conran's latest – and most hyped – culinary venture, and the place and the pace is bright and sharp, the noise just short of deafening.

The food doesn't disappoint. Seafood is the star of the starters, except for a dull langoustine salad, a reinvention of the prawn cocktail. Steamed mussels with pesto, only £3.95, was fab. The Quaglino's salad (£2.50) of creamily dressed lettuce and

avocado swathed with shaved parmesan would be best as a starter. Deep-fried plaice with pommes frites (£10.50), was one of the most gorgeous, crispiest pieces of fish ever eaten, with near perfect chips. Rabbit with prosciutto and herbs came stuffed with sage, wrapped in bacon to keep the flesh soft and presented with roast carrots, onions and endive.

Prices don't seem exorbitant until the bill with 15% automatically added arrives. Then it'll add up to £30 a head without trying. In theory, you don't have to book for the balcony bar where you can join the crush of Mayfair types, have cheaper antipasti beside the grand piano and look down on the exhilarating scene below. The main drawback is the difficulty of booking a table.

Sugar Club

33A All Saints Road, W11

1996

Spawned from its namesake in New Zealand, Sugar Club brings a blast of fresh antipodean air into All Saints Road. It's a relaxing place to enjoy a menu strong on starters and afters. Wonderful ciabatta rolls with chives kicked off the meal very promisingly. Scallops with a hot, sweet, Thai-type sauce packing plenty of chilli and lemongrass, served with crème fraiche to cool them down, nudged into top spot. We spent just over £15 each on really successful original food, knocked back too much house rose – recommended – and left debilitated by enjoyment but glad to have joined the club.

Moro

34-36 Exmouth Market, EC1

1998

Moro attracted a great deal of attention when it was opened in May 1997 by a team including cooks Jake Hodges plus husband and wife Sam and Sam Clark (ex of the River Café and the Eagle). It is fashionably minimal and light, with cream and green walls, a long metal-topped bar , an open kitchen and a plain wooden floor. A modish metropolitan crowd fills the space. The innovative, frequently changing menu incorporates influences from Spain,North Africa and other parts of the Med.

FOOD & DRINK

A high-point is the expert buying of first-rate Spanish produce: a starter of cecina (dry-cured beef) with artichokes and chilli (£5.50) featured superb, richly-flavoured meat; for afters, cheese (£3.50), including some wonderfully pungent Asturian Picos de Europa goat's cheese.

Mash

19-21 Great Portland Street, W1
1999

If you regard airport lounge decor of the 1970s as chic (and you wouldn't be alone), this is for you. The latest in Oliver Peyton's chain of high-profile venues is split-level, with a huge bar on the ground floor and a first-floor restaurant coloured in brash orange, maroon and olive, with Formica here and steel or concrete there. Once we'd got past the confusing greeting system, we were treated to efficient service and good food.

The menu ranges disconcertingly far and wide, over breakfast, brunch, bar snacks, cocktails, pizzas, pastas and various options from the wood-burning oven. House beer – brewed here in visible tanks – are a bonus, and the wine and list is extensive.

Shoreditch Electricity Showrooms

39A Hoxton Square, N1
1999

Very much the bar of the moment in these fashionable parts, this place is so cool that it hasn't even bothered to change its name or alter its appearance much. The lightbulbs hanging from the high ceiling, still in their GEC packaging as makeshift shades, are a witty reminder of the place's former use. Attractively battered sofas and old tables and chairs spread back from the vast windows towards the bar, where you'll find a decent range of draught beers ontap (Kirin, at £2.40 a pint, and Bomabadier bitter, £2.20) and plenty of bottled varieties (including Mexican Negra Modello, £2.30).

Drinkers in one corner are silhouetted against a lurid, kitsch alpine scene. Modish food is served from an open kitchen. There's a small seating area at the back with seats in booths, and there are plans to set up a cocktail lounge (even a swing bar, perhaps) in the basement.

Hakkasan

8 Hanway Place, W1
2002

The latest brainchild of Wagamama creator, Alan Yau, this stylish restaurant has wowed the critics with its fabulous decor and funky Chinese food.

The entrance, down an unlikely staircase with smoky-green slate walls, lit here and there by luminous red panels, is stunning. The first glimpse of the interior will take your breath away. The warehouse-like space, designed by Christian Liaigre, is divided into bar, lounge and dining areas by the skilful use of latticed screens that cleverly allude to the design of traditional Chinese courtyard houses. Backlit blue glass panels add to the atmosphere, shedding a curious light over the dining area.

Over the course of several dim sum lunches, the food has always impressed. Dim sum are roughly twice as expensive as those in Chinatown, but in surroundings like these, who cares?

Sketch

9 Conduit Street, W1
2004

Sketch must be the most famous restaurant to open in London in 2003, garnering more column inches, it seems, than Becks's move to Real Madrid. It's quite a complex, with two bars, a tea room, and two restaurants. The astonishingly expensive Lecture Room is the one that's received all the press, but the ground-floor Gallery is a no-less interesting affair – and much cheaper.

Like everything else at Sketch, the menu is big on shock value. How about 'pardon pepper', with lardo colonato or tonka parfait? There's a Japanese influence in the presentation: lots of itsy-bitsy stuff on geometric plates. And there's no such thing as a simple dish; most have several components, and they're not always easy to identify. Would you be able to spot a lemon balm nage or a soup of chervil root? Us neither.

But to judge Sketch on its cooking alone is to miss the point. People come here to be and be seen. And it's worth visiting just to see the futuristic *2001: A Space Odyssey* design – a series of startlingly white rooms housing vintage furniture classics; fibreglass, pod-like toilets and trippy wall projections.

The Wolseley

160 Piccadilly, W1
2005

Housed in a former car showroom and bank, the Wolseley – the latest offspring of top restaurateurs Chris Corbin and Jeremy King – has fast become one of London's prized dining spots. The art deco interior recreates prewar grandeur with vaulted ceilings, grand pillars, polished marble and weighty chandeliers. Despite the opulence, the vibe is very friendly, and customers can enjoy food from the café menu without having to book.

It's open from breakfast onwards, and the afternoon tea ritual is truly memorable. A superb selection of fresh finger sandwiches, filled with smoked salmon, succulent chicken pieces and sliced cucumber, said so much about stylish simplicity. Just as scrumptious were dainty French cakes, excellent macaroons and almond meringues.

The Wolseley

FOOD & DRINK

Made in London

The big-brand brewers and biscuit makers have left town, to be replaced by smaller-scale producers creating artisanal fare.

By Jenni Muir

Some say you could smell the biscuits for years after the Peek Frean's factory in Bermondsey closed down. Garibaldi. Bourbon. Infused in the brickwork of the building and those on surrounding streets. Peek Frean & Company lasted 123 years at 100 Clements Road, SE16, having been founded at Dockhead in 1857. Right up until 1989, it was providing employment for Londoners (4,000 at its height), pioneering the provision of medical and dental services, decent working hours, holiday pay and tea breaks for staff, and scenting the Bermondsey air with the sweet fragrance of baking biscuits and, from the 1930s, Twiglets and Cheeselets.

Some say SE16 was no place for a food factory. Overheads. Transport problems. The general manager at the time of Peek Frean's closure even suggested people had stopped eating biscuits. But some of the company's brands survive, made by other factories in other places, even other countries. Today they'd say Peek Frean's was a victim of asset stripping. Its parent company Nabisco was bought, and anything of value – like a sizeable piece of property in London – was sold off.

The value of land, the cost of rent – it's a challenge for everyone who tries to do business in the capital. Wouldn't it be better to cash in and move out to the less salubrious parts of the home counties? Young's finally did. After 175 years at the Ram Brewery in Wandsworth, the company shifted its brewing operation to a site in

Bedfordshire, and sold its old site to property developer Minerva for a whopping £69m. Even the softest of hearts would agree that the draught horses and drays that until the end delivered kegs to nearby pubs were hardly efficient on our modern road system. The site is being turned into a mixed-use development, with restaurants, shops and flats (including affordable housing); the poignant postscript was that chairman John Young died days before the closure of the brewery, while the final brew was being run.

At the time the brewery was founded, proximity to the Thames was key for incoming and outgoing goods. It was the same with other food and drink businesses. You may not have heard of the Liebig Extract of Meat Company, but it has left an enduring mark on London. In 1928, it moved into a Thames-side building its owners had commissioned for processing its various 'energy of beef' products, made from the comparatively inexpensive carcasses shipped to the UK from South America. The building had a number of wooden loading bays on each floor: they are still there, but Liebig soon moved on. Later, the building spent some time as a caviar storehouse, and was briefly used to produce long eggs for Dewhurst pies, but it was derelict by the mid'70s. Now known as the Oxo Tower, it has proved more successful as a mixed-use property development, design workshops and smart restaurant destination than it ever did as a food factory.

Not every company seems fated to leave, however. Beefeater is still proudly distilling London dry gin in Kennington, near the Oval cricket ground. Fuller's still runs its Griffin Brewery in Chiswick. Tate & Lyle has recently celebrated 125 years producing golden syrup in the Newham area – you can even see a giant tin on the side of the refinery opposite West Silvertown DLR. And although it has been forced to vacate one building to make way for the Olympic development, the fourth generation of H Forman & Son – Britain's first salmon smokery – has no intention of moving production of its distinctively mild 'London cure' from the East End.

There is also an increasing number of small artisan food businesses setting up to supply the capital's discerning foodies through the growing network of farmers' markets, fine food shops, gastropubs, cafés and restaurants. Although they face the same challenges of high rent and overheads, the local focus on sales and delivery makes their central location an advantage.

Leading the pack is gourmet coffee company Union Hand-Roasted, founded by Jeremy Torz and Steven Macatonia and based in E16. Inspired by San Francisco's micro-roastery cafés, the pair set up their own business, which has become the industry pace-setter for ethical sourcing of coffee beans. Over the past ten to 15 years, London has also developed an enviable cache of craft bakeries – Flour Power City, Born and Bread, the Flour Station, Gail Force, Clarke's, Celtic Bakers and more – and a continually expanding list of world-standard chocolatiers, including Paul A Young, William Curley, Demarquette and Melt.

Indeed, London's new artisan food producers are as diverse, cosmopolitan and sophisticated as the city itself. No smart city breakfast table is complete without a jar of intensely fruity London marmalade, or Kentish bramble jam, from England Preserves of New Cross Gate. Need a readymeal for a quick supper after a long day at the office? Try the Two Fishwives fish pies and fish cakes, or La Tua's tortelloni and ravioli – all made in Park Royal. The city's embrace of all things Asian includes Geeta's fabulous mango chutney produced by the North Circular, St John and Dolly Smith's brinjal and lime pickles made by hand on a stovetop in Ealing, and Cyrus Todiwala's unique venison and wild boar pickles produced at his E1 restaurant, Café Spice Namaste. Fancy a drink? The beers of Charlton's Meantime Brewing includes German-style Helles light beer, Grand Cru wheat beer, and eyebrow-raising chocolate- and coffee-flavoured varieties.

And of the future? Though London's food factories have all but disappeared, it's worth remembering that several of them were built on the sites of market gardens, and it's locally grown fresh produce that the city really lacks. Not-for-

Tate & Lyle still has a factory in London, unlike Peek Frean's.

profit organisation Sustain: the Alliance for Better Food and Farming argues that by following the examples of cities including New York and Chicago, London could commercially produce salads, vegetables and even fish in an environmentally-friendly manner. It is hoping to persuade town planners, architects and policy makers to buy into its vision of urban agriculture and incorporate holistic food production schemes within their projects. The Royal Parks and Federation of City Farms and Gardens are already on board, and chefs such as Oliver Rowe at Konstam are already seeking out 'local' produce such as mushrooms grown under the North Circular in East Ham, and chicken reared in Waltham Abbey, while the rest of us plunder Stoke Newington's community orchards, Carshalton's lavender fields and a remarkable number of postcode-specific honeys. Food not just made in London, but grown in London too.

Be here now!

How did a drab, postwar capital of a defunct empire
reinvent itself as the cultural envy of the world?

By Lisa Mullen

o London Like a Local! That's the message
pumped out across the globe by the capital's
tourist office, Visit London, and it says a lot
about the city's confident modern identity. Yes, we
tell the world, we have all the Princess Di tea towels
and Beefeater pencil sharpeners your heritage-
hungry little hearts could desire, but there's more
to us than shortbread and Sherlock Holmes.
We have art! We have shopping! We have fun!

This is a huge shift in perception. It's true
that, back in 1968, London was already
enjoying a boom in tourism: visitor numbers
were cranking up gradually from a postwar slump
(a mere 1.6m people came in 1964), thanks to
Swinging London, increased prosperity and
cheaper air travel. A boom in hotel building in the
1970s testified to the city's growing popularity, but
the idea that those precious dollars, francs and yen
could be spent in places frequented by the locals
would have seemed laughable. London had one

An icon of new London: the Millennium Bridge.

thing to offer tourists, and one thing only: history. They wanted to snap Big Ben and the Tower, ride on a double decker, see the waxworks and then scurry back to their hotels, hoping against hope that dinner would be vaguely edible. For kicks, they might take in a musical, sample Soho's strip clubs or sit in the hotel bar under a 'residents only' sign, safe in the knowledge that no 'locals' would get past the doorman.

How times have changed. The latest statistics show that 15.6m visitors now come to London every year, and the trend is upwards. The money they spend adds up to £15bn, or ten per cent of the city's GDP. They adore the free admission to our major museums and galleries; they flock to new attractions such as the London Eye, Shakespeare's Globe and Tate Modern; they compete for tables in the 43 Michelin-starred restaurants.

Not only that, but today's trendiest hotels make a point of appealing to the local crowd too, with designer destinations such as St Martin's Lane and Soho Hotel offering style bars,

film screenings and other entertainments to keep Londoners coming back. And of course, more and more of those Londoners were originally from overseas themselves, attracted here as immigrants by much the same things that make London a great place to visit. At the last count in 2006, 2,288,000 of a total of 7.5m Londoners were born in other countries; collectively, we speak 300 languages. London has become the most diverse city the planet has ever seen.

This cultural vibrancy is reflected in our street fashion, our music and, perhaps most of all, our food. But surveying the vast range of cuisines we have to choose from, it's easy to forget how recently London was a gastronomic wasteland. A glance at *Time Out*'s 1978 restaurant coverage paints a gloomy picture. Beyond trattorias and chop houses, beyond Indian and Chinese, you had… La Germainerie on Chancery Lane, which had decor

majoring on 'cuckoo clocks, clogs, grinding wheels, stags' heads etc'. And, lest we forget, it was in 1979 that the first Garfunkel's opened its doors.

By 1988, things had improved vastly. London could field a United Nations of cuisines and exotic produce, available, at a price, all year round. Meanwhile, the charm of nouvelle cuisine was already starting to pall. 'When pub food becomes nouvelle, what will be on the menu?' restaurant critic Joanne Glaseby wondered. 'How could you nouvelle shepherd's pie?' In a way, her words were prophetic: the 1990s saw the return of upmarket comfort food, with the Ivy's shepherd's pie leading the trend, and pub grub did indeed transform in 1991, when the first gastropub, the Eagle in Farringdon, started serving well-priced, quality food in a relaxed environment.

Local colour

In recent years, the unveiling of a new gastropub has often been the harbinger of gentrification in a run-down part of London. Back in 1968, large tracts of the city centre, including now-expensive Islington and Camden Town, were still squalid slums populated by impoverished families left behind by the middle-class flight to the suburbs. In the intervening 40 years, the city's expanding wealth has almost completed the process of filling these wealth gaps, and this regeneration has fostered a strong sense of local community centred on the revival of the high street. Along with gastropubs came the new delis, which catered to Londoners' increasingly sophisticated appetites. And there were exciting new local entertainment options too, especially comedy clubs like the Balham Banana and Greenwich's Up the Creek, both of which were products of the late '80s/early '90s alternative comedy boom. The revival of local cinemas in the 1990s, like the Electric on Portobello Road and Brixton's Ritzy, echoed this trend.

But the rebirth of the London's 'villages' didn't stop tills ringing in the West End. Oxford Street,

From left: National Theatre, British Museum's Great Court, GLA headquarters, firework display over the Thames, Borough Market.

once a dingy, hostile place, is now the busiest shopping street in Europe, and international chains like Gap, Zara and Uniqlo consider it essential to maintain a flagship there.

At the other end of the scale, London's markets are also thriving: more and more farmers' markets are springing up to feed our penchant for fresh local produce, while former fruit and veg markets like Borough have reinvented themselves as gourmet destinations. And although traditional clothing markets like Petticoat Lane have been superceded by upstart traders wheeling and dealing at car boot sales and craft fairs, Brick Lane has benefited from a surge of interest in vintage clothes and retro furniture, especially the style that's come to be known as mid-century modern. Even Spitalfields – in the 1960s, an area of extreme deprivation – has transformed into a fashionable lifestyle hub, piggybacking on the rise and rise of east London's style credentials.

Money, money, money

That ongoing eastern renaissance was pioneered in Hoxton in the mid 1990s by new breeds of artist and website designer looking for affordable premises. But its growth was fed by a completely different London subset: the City millionaires. Since the Big Bang in 1986, when the London Stock Exchange

'2,288,000 people out of a total 7.5m Londoners are born in other countries – it has become the most diverse city on the planet.'

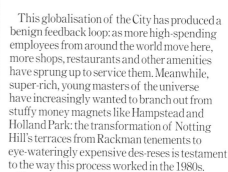

This globalisation of the City has produced a benign feedback loop: as more high-spending employees from around the world move here, more shops, restaurants and other amenities have sprung up to service them. Meanwhile, super-rich, young masters of the universe have increasingly wanted to branch out from stuffy money magnets like Hampstead and Holland Park: the transformation of Notting Hill's terraces from Rackman tenements to eye-wateringly expensive des-reses is testament to the way this process worked in the 1980s.

The recolonisation of the post-industrial hinterlands of central London is now complete. When British Telecom split London's phone numbers into an inner and outer code in 1990, the issue was still touchy enough to warrant an advertising campaign that stressed the desirability of 'central London' rather than the stigma of 'inner city'. It's impossible to imagine anyone succumbing to such status anxiety now: even King's Cross has succumbed to a cleaning-up process designed to co-incide with the arrival of the first Eurostar trains at St Pancras.

Fun, fun, fun

It's these newly promoted areas that tend to host the big events that come to define not just their identity, but the essential nature of London itself. The Notting Hill Carnival has developed from a local expression of Caribbean pride in the '60s, to a focus of multicultural unease in the '80s, and finally into the chaotic, sprawling street party it is today, constantly threatening to collapse under its own success. Clerkenwell began something similarly local when it launched an Architecture Biennale, but soon gave in to the same widening-out process: in 2008 it spread its

abolished fixed commission charges and ushered in a thousand clichés about greed, striped shirts and barrowboys, the City has become Europe's undisputed banking and business centre. The headquarters of more than 100 of Europe's 500 largest companies are in London, and a quarter of the world's largest financial companies have their European headquarters here, lured by the square meterage of modern, open-plan office space that has been provided around Canary Wharf and Broadgate. The London foreign exchange market is the largest in the world, with an average daily turnover of $504bn, more than New York and Tokyo combined. Money breeds money: 550 international banks and 170 global securities houses have set up offices in London – twice the number on Wall Street.

CONSUME

wings to encompass the whole of London, and threw up all kinds of sub-projects and local initiatives.

Say what you like about him, Ken Livingstone always understood the importance of bread and circuses. Noting the success of free Hyde Park gigs between 1968 and 1976, which saw everyone from the Stones to Pink Floyd rolling up to play to vast crowds, Ken's GLC arranged a number of free concerts and festivals in a last-ditch bid for popularity in the 1980s, just before being abolished. In the 21st century, his tenure as Mayor saw London once again embrace the notion of outdoor festivals, drizzle or no drizzle – and he certainly understood the city's need for a proper fireworks party on New Year's Eve.

At his behest, too, Trafalgar Square was transformed from a smog-choked roundabout best known for political protest, to a venue for music, screenings and art installations. For the 2006 London Design Festival, Tom Dixon filled the Square with a mountain of free chairs for people to take away; he repeated the trick (and the subsequent round-the-square queues) the following year by creating a first-come-first-served chandelier of giant energy-saving lightbulbs. Also in 2007, the people at Visit London arranged for the Square to be turfed, and provided deckchairs to help visitors appreciate the park-like atmosphere; and in 2004, artist Doug Fishbone adorned the space with 3,000 bananas in what

From left: Trafalgar Square Festival, Lord Mayor's Show, London Eye, Piccadilly Circus.

he termed a 'cutting-edge, fruit-based masterpiece'. And when Londoners are not gathering at the Square for a gig like the Pet Shop Boys' gigantic 2004 free event (where they provided the soundtrack to Eisenstein's silent film *Battleship Potemkin*), they are rallying there in city solidarity, as they did when the successful outcome of our 2012 Olympic bid was announced.

GLA-sponsored multicultural events such as the St Patrick's Day parade and London Mela, both established since 2000, have come to see like age-old fixtures on the calendar, and our appetite for a communal knees-up has also been answered by the Deptford X art event each September, and the Greenwich and Docklands International Festival (established in 2004 and featuring a wide programme of outdoor art events) each une. Meanwhile, the outdoor art fair, Freize, inaugurated only in 2003, is already a fashionable must-see for the international collector, as well as an accessible Regent's Park entertainment for the rest of us.

The downside of this renaissance is obvious to anyone who has tried to survive in London on an average wage: official figures rank the capital as one of the priciest cities in the world. Living costs are 26 per cent higher than they are in New York, for instance, not just in terms of property, but also for eating out, travel (a non-Oyster card tube journey costs £4, whereas an undiscounted ride on the New York subway is around £1) or any other urban necessity. Meanwhile, London salaries rank only tenth on the global scale. In a 2007 ranking of the most expensive cities in the world, London came second behind Moscow, and two places ahead of Tokyo.

Despite high prices and the strong pound, there will always be middle-aged Americans, deeply suspicious of English food and plumbing, who nevertheless crave quaintness and Lloyd Webber and bobbies; indeed, the United States remains London's biggest tourist market, with 2.5m Americans coming here to spend almost £1.6bn. But the new economic superpowers, China and India, are also sending increasing numbers of tourists our way, and they're as interested in our global and technological chops as they are in our heritage. And, tellingly, it's the number of European visitors that is growing fastest. Many of them are French, German, Spanish, Italian and, increasingly, Polish youngsters. This is the constituency that Visit London is aiming at with its 'Do London Like a Local' campaign. They may not have the largest disposable income to spend, but they're often coming two or three times a year.

And that's how London works its magic. Somehow the city charms everyone who comes here into believing that there's nowhere quite like it in the world – and after that, making the leap from acting 'like a local' to becoming one yourself just seems the obvious thing to do. Why do you love London town? Maybe it's because you're a Londoner…

TIMELINE

1971
'D-Day', 15 February: pounds, shillings and pence replaced by a new system of 100 pence in the pound. Many old coins remained in circulation for a number of years. In 1982, the 20p was introduced, followed by the £1 coin in 1983, with the halfpence withdrawn in 1984.

1973
Biba reopens in Kensington. The iconic fashion store draws people more for its impressive art deco interior than its clothes. The store shuts two years later.

1974
Camden Market opens, selling everything from vintage clothes and antiques to crafts and junk. It now attracts over 100,000 people every week and is a major tourist attraction.

1979
Paul Smith opens his first London boutique in a former bakery in Covent Garden. He has since become London's most commercially successful designer worldwide.

1981
Toy store Hamleys opens on Regent Street.

1983
First London Fashion Week in its present form. The high-profile event is now held twice a year, showcasing top-name designers as well as new talent.

1985
Mohamed Al Fayed buys Harrods for £615m. It is the largest shop in the UK, with more than one million square feet of selling space.

1987
The Conran Shop takes up residence in the Michelin Building on the Fulham Road.

The first Gap store outside the US opens on George Street, bringing preppie chic to the UK.

1988
Sarah Doukas of Storm modelling agency spots 14-year-old Croydon girl Kate Moss at JFK airport.

1992
Victoria Thornton organises the first London Open House weekend, persuading buildings of architectural note to open their doors to the public.

1994
Joe Corre, son of Malcolm McLaren and Vivienne Westwood, and Serena Rees open saucy lingerie shop Agent Provocateur.

1995
First annual 100% Design show held in a small marquee at the Duke of York's barracks, Chelsea. Growing exponentially, by 2006 it has established itself at Earl's Court, attracting 300,000 international visitors and provoking citywide umbrella event the London Design Festival.

1999
Bluewater opens in a disused quarry at Dartford. Europe's largest 'retail leisure destination', it marks a new generation of malls for the UK.

2003
Dr Martens cease production in the UK. From the 1960s to the '90s, their boots were the footwear of choice for skinheads, punks, goths and indie kids. A comeback is rumoured in 2008.

2004
The Apple Store opens on Regent Street.

2005
A riot at the new Ikea flagship store in Edmonton leaves five people hospitalised as shoppers fight for cheap leather sofas.

Topshop becomes a bona fide designer label when it shows at London Fashion Week.

2006
Stella McCartney designs an exclusive range for H&M in a spate of celebrity/high-street collaborations. The clothes sell out within hours… and reappear immediately on eBay.

2007
Primark opens its biggest store in Europe on Oxford Street. The crush to buy £8 jeans is dubbed a 'chavalanche'.

Anatomy of a high street

From a mixed bag of independent shops and cafés that every so often threw up a cultural phenomenon, to a spruced up retail destination of high-end chain stores, the aggrandisement of the King's Road speaks for many of London's local high streets.

By Kate Riordan

KING'S ROAD

There's a Tom Petty and the Heartbreakers song called 'King's Road' which includes the lyrics, 'There was people all around wearin' funny lookin' clothes, some boys, some girls, some I don't know.' An album track, it wasn't released until 1981, but Petty might have been describing this world-famous west London thoroughfare as it was in the late '60s. This was when another American, *Time* magazine journalist Piri Halasz, came to London see what all the fuss was about. The title of the resulting article gave the capital – and eventually the decade – its most hackneyed but lasting adjective: 'London: the Swinging City'.

The King's Road has been in existence for over 350 years, and in that time it has gone almost full circle. It was built by and then named after Charles II, who used it as a private road to shuttle easily between his two palaces at Hampton Court and Whitehall. If the Sex Pistols had been aware of the road's earliest history, they might have enjoyed the delicious irony of those notorious T-shirts sold in Malcolm McClaren's shop Seditionaries, emblazoned with an image of the Queen wearing a safety pin through her lip. That irony seems rather

hollow these days, with the King's Road and its tributary streets returned, if not to the royal family, then to some of London's wealthiest inhabitants.

Back in 1968, a gauche daytripper from a provincial town would have been dumbstruck by the King's Road: girls in miniskirts that barely covered their backsides, and boys in seam-bustingly tight velvet trousers and flamboyant Edwardian jackets, their hair very much over their ostentatiously large collars. Mary Quant's iconic Bazaar boutique had been open at No.138A since 1955; further down, at World's End, No.488 was inhabited by vintage clothes emporium Granny Takes a Trip, which opened its doors in 1965 and immediately became a hangout for the cognoscenti. Top Gear and Hung on You added to the late '60s line-up of contemporary boutiques, and the Chelsea Drug Store – a three-floor emporium where you could browse the records or buy a dress, although most people came to pose over a coffee (not unlike the Chelsea Kitchen) – opened in a radical new glass and aluminium building in 1969. It went on to be a location in the controversial 1971 film *A Clockwork Orange*, and was namechecked

Too Fast to Live Too Young to Die. They'd also taken on one Glen Matlock as a Saturday help, the same Matlock who went on to become bassist for the Sex Pistols (eventually succeeded by Sid Vicious). Two years later, the shop was renamed again, and with rather more brevity. Sex, with its distinctive pink padded sign, was born (though in 1976 it became Seditionaries: Clothes for Heroes).

As well as the infamous Queen and safety pin T-shirt, the shop became notorious for its 'Cambridge Rapist' (after a real case) and gay cowboy designs, brothel creepers and bondage gear, which had replaced the reactionary Teddy Boy garb they had originally peddled. In fact, not many self-respecting punks bought the clothes: not only could they not afford the prices, but the unwritten anarchic code decreed that rips, slashes and daubings should be home-made rather than bought. In 1977, the Pistols' 'God Save the Queen' was released to coincide with the Silver Jubilee; the tabloid press were predictably hysterical.

Surveying the myriad classy chain shops of the King's Road in 2008, it's hard to detect the pulse of the counterculture that was beating here for so long. Thatcher's '80s turned Chelsea from an age-old haunt of bohemians, artists and rebels into the stomping ground of the wealthy. Crumbling stucco was fixed, scruffy flats were gentrified by City traders and, more recently, Chelsea found its name attached to the word 'tractor' – after the hulking 4x4s that crawl along the King's Road during the school run. The alternative scene scuttled east, to Hoxton and Shoreditch.

'Girls in miniskirts that barely covered their backsides, boys in seam-bustingly tight velvet trousers.'

Along with so many others, the Chelsea Drug Store has long gone, the avant-garde building knocked down and a McDonald's now occupying the site, but some things never change. Peter Jones has remained the department store of choice for all good west London housewives since it opened as a draper's in 1877. Antiquarius and the nearby Café Picasso are still going, and although the Pheasantry – where Germaine Greer wrote *The Female Eunuch* – is now a Pizza Express, it looks as elegant as ever. As for No.430 King's Road, you can still buy Vivienne Westwood's designs there. Of course, the shop's name has changed again, and these days it's called World's End – a somehow fitting pair of words that once signified everything that was alternative and unconventional in the swinging city.

in the Rolling Stones' 'You Can't Always Get What You Want'.

Antiques market entrepreneur Bennie Gray opened Antiquarius in 1970 (Alfie's and Gray's followed in '76 and '77, respectively). He remembers, 'It was in the middle of the King's Road, when that road defined trendiness, youthful energy and fashion for the whole world. Every Saturday it had an energy and frisson that has not yet been matched: not just pop music and outlandish clothes, but a whole new lifestyle – and Antiquarius was a part of it. This was an extraordinary period when nostalgia blended with pop culture, and art and antiques became an integral part of the whole King's Road scene.'

In the early 1970s, the threads to be seen in were less vintage-hippy and rather more flash and glitzy. In 1972, Terry de Havilland opened his iconic shoe shop, Cobblers to the World. His vertiginous platform heels and wedges epitomised the new glam-rock look of which David Bowie was the androgynous standard bearer. De Havilland's shop was as fittingly ostentatious as his shoes; a riot of mirror glass and purple velvet banquettes, topped off with a huge chandelier. In addition to Ziggy Stardust, patrons of the shop included Rod Stewart, Led Zeppelin, Anita Pallenberg and Bianca Jagger. He says now, 'The King's Road was the happening place to be, there was so much flamboyance; you just gravitated there. And, of course, all the good looking girls were there too. It was an animal party time.'

At this point, the fashionistas were still buying their clothes from Granny Takes a Trip, as well as from Alkasura, Mr Freedom, Anthony Price and a second-hand clothes shop memorably called El Cheapo. The Sloaney boho girls who bought cowboy boots in the King's Road at the beginning of the 21st century weren't doing anything new: according to Max Decharne's excellent book *King's Road*, the Emperor of Wyoming (Nos.196 and 404) was selling boots, western shirts and even saddles back in 1973.

At No.430 at the same time, Malcolm McClaren and Vivienne Westwood had just changed the name of their shop from Let it Rock to the feistier

THE KING'S ROAD OF YESTERYEAR

1. Granny Takes a Trip
2. Sex/Seditionaries/ Hung on You
3. Roebuck pub
4. Bluebird Garage
5. Alkasura
6. The Pheasantry
7. Mary Quant
8. Peter Jones
9. Chelsea Drug Store
10. Chelsea Potter
11. Picasso Café
12. Antiquarius
13. Top Gear
14. Cobblers to the World
15. World's End pub

Bloody-minded, technically brilliant and a bit batty, Vivienne Westwood is influential beyond the world of fashion. In fact, the past four decades just wouldn't have been the same without her.

Vivienne Westwood

V ivienne Westwood reckons she knows what people think of her. 'I'm this dotty old dame. I'm eccentric. I'm arrogant. I'm a "national treasure." I'm so sick of that title. So patronising.' She sighs. 'I can't be that caricature.'

Well now. It's not as if the 62-year-old British fashion queen hasn't given everyone enough ammunition over the years: turning up at Buckingham Palace wearing no knickers, dressing up as Margaret Thatcher, charging around London on her pushbike in strange clothes and all weathers, marrying a bisexual man half her age, protesting against redundancies at the Natural History Museum with just a fig leaf to cover her modesty… You don't get that with Paul Smith.

Then, of course, there are the clothes: Nazi military decoration, granny-pants with penises drawn on them, 'rubber wear for the office', cardigans made out of dishcloths with Vim lids for buttons, T-shirts celebrating 'The Cambridge Rapist'… So far, so caricatured. And unfortunately, these are the only things that most people outside the hallowed world of fashion know her for. What's been far less appreciated is her staggering technical brilliance, her relentless commitment to originality and her indelible impact on the way we've dressed for the last 30-odd years.

Next week, the balance gets righted with a huge retrospective of Westwood's work at the Victoria & Albert Museum, the first for a British designer, and an enormous honour. 'It looks incredible,' she says. She shakes her head at the wonder of it.

We're upstairs in Westwood's Chelsea HQ, a nondescript postwar industrial site a short walk from the King's Road, where she made her name via Sex, Seditionaries and Too Fast to Live Too Young to Die, the punk/bondage boutiques she ran with Malcolm McLaren in the 1970s. Alexandra, Westwood's wirehaired fox terrier, patters around her feet as she talks. And talks, and talks.

She's enormously entertaining, not to say rather contradictory. She claims that now, designers make things no one could possibly want to wear, then admits that she never thinks about her customer. She grumbles that fashion can't be taught in institutions, then says she's just got off the plane from Berlin, where she lectures at the Hochschule der Künste.

Contrariness is in Westwood's blood. Throughout her career she's followed McLaren's original edict 'to annoy people', frequently taking the path of most resistance. Summer collections are often more black than white. In the '80s, when everyone else 'did' aspirational power dressing, she put out a wardrobe of poor rags and flat shoes. And when the comfy sportswear craze hit big in the '90s, Westwood preferred exquisitely tailored 19th-century crinolines.

Throughout, she epitomised a kind of maverick, bloody-minded Britishness. We can see echoes of her attitudes in, say, Morrissey or Tracey Emin or Alexander McQueen. Indeed, Westwood could only have emerged from a society built on tradition and class difference, one that reveres liberalism on one hand but tends to reject eccentricity on the other. Her collections of royal tweeds, Scottish tartans and Henley stripes only make sense against our background of class obsession and grudging sentimentality for the monarchy.

Yet for all her cocking a snook at the establishment, Westwood has always wanted mainstream approval. While other designers yachted it up off St Tropez, she ran her company from her personal account at the Chelsea NatWest and lived in a one-bedroom council flat in Clapham. Even a decade ago, she was so poor, one dinner guest was flabbergasted to be dished up a main course of fried parsley and garlic. For ages, her talents were overshadowed by her past. 'Vivienne is constantly innovating,' says the designer John Galliano. 'But her work in the punk and New Romantic periods

defined the era. It's impossible to think of the spirit of that time without thinking of Vivienne's work.'

These days, Westwood dresses Sarah Jessica Parker rather than Sid Vicious, and the time of sticking punky safety pins through pictures of the Queen has long gone. In fact, now she's invited to HRH's for lunch. She was there last month, along with 179 of Britain's 'women of achievement', where she chit-chatted to Kate Moss about a charity fundraiser and discussed the anthropology of manners with Kate Adie. But the enfant terrible isn't in danger of becoming the *pensionnée normale* just yet. 'I took the opportunity to tell Mrs Blair exactly what I thought of Tony,' she says. 'He hasn't got a clue what culture is, and his dress sense is appalling. He does seem a foolish person… sorry, I don't mean foolish person… an arsehole!'

What with the V&A exhibition, the mainstream praise, an OBE and – finally – a proper turnover (£48.7m last year), you might wonder what there is left for Westwood to achieve. But her driving force remains not clothes, but a passion for knowledge and literature. 'The best accessory is a book,' she has said, frequently rubbishing her job to sing the

'I took the opportunity to tell Mrs Blair exactly what I thought of Tony. He hasn't got a clue what culture is, and his dress sense is appalling.'

praises of Bertrand Russell, or John Stuart Mill. She's currently finishing *IBM and the Holocaust*, an investigation into the computer giant's collaboration with Nazi Germany, a book you don't imagine is on many designers' bedside tables.

'If I were to die having only worked on my fashion career, I wouldn't feel as if I'd achieved anything at all,' she says. She hasn't quite given up on the idea of opening a latter-day salon, her version of the 17th-century French power bases where writers and intellectuals met and exchanged ideas. 'If I had to choose between fashion and books,' she says, 'obviously, I would give up the clothes just like that.'

But for now, and for the last 34 years celebrated at the V&A, there remains Vivienne Westwood: the Undisputed Queen of Design and her marvellous, magical fashions, eccentric and arrogant British caricature though she may be.

'There was a quotation from Mark Twain, "I am always embarrassed when people flatter me. I never think they've said enough." Isn't that brilliant?' She thinks about this. 'People say all these nice things about you. But they never really understand how brilliant or important you are.'

Original interview by Johnny Davis.

Isabella Blow on Alexander McQueen

CONSUME

My relationship with Alexander McQueen began in 1994, when I went to a Saint Martins' graduate show. I couldn't get a seat, so I sat on the stairs and I was just watching, when I suddenly thought: I really like those clothes, they are amazing. It was his first collection. It was the tailoring and the movement that initially drew me to them. I tried to get hold of him and I kept calling his mother, but he was on holiday. She kept saying: 'He's not here, he's not here.' She told him: 'This crazy person is trying to get hold of you.' I eventually got to meet him and I decided to buy the collection: I bought one thing a month and paid him £100 a week. He'd bring an outfit in a bin liner, I'd look at it and then he'd come to the cashpoint with me.

Shortly afterwards, he moved into my house in Elizabeth Street, Belgravia, and I used to cook dinner for him and other designers. Philip Treacy was there, Hussein Chalayan at one point, I think, and Rifat Ozbek and Manolo Blahnik used to drop in. He was exactly the same back in those days as he is today: really funny, very witty, as raw as he is soft – he's still got that great mixture of fragility and strength.

We like the same things: we love the country and we love animals. In fact, he's crazy about animals: he's got masses of stuffed ones around his house (near Hackney's Victoria Park). There are two deer when you walk in. He loves anything: pigs, dogs, birds, reptiles, and he collects crocodiles. I gave him an amazing crocodile with an open mouth as a gift, but when I went there recently I noticed his paws were falling off, so it doesn't look as good as it did.

Nothing annoys me about him, except maybe the fact that he snores. We've never disagreed for more than about 20 minutes. I might have overstepped the mark a few times. He's very sensitive and very private, but occasionally, just like brothers and sisters do, we've bickered. I was like

McQueen's avant-garde (some said unwearable) spring/summer 2001 collection thrilled audiences at London Fashion Week in September 2000.

'Going for a fitting with him is great: you have these fantastic moments when he's breathing like a pig, concentrating.'

a mentor and then a mother, and now we are equally respectful of each other – I think it's changed quite a lot. It's very balanced now. We don't see each other as much as we used to; these days we speak at least once a week, but we used to speak four times a day. It's like vampires: you need somebody and then you don't need the drug any more. He rang me out of the blue to see what I was doing and I said I really needed a holiday; he offered to send a plane for me to go to Mallorca, which was so sweet.

We've had some of the most fantastic times together in the past. I used to go and have tea with his parents in Stepney – his mother's lovely. She has a wicked sense of humour, and she's got those McQueen blue eyes. Very comely, and the minute you enter she's always got a joke. I think Alexander is very like his mother.

The most exciting time I've had with him was when we learnt falconry together at my house in Gloucestershire, with two local mechanics who were obsessed about training wild birds. We did it for about two years. He loved it. He was fantastic too – he was very good at getting them back. The birds, that is.

Yes, he is richer than me now. Ha! All I can say is that he can keep the riches and I'll wear the rags. I've probably got about 40 McQueen pieces in my wardrobe altogether. He gives me some clothes, loans me others, and I have to fight for them. I have a very good relationship with Gucci: we have an agreement and I have an allowance (about three pieces a season). If I go over that, I have to pay for them. Going for a fitting with him is great: you have these fantastic moments when he's breathing like a pig, concentrating. It's wonderful. He sees everybody's body as a silhouette; Plum Sykes told me she had ten fittings for her wedding dress.

He's been a success at such a young age; his dreams have come true. I think he will be remembered more like Yves Saint Laurent than Chanel – he changed the way we look at women, because he pulled the whole silhouette down beneath the hip and altered the way we walk. His influence is monumental.

Isabella Blow was one of London's most extravagant and influential fashion editors. She died in 2007, aged 49.

Kate Moss

Would it be a low blow to mention drugs and the Priory in the first sentence of a Kate Moss profile? Where else would you like us to start? Recalling her passage from Croydon, where it all began? ('My mum kept saying, "I'm not giving you any more bloody fivers to go up to London to do modelling."') With clichés about her look? Or would questions about her wilder moments with partners such as Johnny Depp satisfy more?

We also know that drugs have played their part in her working life. But despite the media hysteria last year, it would appear that she hasn't been fucked up by the ten years of fashion nonsense she's experienced since photographer Corinne Day took her to Camber Sands for the *Face* magazine's cover in July 1990 and made her into a superstar.

'That shoot took two months and Kate just wanted a dirty weekend with her boyfriend when we did it,' remembers Day. 'I didn't know what we were creating,' admits Moss. 'I was just having a laugh. Corinne just wanted to bring out everything that I hated when I was 15. My bow legs, the mole on my breast, the way I laughed. But it feels natural for us to be back together. Corinne's certainly got quicker at taking pictures.'

After seven years in New York, Moss was to have an epiphany of her own last summer. 'I was in denial, pretending I lived in London but actually living out of a hotel in New York for most of the time.' In July of last year, Moss rang up her agency one morning and announced she was giving it all up. 'I quit because I thought: I fucking hate it.'

This time around, however, she wanted to do things differently. Looking around her, she'd seen the detrimental effect fashion had had on people she knew; the dangers of a hedonistic, 24/7 fashion lifestyle. 'In fashion, excess is not for creative purposes, whatever people may say. It's about escapism from the bullshit. You just have to get out of it to deal with it. And I think that's what a lot of the people in the fashion business that I know do it for. I know that's why I did it. It's a sin to be tired.'

Moss knew she had to have more control over the work she did. 'In the past, I've felt that I was sometimes manipulated into doing something I didn't want to do.'

Original article by Christopher Hemblade.

CONSUME

Streets of style

Armed with an anything-goes attitude, unbridled creativity and plenty of hair gel and eyeliner (and that's just the boys), Londoners have always brought a colourful and confident swagger to the capital.

By Terry Jones

My relationship with London style probably goes back to the '60s: growing up and coming to London, then marrying a Londoner. At that time, fashion was coming out of Chelsea. Chelsea Antiques Market was the place we'd make for to get our clothes, before the inception of Kensington Market. The vibe of London was really exciting. It had a naive energy.

As the '70s came on, I was working as an art director, first with *Vanity Fair*, then on to British *Vogue*. What I saw happening on the streets of London was completely different from cities such as Milan and Paris that I was visiting for work. It was clear that in the UK the music of the time had a really raw energy, and that was crossing over into fashion. Punk kicked in in '76, and although business and high-street fashion were getting boring, what was going on in the street suddenly became really exciting. The recession meant people were getting creative without money; punk crossed over with the reggae scene; and '76 and '77 shook up the establishment of fashion.

Street style seemed to be expressing itself far more assertively than before. I tried to get *Vogue* interested in it, without success, so I produced a book called *Not Another Punk Book* (a forerunner of *i-D*) to record what was going on. But things on the street were moving fast, and I came up with the idea that it should all be documented. I met up with people like Alex McDowell (a painter from St Martins who started Rocking Russian Design, producing record sleeves for, among others, the Rich Kids) and rock photographer Dennis Morris, and together we started to put together *i-D*.

The magazine first appeared in 1980. But it was not alone. That same year Nick Logan launched the *Face*, with more of a slant towards music, and Carey Labovitch and her partner Simon Tesler started *Blitz*, a media-savvy lifestyle magazine, initially quarterly then bi-monthly. Though the *Face* and *Blitz* were certainly glossier than *i-D*, and Neville Brody made a lasting impact with his graphics for the

Face, of the three magazines, only *i-D* survives. *Blitz* closed in 1991, the *Face* in 2004.

The '80s continued to get more exciting with a wave of students that came out of Saint Martins in '83-'84 – journalists and art directors such as Robin Derrick, Caryn Franklin, Moira Bogue, Dylan, Jones and Stephen Male, stylist Simon Foxton, and designers such as Stephen Jones and Bodymap. It coincided with the Blitz club period, and that whole area of Covent Garden and Soho

'We had the Recyclers, the Grebos, the Rockers, the Bikers, the Punks, the Psychobillies, the Rockabillies, the Dandies… we just rattled out a whole list of tribes and invented new ones.'

became like a catwalk. It had a very different vibe from the tourist destination it was to become.

There wasn't really a dominant look, it was a complete mix of styles. The ethos of *i-D* tried to reflect this by not putting things into categories, but showing the street for its variety. There were Psychobillies, which was a spin off of rockabilly (focused around the band the Stray Cats). Duran Duran and Spandau Ballet were just starting, so Perry Haines, one of the first editors of *i-D*, came up with the expression New Romantics. And of course, there was Vivienne Westwood. Her shows were spectacular, especially the Buffalo collection. The end of King's Road around her World's End shop was a magnet for creativity – at least until they put the rent up in the mid '80s.

Because *i-D* was one of the first magazines that dealt with street style, it attracted people. People found us. Nick Knight, now a major-league fashion photographer, walked in off the street from Bournemouth and asked us to publish his skinhead pictures. I wasn't interested in those,

but he went on to do a Sade cover in 1983, a year before she got her first record deal. We had Mario Testino, who shot John Galliano's first collection. Suzie Bick, the London supermodel of the moment. Stylist Ray Petri, who worked with the *Face* and *i-D*.

When Madonna came in for her first cover shoot, it was before anyone knew who she was. She'd had her hair done at Antenna, a hip hairdresser in Notting Hill that was doing hair extensions. Boy George's then boyfriend Marilyn had his weave done there, and when people saw the *i-D* cover, everyone thought it was him. They didn't know Madonna. Now a lot of younger people probably don't know Marilyn.

At the end of the '90s, I was asked to put together a video on street style. I decided to go back through the pages of *i-D*, this time categorising the different styles and giving them name tags. I called it the Tribes. We had the Recyclers, people who made fashion out of salvage, the Grebos, a greasy denim biker look, and obviously the

Rockers, the Bikers, the Punks, the Psychobillies, the Rockabillies, the Dandies… We just rattled out the whole list and invented new ones.

Today we are in a revival period. What's happening in fashion is what's happening in food. Go into a restaurant and you are offered dishes like bangers and mash, apple crumble and other home comforts. Five years ago it would have been rocket with grated parmesan. I think the evolution of fashion is very much like the kitchen. There's a Punk revival going on, but this time round it feels

'The days when Caroline Baker would get arrested for wearing pyjamas and a man's dressing gown at five o'clock in the afternoon are over. That was 1976.'

CONSUME

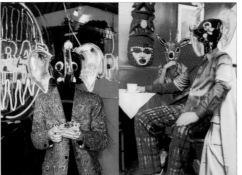

reassuring rather than shocking. In *i-D* we are currently featuring kids who have been born within the lifetime of *i-D*, from the parents of the Buffalo scene; they are educated in the fashion scene to an almost trainspotter level.

Though former London stars such as Stephen Jones, Alexander McQueen, Matthew Williamson and Julien Macdonald have moved onto an international playing field, there's a new group of designers making London exciting again: Giles Deacon, Marios Schwab, Richard Nicholl, Gareth Pugh… Personalities come and go in fashion, headlining, if you like, but there are important voices who persist. Katharine Hamnett, who was famous for her political slogan T-shirts in the '80s, still has a lot to say.

A lot more people are very passionate about style and fashion these days. And it isn't just a London thing. I went to Mayrhofen in the Tyrol recently for their annual Snow Bombing Festival, where 3,000 people, predominantly Brits, turn up. The town was totally different from at any other

time of year. People were individually and extrovertly dressed. It looked like clubland. Fashion is a way of expressing your individualism, and that creativity continues to be generated in London which is, on the whole, more tolerant than a lot of other places. You can walk around London dressed how you like. The days where Caroline Baker would get arrested for wearing pyjamas and a man's dressing gown at five o'clock in the afternoon are over. That was 1976. It wasn't even punk – she was just doing something eccentric.

Today you'd be hard pressed to shock in London. And no one could never achieve the heights of Leigh Bowery and Trojan when they were dressing up to go to Taboo in 1985. Someone in London today being eccentric is probably someone who is trying too hard. Everything has become much cooler – but it will be interesting to see how the next generation decide to mix it up.

Terry Jones founded *i-D* magazine in 1980. He remains its creative director.

Kensington Market

Ya Ya

Not even the owners of Kensington Market – Petticoat Lane Rentals – know its exact date of conception, placing it in the late 1960s; but its familiar red, white and blue façade, tucked away at the 'naicer' end of Kensington High Street, is surely well known to all. It has lived through many eras, although cheesecloth and denim have been sure-fire sellers for years. But with the punk explosion in the late 1970s, and a whole wealth of new, radical clothing, the market entered a new lease of life.

Many of the standard 'den and cheese' concessions faded away with the odour of joss sticks, making room for tiny little stalls crammed full of unusual second-hand clothing, fiercely fought over by stall-owners at jumble sales and markets nationwide.

In the past few years, a whole new breed of stall-owners has been appearing. They sell new clothes, designed by the stallholders themselves, and always one jump ahead of, if not dictating, the current fashions. Some of the stalls sell overpriced rubbish that is a laugh to look at but not funny on the pocket. Someone, though, must buy such outfits – the stalls are still going.

The market nowadays is rather reminiscent of a cottage industry: lots of people doing their own thing in a busy, optimistic fashion. The atmosphere is always alive and throbbing, and not just from the conflicting music that booms out of almost every stall. The busiest day is Saturday, when money changes hands thick and fast, and the social scene in the market is in full swing.

Kensington Market has a lot to offer the bargain hunter who does not want to shop in the expensive King's Road or clone-like Top Shop/Man. The clothes are original, if sometimes a bit pricey, but that's only my own opinion – one's woman's meat could be another's poison.

NB: One intentional omission from the selective guide that follows is Johnsons on the first floor. This shop has already had plenty of publicity, and anyway, I have always found their clothes overpriced and overrated, although their footwear range is good.

Original report by Lindsey Shapero. Kensington Market remained at 49-53 Kensington High Street until 2000, when it was sold for conversion to flats. It has entered into rock legend because Freddie Mercury once ran a stall and Jimi Hendrix spent his last day there.

Ya Ya, stalls 3-6
The only way to describe the clothes here is gear for loonies: wild, extravagant and totally over-the-top garments designed by Martin Degville and Jane Farrimond of Birmingham.

The clothes are unisex, or maybe unsexed would be more appropriate. Costumes are mainly for nightclubs and parties, priced between £20 and £50 for dresses, and tops at an average of £15.

American Retro, stalls 22-24
Two stalls under the same ownership and title: one a Flip-type clothes mart, and the other a 'head' shop. The clothing is mainly '50s gear for boys and girls, and all items with a red 'X' have been reduced to £5.

The 'head' section comprises one of the largest ranges of cigarette papers around, including leopard skins and three fruit-flavoured papers. Pipes, stash boxes and roach clips are well represented, despite the sign 'Nothing sold here is intended to be used for any illegal purpose'.

Apart from gear gear, there is also a good selection of James Dean and Marilyn Monroe cards and posters, plus anti-nuke and art cards. The earrings are fun: spikes, daggers, taps and the old cannibis leaf in silver and gold, and not too pricey.

Rock-A-Cha, stalls 150 & 151
Menswear with a strong emphasis on '50s American style – 'smart but casual'. Clothes are designed by the owners, but made up by tailors in the East End. The clientele is varied, from soul boys to rockabillies in the 15-30 age group. Pegs are £16-£20 and shirts £12; this may seem expensive for a market stall, but the clothes are very well made. Accessories include belts, caps, sunglasses and hair gel.

Black and white photos line the walls, mainly of kids in the '50s from Harlem to Paris. Rockabilly music blares out to keep your toes tappin' while you're buyin'.

Visions, stall 152
Young, trendy hairdressers with 17 years of experience between them. The haircuts I saw under way looked neat and interesting. A cut and blow dry is £8.50 for women and £6.50 for men; tints are £8.50, and wash and blow dry £4.50. As the shop is only small, best to ring for an appointment and full price list.

CONSUME

Britain's first shoppingmall

Brent Cross turned 30 this month. When the north-west London shopping centre opened its doors on 2 March 1976, it was the first time so many shops (75) were enclosed under one roof, not only in the capital, but in the whole of the UK.

At 28 myself, I feel like we've grown up together. Approached from the North Circular, it's still not winning any prizes for aesthetics, but the welcome sign on the centre's wall – a big red cross emblazoned on a concrete slab – always lifts my spirits and takes me back to the early '80s, when I first fell for Brent Cross's subtle charms.

The centre was designed by the Bernard Engle Partnership (which also redeveloped the town centres of Lewisham and Staines in the '60s and '70s). Like much of the architecture of this period, it is big, hulking and chiefly made from concrete (55,000 cubic metres of the stuff). It was the brainchild of Sydney Mason, then chairman of property developer Hammerson (the company that also owns Birmingham's Bullring), and was inspired by the big American malls of the '50s. Though it was 1959 when Hammerson began its search for a suitable site for its visionary scheme, it wasn't until 1972, when the concept was beginning to seem outdated, that construction commenced on a large enough area on land previously used by Hackney & Hendon Greyhound Stadium.

Ironically, a visit to Brent Cross in my formative years was never about the shopping. As far as I was concerned, it was all about the fountain. No longer extant (apparently, it was in the way, the racket it made gave everyone 'Brent Cross headache', and, as with all fun things, there were health and safety concerns), there was a time when no corner of the centre could provide relief from its watery hiss. As you approached – in my case, straining at the safety reins – the noise grew louder until you caught sight of the vapour and then suddenly the whole jet, shooting up to the rainbow-tiled domed ceiling. Around the pool beneath, full of wishing-well coppers, was an area of plush red carpet, the few steps down to it equipped with a shiny brass banister rail. This, I firmly believed, had to be the very pinnacle of luxury. Like the ostentatiously grand cinemas of the 1930s to our cash-strapped forebears, Brent Cross, only just preceding the 1978-79 Winter of Discontent with its power cuts, uncollected rubbish and three-day week, was an exquisite breath of temperature-controlled air.

Not everyone welcomed the concept at the time. In the week that it opened, the *Economist* wrote: 'The Brent Cross shopping centre, legacy of a dead planning fad, opened this week. Eager shoppers thronged its precincts. But whether anyone will make much money out of it remains to be seen.' Even a year later, the sceptics still doubted it was more than a passing fancy: 'Despite its probable success, Brent Cross is likely to remain unique.' (The *Economist* again).

Thirty years on, the centre – now joined by scores more across the nation – is still going strong. The average spend per (purchasing) visitor is the highest in the UK, at £90. Roughly £700m a year whizzes through the tills – about ten times more than turnover in the first year of business.

When I visit on a Tuesday morning, it seems relatively unchanged. There is still a hum of activity reverberating off the smooth, marble-effect floors and an absence of muzak in the air. Barring the Christmas period, the original no-music policy has stood firm – as has the free

> 'Around the pool was a plush red carpet, the few steps down to it equipped with a shiny brass banister rail. This had to be the very pinnacle of luxury.'

parking outside (a maximum 8,000 spaces). The sit-down cafés are still a few steps lower than the walkways, but gone is the neon-signed Rivoli, to be replaced, inevitably, by Costa Coffee and Starbucks. Two stalwarts of the centre – John Lewis and Fenwicks – face each other squarely from either end of the centre as they always have, like opposing armies.

At the information point, an elderly Jewish-American couple ask where to buy a toaster. Given a choice of two shops, the American asks which is the cheapest. With a barely perceptible tilt, the man at information nods backwards. Staff seem a bit more willing to help than in the frenzied West End; a cleaner leads me from one end of the centre to the other when I can't find the place I'm looking for.

Brent Cross customers are rather sedate on a weekday: middle-aged ladies in good coats who wouldn't last two seconds in the throng of Oxford Street. Head of marketing, Norman Black, a local boy himself (and one who sheepishly admits to being once chucked out as a youth for messing around), says the locality means Brent Cross attracts a lot of shoppers from the Jewish community, but otherwise it's a pretty diverse crowd. They fall into two main groups: 'middle-market suburbanite couples and young families who might drive a Mondeo', and much wealthier couples, whose children are probably grown up.

Many original shops – Waitrose, M&S, Russell & Bromley and the department stores – have kept loyal customers returning, and new names such as Apple, Office, The White Company, Carluccio's, Reiss and the soon-to-open Rigby & Peller attract a younger, affluent set.

Competition from malls such as the Bluewater behemoth at Dartford and Watford's Harlequin Centre haven't made much of a dent either. 'Brent Cross might be the oldest, but it's not the most traditional; we think we're more like the north-west London equivalent of the West End,' says Black. 'Coming here is still about treat or indulgence shopping. Some of the other shopping centres are more everyday.'

The local area is earmarked for the largest regeneration plan since the war, into which £2.5bn will be sunk. As well as better public transport and 8,000 new homes, ardent shoppers will get a new open-air, car-free 'high street', whose paths will blend seamlessly with those in the existing indoor malls at Brent Cross. You'll have to wait around 15 years to see major changes, when the centre's facilities will be extended out towards the local river on land already owned by the shopping centre but currently restricted to use as an occasional car park. Interestingly, the number of parking spaces will not increase, so public transport will play an important role in the new plans.

Despite all this upward mobility and forward thinking, however, there's still something oddly comforting and even homely about Brent Cross. Perhaps it's knowing it's been there the longest, perhaps it's down to the details. Whatever it is, Brent Cross just seems to have more soul than the new breed of megacentres. Forty-one of its current workforce have been there since the start, and although room has been made for chains to move in, there is also a niche for independents.

The suburb of Brent, which was in existence long before 1976, has become synonymous with its shopping centre, one much loved by Londoners. After all, 20m visitors a year can't be wrong.

Original article by Kate Riordan.

Memory bank
Lynne Franks on Lynne Franks

I was running my PR company in the '70s and '80s – I was *Time Out*'s PR at one point when they were doing a lot of street performances and activities. I was friends with fashion designers: Katharine Hamnett, Wendy Dagworthy, Jasper Conran, and doing PR for them too.

London Fashion Week was just a few exhibitions when I first got involved. It was really frustrating for the designers trying to find a venue they could afford, and then, when they did, they'd be spread out all over London. I took it upon myself to go and find a space where you could put a tent up, like in Paris. The first one I used was the front lawn at the Commonwealth Institute, until it started sinking; then we moved to the Duke of York's barracks in Chelsea.

With funding from some of my clients, we eventually took over the schedule and ran it. Through what became the British Fashion Council, we also created the British Fashion Awards. Katharine Hamnett won the first year, in 1984, and I even got it on television.

I loved the '80s, it was a lot of fun. I used to see London taxis going about with Lynne Franks PR on the side, and still to this day I don't know how that happened. My company seemed to be involved in everything that was happening in the city: launches, events and parties. I think that, in a way, Lynne Franks PR had a lot to do with London's shift to the design city it is today.

Lynne Franks is a lifestyle guru. She was one of the highest profile PRs of the 1980s and early '90s. Jennifer Saunders is rumoured to have taken her as inspiration for the hit comedy Absolutely Fabulous*.*

It's an ad, ad world

Saluting London's best-loved shops and services.

At this moment something totally undemocratic is going on.

Central government is about to put a bill through parliament to cast aside your right to cast a vote.

Next year's London elections will be cancelled without your say so.

At the same time the GLC will be sending people out on the street asking you to sign a petition.

Sign it if you want to retain the right to have a say in London's future.

This government might get your vote but it doesn't have the right to take it.

SAY NO TO NO SAY.

THIS IS THE LAST TIME YOU'LL BE ASKED IF YOU WANT A SAY IN WHO RUNS LONDON.

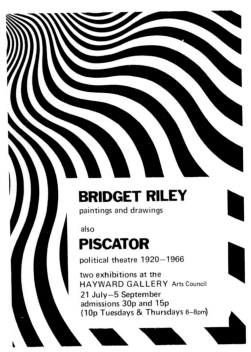

BRIDGET RILEY

paintings and drawings

also

PISCATOR

political theatre 1920—1966

two exhibitions at the
HAYWARD GALLERY Arts Council
21 July–5 September
admissions 30p and 15p
(10p Tuesdays & Thursdays 6–8pm)

FINEST QUALITY

FLIP JEANS!

ALL STYLES IN **100% COTTON** PRE-SHRUNK AND READY-TO-WEAR!

MADE IN U.S.A.! STYLED EXCLUSIVELY FOR FLIP IN AMERICA!

Satisfaction **GUARANTEED** *or a* **NEW PAIR** *FREE!*

FLIP JEANS! – *"You've tried the rest...* NOW TRY THE **BEST!"*

14 oz. Denim

ALL FLIP JEANS ARE: Made from 100% Highest Quality Cotton (14 oz. Denim).. * Fully Pre-shrunk and Ready-to-Wear.. * Riveted for long-lasting wear.. * Extra long leg length (36") to ensure a great fit in all sizes!

EASY-FIT 50'S CUT – Available in these fabrics:
● FLIP "Super-Wash" Denim (soft blue)
● FLIP Hickory-Stripe (blue & white pinstripe)
● FLIP Weave — Our exclusive Herringbone weave – great looking and incredibly tough!
● FLIP "Rock 'n' Roll" RAINBOW – Dyed cotton in a whole range of the LATEST & GREATEST fashion colours from the U.S.A.!

WESTERN-CUT STRAIGHT-LEG – Available in:
● FLIP "Super-Wash" Denim
● FLIP "Rock 'n' Roll" RAINBOW Dyed range

ALL STYLES ONLY £14.95

Try a Pair! **Satisfaction GUARANTEED!**

« QUALITY • STYLE • DISCOUNT PRICES »

FLIP

THIS BRANCH IS NOW OPEN ON SUNDAYS!
11 A.M. – 6:30 P.M.

CLOTHING WAREHOUSE
98 Curtain Road, London, E.C.2
-OPEN 7 DAYS A WEEK!-
MON.-SAT: SUNDAYS!
10 AM-6:30 PM 10 AM-3PM
BUS ROUTES: 6, 22, 35, 48, 149.
NEAR OLD ST. & LIVERPOOL ST. STATIONS.

CHELSEA
191 Kings Road, London, S.W.3
MON.-SAT. 10 A.M.-6:30 P.M.
● SLOANE SQ.
ALL MAJOR CREDIT CARDS ACCEPTED

COVENT GARDEN
125 Longacre, London, W.C.2
OPEN UNTIL MIDNITE
6 DAYS A WEEK!
MON. - SAT. 10 A.M. - 12 MIDNITE
● LEICESTER SQ./ COVENT GDN.

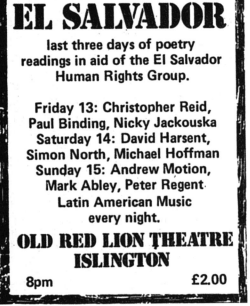

POETS FOR EL SALVADOR

last three days of poetry readings in aid of the El Salvador Human Rights Group.

Friday 13: Christopher Reid, Paul Binding, Nicky Jackouska
Saturday 14: David Harsent, Simon North, Michael Hoffman
Sunday 15: Andrew Motion, Mark Abley, Peter Regent·
Latin American Music every night.

OLD RED LION THEATRE ISLINGTON

8pm   £2.00

CONSUME

CONSUME

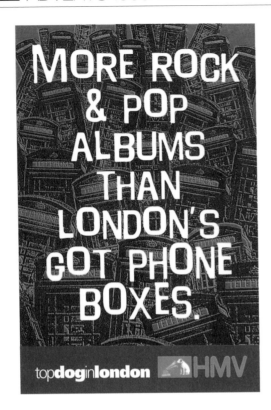

MORE ROCK & POP ALBUMS THAN LONDON'S GOT PHONE BOXES.

topdoginlondon HMV

London's historic new shopping experience

Covent Garden is really back–in style.

For inside the beautifully restored Covent Garden Market Building you'll find literally dozens of London's finest shops, together with many colourful and original market stalls– and they're

open until 8.00pm Monday to Saturday.

Food and fashion, books, crafts, toys and some of the best specialist shops in town all have a place in the old Covent Garden Market as well as a lively pub, wine bars, restaurants and cafés.

So look in and see us soon. You certainly won't be alone.

Already Covent Garden is far and away the most exciting area the capital has seen in years.

Covent Garden Market is close to the Strand and is within easy distance of well over thirty bus routes in Central London, and just 1 minute from Covent Garden tube.

GLC Greater London Council

COVENT GARDEN MARKET

**The King's Road –
first it had pop,
then it had punks,
now it's got Penguins!**

**The Penguin Bookshop
157 King's Road
London SW7**

Stocking over 4000 Penguins, Pelicans, Puffins and other publisher's paperbacks as well as some hardbacks, the bookshop caters for all tastes in books.

So whatever the need, there's now the read down the King's Road.

Come and pay us a visit!

Neal's Yard
THERAPY ROOMS

**2 Neal's Yard, Covent Garden, London WC2H 9DP
Telephone: 01-379 7662**

**ACUPUNCTURE, ALEXANDER TECHNIQUE,
APPLIED KINESOLOGY, AROMATHERAPY,
BACH FLOWER REMEDIES,
BIODYNAMIC THERAPY, CHIROPRACTIC,
CRANIAL OSTEOPATHY, HERBALISM,
HOMOEOPATHY, IRIDOLOGY, MASSAGE,
HEALING, NATUROPATHY, NUTRITION & DIET,
OSTEOPATHY, POLARITY THERAPY,
PSYCHOTHERAPY, RELAXATION,
REFLEXOLOGY, ROLFING, SHIATSU,
TOUCH FOR HEALTH.**

Here at Neal's Yard we can offer you a wide range of Natural Therapies which can assist in the restoration of health and in the establishment of well-being.

We have qualified experienced therapists who charge reasonable fees.

For further details please 'phone or visit.

Open 9am to 9pm weekdays.

All ads reproduced from past issues of *Time Out*.

CONSUME

Talk of the town

The consumer obsessions and high-street sensations of the past 40 years.

CONSUME

Polaroid camera

See your photos instantly! During the 1970s heyday of Polaroid cameras, more than a billion were sold worldwide every year. Their square format and washed out colours defined an era of family photo albums. Sadly, due to the expense of the film and popularity of the digital camera, Polaroid announced in 2008 that it would cease production of its unique camera film.

Duvets

Attempts in the 18th century to introduce the continental quilt to the English were viewed with suspicion, but in the 1970s we finally ditched the sheets and blankets and snuggled up to the Scandinavian import.

Raleigh Chopper

The three-gear Mk2 Raleigh Chopper, with its distinctive high

handlebars,L-shaped seat and central gearstick, was the Christmas present of choice for several years from 1972. A Mk3 version was launched in 2004, after 25 years out of production, clearly aimed at nostalgic dads.

VHS vs Betamax

The battle between the two videotape behemoths, Sony's Betamax format and JVC's VHS, lasted an entire decade from 1975 to 1985. VHS's ultimate triumph now seems a feeble victory in the face of DVDs, themselves looking towards an inevitable redundancy thanks to downloads.

Skateboards

First introduced in California in the 1950s, when surfers thought it would be cool to take their boards on land, skateboarding only crossed the Atlantic in the early '70s – when the introduction of polyurethane wheels offered novices a smoother and safer ride.

Continental lager

Though it was in 1968 that Carlsberg and Heineken were first brewed under licence in the UK, it took the long

hot summer of 1976 for Londoners to realise that an ice-cold lager, not warm beer, was the drink that refreshed.

Ready meals

Supermarkets started stocking ready meals for eager diners in the 1970s, but it was the invention of the microwave oven that turbocharged their popularity: they are now consumed by more than 77 per cent of UK households.

Microwave ovens

Introduced in 1974, the microwave oven became a common device in urban myths – such as the exploding poodle put in to dry. The microwave's other claim to fame is cutting the cooking time of a Christmas pudding from two hours to ten minutes – a miracle that outstrips the Virgin birth.

The Walkman

Invented in 1979 by a Japanese opera lover, the portable personal stereo revolutionised how we listen to music. From the Walkman (Sony or otherwise) evolved the bulky CD Discman, the MiniDisc Walkman, and today's ubiquitous iPod.

SodaStream

The bubbles didn't last and the flavour was a poor substitute for the Real Thing, but we still got busy with the fizzy in the '80s. Bubbling away in the noughties, SodaStream now markets itself as the eco-friendly, waste-free soft drink of choice.

BT phone cards

BT phone cards were introduced in 1981. By 1991, sales reached 74 million (boosted by Bob 'It's good to talk' Hoskins-fronted ads), but they slumped to just 7.2 million in 200, when mobile phones forced them to ring off one last time. Many originals are now collectors' items, with one card fetching £3,000.

Commodore 64 home computer

White-hot technology because of, not despite, its cassette drive operating system. The exciting eight-bit home computer, launched in 1982, outsold IBM PCs and Apple computers, with 40 per cent of the market in the mid '80s.

Mountain bikes

With mountain bikes' extreme sport image, two wheels were suddenly cool again. Prices in 1983 were astronomical, and as a consequence the Brick Lane black market in 'second-hand' bikes took off.

Sinclair C5

Sir Clive Sinclair's 1985 battery-powered three-wheeler vehicle, designed as a cost-effective, congestion-beating road vehicle that could be driven without a licence, was less Smart car than silly trike.

Dyson vacuum cleaners

Despite trick campaigns from rival companies, James Dyson's Dual Cyclone System super suction bagless vacuum cleaner, launched in 1993, was brilliant enough to hoover up the competition and ensure Dyson a role as Design Museum trustee.

Futons

Where 1970s small ads were dominated by pine bed shops, in the late '80s, futons were the sleeping arrangement of choice for all modern homes, part of a long-lasting love affair with all things Japanese. *Time Out* even felt the need to explain to its readers exactly how this weird import worked.

Trivial Pursuit

The board game phenomenon of 1981, 'Triv' was, for a few years, bigger than Monopoly (still the best-selling game of all time), bigger than Scrabble, bigger than Risk.

easyJet

EasyJet wasn't the first budget airline to take to the skies – Ryanair, founded in 1985 by Tony Ryan, preceded Stelios Haji-Ioannou's outfit by a decade – but the latter's great service, teamed with maximum exposure and a vibrant orange livery, has made it synonymous with the weekend city break.

Sun-dried tomatoes

In the mid '90s, no self-respecting desk lunch was without one of these red and wrinkled Mediterranean imports hidden in a salad, panini or pasta.

Amazon

When Amazon.co.uk started trading in 1995, many of London's independent bookshops shut within months. Idiosyncratic independents like Persephone Books and Skoob have fought back in recent years, proving that the pleasure of browsing a bookshelf has not been forgotten.

Bottled water

The mid 1980s craze for bottled water continues, despite being around 10,000 times more expensive than its tap water equivalent (glass for glass). Bottled water is the world's fastest selling drinks sector, worth £1.2 bn a year, even outselling Coca-Cola in London.

PS1

The best console ever? Bringing arcade quality gaming into the living room, the PS1 was the first console to sell over 100 million units. The 32-bit, CD-based console was launched in the UK in 1995, and because of its huge popularity with the Playstation generation, did not cease production until over a decade later in 2006.

eBay

The very first item sold on eBay was a broken laser pointer for

$14.83 in 1995. Astonished, computer programmer and eBay creator Pierre Omidyar emailed the winning bidder to ask if he understood that the laser pointer was broken. In his reply, the buyer explained: 'I'm a collector of broken laser pointers.' Now eBay has approximately 84m users worldwide, who between them trade more than £960 worth of goods on the site every second.

Juicy Salif lemon squeezer

In 1989, Philippe Starck's angular design for Alessi made an icon of an everyday object and encapsulated a new era of rampant design consumption. London's Design Museum opened in the same year, further feeding the hunger for Tizio lamps.

Oyster cards

The schadenfreude watching tourists try to swipe their one-day paper travel card is an unexpected commuting pleasure that almost compensates for the irritation felt when you realise you've run out of money on yours on the bus home.

iMac G3 computer

Chingford designer and Apple head designer Jonathan Ive reportedly visited sweet factories in search of the perfect lustre for the 1998 iMac G3's gumdrop finish. The round edges and translucent candy colours broke the beige box mould for electronic goods, and established Apple Macs as the creative industries' computer of choice.

Birkenstocks

2003 saw fashion folk queuing down Neal Street to buy a pair of the sensible Germany sandals that had unaccountably been deemed essential footwear. The 200-year-old manufacturer was just as surprised and eventually moved from its tiny store to more spacious premises in 2005…Just as London discovered Crocs.

Compiled by Fiona McAuslan.

CONSUME

Terence Conran

CONSUME

When the *Penguin Book of Saints* is revised in a few decades' time, we may see an entry for St Terence of the High Street: the blurb would read that he changed the face of retailing in this country and, along the way, as guru of the role of design in enhancing the quality of life, raised consumers' consciousness about design.

This, Sir Terence Conran would dismiss at a stroke. He disavows notions of grandeur. But he is certainly a power in the land, from his role as chairman of the Storehouse Group – embracing Habitat, the Conran Shop, Heal's, Mothercare, BHS, Richards and menswear shops Blazer – to Conran Design Associates; running restaurants Neal Street and Bibendum; as designer and captain of industry; and as crusading aesthete and hedonist (the evidence of good living is comfortably apparent).

The first Habitat opened in the Fulham Road in 1964. 'Shops at that time were very prim – they had a few things on display; stock was kept in the stock room, and sales assistants went to get what you wanted,' says Conran. 'We took exactly the opposite attitude. We put everything on the shelves. This stockiness, the warehouse feel, was very attractive to people; the merchandise was very accessible. Because it was there in quantity, it looked cheaper than just one single piece by itself.'

Sir Terence Conran in the Bibendum armchair. The chair was originally designed in the 1920s by Eileen Gray, but it wasn't until the '70s, when it was put back into production, that it became a desirable design icon.

Conran's infatuation with France from early travels there had excited his retailing ideas. 'I always loved market stalls and markets, and wanted the shop to have that sort of feel about it.' He had seen all the wonderful, functional cooking equipment on sale in France and Italy, and now offered it to the consumer, along with bright furniture, fabrics and colourful accessories: merchandise that just wasn't on sale anywhere else in the country, displayed in bulk in a store that had been carefully designed, where you could wander around and serve yourself.

'Everything was edited and selected in a way that we believed would appeal to what we knew would be a fairly narrow market at that time. It tucked into a moderately sophisticated person's knowledge. They had a well-trained eye. They saw things for sale there that they'd seen on holiday in France and Italy. The place had a certain spirit that was immediately attractive to the sort of people who lived in that area of London, where Italian restaurants had just started opening. Just a nice atmosphere.'

Habitat has made stylish merchandise affordable to a large number of people and established a new yardstick of aspirational, middle-class style. 'Retailers constantly underestimate the potential of what people might like. I'm a firm believer that people's tastes are formed by what they're offered. There isn't anything in the English genes that makes them have less taste than the Italians or the French.'

The Habitat style has spawned many imitators, like the DIY warehouses, who tend to do it less well, with less 'conviction', offering maybe very cheap products but often inferior designs and quality. Stephen Bayley, director of the Conran Foundation, was right when he said, 'Conran set new standards. Culturally he did for the home what Elizabeth David did for food.'

Since the early '80s, Conran has checked into the big league. He now bears the weight of mergers and takeover bids, and still is a design mandarin and patron, with his Deisign Museum opening next July in his conversion of Butlers Wharf.

Stephen Bayley has described Conran as combining 'puritanism with the tastes of a voluptuary'. The affable, hedonist Mr Bibendum and the shrewd St Terence of integrity. A very complementary combination. As hagiographies go, his most interesting. We have every reason to bless St Tel. *Nunc est bibendum*: let's drink to that.

Original interview by Joanne Glasbey.

Citizen kid

Free travel, fantastic playgrounds, funky shops and grown-up food:
the capital's children have never had it so good. Or have they?

By Ronnie Haydon

Jumping for joy:
attractions for children
now include (clockwise
from centre) free
museums and galleries
like the National Gallery;
specialist shoe shops;
the Unicorn Theatre;
activites along the
South Bank; the Diana,
Princess of Wales
Memorial Playground;
boutique clothes stores;
the Polka Theatre; and
Kew Gardens.

Parents barging through the rush hour to the childminder's might pause to reflect that another august publication celebrates its 40th in 2008. Judith Kerr's *The Tiger Who Came to Tea* was also published in 1968. A favourite among preschoolers, the picture book is a quaint period piece for their parents: a childhood shaped by an apron-clad, stay-at-home mother waiting till father gets home. Four decades on, life like the one enjoyed by the little girl Sophy is almost as unlikely as a tiger drinking all the water in the tap.

Quite apart from changes on the domestic front – and the thorny issues of screen-based versus outdoors fun, homecooked versus microwave-ready meals, over-sanitised surroundings versus healthy pecks of dirt – a child's experience of life outside the home has been revolutionised. Kids are now citizens in their own right, with a wealth of

organisations devoted to their right to consume, to play and to be entertained. Have children never had it so good?

As consumers, modern children are revered. Consider the now obsolete image of children banished to the beer garden with lemonade and crisps while parents enjoy a peaceful pint. As attractive as that may sound to parents, so many hostelries now have a family space, or are of the gastro persuasion, that it's never been easier to enjoy a pub lunch en famille. In restaurants, the die becomes ever more weighted in the minor diner's favour. True, there are a lot of nuggety kiddie menus about, but 40 years ago, even those were too much to hope for. But the pinnacle of children's menus, at Le Cercle, a French restaurant in Chelsea, has a free fixed menu of five smaller dishes for children under 12. They must lunch with a paying

'When a playground consisted of heavy roundabouts set into unforgiving concrete, children were all over them. Today, parents hover oppressively on the bouncy rubber surface underneath handsome wooden playframes.'

adult, *naturellement*, but this is an adult restaurant that likes to treat children as discerning eaters. Other admirable places, such as Giraffe and Carluccio's, come down on the side of an amiable family vibe, where a wide-ranging menu steers a confident path through the exotically unfamiliar and nursery teas, without offending anyone.

Out on the high street, children are showered with largesse. Whole areas of London, such as Wandsworth, Dulwich, Crouch End and West Kilburn, have become known for a preponderance of middle-class families – drawn there to breed by good schools, good parks, delis, cafés – spawning in their turn ranks of child-specific boutiques and lifestyle shops. High Street brands such as Fat Face, Zara and Jigsaw now do whole mini-me ranges. Westbourne Grove's elegantly vintage Jigsaw has a silver slide for their younger customers to enjoy in between trying on the winsome fashions. In the pages of Sunday supplements, tow-haired tots model casuals by DKNY and Diesel, usually under straplines referring to 'pint-sized fashionistas'. It's all a far cry from their parents' memories of Aertex shirts, Ladybird polyester playwear and sensible frocks knocked up on the Singer.

Away from rapacious consumerism on the higher plains of the Arts, the picture, in London at least, is richer and rosier. A child of the 1960s and '70s might have been lucky enough either to attend an annual panto or to be subjected to a worthy TIE (Theatre in Education) performance in his school. Today, a far wider young audience is reached by original productions in purpose-built theatres. The most impressive example of this new accessibility and flair is the Unicorn Theatre, which moved into cool concrete premises near London Bridge in 2005. The Unicorn is, in fact, the UK's oldest professional theatre company for children – founded in 1947 by Caryl Jenner – with a repertoire that always went beyond panto and TIE but struggled to do so. Today, places like the Unicorn, the Polka in Wimbledon and the Half Moon in Stepney bring the magic of theatre to hundreds of thousands of young people, courtesy of highly regarded education programmes established and supported by government and private funding.

Galleries, meanwhile, roll out art trollies at weekends for children to help themselves to drawing materials, and run after-school sketching and painting clubs. Dance centres run classes for children as young as two. A musical education can be delivered by a score of colleges and conservatoires. Drama clubs and theatre schools attract increasing numbers of new students every term – and whenever there's a new reality telly show searching for a West End star.

It cannot be denied that the majority of such artistic opportunities are delivered to the aspirant middle classes, who sign up their children to ever more character-building arts and educational programmes in a panicky response to a digital world. More sobering is the fact that there have to be 'initiatives' to get children drawing, reading, using their imaginations, even walking, for heaven's sake, because the default position for today's child is sitting indoors, eyes on screen.

This is unfortunate, given that playgrounds are altogether safer, cleaner and more attractive than they were just 20 years ago. Some won't even let adults in unaccompanied by a child (the unique Diana, Princess of Wales Memorial Playground in Kensington Gardens, and Bloomsbury's Coram's Fields). When a playground consisted of vertiginous metal slides and heavy roundabouts set into unforgiving concrete, children were all over them. Today, parents hover oppressively on the bouncy rubber surface underneath handsome wooden playframes. Very few will let their under-12s go to the local park – or anywhere else – by themselves. Even though the tube is now free for under-11s and buses are free up to 18, parents who let their primary school-age children actually take public transport on their own are regarded with suspicion. The more attractive city life becomes to children, the less they are allowed to get out and sample it on their own terms.

Are children, in this multiple-choice world, worse off than little Sophy, sipping tea with Mother and passing the time imagining friendly tigers? Her 1960s life looks slightly joyless to children who have flown to Disneyworld and can manipulate the PS2 before they're out of Pampers, but research has concluded that children of the noughties aren't any happier. Certainly their parents are making heavier weather of keeping them healthy, fit and resourceful. Perhaps that's why so many are casting a wistful eye back to when family life was simpler. They may cite environmental concerns when choosing the new generation of washable nappies, stepping out to buy locally grown produce and enduring rainy British camping holidays, but the truth might be that they've seen what the modern world holds for their children, and they're not sure it's all good.

Ronnie Haydon is the editor of *Time Out*'s *London for Children* guide.

HEDONISM INTRODUCTION
SEX CITYSCAPE FASHION
SOCIETY SHOPPING COMEDY
DRAMA PROTEST & POLITICS
VISUAL ARTS PERFORMANCE
LITERATURE GANGS OPINION
COCKNEYS BARS ON SCREEN
DANCE MUSIC TELEVISION
BUILDINGS CLUBS NIGHTLIFE
SPORT & FITNESS MEMORIES
STYLE FOOD & DRINK GIGS
CONSUME RIOTS **REFERENCE**

Upfront

A graphic selection of *Time Out* magazine covers from 1968 to 2008.

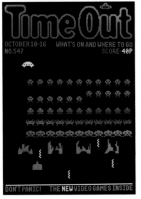

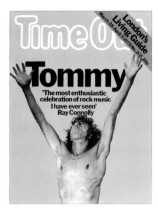

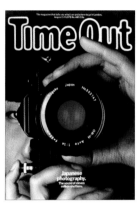

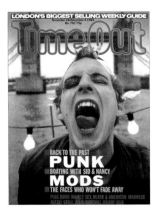

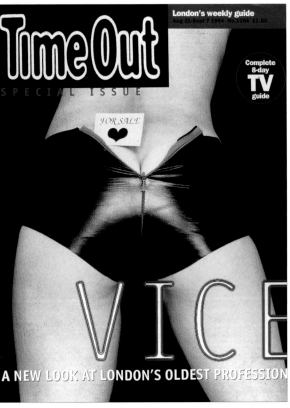

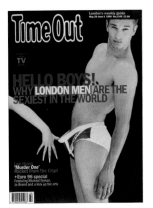

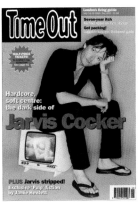

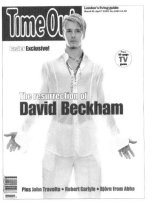

LONDON'S WEEKLY LISTINGS BIBLE
JULY 13-20 2005
No.1821 £2.50

Time Out
London

REFERENCE

OUR CITY

LONDON CARRIES ON

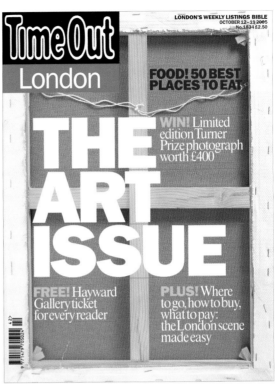

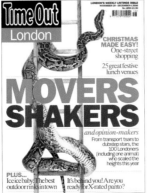

Contributors

Geoff Andrew is Head of Film Programme at BFI Southbank, contributing editor to *Time Out*, consultant editor of the *Time Out Film Guide*, and the author of numerous books on the cinema, including monographs on Nicholas Ray, Abbas Kiarostami and Kieslowski's *Three Colours Trilogy*. He has contributed to many journals and anthologies, and writes regularly for *Sight & Sound*.

Paul Burston is Gay & Lesbian Editor of *Time Out*, and writes for various publications including the *Times* and the *Independent on Sunday*. In 2008, for the second year running, he was named one of the 101 most influential gay people in Britain in the *Independent*'s annual Pink List. His most recent novel, *Lovers & Losers*, was shortlisted for the Stonewall Award. He got hitched in September 2007, and is currently at work on a fourth novel, *The Gay Divorcee*. He hopes it isn't prophetic.

Jessica Cargill Thompson was Features Editor, then Deputy Editor of *Time Out* from 2000 to 2007. Having begun her career in the construction press, she now contributes to a number of architectural publications, including *Building Design*, *Blueprint* and *Elle Decoration*. Her book *40 Architects Under 40* (Taschen) was published in 2000.

Publisher, poet and entrepreneur **Felix Dennis** is the founder of Dennis Publishing, which produces titles such as *The Week*, *Maxim* and *Auto Express*. As one of the editors of *Oz* magazine, he was imprisoned in 1971 after was then the longest obscenity trial in English history. He has written the bestselling book *How to Get Rich* (Ebury, 2006), and poetry collections *A Glass Half Full* (Hutchinson, 2002) and *Homeless in my Heart* (Ebury, 2008).

Jonathan Derbyshire is a writer and critic. He has written for the *Financial Times*, the *Guardian*, the *New Statesman*, *New York Sun*, *Prospect* and the *Times Literary Supplement*. He edited *Time Out*'s *1000 Books to Change Your Life* (2007) and is a contributing editor to *Granta*.

Jane Edwardes is Theatre Editor of *Time Out*. She edited the *Faber Book of Monologues*, for both men and women, and has been a contributor to *Contemporary British Theatre* and *Contemporary Dramatists*. She often lectures on theatre to visiting American students.

Journalist and travel writer **Robert Elms** made his name on the *Face* in the 1980s. Since then he has written the novel *In Search of the Crack* (Penguin, 1989) and *The Way We Wore: A Life in Threads* (Picador, 2006). He continues to write for a number of publications, including *GQ* and the *Sunday Times*, and broadcasts a daily show on BBC London.

Mark Fisher is acting deputy editor of the *Wire*. He is also a visiting fellow at the Centre for Cultural Studies at Goldsmiths, University of London. His writing appears regularly in *Frieze, Sight & Sound and Fact* magazine, but he is best known for his weblog, which can be found at http://k-punk.abstractdynamics.org.

Kate Gavron is the co-author (with Michael Young and Geoff Dench) of *The New East End* (Profile, 2006). She chairs the board of Carcanet Press, is vice-chair of the Runnymede Trust and is a trustee and fellow of the Young Foundation.

Piers Gough, CBE, set up practice with his partners in CZWG while still studying at the Architectural Association in the swinging '60s. Projects have escalated from groovy boutiques to witty, iconic buildings and successful masterplans via Docklands housing, lofts and the park-on-a-bridge in Mile End.

Ronnie Haydon is the editor of *Time Out London for Children* and *Time Out Family Breaks in Britain*. She also writes about children's theatre for *Time Out* magazine.

Michael Hodges is Editor-at-Large of *Time Out* and the re-launch editor of *Time Out Beirut*. He is the author of *AK-47: The Story of the People's Gun* (Hodder & Stoughton, 2007). Awards include PPA British Magazine Writer of the Year 2000 and CRE Race in the Media winner 2006 for his exposure of fascism in London. He is a former editor of *Jack*, and has written for the *Sunday Times*, *Observer* and *Independent*.

Alkarim Jivani was a TV Editor at *Time Out* from 1987 to 2007, and is currently working on various book projects. He is a frequent contributor to *Front Row* and *Nightwaves*, and was a regular on *Newsnight Review*. He is the author of two books: *It's Not Unusual: A History of Lesbian and Gay Britain in the Twentieth Century*, and *Classic TV Series*.

Sarah Kent was Visual Arts Editor of *Time Out* for 30 years. She now works freelance, giving lectures, writing catalogue essays and contributing to magazines such as *Modern Painters* and *Art World*. Her books include *Women's Images of Men* (with Jacqueline Morreau) and *Shark Infested Waters: The Saatchi Collection of British Art in the 90s*.

John Lewis is a former *Time Out* music critic, who now writes about music, sport, parenthood and the arts for *Uncut*, the *Guardian*, the *Times*, the *FT*, the *Independent on Sunday*, *GQ*, *Sight & Sound*, *Metro* and several other publications. He is also deputy editor of *Time Out*'s *1000 Songs To Change Your Life* (2008).

Jonathan Meades's last books were the novel *The Fowler Family Business*, a novel, and *Incest and Morris Dancing*, a compilation of his food writing: he was restaurant critic of the *Times* from 1986 to 2001. A selection of his television shows has just been released on DVD by 2Entertain.

Jenni Muir is a writer and editor specialising in food, health and luxury travel. A regular contributor to *Time Out* and blogger for http://bbcgoodfood. com, she edited the *Time Out Eating & Drinking Guide 2009*, and can often be found helping celebrity chefs put their ideas into print.

Lisa Mullen is a freelance journalist. A former staff writer at *Time Out*, she is currently a regular contributor to *Time Out*, *Elle*, *Sight & Sound* and the *Times*.

Peter Murray is exhibition director of New London Architecture and chairman of architectural communications company Wordsearch. He has edited *Building Design* and the *RIBA Journal*, and in 1983 he launched *Blueprint* magazine. In 2004, he started the London Architecture Biennale, which has grown into the citywide London Festival of Architecture.

Nicholas Royle's latest books are *Mortality* (Serpent's Tail, 2006), a short-story collection, and *The Appetite* (Gray Friar Press, 2008), a novella. He is the film critic for the *London Magazine*.

Sukhdev Sandhu is the author of *London Calling: How Black and Asian Writers Imagined a City* (HarperCollins, 2003), *I'll Get My Coat* (with Usman Saeed, Book Works, 2005), and *Night Haunts: A Journey through the London Night* (Verso, 2007). He is also the *Daily Telegraph*'s chief film critic.

DJ Taylor's books include *Orwell: The Life* (Owl Books), which won the 2003 Whitbread biography prize, and *Kept: A Victorian Mystery* (Vintage, 2006). His new novel, *Ask Alice*, appears in 2009.

Rebecca Taylor is News Editor of *Time Out*. She spent many years in Tokyo working on the *Japan Times*. She has also worked as a reporter for the BBC World Service, and as a freelance writer for various publications and newspapers, including the *Guardian*, the *Times* and *Elle*.

Ossian Ward is Visual Arts Editor of *Time Out* and a writer on contemporary art. Formerly editor of *ArtReview* and the *V&A Magazine*, he has worked at the *Art Newspaper* and now edits *The* Artists' *Yearbook*, a biennial publication by Thames & Hudson.

Peter Watts is Features Writer of *Time Out* and a former Shed Ender. He has written about football for the *Sunday Times*, *Goal* and *Chelsea Independent* fanzine.

Patrick West writes weekly about television for http://spiked-online.com and is the author of three books: *Conspicuous Compassion* (Civitas, 2004), *The Poverty of Multiculturalism* (Civitas, 2005), *Beating Them at Their Own Game* (Liberties Press, 2006).

Other contributors
Simone Baird, Laura Lee Davies, Guy Dimond, Charlie Godfrey-Faussett, Malcolm Hay, Martin Hoyle, Donald Hutera, Brian Logan, Fiona McAuslan, Lisa Mullen, John O'Connell, Sharon O'Connell, Kate Riordan, Andrew Shields, Helen Sumpter, John Sunyer, Dave Swindells.

Interviewees
Brian Bleasdale, Mark Glazebrook, Sue Davies, Piers Gough, Jim, Terry Jones, Nicholas Logsdail, Geoff Martin, Gillian Moore, Danny Rampling.

Memory banks
Immodesty Blaize, Nick Broomfield, Adam Buxton, Omid Djalili, Lynne Franks, Goldie, Jeremy Hardy, Lee Hurst, Oliver Peyton, Ansar Ahmed Ullah, Jonny Woo.

Index

Note: page numbers in **bold** indicate section(s) giving key information on a topic; *italics* indicate photos.

E

F

G

H

M

N

O

P

INDEX

T

U

V

W

Y